IN THE
ALMOST
PROMISED
LAND

IN THE ALMOST PROMISED LAND

American Jews and Blacks, 1915-1935

HASIA R. DINER

 Contributions in American History, Number 59

GREENWOOD PRESS
Westport, Connecticut ● London, England

Library of Congress Cataloging in Publication Data

Diner, Hasia R
    In the almost promised land.

    (Contributions in American History; no. 59)
    Bibliography: p.
    Includes index.
    1. Afro-Americans—Relations with Jews. I. Title.
E184.J5D49   301.15'43'9730496073   76-46767
ISBN 0-8371-9400-8

Library of Congress Catalog Card Number: 76-46767
ISBN: 0-8371-9400-8

First published in 1977

Greenwood Press, Inc.
51 Riverside Avenue, Westport, Connecticut 06880

Printed in the United States of America

To My Mother and to the Memory of My Father

contents

acknowledgments

It seems almost impossible after so many years of working on a project of this length, which has gone through numerous changes and alterations, to remember and give full credit to all the people who helped me—whether with a constructive comment, a perplexing question, or a useful reference source. The friends who lived through this project with me and shared my ideas and thoughts know who they are and know how much I appreciated the insights of both the professional historians and those who were interested in the subject for its own sake.

I would like to thank the Ford Foundation for providing me with a Dissertation Fellowship in Ethnic History in 1972-1973, which allowed me to pursue my research full time. I began this study at the University of Illinois—Chicago Circle under the supervision of Leo Schelbert.

The staffs of many libraries listened to my problems, tried to answer my questions, and directed me to pertinent sources. The bulk of the research was carried on at the Library of Congress and I would like to express particular thanks to the Manuscript Division, to the Hebraic Division, and to Ms. Kay Blair of Inter-Library Loan who helped me get a wealth of material. Ms. Fannie Zelcer of the American Jewish Archives at Hebrew Union College, Cincinnati, facilitated my study of the Louis Marshall Papers, as well as several other collections. The staff of the Herbert Lehman Collection at Columbia University went out of its way to provide the material I needed, as did the YIVO in New York, and the American Jewish Historical Society in Waltham, Massachusetts. Mr. Milton Himmelfarb of the American Jewish Committee not only allowed access to the records of the Committee, but shared with me his ideas on a subject he has been intimately involved in.

Special thanks must also go to Mr. James Marshall for permission to see his father's papers.

Karen Wickre of George Washington University helped me greatly in proofreading and checking the accuracy of this book.

Perhaps one of the most stimulating research experiences involved in preparing this manuscript was my conversation with Mr. Charles "Sacha" Zimmermann, the retired president of the International Ladies' Garment Workers' Union, Local #22. He brought to life an era of labor organizing which helped me understand so much better the people I was writing about.

Richard Fried of the University of Illinois—Chicago Circle took a great deal of time and care in evaluating this manuscript when it was a doctoral dissertation, and I thank him.

I would also like to extend very special thanks to Ira Berlin for the interest he showed in this project and for the extensive and probing questions which he raised concerning numerous points. I appreciate his time, effort, and encouragement.

No one aided me more in this project, in every stage and at every point, than Steven Diner. His help as an editor and as a critic were invaluable. His emotional support and encouragement were boundless. I thank him for his patience, his faith in me, and his enthusiasm for my work.

introduction

In the late 1960s a public discussion raged over the nature of Jewish-black relations. Anyone reading the scores of magazine and newspaper accounts could reasonably conclude that Jews and blacks were embroiled in an antagonistic quest for power, leadership, and jobs. While some Jews refused to participate in the escalating debate, many others registered shock and dismay at the widening rift between the two groups and the growing anti-Semitism among blacks.

In 1966 when Stokely Carmichael of the Student Nonviolent Coordinating Committee proclaimed the birth of "Black Power," American Jews stridently protested that *they* ought not be excluded from leadership in the civil rights movement. When the Coalition for New Politics, under the sway of black militants, passed a resolution in 1968 condemning Zionism and Israel, American Jews cried out in betrayal. When the experimental school district of Ocean Hill-Brownsville became a storm center of conflict over educational policy in New York City, Jews blasted the infusion of anti-Semitism by blacks. When government bureaucracies, universities, public school systems and similar institutions formulated plans of affirmative action for blacks and other racial minority groups, Jews declared that they would be the major victims of this new form of racism.

The anger, bitterness, and recrimination which emanated from organized Jewish communities did not merely express fear of "just" one more instance of anti-Semitism. This anger was special; the bitterness unique. It reflected a sense of betrayal by a group with whom Jews believed they shared a special bond of history and a commonality of interest. For almost a century the leaders of American Jewry slowly and patiently had attempted to forge an alliance with blacks within the civil rights movement, charitable and philanthropic agencies, and organized labor. In politics Jews helped construct the twentieth-century, urban-based Democratic coalition and have been among its most persistent supporters. They played a vital role in bringing black people into that coalition and in placing the political concerns of blacks high on the mid-twentieth-century liberal agenda. Anti-white militants and black separatists in the 1960s condemned the emasculating white liberal "friends" of blacks with greater animosity than they showed to avowed white racists, thus severely straining the liberal coalition. For decades Jewish leaders had attached great importance to their alliance with blacks, and it was small wonder that they should respond with bitterness and resentment to its apparent collapse.

This book poses two questions in trying to understand the nature of that alliance. How did Jews go about attempting to create a fellowship with blacks in the first decades of the twentieth century? More important, why did Jews, a group clearly set on the path of economic mobility, want to publicly link their fate in American society with blacks, who were undeniably relegated to an inferior role in the economic, political, and social life of the nation? The book demonstrates that Jewish ends were served by involvement with blacks.

Underlying these questions and the answers advanced are certain assumptions which generally have not figured in the thinking of most historians and social commentators. While almost all historians have accepted the proposition that ethnicity has, in large measure, determined a group's voting pattern or its integration into the American economy, few have tackled the possibility that the culture and history of an ethnic group has in some way shaped its dealings with blacks. While ethnicity is considered a valid explanation for many things, when American historians have written about race they have talked in two categories only—black and white. This assumes that Irish, Italian, Polish, or Jewish immigrants and their children defined themselves as members of a particular group in the voting booth, in church, or on the housing market, but when confronted with blacks, they acted with one mind. This kind of analysis ignores the subtleties and complexities of American ethnic identity. Clearly, in the case of Jews, the way they talked about the race question and the manner in which they chose to involve themselves in the racial issues of the day, demonstrated that they were not reacting *just* as whites. There was a Jewish element to their attitudes; a Jewish motivation behind their behavior.

This study assumes that Jewish immigrants, their children, and even their grandchildren were constantly attempting to define for themselves a meaningful role in American society; that they were striving to prove their worth to their adoptive nation. Through the first decades of the twentieth century Jews clearly felt ill at ease in America. They sensed in varying degrees of intensity that they did not belong. Hence they constantly sought to achieve an equilibrium between Jewishness and the demands of American life. Much American Jewish behavior in these years, especially that behavior intended for public view, concerned itself with the goal of coming to terms with America, with acculturating psychologically to its pressures. Few acts were committed for their own sake; few statements articulated without bearing on this task. Jewish interest and involvement with blacks must be viewed within this context.

Another assumption which lies at the heart of this book is that many of these individuals were unconscious or only partly conscious of their motivation. Few of the Jews who plunged into black affairs paused to reflect about why they were doing it. Those who commented on their reasons tended either to see themselves as altruists or to believe that Jewish concern for black people was "natural," growing out of a parallel historic experience of suffering and oppression. I believe that these sentiments, while overstated and unrealistic, were genuine; that the Jewish activists really believed that their involvement lacked an ulterior motive. Yet looking back and surveying the pattern of involvement over decades, one can discern certain reasons for Jewish interest which the protagonists themselves could not or would not see.

Attention should be called to what I have not attempted. This study does not purport that all Jewish leaders were committed to black causes. It does not maintain that being Jewish immediately caused Jews to enter black affairs. The book does assert that for many American Jewish leaders black issues provided an attractive forum in which to work out certain tensions of acculturation. Some members of the Jewish elite chose other paths. There is no evidence that prominent Jews like financier Bernard Baruch, Supreme Court Justice Benjamin Cardozo, or New Deal Brain Truster Benjamin V. Cohen actively joined efforts to improve American race relations or the status of black people. Southern Jews, for the most part, also ignored the race issue and, in fact, there is no proof that they felt significantly less anti-

black than their white Christian neighbors. They wanted to accul-
turate to a very different society than the Jews of New York or Chicago, and for them active identification with blacks did not serve their
needs. The leaders of religiously orthodox Jews rarely supported black
civil rights and philanthropic efforts, because they sought to avoid
real involvement in most American secular issues. Unlike most Jews,
they were content to live apart from the American mainstream and
therefore had no need to utilize black causes. These people were,
nonetheless, the exceptions among American Jewish leaders.

Jewish leaders representing different socioeconomic classes, ideologies, and cultural experiences committed themselves to black
betterment and gave time, money, and energy to black organizations.
The spectrum was so wide and the involvement so extensive that one
must conclude that these leaders acted out of peculiarly Jewish
motives. Indeed, this was their own explanation and that of their
black allies.

Secondly, I deal with the leadership of American Jewry and not the
masses. I focus on the most visible of American Jews—the public figures and the molders of public opinion, because they felt the pressures
of acculturation most keenly. In fact, some of the evidence suggests
that real differences in Jewish relations with blacks separated the
leadership and the masses. Many Jewish leaders and organs of public
opinion severely criticized Jewish merchants in black neighborhoods
and expressed little sympathy for their needs. The book does, however, deal with both the leadership of working-class, Yiddish-speaking Jews and those who were affluent and highly Americanized.

Thirdly, I do not try to prove that Jews were the only whites who
actively joined in black affairs in the first decades of the twentieth century. New England Protestants like Oswald Garrison Villard, Mary
White Ovington, Moorfield Storey and other white Christians vigorously fought racism in the early 1900s, while John F. Slater, George F.
Peabody, and Andrew Carnegie donated huge sums to black education. These individuals had their own reasons for identifying with
black causes. However, of the whites who actively worked in black
projects in these years, Jews appear to be the only ones for whom these
activities stemmed from their ethnic identity, unless one considers the
descendants of New England Protestant abolitionists an ethnic group.
In any event, there was no comparable effort among the leaders of

other groups that immigrated in the nineteenth or early twentieth century. Jews were not the only whites committed to black causes, but they were the only white ethnic group in which large numbers of leaders publicly displayed interest and sympathy for the plight of black Americans.

I also make no effort to pass judgment on whether Jews were "good" or "bad" to blacks. How one judges their involvement and interest is a function of one's own values and contemporary prejudices. The historian's task is to describe, as far as possible, the kind of involvement and interest and to explain why it occurred.

Finally, this study is not about blacks per se. It is about the way Jewish leaders played with the issues of racism and black status as a way of working out certain problems and tensions of American life. Blacks appear in this study as a medium by which Jewish leaders tried to solve certain dilemmas engendered by their ambiguous position. Only a minimal attempt is made to assess how black leaders reacted to Jewish involvement and how they perceived Jews. That is another issue which clearly warrants investigation.

For Jewish leaders in the early twentieth century, the issues of black America provided an attractive and appropriate forum to adapt and blend their cultural heritage with contemporary realities. In the first place, many of the issues raised by black civil rights groups spoke directly to problems faced by American Jews. Job discrimination, restrictive housing markets, exclusion from universities and professional schools were concerns of Jews also. Jewish leaders clearly perceived that the removal of civil disabilities from one group would have a beneficial effect on their own security and well-being.

While Jewish organizations pressed hard for their own rights, they displayed a certain reticence to discuss anti-Semitism publicly. They feared that too much discussion of the subject might stimulate anti-Jewish sentiment where it had not yet appeared. They feared that if they put too much pressure on American society a reaction could set in. Jews would come to be viewed as too "pushy," too "demanding." Feeling real bitterness over American anti-Semitism but afraid to vent the full extent of their anxiety, many Jewish leaders resolved this dilemma by expressing their frustration through the problems of blacks. They seized upon the issues of racism partly as a way to launch a vicarious attack on a nation which, they, believed, had not lived up to their expectations. Yet however much American Jews feared latent anti-Semitism, by the early twentieth century they were convinced that the fate of world Jewry was tied to the United States. In the years after World War I, with the rise of Naziism in Germany and the rigors of creating a homeland in Palestine, they increasingly held up America as the only practical answer to the problem of Jewish survival. American Jews realized that they were in the United States for good and strove to prove their worth to their Gentile neighbors. Through race issues, Jews could show America how useful they were. They could cite the achievements of many Jewish leaders in the fields of black civil rights, black philanthropy, and the unionization of black workers. In attacking racism they could prove how American they had become, quoting the Constitution and other documents of the American creed. In doing this, they not only drew links between themselves and the rhetoric of American democracy, but they illustrated the compatability of their own heritage and culture with that of America. Rabbi Stephen Wise of New York's Free Synagogue once mused that "there is so much that is parallel between the ideology of the Jewish outlook . . . and the spirit of the American commonwealth that the Jew need find no difficulty in assimilating the American spirit without surrendering the heart and center of the people's life and spirit." By stressing the Jewish influence in black affairs, Jews actually sought to demonstrate that *they* were the "true" Americans, that *they* were living out the "true" meaning of America.

In proclaiming through the medium of black concerns that Jews were "more American" than the Americans, Jewish leaders were fulfilling yet another need. They were as concerned with preserving that which was distinctly Jewish as they were with adapting the group to American life. They believed that the essence of the Jewish tradition involved a commitment to human rights and philanthropy. Jews must expose the world to high moral standards, for this was their role as God's Chosen People. In America, the desperate plight of blacks provided the forum in which Jews could illustrate their moral and ethical superiority, their "Chosenness." Thus, through the race issue, the leaders of American Jewry hoped that their culture and heritage could be passed on to future generations of American Jews. Racism was labeled "un-Jewish" and pointedly linked with anti-Semitism in Europe. The Jewish media pointed out that discrimination against black people was often supported by Christian churches and, at the same time, dismissed examples of racism by Jews as aberrant and abnormal. Jewish organs of public opinion insisted that Jews and blacks understood each other because both had been victims of oppression for hundreds of years. Both remained isolated from the centers of power in America. Both were shunned by the masses of white Christians. The mission of the Jews was to help the blacks who were even more afflicted, more persecuted than themselves. This, they argued, grew out of a tradition which had sustained the group for hundreds of years.

These uses of black issues in acculturating to American life did not develop from a consciously devised scheme. The leaders of American Jewry sincerely believed that they were the special friends and outspoken champions of blacks. They sensed that their own history and tradition had uniquely equipped them to empathize and aid black people. But the Jewish involvement with black causes stemmed from more than sympathy and understanding. Black issues proved ideal for Jewish leaders actively seeking to build bridges between the Jewish and the American worlds.

chapter 1

JEWS AND BLACKS IN AMERICAN SOCIETY

To the casual observer in 1915 there was little similarity between the status of Jews and blacks in America. Jews, mostly immigrant workers from central and eastern Europe, clustered in northern cities. Some had attained wealth and prominence in the years preceding World War I. Blacks, on the other hand, lived predominantly in the rural South and most remained trapped at the bottom of the American social and economic ladder. Yet when Leo Frank, a young Jewish entrepreneur in Atlanta, was lynched in September 1915 by a mob of white southerners, many Jews began to wonder how dissimilar their positions really were.

After the Frank lynching the leaders of American Jewry and the elite of the Jewish world became acutely conscious of the similarities and differences between themselves and blacks. While Jews had been involved in black affairs for years before the Frank murder, and since the beginning of the twentieth century had participated vigorously in efforts to change the racial status quo in America, that affair precipitated an upsurge of Jewish interest in blacks. They recognized that both identifiably separate groups were profoundly affected by their marginal status in the society.

JEWS IN CHRISTIAN AMERICA: 1915

Diversity characterized the American Jewish world, composed of several distinct groups, each with different ideas about the nature of Jewish life and the meaning of Jewish identity. Yet statistics in 1915 showed that most American Jews shared certain demographic traits. Of the 2,933,874 Jews who lived in the United States in 1914 and who made up 2.5 percent of the American population, the vast majority were immigrants. The flow of Jews to America had been continuous since the late nineteenth century. Only in 1915 did it show signs of slackening, a temporary result of the outbreak of war in Europe. Except for the half-decade of World War I, the history of American Jewry through the mid-1920s was shaped by constant immigration. From 1881, a year of violent anti-Jewish riots in Russia, to 1910, 1,562,800 Jewish newcomers arrived in America. Of them, 840,260 migrated from Russia and 130,142 from Austria-Hungary. Massive numbers of Polish Jews also came; they were included in the statistics of Russia and Austria, depending on the part of Poland from which they hailed. Fleeing from the hardships of World War I, 136,654 Jews came in 1915 alone, 102,638 from Russia. This added up to the third largest year of Jewish influx into the United States in the twentieth century, surpassed only by 1906 with 152,491 and 1907 with 148,131 Jewish immigrants.[1]

Jews migrated to America in family units. Beginning in 1899 every yearly flood of Jewish newcomers from eastern Europe contained an almost equal number of men and women and a substantial number of children. Unlike more typical peasant immigrants, Jews had come to the United States to stay. For every one hundred immigrants who came to America in 1914 almost twenty-five returned, while among Jews only five out of one hundred went back. Contemporary sociologists noted that Jewish immigrants brought with them the full range of community institutions and the new arrivals represented all classes: intellectuals and leaders joined the masses in the exodus to America.[2]

Jewish immigrants headed overwhelmingly to the cities. Of more than 130,000 Jews who immigrated in 1914, 78,575 settled in New York City, 14,485 in Philadelphia, and another 10,469 in Chicago. These industrial cities of the East and Middle West already housed the existing centers of the Jewish population. In 1915, 975,000 Jews resided in New York, making up about 28 percent of the city's total population. Other cities with large Jewish concentrations at that time included Chicago with 200,000 Jews; Baltimore, which had 50,000; Philadelphia, 150,000; Detroit, 25,000; Boston 60,000; Cleveland,

60,000; and St. Louis with 40,000.[3] Jews streamed to these big cities because their skills met existing labor needs.

Jews were not attracted to agriculture. For centuries few Jews had tilled the soil in Europe. In some areas the state forbade them from owning or working the land, and Jewish law and tradition frowned upon Jews farming outside Palestine. Thus, only the smallest number of Jews went to the agricultural states and most of them were petty merchants. In 1914 only 112 Jewish immigrants were bound for Kentucky, 127 for Alabama, and 160 for Louisiana, with none heading for Mississippi, Arkansas, or West Virginia.

Jewish immigrants clustered in certain skilled trades. In 1910 37 percent of all Jewish immigrants were skilled workers. Nearly half were in the needle trades, and of these 36.6 percent listed themselves as tailors, while the rest made a living as capmakers, milliners, seamstresses, and other related specialists. Another 10.3 percent of the skilled workers were carpenters, 5.9 percent shoemakers, 4.3 percent clerks, and 4.1 percent painters and glaziers.[4]

While most American Jews in 1915 were relegated to the working class, they eagerly aspired to move up to middle-class status. In the second decade of the twentieth century Jews experienced a gradual rise in economic condition. Some Jews moved from the role of worker to petty merchant or small businessman. Figures for many of New York's Jewish charitable organizations indicated a dramatic drop in the number of poor people. In this same period the predominantly Jewish labor unions in the needle trades had begun to organize extensively and, where they were effective, brought a constant though modest increase in wages and benefits. Furthermore, if the immigrants were workers, Jewish children did not follow their parents into garment factories. Instead they turned to white collar and professional jobs. The earliest figures on Jewish enrollments in American colleges and universities compiled in 1918 revealed that Jews made up 9.7 percent of the American college enrollment. Jewish students accounted for 23.4 percent of all the students of dentistry, 27.9 percent of the pharmacy students, 21.6 percent of all law students, and 16.4 percent of all those studying medicine. Clearly, this group eagerly sought economic mobility.[5]

The bulk of American Jews in 1915 clustered in the skilled and semi-skilled trades, especially in New York's garment industry, but an extremely small highly visible group of Jews were among the financial elite of American society. The Schiffs, the Warburgs, the Lehmans, the Seligmans, the Loebs, and the Lewisohns, who were among the wealthiest families of New York, differed from the masses of Jewish immigrants in more ways than economic status. They also defined Jewish identity in a way that differed strikingly from that of the Eastern European immigrants.

Throughout Jewish history, especially since their exile in the first century A.D., Jews had pondered the question, "Who is a Jew?" For some, Judaism represented a specific religious faith, governed by Mosaic law and its various elaborations. For others, Jewishness encompassed a cultural heritage and national identity, emphasizing the common origins of all Jews, with religion itself sometimes playing a minor role. Jews had debated this question wherever they had lived, and the divisions among American Jews in 1915 echoed this centuries-old debate.

The American Jewish community especially mirrored the conflicting currents of Jewish life in nineteenth-century Europe. The Jews of western and central Europe (the "German" Jews) had been deeply influenced by the European Enlightenment and the liberalism of the late eighteenth century. While the traditional barriers to Jews had not crumbled totally, Jews there could overcome the limitations of ghetto existence. They entered the professions, the literary world, and wealthy social circles. They partook of many educational and social opportunities in the secular world and were deeply influenced by their Christian acquaintances. Trying to harmonize their ancient faith with their newly gained status, the Jewish intellectual and religious elite developed the notion that Judaism was purely a religion. They wanted it to be simply one of many acceptable denominations in German society, rather than a separate culture or a distinct way of life. Their nationality was German, they argued, and their way of life did not differ from that of the German bourgeoisie. Therefore they instituted numerous religious reforms. Men and women sat next to each other in services. They used the German language in their worship and the traditional liturgy was augmented by organ and choir. They eliminated many of the restraints of Jewish law on diet and Sabbath observance. This Reform movement within Judaism developed among western European Jews, both those who remained in Europe and those who emigrated to the United States after 1830. In America rabbis like Isaac M. Wise, Emil Hirsch, David Einhorn, and Bernard Felsenthal advocated reform and built Hebrew Union College in Cincinnati to train their rabbis and teachers.[6]

While the Jews of central Europe attempted to blend their spiritual heritage with their rising status, their coreligionists in the east lived through very different experiences. The age of liberalism had not penetrated czarist Russia and the other lands of eastern Europe. There the ghetto walls were not broken and within the confines of the *shtetl* (hamlet) Jewish life was bounded by poverty, tradition, and the extreme anti-Semitism of the surrounding Christian world. These Jews (referred to usually as the "Russian" Jews) clung tenaciously to all religious precepts and made no efforts to modernize the faith. To them Judaism was not merely a religion, not just an organized ritual of worship: it was a total way of life, governing every aspect of existence—material and spiritual.

Some Jews in eastern Europe in the nineteenth century, especially the young, were not immune to new ideas. Many were attracted to socialism, which promised to transform the society in which they lived, or to Zionism, which dreamt of the creation of new societies. Both left-wing radicalism and Zionism shaped the political and ideological lives of many Jews who emigrated to the United States beginning in the 1880s.[7]

On the whole, though, the Jews of eastern Europe were orthodox in religion, living in constant fear of violence from their anti-Semitic neighbors, and lacking exposure to Western ideas. The great majority of Jews in the United States in 1915 were such people. Relations between eastern and western European Jews during the nineteenth century in Europe had been hostile. Reform Jews of western and central Europe viewed the eastern Europeans as medieval throwbacks retarding the progress of all Jews. Russian Jews, on the other hand, viewed those from western Europe as apostates who had no right to call themselves Jews.

These conflicts, originally based on European problems and conflicting definitions of Jewish identity, took on added significance in the United States. In 1915 American Jewry was composed of eastern and western Europeans. Since the German Jews had been in the United States for one or two generations by then, the old antagonism was redefined as a conflict between immigrant and Americanized Jews. Much of this hostility erupted in New York, the center of American Jewry, where new idioms and arguments exacerbated the old antagonism. Since many of the eastern European Jews in New York lived on Manhattan's lower East Side, they came to be called, quite derisively, the "downtown Jews" by their uptown American coreligionists. In turn, the Russian Jews often referred to the Germans as *Yahudim*, the Hebrew word for Jews, which here denoted their superficially elegant and American manners and their lack of a real commitment to Judaism. German Jews had been in the United States for several decades by the time of the massive immigration from eastern Europe. They had established their Reform religious institutions. Some had moved into circles of wealth and prominence; most of the others were comfortably middle class. They had adopted the trappings and respectability of the dominant culture as they had done in Germany. The influx of the Russian and Polish Jews from the 1880s to the 1920s put these well-established, Americanized Jews in an uncomfortable position. The century-old conflict between them and the eastern Europeans was transformed into embarrassment at the "strange customs" and "alien ways" of the newcomers.

The efforts of the German Jews to transform the eastern European Jews, to Americanize them, and to bring them into the middle class dominated the relationship. The German Jews were thus responsible for myriad projects—settlement houses, training schools, camps, nurseries—designed to educate the newly arrived immigrants and to speed up their institutional adjustment to America. Adolph Radin, founder of the Russian-American Hebrew Association, claimed in 1890 that his organization was going "to exercise a civilizing and elevating influence upon the immigrants and to Americanize them." In 1894 the *American Hebrew*, an English-language magazine, attempted to characterize the relationship between the two groups of Jews and noted:

> The thoroughly acclimed American Jew is oftentimes almost as peculiar among Jews generally as the race is singular among mankind. . . . He stands apart from the seething mass of Jewish immigrants . . . and looks upon them as in a stage of development pitifully low . . . He is closer to the Christian sentiment

around him than to the Judaism of these miserable darkened Hebrews.

Jacob Schiff, generally acknowledged leader of the German Jews, embarked on a massive, nationwide crusade in 1915 to discourage Jewish parents from speaking Yiddish with their children to hasten the process of acculturation.[8]

Ideological differences also fragmented American Jewry. Politically, many of the eastern European Jewish immigrants were radicals. While the vast majority voted for candidates of the two major parties, a significant minority espoused socialism. In 1916 New York's lower East Side sent Meyer London, a socialist labor lawyer, to Congress. The major Yiddish newspaper in New York and the United States was the socialist *Jewish Daily Forward*. Avowed socialists, publicly aligned with Eugene V. Debs' Socialist Party of America, led the two largest Jewish trade unions—the International Ladies' Garment Workers' Union and the Amalgamated Clothing Workers of America.

Socialism proved such an attractive political philosophy to these immigrant Jews because of the brutal sweatshop conditions under which so many worked, usually in factories owned by other Jews. The radicals boasted an articulate leadership, first converted to left-wing thought in czarist Russia. Among these leaders were Abraham Cahan, editor of the *Jewish Daily Forward*, and labor organizers Baruch Charney Vladeck, Morris Hillquit, and Sidney Hillman. The socialist leaders were deeply committed to Jewish culture, yet professed atheism and disparaged the hundreds of rabbis and houses of worship of the lower East Side.

Even those Jews who identified themselves with the left splintered into numerous ideological factions. All shades of left-wing thought and action were represented: left-wing unionism, social democracy, anarchism, communism. Each of these groups in turn created institutions to foster their ideology. Newspapers and magazines, schools and summer camps all flourished in order to win adherents and provide services for members.

Yiddishists—Jews who believed themselves bound to Jewishness through the medium of the Yiddish language—were closely aligned with the socialists. They saw Yiddish culture as a workers' culture and the expression of the Jewish folk spirit. Their heroes included Yiddish writers like Sholem Aleichem, I. L. Peretz, and Mendele Mokher Seforim, who had elevated Yiddish to high literary levels. The Yiddishists also formed organizations and institutions like the Workmen's Circle (Arbeiter Ring), a mutual aid insurance society which maintained extensive educational and recreational programs.[9]

The Zionists, on the other hand, differed fundamentally both from the Yiddishists and the left. They believed that Jewish destiny lay in the creation of a Jewish homeland in Palestine. The Zionists themselves were splintered. Labor Zionism attracted mostly eastern Europeans who envisioned a socialist homeland in Palestine. Territorialists hoped to establish a Jewish colony anywhere feasible and not necessarily in Palestine (Jewish homelands in Uganda, Mexico, and other parts of Central America had been suggested at various times). American-born Zionists like Henrietta Szold and Louis D. Brandeis saw Palestine as a potential refuge for the Jews of eastern Europe, but of no substantive importance for themselves or other American Jews. Many Zionists were political Zionists who anticipated the establishment of the Jewish homeland as a separate political entity. Others opposed this and merely called for Jewish settlement in Palestine under Turkish rule. All Zionists, however, stressed the rejuvenation of Hebrew as a spoken language and encouraged American Jews to aid the newly developing agricultural settlements in Palestine.[10]

This fragmentation of American Jewry often hampered concerted action. It created unnecessary hostility and exacerbated existing animosities. On the other hand, the many divisions of American Jewry led to the development of an extensive and complex organizational network. Since Jews were divided by geographic background, language, length of time in America, class, and ideology, each splinter group proceeded to build formal organizations and institutions. The *Jewish Communal Register of New York City* in 1917 listed 3,637 organizations—religious, recreational, cultural, educational, charitable, political, burial, mutual aid—in New York alone. In that year, seventy-six national Jewish organizations, fifty-four of which had over 5,000 branches combined, estimated their membership at over one million. In 1915 more than 200 *new* local Jewish organizations were established across the country and, at that time, thirty-one Jewish publications began to circulate for the first time.[11] These organizations ranged from youth groups and orphanages to the Jewish sanitarium in Denver to important political and social organizations like the American Jewish Committee, the B'nai Brith with its Anti-Defamation League, and the American Jewish Congress. The B'nai Brith was the oldest of the large national Jewish organizations. It was founded in the mid-nineteenth century as a mutual aid and fraternal society consisting of lodges scattered across the United States. In 1913, after the arrest of Leo Frank in Atlanta, the B'nai Brith established the Anti-Defamation League dedicated "to stop by appeals to law, the defamation of the Jewish people." In its earliest years, the ADL concerned itself with combating the negative Jewish stereotypes which abounded in the press and on the stage.

Perhaps the most important national Jewish organization was the American Jewish Committee, organized in 1906. Composed mostly of the elite of the western European Jews, its wide range of activities was designed "to safeguard the civil and religious rights of Jews, to combat discrimination and to allay prejudice." While the scope of its work was international, it focused mainly on the United States, where it depended on the personal contacts of its influential membership and used personal pressure rather than litigation to confront anti-Semitism. The American Jewish Congress, founded in 1922, was more heavily eastern European and saw itself as a mass-based, democratic organization. Its leaders included some of the most prominent American Zionists like Rabbi Stephen Wise, but its goals differed little from the Committee's.[12]

The diversity of American Jewry resulted directly in the extensive and rich organizational life. The highly developed communal structure in turn produced a sophisticated and articulate leadership class. Leaders like Louis Marshall of the Committee, Stephen Wise of the Congress, David Dubinsky, Morris Hillquit, Sidney Hillman, Benjamin Schlesinger, Meyer London, and Baruch Charney Vladeck of the immigrant Jewish labor movement, Henrietta Szold, Louis Brandeis, Horace Kallen, Julian Mack, and Felix Frankfurter of the Zionist movement were but some of the most influential American Jews who represented the various communities.

Although the American Jewish world was diverse, it could nevertheless demonstrate solidarity when necessary. Jewish communities in various cities united to organize and coordinate charities. The federation of Jewish philanthropies began in 1895 in Boston; eastern and western European Jews worked together to rationalize the distribution of charity to the city's Jewish poor. Jewish philanthropy in Cincinnati was federated in 1896, Philadelphia in 1901, Cleveland in 1904, and Baltimore in 1906. In 1914 the American Jewish Joint Distribution Committee attempted to relieve the suffering of European Jews caught between the armies of World War I. Despite differences of opinion, despite struggles between eastern and western Europeans, Yiddishists and Americanists, Zionists and anti-Zionists, the JDC collected and distributed millions of dollars in relief money. New York Jews also overcame diversity to create the Kehillah (in Europe, the *kehillah*, Hebrew for congregation, was the officially sanctioned Jewish community). In 1911 the uptown and the downtown Jews established a central unifying community organization, intended to defend Jews from anti-Semitic critics as well as to regulate and coordinate internal Jewish affairs like charity and education.[13]

These various Jewish communities, although divided and fragmented, could work together for various reasons. First, they were all Jews and shared a common history spanning several centuries of exile and oppression. All ultimately drew their inspiration from the same sources—the Old Testament and the Mosaic code. In America all were urbanites and tended to be liberals in politics. While a real gulf separated the various groups, no taboo existed against intermarriage, and in the generations after immigration marriage between eastern and western Europeans became commonplace as the distinctions blurred.

They also shared a *recent* history of suffering and discrimination and felt anxious about the fate of contemporary Jewry in Europe and America. The recognition and fear of anti-Semitism transformed a vague sense of coreligion into a workable unity. The two major examples of united action—the JDC and the Kehillah—were both reactions to anti-Semitism. The Joint Distribution Committee responded to the desperate situation of millions of Jews trapped between the various armies of World War I. Nearly three and a half million Jews lived on the Eastern Front and were caught between the forces of Germany-Austria and Russia. As early as December 1915, 600,000 Jews were uprooted by the Russian army alone. By 1916 most of the Jewish Pale of settlement was controlled by the Germans, who evacuated at least 70,000 Jews to Germany as semi-forced labor. In that same year over half the Jews in Galicia were refugees. Jewish communities were physically destroyed. Jews were accused of disloyalty by each new set of invaders.[14]

The New York Kehillah was also a response to anti-Semitism. In October 1908 the Police Commissioner of New York, Theodore Bingham, declared that nearly half of the criminal population of New York was Jewish. This statement set off a furor in the Jewish communities of the city and when Rabbi Judah Magnes of the ultra-reformed, affluent Temple Emanu-El spoke to a group of "downtown" Jews at Clinton Hall on the lower East Side, he sketched his vision of a Kehillah which could provide for the common defense of all Jews. Magnes hoped that the Kehillah could "wipe out invidious distinctions between east European and west European, foreigner and native, Uptown and Downtown Jew, rich and poor: and make us realize that the Jews are one people with a common history and with common hopes."[15]

In 1915 those common hopes focused most sharply on the United States. Anti-Semitism was on the upsurge in Europe, Palestine seemed far from a practical reality as a Jewish homeland, and so it was to America that most Jews directed their aspirations. Leaders of American Jewry thus were sensitive to any anti-Semitic rumblings in the United States and kept a close watch on anti-Jewish activities in all sectors of the society. American Jewish leaders were less than optimistic about the future of American Jewry in that year and doubted that the American rhetoric of democracy and equality really applied to them. Optimism was clearly unwarranted. In fact, the lynching of Leo Frank in 1915 ushered in two of the most blatantly anti-Semitic decades in American history.

Anti-Semitism had long existed in America. Histories of American Jewry always opened with the prophetic anecdote that in 1654, when the first group of Portuguese Jews landed in New Amsterdam, they were greeted by a hostile Peter Stuyvesant, who grudgingly allowed them to remain "provided that the poor among them shall not become a burden to the company [Dutch West India Company] or to the community, but be supported by their own nation." Since Jews made up such a small portion of American society until after the Civil War, anti-Semitism remained fairly dormant, but with the migration of eastern European Jews to the United States in the post-war decades it appeared in more overt forms.[16]

American anti-Semitism seemed to accompany other social movements which flourished in the years from the Civil War until World War I. Anti-Semites seized upon certain pervasive, Jewish stereotypes, utilizing these images for their own political purposes. On the one hand, the image of Jews as money-hungry, aggressive and vulgar capitalists was used both by the declining New England elites, epitomized by Henry Adams, and by dispossessed agrarians of the South such as the Populists. On the other hand, the specter of clannish, medieval, and unassimilable Jews who could not be Americanized figured in the rhetoric of nativists who wished to restrict immigration. They often linked Jews with radicalism and stressed the danger to American institutions from Jewish leftists.[17]

The anti-Semitism of these years pervaded all sectors of American life. Vicious portrayals of Jews abounded in literature, both popular and intellectual. On the stage the stock character of the Jew was a shabby peddler or grotesque pawnbroker, depicted with dirty clothes, a thick accent, and an insatiable desire for money. He was Ikey, Jakey, or Abie, best remembered for his stinginess and greed. Fashionable resorts and clubs frequently refused admission to Jews, who also faced discrimination in the housing market where restrictive covenants were commonplace. Perhaps most serious, Jews met systematic discrimination in professional and business circles. Jewish doctors had a hard time finding internships and residencies, Jewish lawyers were kept out of the most prestigious law firms, and in academia, Jews were repeatedly denied teaching positions. These trends became more pronounced after 1915 as more Jews sought admission to the middle class and to the professions. While the stage Jew faded after World War I, professional and academic discrimination worsened, culminating in the 1920s with the imposition of quotas on Jewish students in many American universities.[18]

In 1915, as Jewish leaders pondered the nature of American anti-Semitism, they and the rest of American Jewry were horrified by the brutal lynching of a fellow Jew. In 1913 Leo Frank, a Northern-born Jewish businessman, owner of a pencil factory in Atlanta, Georgia, was arrested and tried for the rape-murder of Mary Phagan, one of his employees. The case against Frank was flimsy, but the white Christian population of Atlanta hysterically demanded a guilty verdict against Frank, the Jew and northern capitalist. The trial was sensational. The court even lifted the taboo on admitting the testimony of a black man against a white and Frank's janitor, Jim Conley, testified for the prosecution. While the trial was still in progress, Conley, who had sworn in court that he had seen Frank commit the murder, admitted that he had perjured himself and implied that it was he who had actually killed the girl. The jury chose to overlook this admission. Bizarre stories and rumors about Frank's alleged sexual perversions, which stemmed directly from his Jewishness, circulated in Atlanta and throughout the rest of Georgia. [19]

Although Frank was found guilty of the crimes against Mary Phagan, Governor Slayton commuted the death sentence to life imprisonment. This did not end the crusade against Frank, nor did it assuage the anti-Semitism which had engulfed the state. Atlanta newspapers and magazines cried for true revenge. Periodicals like *Tom Watson's Magazine* called for real justice. Spurred on by such incendiary rhetoric, a mob stormed Frank's prison cell in Marietta, Georgia, on August 16, 1915, dragged Frank out, and lynched him.

The Jewish world was aghast. Throughout the case they had compared it to the Dreyfus case in France and to the blood-libel against Mendel Beilis in Russia in 1911. The entire affair and especially its tragic ending caused American Jews—western Europeans and eastern Europeans, immigrants and American-born—to ponder their future in America. The events of the next twenty years in the United States and Europe were to cause American Jewry a great deal more anxiety.

It was not accidental that the years which saw the beginnings of real American anti-Semitism coincided with the slow but substantial movement of American Jews into the middle class and into positions of prominence in American society. Jews were experiencing a continuous, though gradual, economic rise. While the vast majority of Jews in 1915 were immigrant workers, their children deserted the laboring class in droves, attracted to the professions and business. In 1900, 59.6 percent of all American Jews were employed in industry. Thirty years later that number had fallen to 13.7 percent. In 1900 only about 20 percent of the Jews in the United States were in business, but by 1930 over half were. A similar rise occurred in the numbers of Jews in professional positions. [20]

A small number of Jews found themselves among the financial elite of America. While they constituted the smallest percentage of American Jewry, the economic position of individuals like Julius Rosenwald, Jacob Schiff, Felix Warburg, and Herbert Lehman had significance for all Jews. [21] On the one hand, their wealth directly fed anti-Semitic notions about Jews as ruthless capitalists. On the other hand, they used their positions of influence and wealth to improve the conditions of Jewish life in America. Although their ideas on the nature of Jewish identity differed dramatically from those of an Abraham Cahan, they still were considered by many as representative of all American Jews. In 1915 a number of Jews were also beginning to make their mark in academia, especially in newer fields like anthropology and psychology. Franz Boas emerged as the best known of this group. Fields like law, medicine, theater and music also projected a number of Jews into national prominence.

The career of Louis D. Brandeis, who in 1916 was appointed by Woodrow Wilson to the Supreme Court, perhaps best symbolized the rise of elite American Jews to recognition in American society. An urbane Boston lawyer who slowly had come to a consciousness of his ethnic-religious background, Brandeis was initially slated for a cabinet position in the first Wilson administration. Wilson, however, decided to pass over his trusted adviser and ardent admirer because anti-Semitic protests from New England business and community leaders frightened him. Two years later, after a protracted and heated Senate fight, Brandeis' nomination to the Supreme Court was confirmed. [22]

In 1915 American Jewry could look back and see a recent past of growing anti-Semitism in Europe and America. But, troubled as they were by anti-Semitism in America, the contrast with Europe made it seem pale and benign. Jews could also perceive that they were firmly set on the path of educational and economic mobility. In 1915 American Jews could not know the extent to which the next two decades would see the intensification of anti-Semitism, both here and abroad.

BLACKS IN WHITE AMERICA: 1915

For American blacks 1915 was also a year of a significant change. While it did not bring great social and economic upheaval, two events signaled the beginnings of fundamental shifts. In 1915 the master of

Tuskegee, Booker T. Washington, died. In 1915 economic lures in the North began to convince many blacks that the future held little hope for altering the continuous cycle of poverty, disfranchisement, lynching, and Jim Crow in the South. In fact, 1915 can be seen as a midway point in the history of blacks. It had been fifty years since the end of the Civil War and the official end of slavery. It would be yet another fifty years before the passage of comprehensive civil rights legislation would give real strength to the post-Civil War Constitutional amendments. In 1915, it might be said in retrospect, black America stood halfway between slavery and freedom.

"Easily the most striking thing in the history of the American Negro since 1876 is the ascendancy of Mr. Booker T. Washington," wrote his major critic, W.E.B. Du Bois in 1903. Washington's personality, Washington's ideology, and Washington's influence on both blacks and whites dominated the course of black history up to 1915. His public posture of acquiescing to segregation and disfranchisement and his boundless faith in the powers of education made Booker Washington seem the ideal leader for a people in transition—a people which was beginning to emerge from the psychological and economic bonds of slavery. But the ideology of Tuskegee, the "cast down your buckets where you are" approach to race relations, could not flourish without Washington. His death unloosed public criticism of this philosophy among black leaders. [23]

Nineteen fifteen also heralded the beginning of the great migration: a migration of a rural population to the cities, a migration of an agrarian population to industry, and a migration of southern people to the North. In the decade from 1910 to 1920, 454,300 blacks left the South. While the 1920s would witness an even larger flood northward, the process was set in motion before World War I, and 1915 was one of the most intense migratory years of that decade. The immensity of the northward black movement can be seen most clearly by comparing the 1910 and 1920 black urban northern populations. In Chicago in 1910 there were 44,103 blacks. By 1920 that number had jumped by 148.5 percent to 109,594. The 5,741 blacks in Detroit in 1910 were joined by over 35,000 others by 1920, and that city's black population increased a staggering 623.4 percent. Cities like Cincinnati, Cleveland, Philadelphia, and New York experienced similar influxes of southern blacks, and their Negro population jumped by 50.9, 308.0,

50, and 60 percent, respectively. Gary, Indiana, a steaming steel center, saw its black population grow 1,283.6 percent in those ten years. [24]

A combination of factors propelled this massive internal migration. Economic conditions in the South were dismal; agriculture remained continually depressed. Massive crop destructions by the boll weevil and a shortage of capital made the tenant farmer system even less viable than it had been. The limited economic growth that did occur in the South was in industry, but both law and custom excluded Negroes from factory jobs. Shoddy housing, negligible educational opportunities, and sub-standard medical facilities characterized black living conditions. Southern blacks suffered through an unending cycle of discrimination and violence. From 1900 to the eve of World War I, 1,100 blacks had been lynched and the specter of terror loomed throughout the South, Jim Crow segregation was firmly entrenched and blacks were legally defined to be much less than full citizens. [25]

For Negroes the North posed a strikingly different picture. A labor shortage in the North, caused by the cessation of European immigration at the beginning of World War I and expansion of northern industrial plants, proved attractive lures to impoverished southern blacks. Not only were salaries substantially higher, hours shorter, and conditions relatively more tolerable in the North, but greater educational and political opportunities existed. The northern Negro press actively painted the contrast between southern deprivation and the prospects of the North, trying to induce blacks to migrate. One black newspaper, *The Chicago Defender*, ran so many articles contrasting the problems of the South with the promises of the North that several southern cities tried to ban its circulation. [26]

The North was obviously not the idyllic promised land, unconscious of race, which the black press depicted. The years after 1915 saw intensification of black residential segregation in the North, exclusion of blacks from well-paying jobs, and outbreaks of bloody riots in East St. Louis, Chicago, and elsewhere. Yet, in 1915 blacks could still be optimistic about their future in the North. For one thing, in the North blacks at least exercised a modest amount of political influence. They voted, and in 1915 elected the first black to the Chicago City Council. Blacks had begun to flex their muscle in local politics in New York as well, and as their numbers grew, politicians were forced to make some overtures to black communities. [27]

Even more significant, in the North blacks actively could protest the course of race relations. They could meet, discuss grievances, and publish militant statements without having to fear the lynch mob. While vigorous black protest no doubt upset many northern whites, blacks in the North did not hesitate to decry discrimination. Organizations like the National Association for the Advancement of Colored People boldly protested racism. Black writers like W.E.B. DuBois, James Weldon Johnson, Walter White, and Claude McKay could write eloquently about the tragedy of their race and depict movingly the brutality of the white South.

The growth of northern black protest rose to a significant level in 1915 when the NAACP launched a vigorous crusade against D. W. Griffith's film, *The Birth of a Nation*. In the same year the association successfully petitioned the Supreme Court of the United States against the so-called "grandfather clause" which was routinely used to disfranchise blacks in the South. In *Guinn v. United States* the Court for the first time struck down a law robbing blacks of the vote.[28]

Such vigorous action could only have been undertaken by blacks who did not live under the specter of lynching. It was among northern blacks that a vocal, politically articulate leadership class emerged in the years after 1915 and it was in the North that the cultural stirrings of the 1920s "New Negro" renaissance developed.

Nineteen fifteen was a year which signified change for blacks. It saw the shift of leadership away from Tuskegee. It saw the first shifts of population away from the South. It witnessed strident black protest against legal discrimination. The changes in leadership, demography and mood in black America after 1915 were dramatic. Any interested observer would have noted these trends and developments, and among the most interested were the leaders of American Jewry.

THE TWO MINORITIES

Nineteen fifteen proved a turning point for both the Jewish and the black world in America. It was also significant in the relationship between the two groups because only after massive black migration to Northern cities did Jews and blacks really come in contact with each other. Furthermore, with the growth of American anti-Semitism in the decades following 1915, Jews became fascinated with blacks as the symbol of America's failure to live up to its rhetoric of equality and democracy. It was not that Jews were uninterested in blacks before 1915. In fact, since the beginning of the century Jews had contributed heavily to black philanthropy and civil rights efforts. But after 1915, with the Frank case and the increase of blacks in cities like New York and Chicago, Jewish interest intensified.

In the nineteenth century the record of the American Jews on the black issue had been more ambiguous than it would be in the twentieth. There had been Jews who owned and dealt in slaves. There were Jews like Judah P. Benjamin, Secretary of War of the Confederacy, whom Daniel Webster described as an "Israelite with an Egyptian heart," Rabbi Morris Raphall, a New York clergyman who sought to prove that slavery carried Biblical sanction, and David Yulee, U.S. Senator from Florida, who staunchly supported the slave system. On the other hand, the anti-slavery societies attracted Jews like Moses Judah, a New York merchant affiliated with the New York Manumission Society, Moritz Pinner, editor of an abolitionist newspaper in Kansas City, and August Bondi, who joined John Brown in the fight to keep Kansas from becoming a slave state. [29] In the twentieth century, however, *no* representative of the Jewish community publicly sanctioned or approved of the segregation of blacks. No organ of Jewish public opinion failed to express some degree of sympathy and commiseration with the plight of black people.

The sympathy expressed by Jews did not surprise many observers. The parallel between the black and Jewish experiences had been frequently drawn in America, especially in the pre-Civil War years. Because so much eighteenth- and early nineteenth-century American rhetoric drew its inspiration from the Old Testament heritage of the Puritans, the image of black slaves as the Children of Israel appeared repeatedly. One of the earliest anti-slavery pamphlets was Samuel Sewall's tract of 1700, *The Selling of Joseph, A Memorial*. Sermons and editorials on the subject of slavery frequently made the comparison between blacks and Jews. Boston minister Edward Everett once compared the scheme to send freed slaves to Africa with the return of the Children of Israel to Canaan after leaving Egypt. Long before masses of Jews had emigrated to the United States, Negro slaves and black and white abolitionists seized upon the Old Testament imagery of slavery in Egypt for spiritual and propagandist purposes. The music of black slavery abounded with the metaphors and analogies of the exodus from Egypt. Slave leaders like Harriet Tubman of the underground railroad and Gabriel, organizer of an 1800 slave revolt in Virginia, compared the lot of their people with that of the Children of Israel in bondage, and Tubman saw herself as the Moses of her race, leading her people to freedom.[30] Decades after Emancipation, American Jews would point with pride to the fact that the Old Testament had been an inspiration to the cause of abolitionism.

But the Children of Israel who figured so prominently in the sermons and songs of the nineteenth century were not the same Jews who were contributing time, effort, energy, and money to the NAACP, the Urban League, Tuskegee, and dozens of other black endeavors. Several centuries of European life had produced those Jews, and they had but the scantiest exposure to color and race differences before migrating to the United States. One Jewish immigrant from Lithuania wrote an essay for *Opportunity*, the journal of the Urban League, entitled, "I See a Colored Man for the First Time. . . ." He had heard of dark-skinned people, but he imagined "a copper, glowing sun and burnished, brown bodies . . . bodies that would scatter sun and ray-dust as they ran." The writer of the article, U. Katzenelenbogen, had perhaps first learned of the existence of dark-skinned people from the Bible. The Ethiopians appeared frequently in the pages of the Old Testament, where they were not considered to be particularly unpleasant or forbidding. The prophet Amos, speaking for God, asked, "Are you not like the Ethiopians to me, Children of Israel?" The female character of the Song of Songs who, according to rabbinic tradition, represented Israel, stated, "I am black and beautiful, Daughters of Jerusalem." Jeremiah did not intend to insult the Ethiopians when he asked: "Can the Ethiopian change his skin or the leopard his spots?" Post-Biblical Jewish learning also contained references to dark people. According to lore, the Queen of Sheba who bedazzled Solomon was black. The Talmud contains several folktales about white-skinned women giving birth to black-skinned children.[31]

Undoubtedly, many of the Near Eastern peoples with whom Jews traded and fought in Biblical and post-Biblical times were dark-skinned, but the first modern encounter between Jews and nonwhites most probably occurred during the Moorish occupation of Spain. Not only was the relationship harmonious, with intermarriage between Moors and Jews fairly common, but this epoch, called the Golden Age of Spanish Jewry, saw Jews prominent and prosperous in a society which tolerated their religion. [32]

While written and oral accounts of the Spanish era circulated among eastern European Jews, the Moors, historic and almost mystical characters, had no impact on the *shtetl* or ghetto. Jews in central and eastern Europe might have heard of American blacks through letters from friends and relatives in the United States. Jews with cosmopolitan contacts who moved freely in London, Berlin, Paris, or Vienna, undoubtedly heard about American race relations. The masses of Jews might also have read about Negroes in the *Jewish Daily Forward*, which circulated in Europe. Likewise, some American Yiddish novelists who delved into black themes published their works in Warsaw and Vilna.

Theodore Herzl, a polished Viennese journalist, founder of the modern political Zionist movement, included a lengthy reference to blacks in his 1902 utopian novel *Altneuland*. A young Jew, unsure of his place in the world, was transported to Palestine and its New Society. He entered the research laboratory of Dr. Steineck. When asked what the scientist was working on, he answered,

"At the opening up of Africa."

The visitors mistrusted their ears. Was the seeker after scientific truth a bit mad?

"Did you say, at the opening up of Africa?" . . .

"Yes... That is to say, I hope to find the cure for malaria. We have overcome it here in Palestine, thanks to the drainage of the swamps, canalization, and the eucalyptus forests. But conditions are different in Africa. The same measures cannot be taken there because the prerequisite—mass immigration—is not present. The white colonist goes under in Africa. That country can be opened up to civilization only after malaria has been subdued. Only then will enormous areas become available for the surplus populations of Europe. And only then will the proletarian masses find a healthy outlet. Understand?"

Kingscourt laughed, "You want to cart off the whites to the black continent, you wonder worker!"

"Not only the whites!" replied Steineck gravely. "The blacks as well. There is still one problem of racial misfortune unsolved. The depths of that problem, in all their horror, only a Jew can fathom. I mean the negro problem . . . Think of the hair-raising horrors of the slave trade. Human beings, because their skins are black, are stolen, carried off, and sold. Their descendants grow up in alien surroundings despised and hated because their skin is differently pigmented. I am not ashamed to say, though I be thought ridiculous, now that I have lived to see the restoration of the Jews, I should like to pave the way for the restoration of the Negroes." [33]

Other spotty sources of information about blacks also existed. *Uncle Tom's Cabin*, for example, was translated into Yiddish and Hebrew. In fact Mr. Katzenelenbogen, the Lithuanian Jewish immigrant who shared his thought on race with the readers of *Opportunity*, noted that he considered reading the antebellum novel one of the most profound and enduring memories of his childhood. "At once my beating heart (and my tears) went out to her [Stowe] as if she had been a kind, elderly aunty. I saw the . . . colored people . . . in the toils of slavery, lashed and tortured by the planters, downhearted and afraid." [34]

The suffering of American blacks struck a responsive chord in Jews in Europe. But it had an even more profound effect on the leaders of American Jewry. More significant than the literary interest was the fact that a large portion of the leadership and sponsorship of many black civil rights, philanthropic, and labor efforts came from Jews. More profoundly important was the fact that the organs of Jewish public opinion—the Yiddish and English-language Jewish press— were fascinated by black affairs and the problems of racism.

In the years from 1915 to 1935 American Jews, especially the elite, witnessed with dismay growing anti-Semitism at home and abroad. They also experienced steady economic success and greater prominence in society. Out of these contradictory conditions of American life there emerged an intensified Jewish interest in and involvement with black affairs. From these contradictory conditions of American life emerged a need to come to terms with the new reality as well as to preserve the old.

NOTES

1. *American Jewish Yearbook: 5676, 1915-1916* (Philadelphia: Jewish Publication Society of America, 1916), p. 344; Moses Rischin, *The Promised City: New York's Jews, 1870-1914* (Cambridge: Harvard University Press, 1962), pp. 270-271; Maurice J. Karpf, *Jewish Community Organization in the United States: An Outline of Types of Organizations, Activities, and Problems* (New York: Bloch Publishing Company, 1938), pp. 1-8; Marshall Sklare, *America's Jews* (New York: Random House, 1971), p. 38.

2. *American Jewish Yearbook: 5676*, pp. 346-347, 353; Samuel Joseph, *Jewish Immigration to the United States: From 1881-1910* (New York: Columbia University Press, 1914), p. 93; Robert Park and Herbert Miller, *Old World Traits Transplanted* (New York: Harper and Brothers, 1921), pp. 195-211; Maurice Karpf, *Jewish Community Organization*, p. 35.

3. *American Jewish Yearbook: 5676*, p. 353.

4. Samuel Joseph, *Jewish Immigration*, pp. 187-188.

5. *Jewish Communal Survey of Greater New York, 1928* (New York: Bureau of Jewish Social Research, 1928), p. 70; Amalgamated Clothing Workers of America, *Annual Report, 1922-1924* (1924): XLV; Elton Rayack, "The Effect of Unionism on Wages in the Men's Clothing Industry, 1911-1955" (Ph.D. dissertation, University of Chicago, 1957); *New York Herald*, November 26, 1905; Lee J. Levinger, *The Jewish Student in America: A Study Made by the Research Bureau of the B'nai Brith Hillel Foundation* (Cincinnati: B'nai Brith, 1937), pp. 85-86.

6. There is an extensive body of literature dealing with Western European Jews, both in Europe and in America. Two works on the subject are Marvin Lowenthal, *The Jews of Germany* (New York: Longmans, Green and Company, 1936) and Eric E. Hirshler, ed., *Jews from Germany in the United States* (New York: Farrar, Straus, and Cudahy, 1955).

7. Three valuable studies from an immense field are Lucy S. Dawidowicz, ed., *The Golden Tradition: Jewish Life and Thought in Eastern Europe* (New York: Holt, Rinehart and Winston, 1967); Mark Zborowski and Elizabeth Herzog, *Life Is with People* (New York: International Universities Press, 1952); S. N. Dubnow, *History of the Jews in Russia and Poland*, trans. by I. Friedlander, 3 vols. (Philadelphia: Jewish Publication Society of America, 1916-1920). Irving Howe, *World of Our Fathers* (New York: Harcourt Brace Jovanovich, 1976) is the most recent and most complete survey of the eastern European Jewish experience in America.

8. Irving Mandel, "The Attitude of the American Jewish Community to East European Immigration," *American Jewish Archives*, 3 (June 1950): 73-85; Oscar Handlin, *Adventure in Freedom: Three Hundred Years of Jewish Life in America* (New York: McGraw-Hill, 1954), pp. 109-142; Esther Panitz, "In Defense of the Jewish Immigrant: 1891-1924," *American Jewish Historical Quarterly*, 53 (December 1963): 99-130; Esther Panitz, "The Polarity of American Jewish Attitudes Towards Immigration, 1870-1891," in *The Jewish Experience in America*, Vol. IV, ed. by Abraham J. Karp (Waltham, Massachusetts: American Jewish Historical Society, 1969), pp. 31-62; Moses Rischin, *The Promised City*, pp. 95-111.

9. Hertz Burgin, *Die Geschichte Fun der Idisher Arbeiter Bewegung* (New York: United Hebrew Trades, 1915); Abraham M. Rogoff, *Formative Years of the Jewish Labor Movement in the United States: 1890-1900* (Ann Arbor: Edwards Brothers, 1945); Melech Epstein, *Jewish Labor in USA: 1914-1952* (New York: Trade Union Sponsoring Committee, 1953); Judah J. Shapiro, *The Friendly Society: A History of the Workmen's Circle* (New York: Media Judaica, 1970).

10. Isidore S. Meyer, ed., *Early History of Zionism in America* (New York: American Jewish Historical Society, 1958); Arthur Hertzberg, *The Zionist Idea: A Historical Analysis and Reader* (New York: Doubleday and Company, 1959); Ben Halpern, *The Idea of the Jewish State* (Cambridge: Harvard University Press, 1969); Samuel Halperin, *The Political World of American Zionism* (Detroit: Wayne State University Press, 1961); Yonathan Shapiro, *Leadership of the American Zionist Organization, 1897-1930* (Urbana: University of Illinois Press, 1971).

11. *Jewish Communal Register of Greater New York, 1917* (New York: Bureau of Jewish Social Research, 1918), p. 49; *American Jewish Yearbook: 5676*, p. 116; Robert Park and Herbert Miller, *Old World Traits*, p. 210; *Directory of Jewish National and Local Organizations in the United States* (Philadelphia: Jewish Publication Society of America, 1919), p. 303.

12. There is no history of either the B'nai Brith or the American Jewish Congress. The only history of the Anti-Defamation League is a short work by the Anti-Defamation League, *Not the Work of a Day: The Story of the Anti-Defamation League of B'nai Brith* (New York: Anti-Defamation League, 1965). There are several histories of the American Jewish Committee, including Nathan Schachner, *The Price of Liberty: A History of the American Jewish Committee* (New York: American Jewish Committee, 1948); Frederick W. Robin and Selma G. Hirsh, *The Pursuit of Equality: A Half Century of the American Jewish Committee* (New York: Crown Publishers, 1957); Naomi W. Cohen, *Not Free to Desist: The American Jewish Committee, 1906-1966* (Philadelphia: Jewish Publication Society of America, 1972).

13. Joseph Jacobs, "The Federation Movement in American Jewish Philanthropy," *American Jewish Yearbook: 5676*, pp. 159-198; Oscar Handlin, *A Continuing Task: The American Jewish Joint Distribution Committee, 1914-1964* (New York: Random House, 1964); Arthur A. Goren, *New York Jews and the Quest for Community: The Kehillah Experiment, 1908-1922* (New York: Columbia University Press, 1970).

14. Joseph C. Hyman, *Twenty-Five Years of American Aid to Jews Overseas: A Record of the Joint Distribution Committee* (New York: Joint Distribution Committee, 1939); Salo W. Baron, *The Russian Jew: Under Tsars and Soviets* (New York: Macmillan Company, 1964), p. 191.

15. Arthur Goren, *New York Jews*; quoted in Moses Rischin, *The Promised City*, p. 243.

16. Lee J. Levinger, *Anti-Semitism in the United States: Its History and Causes* (New York: Bloch Publishing Company, 1925); Jacob J. Weinstein, "Anti-Semitism," in *The American Jew: A Composite Portrait*, ed. by Oscar I. Janowsky (New York: Harper and Brothers, 1942), pp. 183-204; Carey McWilliams, *A Mask for Privilege: Anti-Semitism in America* (Boston: Little, Brown, 1948); John Higham, "Social Discrimination Against Jews in America, 1830-1930," *Publications of the American Jewish Historical Society*, 47 (1957): 1-33; J. Milton Yinger, *Anti-Semitism: A Case Study in Prejudice*

and Discrimination (New York: Freedom Books, 1964).

17. E. Digby Baltzell, *The Protestant Establishment: Aristocracy and Caste in America* (New York: Random House, 1964), pp. 32-37; Richard Hofstadter, *The Age of Reform: From Bryan to F.D.R.* (New York: Alfred A. Knopf, 1955), pp. 77-81; Daniel Bell, "The Grass Roots of American Jew Hatred," *Jewish Frontier*, 11 (June 1944): 15-20; C. Van Woodward, *Tom Watson: Agrarian Rebel* (New York: Macmillan Company, 1938), pp. 442-446; John Higham, *Strangers in the Land: Patterns of American Nativism, 1860-1925* (New Brunswick, N.J.: Rutgers University Press, 1955), pp. 66-67, 92-94, 160-161. The anti-Semitism of the Populists has been minimized by Walter Nugent, *The Tolerant Populists* (Chicago: University of Chicago Press, 1963).

18. Lee J. Levinger, *Anti-Semitism: Yesterday and Tomorrow* (New York: Macmillan Company, 1936), p. 145. One interesting case of academic anti-Semitism is that of Ludwig Lewisohn, who had converted to Christianity as a young man but was still refused several academic posts because of his Jewish origins. See Ludwig Lewisohn, *Up Stream: An American Chronicle* (New York: Boni and Liveright, 1922); Adolph Gillis, *Ludwig Lewisohn: The Artist and His Message* (New York: Duffield and Green, 1933); Fred Mandell, "Ludwig Lewisohn: An Intellectual Biography" (Ph.D. dissertation, University of Chicago, 1972).

19. Leonard Dinnerstein, *The Leo Frank Case* (New York: Columbia University Press, 1968).

20. There are no adequate or systematic surveys of Jewish economic conditions. Jewish economic mobility is a factor referred to constantly in the literature of American Jewish history. It was also a reality as indicated by the statistics of Jewish charity agencies, Jewish labor unions, and Jewish social service organizations. The increase in the numbers of Jewish college students in the first decade of the twentieth century indicated an upward economic trend. A useful statement on Jewish economic mobility up to 1914 is Moses Rischin, *The Promised City*, pp. 51-75; a general survey of Jewish economic change is Nathan Goldberg, *Occupational Patterns of American Jewry* (New York: Jewish Theological Seminary and Peoples' University, 1947).

21. A popular but useful book on the wealthy American Jews is Stephen Birmingham, *"Our Crowd": The Great Jewish Families of New York* (New York: Harper and Row, 1967).

22. Alfred Lief, *Brandeis: The Personal History of an American Ideal* (New York: Stackpole Sons, 1936); Alpheus Thomas Mason, *Brandeis: A Free Man's Life* (New York: Viking Press, 1946); Melvin I. Urofsky, *A Mind of One Piece: Brandeis and American Reform* (New York: Scribner's, 1971). See also E. Digby Baltzell, *The Protestant Establishment*, pp. 187-195.

23. W.E.B. Du Bois, *The Souls of Black Folk: Essays and Sketches* (Chicago: A. C. McClurg and Company, 1903), p. 40; Emmet J. Scott and Lyman Beecher Stowe, *Booker T. Washington, Builder of a Civilization* (Garden City, N.Y.: Doubleday, Page and Company, 1916); Samuel R. Spencer, *Booker T. Washington and the Negro's Place in American Life* (Boston: Little, Brown, 1955); Emma L. Thornbrough, *Booker T. Washington* (Englewood Cliffs, N.J.: Prentice-Hall, 1969); Louis R. Harlan, *Booker T. Washington: The Making of a Black Leader, 1856-1901* (New York: Oxford University Press, 1972).

24. Chicago Commission on Race Relations, *The Negro in Chicago: A Study of Race*

Relations and a Race Riot (Chicago: University of Chicago Press, 1922), pp. 79-89; Philip M. Hauser, "Demographic Factors in the Integration of the Negro," *Daedalus*, 94 (Fall 1965): 847-877; Gunnar Myrdal, *An American Dilemma: The Negro Problem and Modern Democracy*, Vol I (New York: Harper, 1944), pp. 182-204.

25. The causes of black migration have been written about extensively. See, for example, Allan H. Spear, *Black Chicago: The Making of a Negro Ghetto, 1890-1920* (Chicago: University of Chicago Press, 1967), pp. 129-146; Gilbert Osofsky, *Harlem: The Making of a Ghetto: Negro New York, 1890-1930* (New York: Harper and Row, 1966), pp. 17-34. Older studies of black migration and its causes are Carter G. Woodson, *A Century of Negro Migration* (Washington, D.C.: The Association for the Study of Negro Life and History, 1918); Louise V. Kennedy, *The Negro Peasant Turns Cityward: Effects of Recent Migrations to Northern Centers* (New York: Columbia University Press, 1930); Frank A. Ross and Louise V. Kennedy, *A Bibliography of Negro Migration* (New York: Columbia University Press, 1934).

26. Allan H. Spear, *Black Chicago*, pp. 134-136; Chicago Commission on Race Relations, *The Negro in Chicago*, p. 80.

27. Gilbert Osofsky, *Harlem*, pp. 159-178; Allan Spear, *Black Chicago*, pp. 181-200.

28. Charles F. Kellogg, *NAACP: A History of the National Association for the Advancement of Colored People, 1909-1920* (Baltimore: Johns Hopkins University Press, 1967).

29. Kate E. R. Pickard, *The Kidnapped and the Ransomed* (Syracuse: William T. Hamilton, 1856); Max J. Kohler, *The Jews and the Anti-Slavery Movement* (New York: American Jewish Historical Society, 1896); Louis Ruchames, "The Abolitionists and the Jews," *Publications of the American Jewish Historical Society*, 42 (December 1952); Bertram W. Korn, *American Jewry and the Civil War* (Cleveland: World Publishing Company, 1961); Bertram W. Korn, *Jews and Negro Slavery in the Old South, 1789-1865* (Elkins Park, Pennsylvania: Reform Congregation Keneseth Israel, 1961).

30. Sermon, *Boston Daily Atlas*, 1853, p. 1; Miles Mark Fisher, *Negro Slave Songs in the United States* (Ithaca: Cornell University Press, 1953); Sarah Elizabeth Bradford, *Harriet Tubman, the Moses of Her People* (New York: Corinth Books, 1961).

31. *Opportunity*, 6 (September 1928): 261-262; *Amos* 9:07; *Song of Songs* 1:05; *Jeremiah* 13:3; Joshua Trachtenberg, *Jewish Magic and Superstition: A Study in Folk Religion* (New York: Behrman's Jewish Book House, 1939), p. 187.

32. Joseph Krauskopf, *The Jews and Moors in Spain* (Kansas City: M. Berkowitz and Company, 1887); Cecil Roth, *The Spanish Inquisition* (London: R. Hale, 1937); Paul Borchsenius, *The Three Rings: The History of the Spanish Jews* (London: George Allen and Unwin, 1963).

33. Theodore Herzl, *Altneuland* (New York: Bloch Publishing Company, 1941), p. 169.

34. *Opportunity*, 6 (September 1928): 261-262; Yitzhak E. Ronch, *Amerike in Der Yiddisher Literatur* (New York: I. E. Ronch Book Committee, 1945), p. 204.

chapter 2

"THE SOULS OF TWO NATIONS":
IMAGES OF BLACKS IN THE
YIDDISH PRESS

If any medium attempted to blend the old and the new, to reconcile tradition with American concerns, it was the Yiddish press. These newspapers became intrigued with blacks. The writers and editors repeatedly focused on the problems of prejudice and racism in America and on the valiant advances made by blacks in overcoming discrimination. The Yiddish press tried to give more than merely adequate coverage to one of the most important issues of the day. The plight of American blacks struck a responsive chord in the Yiddish papers because they perceived numerous similarities between the suffering of blacks in America and of Jews in Europe. The Yiddish papers also used the issues of racism and the denial of equal rights to blacks as a way to condemn an American society which failed to measure up to the expectations and dreams of an immigrant generation.

For immigrant Jews the Yiddish press was one of the most significant social and educational institutions of America. From it, they learned about events in Europe, where many friends and relatives still lived. In the pages of the various Yiddish dailies, they learned about American politics, American economic and social conditions. They read about such new issues as women's suffrage, unemployment compensation, the political machine, election campaigns, and the like.

In the early decades of the twentieth century the New York Yiddish press played an important part in the cultural and intellectual life of the Jewish American world. Yiddish writers and intellectuals attached themselves to particular newspapers. According to one study of American Yiddish literature:

In Yiddish all literature stemmed from journalism. The newspapers . . . published the works of the new writers who made
their debut in America. They were the meeting ground of the
novelist, the poet, the critic, and the reader . . . *practically every*
Yiddish short story, novel, poem, and critical essay appeared
first in the press.

Each newspaper expressed its distinct ideology. The religious papers
took an active role in the establishment of schools of Jewish learning
in New York, while the socialist press lent a hand in the development
of trade unionism among Jewish garment workers. Hutchins Hapgood, an American journalist, noted in his 1902 study of New York's
"Jewish Quarter" that the Yiddish newspapers had a "strong interest
in great freedom of expression. They are controlled by passion."[1]
   Of all the institutions of immigrant Jewish life in the United States,
the press was most thoroughly a product of the American experience.
There had been nothing in Europe which resembled the New York
Yiddish newspapers. An active and vital Yiddish press flourished in
America several decades before one did in Russia. In Europe, most
Jewish intellectuals and writers looked down on Yiddish, considering
it a mongrelization of German and Hebrew. They wrote in Russian,
Polish, or German. A very small band of Zionist intellectuals began to
revive Hebrew as a literary vehicle in the late nineteenth century. Yiddish, however, they deprecated as the language of common people.
   The first American Yiddish newspapers were written in *Deitshmer-*
ish, a sort of German with Hebrew characters, which eastern European immigrants had great difficulty understanding. These newspapers, like the *Judische Post* of Boston, appeared first in the 1870s
but could not survive the massive wave of Yiddish-speaking immigrants from the 1880s through the early 1920s. Although the first real
Yiddish daily was the orthodox *Yiddishe Tageblatt*, founded in 1885
by Kasriel Sarasohn, the Yiddish press rose to its heights in the hands
of socialists. Radicals keenly appreciated the potential of Yiddish in
spreading socialism among the Jewish masses, and in the 1880s and
early 1890s several Yiddish socialist non-dailies appeared in New
York. In 1894 *Das Abendblatt*, the first socialist daily, began publication.[2]
   The growth of the number of Yiddish daily newspapers during the

early twentieth century demonstrated the importance of the press in the Jewish world and indicated the continuous appetite of the Yiddish-speaking masses for news. By 1900 five Yiddish dailies circulated, and by the end of the second decade of the century, eleven. In 1933, almost a decade after massive immigration had been checked, eight dailies found their way to Yiddish readers.[3]

At the height of their success in 1925 the Yiddish newspapers serviced over 550,000 readers. According to a 1925 survey of the Yiddish press, the largest number of readers of the press fell between the ages of twenty-six and thirty-five and between forty-one and fifty. Forty-eight percent of the readers were Russian-born, 42 percent Polish, and only 9 percent American. More than 70 percent of the readers had lived in the United States for at least eleven years. Only 13 percent knew no English and 77 percent also read English-language newspapers regularly. Thus the readership of the press had some familiarity with American institutions and with English, yet chose to continue reading Yiddish. This active language maintenance displayed the intense desire of eastern European Jews to keep Yiddish alive as a symbol of a living culture.

The Jewish reading public also had particular needs not met by English papers. Nowhere else could readers find the same extensive coverage of Jewish events in the United States, Europe, and Palestine. The Yiddish press also gave a Jewish twist to standard news items, discussing, for example, how particular political candidates or proposed municipal laws would affect the Jewish community. The editors of the Yiddish press knew their readers and consciously addressed an audience substantially set on the road to Americanization. The purpose of the Yiddish press was, in part, to speed up that process.[4] Sociologist Robert Park, in his classic study of the immigrant press in the 1920s, applauded this goal of Yiddish American journalism:

> In the Yiddish press the foreign-language newspaper may be said to have achieved form. All the tendencies and all the motives, which other divisions of the immigrant press exhibit imperfectly, are here outstanding and manifest. No other press has attained so complete a simplification of the racial language, nor created so large a reading public. No other foreign-language press has succeeded in reflecting so much of the intimate life of

the people which it represents, or reacted so powerfully upon the opinion, thought, and aspiration of the public for which it exists. This is particularly true of the Yiddish daily newspapers in New York City.[5]

Because they articulated social goals for their newspapers, the editors and writers of the Yiddish press emerged as distinct leaders of the immigrant Jewish community. Like leaders of all the other communities, these journalists strove to define a meaningful role and position for themselves. More important, they used the Yiddish press as a way to confront the central questions of American life and decide how Jews would fit in with the values of their adoptive land. Perhaps more than any other distinctly American issue, the questions of racism and the status of blacks provided a forum in which Yiddish journalists could try to define the nature of their relationship to America. All of the newspapers, despite their ideological differences and regardless of their definition of Jewish culture and identity, seized on the image of American blacks and stressed the close parallels between them and Jews.[6]

THREE YIDDISH NEWSPAPERS

The *Yiddishe Tageblatt* (its official English title was *The Jewish Daily News*), founded in 1885, was religiously orthodox, suspending publication on Saturdays and Jewish holidays. While it heralded itself as "the American newspaper printed in Yiddish," it remained old-world and sectarian. It constantly preached against the Reform movement in Judaism and singled out Reform rabbis as the greatest enemies of the Jewish religion. It harshly condemned Jacob Schiff, a pillar of the Reform, German-Jewish world, for making anti-Zionist remarks, and relentlessly rebuked Jewish radicals and socialists. The *Tageblatt* maintained a conservative stance on American domestic issues, supporting the Republican party and condemning most labor unions. It especially decried strikes in the garment trade. Very concerned with the image of Jews in the United States, it insisted that Jews not involve themselves in radicalism or socialism because, the *Tageblatt* held, such action would only fan the flames of anti-Semitism. The other, less religious Yiddish newspapers often mocked the orthodoxy of the *Tageblatt*.

The *Tageblatt*, which was published in New York but circulated nationally, had a fairly small readership when it began publication. In 1888, its third year, it sold 3,750 copies a day. Since it was the first Yiddish daily, it faced the task of stimulating a taste for newspaper reading among the Yiddish-speaking immigrants. It was quite successful. By 1900, its readership rose to 40,000; in 1905, 48,031; and in 1911, it reached its height of popularity with an audience of 69,000.[7]

In 1928, the *Tageblatt* merged with another Yiddish newspaper, the *Morgen Journal* (the *Morning Journal*), the only Yiddish morning daily in New York. According to Robert Park, the *Jewish Morning Journal*, "is the New York *Times* of the East Side Jewish population . . . It is enterprising as a news-gatherer, conservative but intelligent in its editorial policies, and it is the natural medium for communication between the employer and the employee." The *Morgen Journal*, founded in 1901, maintained an editorial policy similar to that of the *Tageblatt*. It, too, supported the Republican party and orthodox religion. Its first editor-publisher, Jacob Saphirstein from Bialystock, Russia, stated that the paper's goal was to prove that "Orthodox Judaism and patriotic Americanism" could coexist harmoniously. It began with an impressive circulation. In 1905, just four years after its founding, 53,379 people read it. By 1911, the readership reached 80,127; by 1913, 96,675. The zenith of the *Morgen Journal*'s circulation was 1916, when it totaled 111,000. This newspaper outsold the *Tageblatt* because, as a morning paper, it met the needs of job-hunters. After the 1928 merger, its editorial policies changed little.[8]

Perhaps the most influential and certainly the most enduring Yiddish daily newspaper was the *Jewish Daily Forward*. The *Forward*, as it was most commonly referred to, was founded in 1897. Socialist in ideology, it included in its pantheon Karl Marx and Eugene V. Debs. It spoke to the thousands of Jewish garment workers in New York and other large American cities and played a dynamic part in the conversion of those workers to socialism, exerting its influence in shaping the policies of the ILGWU, the Amalgamated Clothing Workers, and the United Hebrew Trades. This newspaper was openly anti-religious, scoffing at the rabbis and brazenly staging dances and parties on the most solemn days of fasting and worship. The *Forward* was also staunchly anti-Zionist until the late 1920s, when it adopted a somewhat more neutral stand on the subject.

While the *Forward* was not the most radical of the New York Yiddish dailies (the *Freiheit*, founded in 1922, was the organ of the Yiddish-speaking communists), it reached more people than any other Yiddish paper. In 1925 it circulated more widely than any other foreign language daily in the United States. Its New York circulation figures alone overshadowed four New York English-language dailies. In 1923 it opened an office in Chicago, and it ran special editions geared for eleven different cities, including Philadelphia. The circulation of the *Forward* jumped from 19,502 in 1900 to 198,982 in 1916. [9]

How can the immense popularity of the *Forward* be accounted for? For one thing, the newspaper, its reporters and editors actively involved themselves in all the events of importance for New York's Yiddish-speaking community. The *Forward* aggressively pushed for the development of a Yiddish theater in New York. It sponsored such significant Yiddish creative writers and essayists as Sholem Asch, B. Z. Goldberg, S. Niger, and Mane Leib. It left its mark on Jewish unionism, Jewish socialist politics, and Jewish culture.

Perhaps an equally important factor in the *Forward*'s appeal was the dynamism and creativity of its editor, Abraham Cahan, who directed the newspaper from its earliest years until his death in 1951. Cahan, a writer, intellectual, and committed socialist, emigrated to the United States in the 1880s to escape czarist political suppression. He was one of the first Jewish radical intellectuals to recognize the potential of Yiddish as a vehicle to convert the masses to socialism. Throughout his editorial career he firmly believed in writing at the level and in the language of the readers. He once advised his staff: "... if you want the public to read this paper and assimilate socialism, you've got to write of things of everyday life, in terms of what they see and feel and find all about them." Cahan himself was a polished writer. His full-length novel, *The Rise of David Levinsky*, and his shorter works, *Yekl* and *The Imported Bridegroom*, won the praise of such liberal American writers as Hutchins Hapgood and William Dean Howells. Cahan had his hand in all Jewish communal affairs in New York and made the *Forward* one of the central institutions of American Jewish life. [10]

The Yiddish newspapers were somewhat smaller than standard newspapers, although the *Forward*, the longest, averaged around sixteen pages a day and more on Sundays. Most front-page stories were Jewish-oriented. Except when there were major national or international events, the headline and lead stories usually involved some Jewish problem or personality. Reports of pogroms in eastern Europe or the signing of the Balfour Declaration, which might have warranted only secondary attention in other papers, were front-page headlines in the Yiddish papers. All three of the newspapers presented the news in sensational, almost yellow journalism. All three emphasized crime, portraying events in macabre and often lurid detail.

The purposes of the Yiddish press were complex. It was designed to supplement the newspaper reading of some of its readers and give them Jewish news. Other readers had no other source of news, so the Yiddish writers balanced items of strictly Jewish interest with those of general importance. The papers focused sharply on national and foreign events in both the news and editorial sections, detailing the whole range of timely happenings. The Jewish orientation of the newspapers was, however, omnipresent. Many of the items inherently contained no particularly Jewish themes, yet the writers added a Jewish note, drawing parallels between a general news event and something from Jewish history or some aspect of Jewish culture. This was especially true in editorials and features on the subject of blacks and race relations in America.

A large part of the Yiddish newspaper consisted of feature items ranging widely in subject matter. Frequently, sketches from Jewish history, American history, and American social behavior appeared and, in the *Forward*, histories of radicalism and socialism. The newspapers often published articles devoted to science for laymen as well as frequent health columns. A regular feature of the *Forward* consisted of a gallery of snapshots of missing men being sought by their families, and all three newspapers ran the names of immigrants searching for relatives in America. Women's pages with short, human interest vignettes, recipes, fashion, and child-rearing articles ran in all the papers, and, in the socialist Yiddish press, accounts of the suffrage movement and great women in history were featured. A humorous page with jokes and cartoons and a special page devoted to photographs of the news and of particularly bizarre characters also appeared. All three newspapers printed English pages. The *Forward* began its English page in the 1920s, while the *Tageblatt* began one much earlier.

Despite extensive coverage of non-Jewish events and personalities, these were Jewish newspapers, geared to Jewish readers who were actively involved with Jewish life and culture. One subject, which superficially had no special significance for Jews but which the Yiddish press treated extensively and passionately was the status of blacks in American society. [11]

BLACKS IN THE YIDDISH PRESS

No matter what the ideology of the Yiddish papers, they approached this subject with a certain uniformity. Even though the *Forward*, the *Morgen Journal*, and the *Tageblatt* agreed upon very little, race and the lot of black Americans proved a striking exception. Out of their fascination with questions of race five themes dominated the Yiddish press reaction to blacks and were woven into dozens of news articles, editorials and features. First and most often the Yiddish newspapers saw blacks as the physical, political, and economic victims of American racism. Secondly, with thrilling praise they chronicled Negro achievements, past and present. Thirdly, with a sensationalistic flair they reported a high incidence of black crime. These newspapers at the same time were also very concerned with the relationship between Jews and blacks and pondered how the two groups intersected. Finally, Yiddish writers played on the similarities between blacks and Jews, projecting the image of blacks as America's Jews.

In exploring these five themes and in probing the meaning of race in America, the Yiddish writers raised questions which affected not only blacks, but which related directly to the experiences of Jews in Europe as well as in the United States. The image of the suffering black race dominated the pages of the Yiddish press, which devoted more space to black victimization than to any other aspect of the race question.

Blacks: The Victims of American Intolerance

If one of the functions of the Yiddish press was to Americanize the Jewish immigrants and to provide them with positive images of the institutions and heritage of America, frequent and repetitive articles on black oppression, both historically and in contemporary America, presented very negative pictures. In fact, the Yiddish writers noted repeatedly that racism ran so deep in American culture that the history of America and the oppression of black people were inextricably linked. Both the *Forward* and the *Morgen Journal* ran lengthy pieces on the history of the slave trade and slavery. Hillel Rogoff, a writer for the *Forward*, labeled the slave trade "the blackest chapter in American history," and other journalists lamented that the Africans had been mercilessly kidnapped from their own happy home. Articles such as these far from glorified American history, but if there was anything noble in that history it could be found in the movement to abolish slavery. Biographies of Harriet Beecher Stowe, Frederick Douglass, John Brown, William Lloyd Garrison, and Wendell Phillips appeared in both newspapers and portrayed these abolitionists in heroic terms. Even the conservative *Morgen Journal* noted that many great heroes of American history—Washington and Jefferson, for example—were slave owners and had refused to extend democracy "to millions of human beings who were considered property." Abraham Lincoln, however, emerged as the champion of liberalism who freed the slaves and, in the words of the *Morgen Journal*, "carried out the ideas of John Brown."[12]

Slavery's links extended to the present. Continuing their fascination with the subject, the papers featured interviews with former slaves, who reminisced about life under slavery. These freedmen talked to a *Forward* correspondent about their former masters in mixed tones. They claimed that they had found both brutality and paternalism in the slave experience. In the Yiddish newspapers, short news articles announced the deaths of former slaves. One such item told of a "Negro That President Lincoln Freed," who had worked until the age of 100. Not only were the newspapers interested in the existence of former slaves, but they also pointed out the continuity from antebellum slavery to contemporary racism. Readers were told, for example, that Wall Street had once housed a slave market,

"Where Negroes Were Bought and Sold, Retail and Wholesale." The article concluded with a discussion of recent incidents of police brutality to Negroes in the same Wall Street area, noting that legal emancipation had made very little difference in the treatment of black people. The heritage of slavery persisted in all areas of American life. It was responsible for the economic and political plight of Negro Americans, and the extreme feelings engendered by slavery and the Civil War had not dissipated over the course of decades. When, in 1928, the city of Atlanta banned the film *Uncle Tom's Cabin*, the *Forward* editorialized: "That such a picture . . . should be banned in the South is no surprise. The book is always hated in that part of the country. Many residents of the South believe even today that the book was responsible for the Civil War . . . . The picture was banned because it reveals a wound which the white there does not want to see."[13]

The post-Civil War period and the growth of the Ku Klux Klan aroused the interest of the Yiddish newspapers. Partly because of the revival of the Klan in 1915, which espoused anti-Semitism in the same breath as anti-black feeling, and partly because of the general concern with black victimization, frequent articles discussed the history of the Klan and the differences between the Klan of Reconstruction and that of Hiram Wesley Evans, the Imperial Wizard of the 1920s. Generally, the Yiddish newspapers saw the contemporary Klan as an anti-Semitic organization, although "it carries on heated agitation not just against Jews, but against Catholics, Negroes, and liberals . . . . This is a small piece of consolation that at least we are not alone in this misfortune." Given the Klan's attachment to macabre rituals, concocted titles, flowing robes, and clandestine activities, articles on the Klan were often laced with humor. The *Tageblatt* delighted in recounting that a group of blacks had challenged a KKK branch to a baseball game, and that on several instances Klansmen had donated money to black churches.

Most Klan activities were far from humorous and the Yiddish press expressed considerable alarm at the growing political power of the Klan in states such as Oklahoma and Louisiana. It registered particular shock when the Klan opened up a chapter in New York City and detailed the physical brutality of the Klan toward blacks, both in and outside the South. The *Tageblatt*, for example, decried the terrorizing

of Negro residents of Camden, New Jersey, by the Klan and graphically portrayed the city's black population fleeing from a burning cross.
Morgen Journal correspondent Samuel Bloom, who covered the
South and race relations in the 1920s, described the Klan as "an organization which has taken for itself the roles of spy, sheriff, prosecutor,
judge, jury, and executioner."[14]

The issue which crystallized all thinking on racist violence was that
of lynching. The Yiddish writers took the word *lynch*, put it into Yiddish letters and incorporated it into proper grammatical form. *Mob*
also became standard terminology and was used repeatedly in the
context of mass brutality to blacks. Frequent news items, replete with
gory details, as well as vivid features and passionate editorials about
lynchings spread across the Yiddish newspapers. The papers kept
abreast of statistics on lynching and every year reprinted Tuskegee
Institute's report on lynching. If there had been a decline in the number, the headline of the article read, for example, "'Only' 16 Lynchings in 1927," stressing that even a reduced number was far too much.
The number of lynchings occasionally served as a barometer of reac-
tionary tide in the United States, and in 1926 the *Forward* hoped that
the general climate of the country had improved because of a significant lynching decrease.[15]

Lynchings were always highlighted by their bloodiest and most
tragic details. When the *Forward* described one 1921 lynching in
Georgia, it declared that one's "Hair Stands Up When You Read
About the Slaughter of Negroes in Georgia." The whites who participated in these barbaric public murders were sarcastically labeled
"civilized whites," and all the newspapers noted that their ranks were
filled with the most respectable citizens of southern towns. Ministers,
town officials, doctors, lawyers, businessmen—all joined in the lynchings and the Yiddish newspapers cried out in horror over the openness
which pervaded such affairs. Most articles dwelt on the actual murders, how they were committed, the reaction of the victims, and what
the mob did with the body. One Negro, lynched in Missouri in 1935,
sang religious songs and prayed throughout the ordeal, while during a
1916 Waco, Texas, lynching the victim screamed so loud that "the
cries . . . were carried for blocks and blocks, but they were quickly
drowned by the cheers of the excited mob." Lynchings provided

amusement and sport for a great number of southerners, who laughed and frolicked during these all too frequent "folk holidays."[16]

Blacks appeared as the defenseless victims of this "American shame," this "stain on the American flag." Lynching was a specter which hung over the heads of American blacks and Negroes lived in constant fear of it. One *Forward* reporter told of a black in Atlantic City who died of a heart attack just hearing a crowd yell, "lynch the nigger!" The black population of Irvine, Texas, reportedly fled after a lynching, fearing more violence. The Yiddish newspapers also hailed Northern judges who refused to extradite blacks who had fled the South under suspicion of murder, because they would be met not with impartial justice but with the noose of the lynch mob. The *Morgen Journal-Tageblatt* felt that it was fitting and proper that "more developed and more liberal states look down on the legal structure of Southern states, because of . . . injustices and illegal actions towards Negroes." The Yiddish journalists assumed that black leaders were preoccupied with the lynching issue. In 1919, the *Forward* ran a half-page article on what Dr. Burghardt Du Bois . . . "the Secretary of the Society to Uplift the Social Situation of the Negroes," thought about the epidemic of lynching and what he and other black leaders proposed to do about it.[17]

Dr. Du Bois had agreed that lynching posed the major immediate problem of American Negroes and America had a responsibility to eradicate it. The Yiddish newspapers, in articles and editorials, heartily concurred with Du Bois and other black leaders that the cause of lynching was not black criminality. While the majority of lynching news items in the press involved blacks who had been accused of crimes of physical violence against whites, especially murder or rape, the articles always stressed the *suspicion* of crime rather than conviction.[18] The innocence or guilt of a black, however, was unimportant and could never justify a lynching, although the newspapers seemed particularly horrified when a black was murdered before guilt had even been established. The Yiddish press was even more dismayed when the victim had been proven innocent, or when there was no crime but only some violation of social mores of southern life. Lynchings had been precipitated by a black merely walking next to a white woman or, in one case, when three blacks were friendly toward a

group of white men. One black was lynched over a three dollar robbery and another met his fate for agreeing to testify in a kidnapping
case. A black woman was murdered because her son had been accused
of killing a white man; several blacks in Georgia were lynched for
allegedly voting Republican; and Eli Cooper of Dublin, Georgia, was
pulled out of church and lynched though "no one knows what his
crime was." [19]

Not only did the news sections of the Yiddish press report extensively on lynchings, but editorials cried out in impassioned tones. The
same liberal use of gruesome details and bloody minutiae appeared
here. The whites were always "mad beasts" and feature articles,
focusing on specific lynchings, always stressed the innocence of the
victim or the righteousness of his crime. One lengthy *Forward* article
described the lynching of a young black tenant farmer who had murdered his boss in self-defense after he and his family had lived in
grinding poverty and economic oppression for years. While the
editors reported decreases in lynching figures with pleasure, they realized that this could be reversed at any time and that America had not
really experienced a change of heart or a prick of conscience in regard
to race. The *Forward*, for example, noted:

> Only sixty-one lynchings occurred in America last year. And
> this is great progress. There were times in America, not long
> ago, when the lynchings numbered into the hundreds. This fact
> would be a lot more cheering if it was evidence of a change in
> attitude, that the South had become civilized, progressive, and
> humane and that the former slave drivers had lost their desire
> for burnt Negro flesh. This is however far from certain. [20]

In 1917, a reader wrote to the *Tageblatt* from Houston, Texas,
suggesting that the newspaper might be unaware of the excesses of
black criminality and should be perhaps less vehement in its condemnation of lynching. The editors responded:

> Let us remember that Negroes are not the only people commit-
> ting rape and murder. There are others whose skins are pure
> white. These are brought to trial and punished. There is one law

and that law applies to all . . . That idea must prevail or else the state cannot exist.

The Yiddish newspapers reserved their greatest anger for the state and local governments of the South. Not only did southern officials usually allow lynchers to commit their crimes, as evidenced by the fact that blacks were often lynched while in jail or in police custody, but they never arrested lynchers. [21] The newspapers reported that local officials themselves participated in lynchings and then refused to acknowledge that a crime had ever been committed. Occasionally, sheriffs or police officers tried to prevent lynchings and they, in turn, won the praise of the Yiddish writers. Southern governors who sent out the state militia to protect a Negro were lauded, while governors who ignored the situation merited utter condemnation. The *Morgen Journal-Tageblatt* vehemently denounced Mississippi's Governor Theodore Bilbo, who claimed that he did not have the time or money to investigate a lynching, and the newspaper cynically noted that the governor had accepted the coroner's report that a "burned Negro died of 'unknown causes.'" [22]

All of the Yiddish newspapers agreed that the problem of lynching could not be left to the local or state governments. The states themselves, even with the best of intentions, could only exert feeble attempts to eradicate it and the only solution lay in a federal anti-lynching law. While the newspapers applauded white liberal southerners who issued statements and organized conferences against lynching, they generally felt that only a rigorously enforced federal statute could eliminate the crime. The newspapers dismissed arguments that such a law was unconstitutional and felt that politicians who opposed the Dyer Bill in the 1920s and the Wagner-Costigan Bill in the 1930s on constitutional grounds were at heart anti-black but afraid to admit it openly. [23]

The Yiddish press agreed that physical victimization was compounded by the racial insensitivity of the American judicial process. Judges and juries freely ordered execution of convicted blacks, while they imposed very light or even suspended sentences on whites convicted of similar crimes. In one case, the *Forward* noted, a white who had murdered a black bellboy in Pittsburgh was sentenced to only eighteen months in prison, and the article concluded: "A Negro's life is worth almost nothing in America." One of the rare Yiddish jokes dealing with blacks depicted a judge, handing down a sentence to a white man who had shot an entire Negro family to death, announcing that the defendant would have to serve thirty days in prison.

Accused: Don't be so severe, your honor, it was a small family.
Judge: Ten days, then, less for good behavior. [24]

The judicial callousness to blacks, the seething prejudice of the southern communities, the omnipresent potential for physical violence, and the insecurity of the Negro's existence in the South all came together for the Yiddish press in the case of the nine young blacks arrested in 1931 in Scottsboro, Alabama. Of all the events in the history of race relations from 1915 to 1935, no single episode received as much attention from the Yiddish press as did the Scottsboro case. Partly because there were Jews involved in the affair—the defense attorneys, Samuel Leibowitz and Joseph Brodsky—and partly because the trial coincided with the earliest Jewish-American awareness of the threat developing in Germany, the case of these unfairly accused blacks captured the imagination of the Yiddish newspapers. News items, features, editorials, photographs and interviews highlighted the case. From the summer of 1931 through the spring of 1935, a total of 104 articles appeared on the case in the *Forward* and the *Morgen Journal-Tageblatt*. The articles universally sympathized with the boys, condemned Alabama "justice" and praised Samuel Leibowitz, attorney for the defense. The socialist *Forward* supported the accused unyieldingly. From the earliest days of the incident, it noted that the "trial was a mockery and the boys are in danger of losing their lives only because they are Negroes." It cynically noted after one of the numerous trials that "Alabama Gives Justice to Negroes—Will Burn Nine at Once on the Electric Chair." The Scottsboro boys never had the slightest chance of getting real justice from the "ignorant and backwards residents there . . . so agitated and so infuriated against Negroes." *Forward* readers had to come to terms with this reality, "no matter how convinced they are that the Negro boys are absolutely innocent of the crime for which they are being tried." The conservative

Morgen Journal-Tageblatt expressed similar sympathy for the "un-lucky Negroes." [25]

The Yiddish press found the race riots, which flared with frighten-ing regularity from 1915 to 1935, equally traumatic. Besides the major riots—East St. Louis, Chicago, Washington, D.C., Omaha, Tulsa, Knoxville, and Elaine, Arkansas—the Yiddish newspapers reported on nineteen other mass race clashes in the South [26] and twenty-six in the North, six of which were in New York City. [27]

Since the East St. Louis riot of July 1917 was the first of the major northern race riots in this period, it particularly shocked the news-papers and evoked a passionate response. The *Morgen Journal* graphically described the mobs of whites, "so large, so agitated, and so blood-thirsty." They "set on fire the Negro quarter and the poor houses. Women and children were not spared by the wild beasts . . . . When Negroes ran out of their burning houses, screaming, they were shot down without mercy." The *Forward* was even more emotional, claiming that "the blood steams in the veins when we read about what is happening in East St. Louis. A regular pogrom on people, who had the misfortune to be born with black skin." The highly conservative *Tageblatt* added its voice to the outrage and asserted, "That which happened in East St. Louis fills every person who has a human heart and soul with horror and shock. In the streets of an American city, over which flies the flag of stars and stripes—the flag of the land of progress and humanity—a slaughter was organized on innocent peo-ple. They were murdered in the streets, shot, hanged, beaten and killed. The ground in East St. Louis drank human blood, shed by citi-zens of the most civilized country in the world." [28]

This inconsistency between the claims of American "civilization" and the reality of race riots was a major motif in the Yiddish press. A *Forward* cartoon, appearing just as the race riot in Washington, D.C., had subsided and the one in Chicago was brewing, showed two Africans with bare breasts and grass skirts sitting under a coconut tree, reading a copy of the *African Press*, which bore the headline: "Race Riots in America." One of the Africans noted, "We are so lucky not to live in a civilized country." Each of the great race battles—Chi-cago, Washington, Omaha, Tulsa—brought forth the same editorial outrage and the same screaming headlines of blood, slaughter, and burning. [29]

One small, less publicized race riot, that of Carteret, New Jersey, in April 1926, particularly caught the imagination of the Yiddish press. Not only did Carteret see a massive outbreak of violence against blacks, with murder and wholesale terror, but the blacks, after hiding in their homes in fear, were forced to leave the town. "Negroes who lived in their homes for twenty years and many who were even born there, were forced to leave . . . in the middle of the night and flee . . . naked and barefoot . . . " This minor riot inspired several editorials in the press. Most likely, the similarity between the violent eviction of blacks from Carteret and the frequent expulsion of Jews from eastern European towns in the nineteenth and early twentieth centuries struck a familiar chord. For eastern European Jews, the sudden expulsion from the town was not an unimaginable event, but a predictable catastrophe.[30]

"What did the Negroes do to deserve such brutality?" asked the *Tageblatt* after racial fighting had broken out in the nation's capital in late July of 1919. The Yiddish writers generally agreed that white hostility was rooted in fear of economic competition. Other columnists pointed out that whites were particularly outraged when blacks began to defend themselves, a phenomenon roundly applauded by the Yiddish newspapers. Whites were reacting to a growth of Negro assertiveness, a product of the war and the admirable service rendered by blacks in the armed forces. One well-known Yiddish journalist, Philip Krantz, speculated in the *Forward* during the Red Summer of 1919 that searching for immediate causes for the riots would prove fruitless. More important, readers should understand "the disease which lies in the deeply embedded prejudice and antipathy of the privileged whites to the 'inferior' black race. Let this prejudice disappear even just a little and such race riots would not occur."[31]

The physical victimization of blacks by lynching, the organized forces of the state, and race riots were depicted as so deeply ingrained in American society that any movement to eliminate them, while greeted approvingly, was inherently doomed to failure. Although the Yiddish press paid much less attention to black economic conditions, a number of articles, especially in the socialist *Forward*, also discussed the pathetic economic plight endured by black Americans. The press always equated contemporary southern black conditions with those of the slavery period. Typical were such articles as "Negro Slavery—

Today," "Negro Slavery in America is Still Not Ended," "In the South Slavery Exists Even to This Day," "Slavelike Laws for the Negroes in the South," "Are the Negroes in America Held Like Slaves?" News reports of "slave farms" in Georgia in 1921 and Florida in 1923, discussions of the virtual servitude of sharecroppers, and details of peonage laws, all confirmed the Yiddish press' belief that "Negro slavery exists, today, by us, in this country." The *Forward* found poverty and economic exploitation among blacks in the South as disturbing as the brutality of lynching. After detailing two particularly horrible cases of black convict labor in 1927, it asked:

> Where is the spirit of freedom with which our America is always priding itself? And where is the holiness of the Constitution which is so often mentioned? And Monday, the 30th of May, the American people decorated the graves of those who fell in the great battle to free the slaves in America and to free America from the stain of the shame of slavery. The slaves are today not free and on America, the stain of the shame of slavery is still evident. [32]

The Yiddish press seemed more optimistic about black economic prospects in the North. The universal feeling in the press during the early years of the great migration seemed to be that economic conditions had been so depressed in the South that any move would help. The writers believed that if blacks left the South in sufficient number, their labor would become more valued there and hence their condition had to improve. With some delight the newspapers observed the panic of the "slave-drivers" as their cheap labor began to desert them. They saw the beginnings of white southern opposition to lynching as a direct result of the exodus. On the other hand, the *Morgen Journal* lamented in 1919 that as black workers became more expensive, "they are being treated even more badly than before." [33]

The Yiddish press considered migration from the South the only feasible solution to the problem, since the government—federal, state, and local—would never help ameliorate Negro poverty. Nor did they believe that blacks should patiently wait for white southerners to experience a change of heart. [34] In fact, the newspapers hailed the mass exodus of blacks as a positive step toward neutralizing race tension. However, the newspapers recognized that black migrants in the North faced a far from hospitable reception. The race riots certainly revealed deep-seated *national* antagonism toward blacks. The Yiddish press especially condemned the racism of northern labor unions. All of the newspapers noted how blacks were frequently used as strikebreakers or were brought in by management to depress wages in a particular industry. Yet the newspapers vociferously condemned the violent reaction of organized labor, which included rioting, physical terror, and exclusion. The *Forward* sadly noted the dilemma of blacks, saying, "If the American Negroes want the unions to open the doors to them, they must first become scabs."[35]

Northern black poverty was generally ironically juxtaposed with the high hopes engendered by migration. A *Forward* photographer in 1923 found an unemployed black man sitting on a Bowery park bench after a futile search for work. He "comes from the South where Negroes are oppressed and kept down. Is it better for him in the 'free' New York? Is hunger an easier slave driver than the human slave drivers in the South?" The writers asked this question over and over again in discussions of the effects of poverty and racism on black housing conditions, health, and employment. The newspapers perceived links between all these phenomena. Prejudice forced blacks out of decent jobs shoving them into congested, unsanitary apartments for which they paid exorbitant rents. The unsanitary conditions caused outbreaks of tuberculosis and other contagious diseases. A *Forward* review of a speech by W.E.B. Du Bois confirmed the newspaper's belief that "the situation is a lot worse than assumed . . . . Half of the male population of Harlem is unemployed. The women are forced to go out and seek work. The homes are neglected. Thousands and thousands of families have already been thrown out of their quarters."[36]

Discussions of black poverty in the North equalled those about the South in terms of suffering and pathos. Not that the Yiddish press felt that blacks were as badly off in the North. Northern conditions were clearly better. Yet, after migration, things had not changed enough to have warranted the earlier optimism. The conditions of black life in America—North and South—were fraught with irony. It was ironic that bloody race riots against Negroes resulted from the mass migration which, at one point, seemed to be the answer to the poverty of the

South. It was ironic that both labor and capitalists hated blacks with equal ferocity and misused them with equivalent crudeness. It was also ironic that American economic productivity so thoroughly depended on the labor of this most despised segment of the society. "The Americans," speculated the *Forward* in 1924, "would love to throw out all the Negroes if they were not so dependent on them." [37]

Blacks were not only the victims of poverty and economic deprivation, but they were also completely excluded from the political system. This fact particularly upset the Yiddish journalists. If anything had been considered unique about America, it had been the openness of the political process. The Yiddish newspapers displayed just how American they had become when they stressed the great gulf between the rhetoric of American democracy and the reality of racism. According to the press, the exclusion of blacks from meaningful roles in American politics and government extended far beyond the South. The *Morgen Journal*'s race specialist, Samuel Bloom, calculated that based on the number of blacks in the United States, "The Negroes should have forty-five Congressmen in the House of Representatives, but in reality, there is not one Negro sitting in the body. Which means, that only one Negro in eight is allowed to vote." Even in the North where blacks had the vote, the political parties cared little about them. The *Forward* particularly blamed the Republican Party. The *Forward*'s reasoning ran thus. No doubt existed that southern racists dominated the Democratic Party. The Republicans by the 1920s, however, had abandoned the vision of Abraham Lincoln in their attempts to make inroads into the South. One way to accomplish this was to ignore blacks and black issues.

Naturally the newspapers reported with unrestrained outrage the open disfranchisement of blacks. The Yiddish press also followed closely the Supreme Court decisions which tried to liberalize the voting situation. The 1915 decision striking down the grandfather clause (which the *Forward* called a "Barbaric Law Against Negroes") was hailed as a "death-blow to the Negro haters in the South." The Yiddish newspapers welcomed this ruling and the 1927 *Nixon v. Herndon* decision which declared the white primary in Texas unconstitutional. The press was not, however, euphoric in thinking that these decisions would really be enforced or that southern states would not legally evade them. *Morgen Journal* correspondent Isaac Zaar noted that "the whites will probably find a way to avoid this [*Nixon v. Herndon*] decision . . . just as they found a way with the other decisions of the federal laws which do not fit with their idea of Negro rights, but for the principle of equality and for the honor of the country it is nice to hear such words from the highest judicial institutions." [38]

The Supreme Court, in fact, was the only political institution whose position on race merited praise from all the Yiddish newspapers. The *Forward*, however, also lauded the Socialist Party of America. It wrote, "There is only one party and one presidential candidate who talks about the questions of racial tolerance . . . . The party is the Socialist Party and the candidate is Norman Thomas." The two major parties, according to all the Yiddish press, indulged in equally repugnant race-baiting. The local southern governments were thoroughly Negrophobic and existed in order to maintain the racial status quo. Northern governments were somewhat more benign, but incidents of discrimination abounded. [39]

Likewise, they found little of merit in presidential action. Theodore Roosevelt, an ex-President, received some praise for his condemnation of the East St. Louis race riot, but Wilson, Harding, Coolidge, Hoover, and Roosevelt all drew condemnation for their insensitivity to blacks. According to the Yiddish press, Wilson, the first southern President of the twentieth century, was an unmitigated racist. After he instituted segregation in the federal service and cut back on black patronage, the *Forward*'s Washington correspondent, "Ben-Zion," commented:

> Once again our president, Woodrow Wilson, showed that he had not forgotten that he was born in the South or that his party receives its strongest support from the South.

When in 1921 Harding suggested in a lecture at a southern black school that the only solution to race tension and lynching was more black education, both the *Forward* and the *Morgen Journal* criticized him. While both newspapers noted that many southerners considered Harding's talk bold, the papers declared vehemently that education was not the issue. According to the *Forward*:

> The Negro demands justice; he demands that the law protect him just as it protects the whites; he demands from the govern-

ment in Washington that it enforce the points written into the
Constitution . . . . But the government does not want to antago-
nize the whites in the South. President Harding knows very well
that the Washington government could do a lot to ease the situation of the Negroes. He knows that education or other "home
remedies" are just a mask, just a way to blind the Negroes.

Hoover fared a little better. The *Forward* praised steps he had taken
as Secretary of Commerce to improve the conditions of black civil
servants. Both the *Forward* and the *Morgen Journal* applauded Mrs.
Hoover's willingness to extend hospitality to the wife of Chicago's
Negro Congressman, Oscar De Priest. These gestures were, however,
just that and the writers shrugged them off as "politics" and not as
signs of egalitarianism. [40]
The victimization of Negroes extended far beyond disfranchisement and political exclusion. It pervaded every aspect of American
life. A significant number of articles discussed *de jure* residential
segregation of blacks in Kentucky, Missouri, and Louisiana. The
newspapers noted that, in the realm of housing, blacks suffered as
much where no legally established "ghettos" existed. Blacks paid exorbitant rents for shoddy appartments, and when they moved into
better neighborhoods, they faced the hostility and violence of their
neighbors. [41] Educational institutions, too, were infected with anti-
Negro prejudice. Harvard, Columbia, and Syracuse Universities and
the United States Military Academy at West Point were all criticized
by the Yiddish newspapers for discrimination against blacks. [42] The
press also noted several instances in 1926, 1929, and 1932 where
Christian churches had expelled black worshippers. To the Yiddish
newspapers, this constituted a particular outrage, and a *Forward*
columnist noted: "They do not even allow the Negro to have a
God." [43]
Social discrimination and segregation found its way into all institutions of American life. Discriminatory practices were cited in such diverse sectors of society as sports, social clubs, the arts, theater. The
Yiddish press believed that white Americans most feared physical
proximity to blacks. American tourists had spread racial hatred in
France in the mid-1920s, when they forced French restaurateurs to re-
fuse to seat Negroes. Diplomats from Africa were snubbed in America, and one Alabama congressman resigned a congressional commit-

tee appointment because he "does not want to sit at one table with a
Negro." Mockingly, the *Forward* noted that a white woman fainted
because she kissed a black man by accident.

The whole complex of Jim Crow laws was constantly condemned. A
correspondent from the *Forward* movingly described his reactions to
a train ride from Washington, D.C. to the South:

> You get into a car in Washington which goes over a bridge cross-
> ing the Potomac. When the car reaches the half-way point of the
> river, you see already how blacks cannot sit with whites. The
> white becomes the privileged one, the black is just a "nigger" . . .
> and the word "nigger" must be said in a despising voice, as
> though he were an ugly creature, a frog instead of a person.
>
> You travel on the train and you see the stations . . . These are
> mostly small wooden buildings, poor and dark with low wooden
> benches. But above the door a sign hangs, "For Whites Only."
> The blacks must enter through a door in the back into a separate
> room. A small wooden booth stands . . . a telephone booth, with
> the inscription, "ONLY FOR WHITES." You want to leave the
> station. There is a wide open exit, without a door. Over the exit
> hangs a large sign, "EXIT ONLY FOR WHITES." The blacks
> are not even allowed to leave by the same side as whites I
> thank God that I was able to leave the South. [44]

Descriptions like this, reports of race riots and lynchings, and tales of
Negro poverty and of official governmental hostility caused the Yiddish press to condemn American society in eloquent and passionate
terms. The pervasiveness of black victimization touched on every
aspect of American life. As early as 1917, the *Forward* saw it as "an
old, painful question, an important problem, which is like a black
stain on the conscience of the nation." [45]

Black Heroes, Black Achievements, and Black Protest

While the image of the southern black—innocent victim hotly pursued by a wild lynch mob—was basically a passive one, the Yiddish
press also presented blacks in particularly aggressive and positive
roles. Just as the press devoted considerable space to analyzing the

forces working *against* blacks, it also considered the movements *among* blacks to reverse the racial status quo. It covered in some detail the efforts of the NAACP, the black socialists and communists, and gave especially voluminous attention to Marcus Garvey's Back-to-Africa movement. In fact, the press framed much of the material about race relations in terms of dynamic black protest against prejudice and oppression. The biographies of black heroes and leaders appeared on the pages of the Yiddish newspapers: Frederick Douglass, Booker T. Washington, and James Weldon Johnson were all lauded and extolled. Black excellence in such diverse fields as music, literature, the arts, and education glowed as evidence that racial thinking was ill-founded, and the Yiddish press greeted the Negro men and women who had overcome racial prejudice and succeeded in their chosen fields with great applause.

All the Yiddish newspapers accepted the reasonableness of the position that blacks should not wait for some vague golden moment in the future when liberal whites would give them their rights. Blacks had to seize the initiative themselves. The papers hailed blacks who vociferously demanded equal treatment as "intelligent Negroes." The Yiddish writers heartily approved of black movements to change the balance of race relations. [46]

The exodus of blacks from the South was seen as one form of protest against racism and poverty. According to the *Forward*, "The Negroes are leaving. One can say that they are escaping, never to come back again." The migration constituted a positive act of protest in two ways: for those blacks who left the South, prospects of greater economic opportunities appeared, greater personal freedom, and greater security. The Yiddish papers generally felt that those blacks who did not join the flood of migrants would also benefit. Their labor would become more valuable, lynchings would decline in number, and gradually the South would become less of an inferno for blacks.

Northern conditions, however, did not obviate the need for black protest. The Yiddish press watched with enthusiasm the development of vocal protest in the black communities. More than anything else the 1919 riots, in which blacks chose to fight back and defend themselves, were defined as a positive step. While the press perceived an element of revenge in this, in both the Chicago and Washington riots evidence of Negro aggressiveness was painted in heroic terms. The

Morgen Journal, for example, noted that a group of Negroes in Washington announced that "they would not take the brutal attacks quietly," and signs appeared in black homes reading: "WHITES! WE ARE WARNING YOU! DO NOT GO OUT OF YOUR HOMES TONIGHT!"[47]

The Yiddish newspapers kept fairly close watch on the activities of black organizations dedicated to ameliorating the racial situation. The *Tageblatt*, for example, covered a 1919 meeting in New York, at which the "Negroes demanded greater social and political rights and the speakers often asked the audience to show their strength if they wanted to get these rights." The organization that sponsored the meeting of over 2,000 Negroes "exists all over the country. Propaganda articles appear from time to time by this group in various journals and newspapers." In 1917 Philip Krantz, a frequent contributor to the *Forward*, described "a great congress of Negroes" and claimed that the sponsoring organization was the "National League for Equal Rights." In 1918 James Weldon Johnson and W.E.B. Du Bois reportedly headed a meeting sponsored by the "National Association for the Development of Black People."

The press reported the activities of black protest organizations in glowing and positive terms. Krantz, who had attended the "great Congress of Negroes," noted that he was one of the few reporters who had been there and he had been very impressed by the gathering and from it he learned "that Negroes are much more capable . . . than the white Americans want it to be known." Krantz was moved by the boldness of the group. After stating that the group had vociferously demanded equal rights, he reflected:

> Yes, equal rights! Unfortunately that is what they lack in our democratic republic. Our black fellow citizens are still being held down, in spite of all the provisions of the United States Constitution, in spite of paper statements about equal recognition of citizens, even if he does not have the luck to be covered with a white skin.[48]

The NAACP especially was hailed. The Yiddish writers discussed and praised its pressure on Congress for an anti-lynching law in the 1920s. Speeches and articles by W.E.B. DuBois in the association's magazine, *Crisis*, received frequent attention, and the *Tageblatt* in 1920 concurred with the *Crisis* editor that "if the South will become civilized . . . she must give full rights to all citizens, regardless of color . . . and end the practice of lynching." After the East St. Louis riot, the *Tageblatt* editorialized with sympathy and solidarity on the NAACP's silent protest down New York's Fifth Avenue:

> Without music, without speeches, without applause, and without resolutions a procession of Negroes marched . . . . It was a quiet protest against Jim Crow cars, against the injustices done to them, a protest against being locked into separate neighborhoods . . . against constant persecution. . . . Especially because it was a silent protest it had greater impact and more deeply touched the human heart. . . . 10,000 Negores marched in line in the mourning parade over East St. Louis and 20,000 other Negroes were standing along the streets through which the procession went. The Negro race silently protested the blood that was spilled. . . . The procession marched to awaken sympathy, to awaken the American conscience that was asleep.[49]

If all the Yiddish newspapers responded positively to the NAACP, only the *Forward* rejoiced at the beginnings of socialist ferment among blacks. A. Philip Randolph, a socialist and organizer of the Brotherhood of Sleeping Car Porters, was a hero to the *Forward*. The *Forward* was so enthusiastic about Randolph and his socialist activities that it agreed to stage a fund-raising campaign for his publication, the *Messenger*. The editors of the *Forward* saw the stirrings of socialism among Negroes as the first step in the death of both racism and capitalism, which, it perceived, were inextricably bound to each other. This development "has thrown a great fear upon the capitalistic parties and the capitalistic press. . . . The capitalistic leaders never expected such a 'problem.'"

Yet the *Forward* joined the *Tageblatt* and the *Morgen Journal* in expressing concern over the movement of some blacks to the Communist party. Although they feared this development, they tried to downplay it, pointing out that whatever minimal enthusiasm blacks exhibited toward communism had been produced by oppression and discrimination in American society. These Yiddish newspapers generally condemned the Communist Party and saw its campaign to attract blacks as opportunistic and insincere. The *Forward*, a social democratic newspaper, launched the most severe criticism of the communists, pointing out the hypocrisy of their overtures toward blacks. Thus the black drift to the extreme left was not considered a legitimate or mass-based form of black protest. Like other Communist Party activities, it was manipulated and contrived. [50]

One Negro movement which was generally scorned by the American press but which aroused a great deal of interest, curiosity, and some admiration among Yiddish journalists was Marcus Garvey's Back-to-Africa movement. The Yiddish press gave considerable news coverage to the annual month-long conventions held in New York in the early years of the 1920s. Sponsored by Garvey, they brought together black leaders from around the world. The Yiddish writers were initially fascinated by the international scope of the color problem and by the determination and boldness of the rhetoric. The pomp and ceremony which marked the meetings captivated the journalists, as did the personality and charisma of the leader of the Universal Negro Improvement Association, Marcus Garvey, referred to as the "Black Messiah," "Black Moses," "the King of the Negroes," the "Negro president," or the "self-crowned emperor of the Negroes." While all of the Yiddish writers scoffed at Garvey after his arrest, deciding in the end that he was a fraud, during the early years of his meteoric career they usually depicted him as an authentic leader. The *Morgen Journal*, for example, heartily approved when Garvey proclaimed, "I am always ready to suffer for my race." The movement Garvey led, its nationalist ideology of the return of black Americans to a non-colonized Africa where they could achieve political, economic, and cultural independence, was warmly received by the pro-Zionist *Tageblatt* and the *Morgen Journal*. In 1920, when the first of Garvey's mammoth conventions met in New York, the *Morgen Journal* noted:

> Most of us will look sympathetically at the great convention of representatives of the black race which is now being held in New York. It might be a bit exaggerated when it is claimed that 400,000 members of the black race are in agreement, and that the founding of a new republic to which masses of blacks from the United States and other countries will migrate may be no

more than a fantasy. But it is certain, that the Negroes may have something to work with and that they are so justified in protesting against bad treatment to seek methods to help themselves, by migration, as every other group, race, or nation has.

In that same year a *Tageblatt* reporter had a personal interview with Garvey and speculated:

The Negro congress in Madison Square Garden, with its protests and nationalistic strivings will ring throughout the world and will shake up the conscience of the white population of America.

Though a *Tageblatt* editor found the pomp and regalia of the Garvey movement a bit bizarre, he declared:

It points out strongly . . . the development of self-consciousness. It shows that yesterday's black slaves feel the humanity in themselves and declare themselves equal with whites, if only they could have a place of their own under the sun where they could live a free life.

Interestingly, Garvey and the Back-to-Africa movement received less press coverage in the *Forward*, which generally showed greater interest in black issues than the other papers. What coverage Garvey and Garveyism got was sarcastic and negative because, as a socialist organ, the *Forward* viewed Garvey's analysis as antithetical to a class analysis. The *Forward* consistently took an anti-Zionist stance in the early 1920s. It viewed *black* Zionism as it viewed *Jewish* Zionism. In contrast, both the *Tageblatt* and the *Morgen Journal*, Zionist publications, applauded all nationalistic yearnings, whether expressed by Jews or by blacks.[51]

Instead of presenting a passive image of blacks, the Yiddish press portrayed an alert and vigilant group, exploring every possible avenue of protest. When Negroes demanded action from government officials to halt lynchings or to investigate race riots, they were supported by the Yiddish press. The newspapers praised black leaders who appeared in Versailles in 1919, attempting to speak for the darker races of the world, and the action of black groups who sought redress in the courts and other political forums. When blacks asserted themselves in politics, the Yiddish newspapers declared it a positive sign. The *Forward*, which enjoyed any significant desertion from the traditional parties, announced with pleasure in 1924 that several black leaders had endorsed Robert La Follette of the Progressive Party for president, and noted that the "Republicans are no longer the friends of the Negroes." A few years earlier, when there had been talk of an independent black political party, the newspaper had also rejoiced, asserting that finally Negroes "have woken up from the sweet sleep in which the Republican Party has held them since the Civil War. . . . It took fifty years until the bluff of the Republicans was exposed."[52]

Assertiveness in politics had paid off for some black leaders: a number of black political figures held either appointive or elective office. The Yiddish press paid fairly close attention to the few black politicians, seeing their power as a potentially important factor in the liberalization of the racial situation. The Yiddish papers were particularly fascinated with Walter Cohen, appointed by Harding as Controller of the Port of New Orleans. At first, the press was in a flurry because it thought that Harding's appointee was Jewish. It quickly learned that he was black. Immediately after Harding announced his appointment, a major move began in and out of Congress to have him removed from office, according to the *Morgen Journal*, "for the . . . 'crime' that he is black," The press followed his career closely and the solidly Republican *Morgen Journal* happily announced that two Republican presidents, Harding and Coolidge, supported Cohen. By doing so, "Washington officially declared war on the K.K.K., whose dark power has . . . been felt in many parts of the country." The *Tageblatt* welcomed the efforts of the National Union for the Improvement of Negroes (probably the NAACP) to keep Cohen from being ousted and felt that if he were removed, "all Negroes will be denied the rights of citizenship."[53]

The Yiddish newspapers hailed black participation in electoral and party politics. They reported the election of blacks to minor positions like judgeships, aldermanic seats, and boards of education in New York and Chicago and, as early as 1924, the *Morgen Journal* editorialized that Harlem should be represented by a black congressman. "It would add to their self-respect when a notable member of their race would be sent as a representative to Washington." This obviously contained an element of Republican self-interest, as did the pronouncement of the *Tageblatt* of the same year: "We would like to see a Negro congressman from a Negro district from the point of view of equality. We would like to see the principle of equality triumph against all who would like to see a land which must be white, Christian, and Protestant." When Illinois' First Congressional District elected Oscar De Priest in 1929, the Socialist *Forward* cheered: "This will not only add to the Congress in Washington some missing color, it will mean that the voice of 10,000,000 people whose rights are being trampled on, will be heard more often and louder."[54]

De Priest was something less than a great leader. He had been arrested in 1917 on a bribery charge, and both the *Forward* and the *Morgen Journal* expressed disappointment that the first black congressman was so tainted. Both papers felt that if a black of greater stature (and integrity) would serve in Congress, the image of the whole race would improve. Historically, great black leaders had appeared on the scene. Frederick Douglass, who merited two full-length biographical articles in the *Forward*, was one. Douglass, referred to as "the greatest Negro orator," had escaped from slavery and had used his great talents and fertile mind to help his people. No less inspiring had been another great black personality, Booker T. Washington. Besides eulogizing Washington in obituaries in 1915, both the *Forward* and the *Morgen Journal-Tageblatt* ran lengthy features on the Tuskegeean in the 1920s and 1930s. They considered Washington "among the greatest American personalities of the last century and the beginning of this one. . . . More than any other Negro leader he personified the tragic situation of the entire race, which had to find its way from slavery to freedom in an environment of hate, discrimination, and inferior treatment." Washington found *his* way and, according to the *Forward*, his "life was fully dedicated to the lofty ideals and to the fruitful work for his race. . . . He made a remarkable journey on the rough way from slave to leader, from lowly janitor to distinguished lecturer, teacher, and civic leader. He is the pride of the black race in America."[55]

This was in many ways uncharacteristic of the *Forward*, which, as a Marxist newspaper, did not believe in the American dream of "rags to riches," nor did it generally ascribe to the notion that individual achievement would help the masses out of poverty. The *Forward* did, however, follow closely the *organized* attempts of black groups to improve their economic lot. The newspaper was an early and ardent supporter of A. Philip Randolph and the Brotherhood of Sleeping Car Porters, a "remarkable union of former slaves and the children of slaves . . . which has already enlisted over 7,000 members." The *Forward* noted all attempts to unionize black workers and discounted widely held notions that blacks were hard to organize and resisted labor unions. The *Forward* felt that the example of the unionization of blacks in the needle trades provided excellent ammunition to refute those arguments. Numerous articles and photographs attempted to prove how actively blacks participated in the ILGWU and how eagerly the ILGWU tried to organize blacks. [56]

All three Yiddish newspapers were captivated by black achievements, especially by Negro distinction in the arts—theater, literature and music. Yiddish journalists saw that the tragic situation of black Americans provided a fertile field for artistic inspiration. [57] According to the Yiddish press, less overt racism pervaded the art world and blacks with talent could demonstrate their ability. The Yiddish newspapers kept close watch on the achievements of black artists and noted prizes and awards won. The exellence which these writers and musicians had demonstrated proved the southern racists wrong. In 1922, when Caribbean black writer Rene Maran won the Prix Goncourt, the *Forward* observed gleefully: "The American critics were so surprised that a Negro could write such good books."

The Yiddish press responded with indignation when racial discrimination occurred in artistic circles. For example, when Charles Gilpin, a black actor, was barred from a banquet, the *Tageblatt* expressed dismay:

> It has always been assumed that art, science and scholarship generally know no racial or color lines. . . . It will be a bad day for progress when color lines will be drawn and racial discrimination will rule. It will be a death blow to advancement in the arts and science. . . . Charles Gilpin is a negro. He has made good. What are we coming to that it is refused to honor him as he deserved.

The *Tageblatt* also protested when the Fontainbleau School of Fine Arts denied admission to sculptor Augusta Savage.[58]

The literary editors of the Yiddish press reviewed the work of black writers and artists, informing the readers about upcoming performances of black musical groups, including some which performed on Station WEVD, New York's Yiddish socialist radio network. Lengthy articles scrutinized the work of Paul Lawrence Dunbar, Walter White, Claude McKay, James Weldon Johnson, Langston Hughes, and Countee Cullen. Each writer received superlative comment and lavish praise. For instance, the *Tageblatt* noted about Dunbar:

> Perhaps none of the Negro poets have sung in more heart-rendering verses and songs such a rich song of his own people. In his singing he poured out the pain and suffering of the black citizens . . . Dunbar sings of the life and striving of his brothers.

In 1926, the *Forward* considered the works of several of the "New Negro" poets and translated into Yiddish poetry by McKay, Cullen, and Hughes, who were called "the young Negro intellectuals."

In the world of performance, Charles Gilpin, Roland Hayes, the Hall-Johnson Singers, and Paul Robeson were frequently discussed and praised. Robeson received the most attention. To the *Forward*'s question, "Who Is Your Favorite Actor?" one reader responded: "Paul Robeson, the magnificent colored actor is perhaps the finest actor today. What a voice! What a physique! What an actor!" More seriously, after Robeson gave a heralded series of concerts in London in 1930, the *Forward* devoted its entire editorial space of the day to a discussion of the man, his music, and the meaning of that music for both blacks and whites.

> From the other side of the ocean, from London, the cry of an oppressed people was brought here, the cry of an insulted and driven race. The cry of pain of a race through the mouth of an artist, through the musical lines of a performer. The cry was directed to the world, the appeal was made to all of mankind, but the first country that must listen should be—America.[59]

If, according to the Yiddish press, Robeson represented the zenith of Negro musical achievement, the 1930 black spectacular *The Green Pastures* was the height of black theatrical production. According to the *Morgen Journal-Tageblatt*, Jewish audiences particularly identified with the play, which attempted to present a folk interpretation of the Bible and found it extremely meaningful and moving. The actor who played "De Lawd," Richard Harrison, and his remarkable performance earned the accolades of the Yiddish critics. His career symbolized to them the problems faced by all blacks in America. A gifted actor who had never had the opportunity to perform in a legitimate theater, he had supported himself with odd jobs in menial positions until the age of 65 when his acting ability was discovered. Yet once he showed the world his great talent, he became universally respected. Prejudice *had* to melt in the face of truth, and performers like Harrison and Robeson, writers like Dunbar and McKay showed the world clearly that there was no basis for racist thinking.[60]

Yiddish writers themselves were not immune to certain stereotyping. The underlying assumption in discussions of black artistry was that blacks reacted more sensitively, felt pain and suffering more sharply, and expressed themselves with greater depth and with more poignancy. About Robeson and his spirituals, *Tageblatt* critic Mordecai Dantzis wrote:

> It is . . . not exaggerated to say that every Black is blessed with singing abilities, with a melodious voice, with a sort of special quality in his heart, which spills out in his throat and chokes up the listeners. . . . Robeson . . . can raise his voice with such power that the walls tremble and the candles quiver. . . . He can lower his voice like a dove . . . and you feel the tears in your eyes.

Descriptions of Negro life in Harlem were replete with dancing, gyrating men and women, the sounds of bongo drums (which one *Tageblatt* writer called "their national instrument") resounded, and exuberant, vibrant music filled the streets. Maurice Schwartz, one of the great stars of the Yiddish stage, claimed in no uncertain terms that rhythm ran in the Negroes' blood. Yet other writers went further and noted that rhythmic Negro music and dance, like jazz, ragtime, the Charleston, the Cakewalk, and the Black Bottom, all provided escape from the dreary life of poverty which trapped most black Americans.

Musical and rhythmic expression were the most distinctive characteristics of black cultural life. Some Yiddish writers felt that music constituted the Negroes' most important and meaningful contribution to American culture.

> Everyone agrees that the Negro has brought his own special tone into American music. Many are of the opinion that the words 'American music' are incorrect. There is no such thing and the little bit that Yankees created in their art is not worth much and does not describe the American soul. Yet, if one is talking about American music today, one is really talking about Negro music, because the blacks have created something unique, their music, which was born on the plantations of the South and in which one can hear the cracks of slave-drivers' whips and the clanging of chains and the pain of expression. [61]

The Yiddish press also extolled black achievements in areas not considered typical or traditional. Blacks who had excelled in the fields of education and scholarship received the praise of the Yiddish journalists. The newspaper writers universally recognized that blacks had demonstrated a tremendous drive for education and, in spite of poverty, in spite of unequal allocation of state funds, and in spite of poor facilities, Negroes in the South were "more attached to school than the whites in the same area." This educational hunger and excellence dealt "a blow to the theory of certain 'race thinkers' who are convinced by reason of 'science' that black-skinned races are by nature inferior to the white race in intelligence and in morality." [62]

Black heroes graced the pages of the Yiddish press in such diverse fields as aviation, business and science. Numerous news items also appared about blacks who had shown extraordinary bravery and courage. Blacks rescued children from precarious situations, black policemen risked their lives to catch dangerous criminals, and many blacks, through ingenuity, thrift, and talent, clawed their way from poverty to wealth. The *Forward* spent several columns detailing the illustrious career of Mrs. C. J. Walker, the Negro cosmetologist, "A

Former Washer-Woman . . . Now one of the Richest Women in America." The *Tageblatt* in 1925 reflected on a John W. Underhill, a black of Mays Landing, New Jersey, who died apparently poor, but left $100,000 in his will, a fortune accumulated by shrewd land investment and earmarked for the poor children of the community. The writer of the short article reflected: "John W. Underhill was only a 'nigger' and of course of no account. But before our 'Super Nordics' continue to speak so glibly of 'inferior races' let them pause for a moment."

From Booker Washington to John W. Underhill, from Frederick Douglass to Paul Robeson to Madame Walker, the Yiddish press sang the praises and chronicled the deeds of the heroes of the black race. The Yiddish press documented the black quest for greater rights and detailed the positive steps blacks were taking to shape their own future, to change the racial imbalance in America. [63]

Yet not all discussions of blacks evoked the sensitive poet, outspoken civil rights leader, or renowned educator. The Yiddish newspapers also presented a more sinister image of blacks in scores of articles on Negro criminality.

Blacks and Crime

There were probably more articles on black crime than on any other single black theme in the Yiddish press. Yet these articles took a very stock form. All were short news items, without any editorial or feature comment. In all likelihood, the Yiddish newspapers got these articles from a wire service or from the English-language newspapers of the day. Extensive reportage of Negro crime appeared in all the newspapers, in the *Morgen Journal*,[64] in the *Tageblatt*[65], the *Morgen Journal-Tageblatt*,[66] and the *Forward*.[67] These articles generally focused on local crimes of blacks in New York or Philadelphia. Consistent with its sensationalistic style, the headlines of these short news items were either gruesome or explosive: "Crazy Negro Kills 4 People in Chicago," "Mad Negro Bites Policeman, Who Dies," "Black Accused of Trying to Chloroform a White Girl and Rape Her," and "Negro Found Guilty of Murder of Girl: Two More Girls Attacked Brutally Yesterday," typifies the Yiddish press style. Usually crime articles, which abounded in these papers, did not specify the ethnicity of the criminal; the only consistent exceptions were stories of crimes committed by blacks and crimes committed by Jews.

While the Yiddish newspapers reported extensively on Negro crime, they occasionally went beyond a facile and alarmist analysis. They universally recognized that many of the blacks arrested were suspected unfairly and that blacks had a difficult time receiving a just hearing in the courts. The press always responded with indignation when blacks were sentenced to death or got lengthy jail terms after only minutes of deliberation by judge or jury. In 1919, for example, the *Tageblatt* reported that in Camden, New Jersey, a "Negro Gets 30 Years in 30 Minutes." With great cynicism, the reporter observed: "Justice in New Jersey is one of the fastest, but this time it broke all records."[68]

Not only was the judicial system riddled with prejudice and racism, but it was black poverty which bred criminality and not inherent race traits. Because of their sensitivity to this fact writers who were generally anxious about urban violence *never* editorialized on the subject of black crime statistics. Over the years the *Forward* ran only two feature stories on the subject. One, in 1918, was part of a series on the criminal court system of New York, and one of the many defendants described was a middle-aged black woman accused of stealing from a dry-goods store. The woman could not afford a lawyer and the article noted that the court appointed attorney "gets nothing from this, so he takes very little interest in the poor client. In this case the lawyer did not ask her a word about the situation." Another *Forward* feature article, which focused on black crime, carried an interview with the mother of a convicted murderer of several policemen. A sympathetic article, it again stressed the poverty which had spawned the black criminal, and it presented a moving picture of the mother who had claimed that she had "raised my children right and I hoped that he would be a respectable person. However he went away to the army and there they taught him to shoot and to murder—nothing else could have been expected of him then."[69]

The Yiddish newspapers implied that blacks themselves suffered the most from black crime. Most reported black crimes took place within families. Stories like "Negro Woman Arrested for Burning Her 8-Week Old Baby," "Negro Kills His Wife in an Argument Over a Rug," "Negro Woman Strangled: Search For Her Husband," ran fre- ·

quently and were as grotesque in detail as those which discussed black crimes against whites. Most intra-racial acts of violence flared in what the press considered unsavory places—poolrooms, cabarets, saloons, back rooms where crap games were taking place. [70]

Besides discussions of the physical crimes blacks perpetrated on each other, the Yiddish press commented extensively on black trickery and deception, again with other blacks as the unsuspecting targets. This received its fullest attention after the arrest and conviction of Marcus Garvey. While much of the Yiddish press initially reacted positively to Garvey, the Yiddish writers universally condemned his fraudulent business dealings which hurt his fellow blacks. Garvey was not the only black charlatan and demagogue whom the newspapers scorned. Several black ministers reportedly claimed supernatural powers only to be proven bluffers and, according to the *Morgen Journal-Tageblatt*, many swindlers in Harlem took vast amounts of money from poor blacks, promising to turn their skin white. In the early 1930s New York's Father Divine was another favorite target of the Yiddish journalists. Divine, they felt, swindled money out of blacks suffering from the depression. He profitably exploited their desperation. The bizarre rituals surrounding his cult and his image in the general press were considered bad publicity for blacks. In spite of their criticism, the newspapers were fascinated by this "Black God of Harlem." Novelist I. J. Singer attended one of Divine's meetings and wrote two lengthy articles stressing that Divine was nothing more than a shrewd faker and deceiver, bilking the poor black masses and fanning the flames of racist thinking. [71]

Much of the criticism leveled in the Yiddish papers at unsavory blacks—criminals, swindlers, operators—noted that these shady characters gave *all* blacks a bad name. When a particularly notorious black criminal was captured by a black judge, the *Forward* commented: "The Negro judge received many thanks from Negroes. The Negroes consider the . . . judge the savior of their race. He washed clean the name of their race in America." This obsession with public relations echoed the attitude that the Yiddish newspapers expressed about Jewish criminals. Not only had these people broken the law, but their very actions set back the progress of the whole group.

The issue of ethnic image and how disastrous the sinister actions of some blacks would be for the whole group also appeared in occasional articles on the "moral" quality of black life. In the Yiddish newspapers it was not infrequent for blacks to be found in disreputable places: cabarets, speakeasies, poolrooms, and the like. The *Forward* ran several long articles on Harlem night life, partly to discourage Jewish youth from slumming there. The newspapers concluded that it was dangerous for whites to patronize Harlem cabarets and saloons, though "The Gay Night Places in Harlem Are For Whites, Not For Blacks." The *Forward*, however, went beyond this and tried to tie this phenomenon into a larger pattern of white economic exploitation of blacks. [72]

In connection with the theme of black immorality the Yiddish newspapers reported, but without editorial comment, scandals involving black marriages and family life. They devoted considerable news space to such items as "Black Has Two Wives In His House, Twenty Children," "Negro Married to 22 Women," or "101 Year Old Negro Gets a Divorce." In an interview in 1916 with a former slave living in Washington's Foggy Bottom district, Ben-Zion, a *Forward* correspondent, noted that the woman had had many husbands; in fact, "she did not know them well, she cannot remember exactly how many she had had, six or seven." Yet the *Forward* again attempted to transcend the immediate and to link the stereotypical notions of black immorality and unstable family life to larger political and economic considerations. Ben-Zion noted that as a slave "Mother Lu" had not been allowed to remain married to any one man. As she saw it, "What would a Negro in those days know of love." [73]

Thus, blacks themselves suffered the most from black crimes—violent physical crimes, crimes of chicanery and deception, or crimes of immorality. However, there was one other group which, according to the Yiddish newspapers, was a major target of black crime—Jews. Most of these crimes were directed at merchants, and usually involved robbery. The papers reported few cases of Negro crimes of passion against Jews. In all of the newspapers for the entire twenty-year period, there were only eight incidents in which Jewish women were attacked or raped by black men. Several other brief news items reported Jews being shot or stabbed by blacks for no apparent reason, and, in spite of the extremely emotional nature of the issue, the Yiddish press never published an editorial on the subject of black crime against Jews. [74]

The bulk of black violence against Jews was economically motivated, and most of the murders or beatings stemmed from attempted
robberies, not just of merchants but of Jews waiting on subway plat-
forms, walking in the hallways of apartment buildings, passing on the
streets, or in their homes. Usually, the robberies involved small
amounts of money. In 1930, for example, the *Morgen Journal* reported that a Brooklyn rabbi had been hit over the head with an axe
and killed for $11.35, while in 1923 Morris Schenwald, a sixty-one
year old Bronx tailor, was stabbed for three dollars. [75] Jewish landlords and rent-collectors were also robbed and murdered, and again
the amount of money involved was not great. In one case, a Brooklyn
rent collector was beaten to death for $700. [76] However, the bulk of
these robbery-murders were directed at Jewish merchants in their
stores. These crimes were perpetrated in delicatessens, bakeries,
groceries, dry-goods stores, tailor shops, and meat markets. The
amounts of cash involved varied but tended to be small, and news
items gave the impression that most of the merchants were small petty
shopkeepers rather than affluent capitalists. On only one occasion did
the Yiddish newspapers actually comment on the prevalence of Negro
crime against Jewish businesses. After a May 1917 attack on a Jewish
girl in Norfolk, Virginia, the *Tageblatt* noted that the police were attempting to locate the Negro attacker of the twelve-year-old
Mendelsson girl. "They will probably find him," commented the
Tageblatt, cynically, "like they have found the other murderers who
have killed so many Jewish grocers." [77]

Black criminality thus was an often reported subject, though it
rarely merited editorialization or comment. It never evoked the same
passionate concern as lynchings or race riots, and all the newspapers
drew a connection between the rate of black crime and the unending
subjection of blacks to poverty, prejudice, and discrimination.

JEWS AND BLACKS: THE RELATIONSHIP

There was no question that the Yiddish newspapers were more
interested in blacks than in any other racial or ethnic group in New
York City in the years from 1915 to 1935. Only sporadic articles on
Italian, Irish, Greek, or Chinese Americans appeared. No group other

than blacks merited detailed and consistent attention. Jews may, in fact, have had more frequent and more intense contact with Italian and Irish Americans, yet those groups appear rarely and without much emotion in the pages of the Yiddish press. The Yiddish dailies expressed unbounded interest in the conditions and problems of Negro life and also in the relationship between their own readers and those very problems. It was perhaps in the exploration of this theme that the Yiddish journalists most creatively dealt with the meaning of American life for Jews. The Yiddish newspapers covered the whole gamut of Jewish-black relationships and interaction. They discussed the aid given by Jews to black causes—to the civil rights movement, to Negro philanthropy and to the unionization of black workers. The newspapers discussed the social and personal relations between the two groups and were generally encouraged by the friendly relations which seemed to be developing. On the other hand, the Yiddish press was fierce in its condemnation of Jewish merchants and business people who profited from black poverty. The papers decried any manifestation of anti-Negro sentiment among Jews and felt that Jews should be immune from racism and aloof from vulgar prejudice. However, the Yiddish newspapers became conscious of the birth of open anti-Semitism among blacks in the mid-1930s. Since this development coincided with the rise of Naziism in Europe, the sting was particularly painful.

The Yiddish papers sensed that a special relationship existed between blacks and Jews and because of this the press believed that the two groups were captivated by each other. This manifested itself in a number of ways, one of which was a symbiotic artistic relationship. On the one hand, Yiddish-speaking New York was enthralled by several black performers who sang Yiddish and Hebrew songs. Reb Tuviah, a black thespian, performed in all the Yiddish theaters, starred in a Yiddish play, "Yenta Telabenta," and according to the *Forward* his rendition of "Eli, Eli" (a traditional prayer of sorrow and mourning) "conveyed more deeply and more movingly the Jewish sorrow, the Jewish martyrdom, the Jewish cry and plea to God, than . . . could have ever been imagined." On the other hand, the world of Jewish entertainment began to incorporate certain elements of black music in the early 1920s. The press was fascinated by stars like Al Jolson, the son of an immigrant cantor, who seemed to blend the

Jewish and Negro entertainment styles. The *Forward* in 1928 noted the heavy Jewish influence in Tin Pan Alley and the fact that many Jewish songwriters wrote songs in the black style. A cartoon in 1920 captured the spirit and summarized the whole trend. A white man and a black man were both singing. The black, wearing a skullcap, was singing "Eli, Eli," while the white man, labeled Rabbi Samson the Cantor, was singing from *Aida*. The cartoon bore the title, "An Upside Down World."

On this artistic level the Yiddish press cited at least one authority who claimed that a real psychological bond linked the artistic hearts of the two peoples. In 1933 the *Morgan Journal-Tageblatt* published an interview with Paul Robeson in which the singer noted that he was hoping to appear in a Jewish opera. Robeson went on to say that he did not like to sing in French, German, or Italian.

> I do not understand the psychology of these people, their history has no parallels with the history of my forebearers who were slaves. The Jewish sigh and tear are close to me. I understand . . . them . . . feel that these people are closer to the traditions of my race.

A few years earlier the *Forward* devoted a lengthy article to Al Jolson, whose talkie, *The Jazz Singer*, about a cantor who had rejected Jewish life to become a black-face entertainer, was immensely popular with Jewish audiences. The reviewer speculated on the seemingly strong Jewish-Negro artistic bond:

> It is a curious thing that there are so many points of resemblance between Jews and Negroes. It is a notable thing that at least three of the most popular makers of music on the American stage should be Jewish boys, two of whom blacken their faces and sing Negro "mammy" songs while the third has written many songs in Negro dialect. How is it that the most famous black face singer in the world, Al Jolson, should be the son of a cantor? How is it that the second most popular black face artist should be an East Side boy, Eddie Cantor and that Irving Berlin, author of so many Negro songs, should be an East Side scion of a line of *Chazonim* [cantors]. . . Is there any incongruity

in this Jewish boy [Jolson] with his face painted like a Southern
Negro singing in the Negro dialect? No, there is not. Indeed I de-
tected again and again the minor key of Jewish music, the wail of
the *Chazan*, the cry of anguish of a people who had suffered.
The son of a line of rabbis well knows how to sing the songs of
the most cruelly wronged people in the world's history.[78]

Another issue which developed the theme of mutual fascination
and interest was the growth of Negro-Jewish synagogues and schools,
especially in New York. While the Yiddish press never took the black
Jewish sect, which sprouted in Harlem in the 1920s, very seriously,
numerous feature-length articles discussed the black Jews and the
kind of Judaism they practiced. Occasionally, reporters from the
Yiddish dailies went to one of the Negro temples and expressed surprise at the strict adherence to Sabbath and dietary law, at the liturgi-
cal purity maintained, and speculated on the origins of the groups.
   The close contact between Jews and blacks may have been one
explanation for the origin of the black Jews. In 1929 a black man,
James Harding, converted to Judaism, assuming the name Jacob
Abramowitz, "because he associated with Jews so long that he wanted
to become a Jew himself."[79] The Yiddish journalists realized that
Jews and blacks, in New York especially, lived and worked in physical
proximity to one another. The Yiddish newspapers did not hesitate to
talk about the actual social relations between them, and even discussed Jewish-black intermarriage. In one case in 1930 a Jewish girl
wrote to the *Forward*'s lovelorn columnist Polly Lerner that her sister
had married a black and the family was quite upset. Polly Lerner did
not categorically condemn the marriage and even admitted that a real
bond of love might exist between the Jewish woman and the black
man. She felt, however, that the marriage almost certainly was
doomed to end tragically if there were children. "The misery that a
'mixed child' would suffer in any world she lives in, is something she
should certainly be warned against," advised the columnist.
   The fact that blacks and Jews lived so close to each other in New
York caused them to learn a great deal about each other. The fairly
accurate and extensive information about blacks in the Yiddish press
certainly indicated this knowledge. The fact that black singers
learned Yiddish songs and Jewish artists were drawn to black artistic

forms was yet another indication. A *Forward* cartoon of 1927 hinted at the penetrating knowledge blacks had of Jews and Jewish anxieties. A Jewish man, attempting to sneak a box of *matzoh* into his fashionable Riverside Drive apartment to escape the view of his Christian neighbors, lest they discover his Jewish identity, was stopped by the black elevator operator. The black smilingly noted to him:

"Mister Taylor, aren'tcha kinda late?"

"Late? Late?"

"Sure. All the other tenants has brought their matzos last week!"[80]

The Yiddish writers seemed to be pleased that so much of the social contact between Jews and blacks was amiable. They were especially elated to report specific instances in which Jews had aided black causes like the civil rights movement. The *Forward*, for example, conducted an interview with Herbert Seligmann, press director of the NAACP, describing him as "A Jewish Young Man, One of the Leaders of the American Negroes." Jewish philanthropic contributions to blacks received extensive coverage. Even the *Forward*, which criticized millionaire Julius Rosenwald as a capitalist and opponent of unionization, praised his massive contributions to black charities. In general, the Yiddish newspapers felt that it was no accident that Jews participated so actively in efforts to improve race relations, that Jews naturally sided with blacks and opposed racism. After reporting that Jewish voters in St. Louis had voted almost unanimously against a racial segregation referendum, the *Tageblatt* editorialized that "this is not because they are afraid, but because the Jew understands more what fairness is. He understands more what equality means. This is because the Jew is always a believer in justice . . . ." In 1925, the *Morgen Journal* talked about an unnamed Jewish professor at Columbia University who was extensively involved in the movement for black rights. This same professor was not particularly interested in Jewish affairs, but he confided to correspondent Samuel Bloom that much Jewishness had remained with him and was expressed in terms of his interest in blacks. During the years of the Scottsboro trial, the Yiddish newspapers applauded the able attorney for the unfairly accused Negroes as a Jew and as a fighter for justice.

Jewish involvement with black causes was rewarded and Yiddish journalists glowingly noted that blacks did recognize the Jewish contribution to their struggle. The *Forward*, depicting a great upsurge in black unionization in 1920, believed that blacks "are placing much hope in the Jewish unions, the Jewish Workmen's Circles, the Jewish socialist organizations." This same editorial continued:

> They are turning to us with more hope than to any other workers' organizations because the Jews can sympathize and empathize more with them. That which the Negroes suffer in America, the Jews in many parts of Europe are now suffering in a more massive degree. Many of us ourselves were oppressed in Old Russia as the Negroes are in free America. We can understand them better and therefore we sound their appeal wide and quickly.

Black recognition of Jewish sympathy and concern received its clearest summation in the Yiddish press in a 1923 *Forward* interview with W.E.B. DuBois. The civil rights leader, author, and sociologist began by saying that "the Negro race looks to Jews for sympathy and understanding."[81]

The Yiddish press realized, however, that all American Jews were not Seligmanns or Spingarns or Rosenwalds and that some Jews were far from sympathetic and understanding to blacks. Anti-Negro sentiment among Jews was a subject of real pain to the Yiddish newspapers and they took every possible opportunity to expose and condemn it. The press reported several incidents in which Jews had treated blacks with rudeness and derision in public. A *Forward* editor noted with disgust that she had heard two wealthy Jewish women discussing their domestic help, using the phrase "a fat nigger." When a black director of a music school was asked to leave a testimonial dinner for Jewish philanthropist Felix Warburg, both the *Morgen Journal* and the *Forward* were outraged, especially since the dinner was sponsored by a Jewish group. The apologies sent by both Warburg and Adolph Zukor did not compensate for the shame and embarrassment.

The newspapers reported a few cases of Jewish violence and insensitivity against blacks. In scattered instances Jews participated in mob action against blacks, shot blacks, or unfairly accused black people. Much of the reported Jewish action against Negroes was less overt, though equally condemned by the Yiddish newspapers. When there were direct or indirect clashes between the two groups, the newspapers did not automatically take the side of their coreligionists. In 1928, for example, a fight developed between a Jewish storekeeper and a Negro woman in Newark. The black population of Newark was incensed against the Jew and a good deal of anti-Jewish rhetoric circulated. Yet the *Morgen Journal* quite calmly analyzed the situation:

> The incident has in our mind a very important meaning. It is a teacher to us. We cannot blame it on the Negroes for acting this way. Do not the whites do the same. When a Negro has a fight with a white woman and especially if it happens in the South, the Negro would surely be lynched. And the white citizens would make the same outcry that all of womanhood must be protected from the black beasts. This is the same thing that the Negroes of Newark are doing. They yell also that all Negro women must be protected from the attacks of white storekeepers. If the Negroes of Newark act this way now, it is the fault of the whites. They provided the first example. [82]

The Yiddish press attributed the existence of anti-black sentiment among Jews to three factors. First, they felt that Jews had learned racism from Americans and, in their drive to become American, they had picked up certain "un-Jewish" ideas. Second, Jews were so insecure about their own status in America that they feared being associated with a group whose status was even lower than their own. Third, much Jewish racism grew out of the type of economic relationship that existed between Jews and blacks. Jews tended to be small, petty merchants with a heavily black clientele, clustered in certain areas of the large northern cities as well as in the South.

The first two factors were treated less frequently and less systematically than the third. The issue of racism as a by-product of Americanization was explicitly discussed for southern Jews but only hinted at for urban northern Jews. The *Forward*, for example, presented a sketch of some young Jewish immigrants who had gone to the South. One of them, Sam, "soon learned to appreciate the unhurried ways of the natives. He enjoyed the deferential attitude of the local Negroes towards any white man." In a somewhat different vein a 1919

Forward piece on the life of a Jewish subway conductor included a sketch of a Negro hobo trying to warm up and sleep in the conductors' rest house. The only one to express sympathy for the poor fellow was the Jewish conductor. But as soon as some of the others began to laugh at him and ask "'Perhaps he is a friend of yours?' the Jewish conductor stopped his pleas in behalf of the black and silently watched the others torment him."[83]

The basic cause of Jewish racism, according to the Yiddish dailies, was economic. Jewish entrepreneurs took advantage of the lack of Negro businesses and opened up stores of all kinds to service black neighborhoods—primarily grocery stores, dry goods stores, delicatessens, and tailor shops. Some Jewish immigrants who wanted to get a foothold in business found the South attractive. With relatively little capital, they opened shops catering to blacks. Since southern whites would not operate Negro businesses, there was a wide-open market.

The economic sources of the conflict went even further than business, and the Yiddish press was acutely aware of the process of neighborhood change, by which predominantly Jewish neighborhoods became black. In no case did they sense it more acutely than in Harlem. They felt that as more and more blacks moved to the area, Jewish businesses would be ruined and community institutions disrupted. In the 1930s, the *Forward* ran a series of retrospective articles on the former Jewish community of Harlem, and though no direct, anti-black material was included, there was a pervasive sense that this neighborhood had once, and not too long before, been one of the finest Jewish centers. It had housed schools, community centers, synagogues, old age homes, orphanages, and myriad other social institutions built by relatively successful Jews. This pattern of Jewish abandonment of a neighborhood in the wake of a heavy black influx was not limited to upper Manhattan but, in the 1920s and 1930s, occurred in Brooklyn, Chicago, and elsewhere. For the Yiddish press, the issue which seemed to crystallize the anguish over this pattern was the conversion of synagogues into black churches. It symbolized more than just blacks moving into Jewish sections. It signified the instability of Jewish communal life in the United States. It also brought to the surface Jewish feelings about blacks which organs like the *Forward*, the *Morgen Journal*, or the *Tageblatt* did not like to acknowledge.[84]

The press condemned Jewish prejudice against blacks in whatever form it appeared. It condemned this racism in particularly harsh language because the Yiddish writers believed that a deep psychological bond existed between the two groups. That bond was meaningful to these intellectuals and journalists because they perceived an undeniable historic parallel between the Jewish and the black experience and because they were convinced that racial liberalism was both a logical extension of Jewish tradition and a useful Jewish contribution to American society.

Blacks As America's Jews: The Historic Parallels

Pervading the hundreds of articles and stories about blacks in the Yiddish newspapers was the suggestion that Jews had a peculiar ability to understand the problems of blacks. That understanding sprang from a similarity of experience, from a shared history of discrimination and oppression. While Jews had met a certain amount of prejudice in the United States and many of the forces of anti-Semitism were also anti-black, the real weight of the parallel was historic. So obvious was the parallel that the Yiddish press believed that blacks were in America what Jews were in Europe—the most oppressed, the most despised, and the most victimized segment of the population. Blacks seemed, in the eyes of the Yiddish writers, America's Jews.

For twenty years the Yiddish newspapers pointed out that *even* in America, blacks and Jews suffered from the same racism and racists—Ku Klux Klansmen, lynchers in the South, bigoted college officials at schools like Harvard, Alabama officials, restrictive housing covenants, or exploitative capitalists. When a *Tageblatt* correspondent went to a 1923 anti-Klan rally attended mostly by white Christians, he happened to sit next to the only black in the hall. Through the reporter's mind ran the thought that he was pleased that someone else had something to protest about. When the meeting condemned Klan anti-Semitism, the Jew felt a bit awkward and did not join in the applause. When the group went on to disparage Klan bigotry against blacks, the black man looked slightly uncomfortable, and he did not applaud.

Any attack on blacks carried with it potential for anti-Semitism. When black leaders criticized a 1925 study which pointed to black cowardice during World War I, the *Forward* commented:

The "accused" have cried out a great protest . . . . The Negroes yell and protest that they were insulted. This would also create a great upset in the Jewish circles if we were insulted like this. I am sure that sooner or later an anti-semitic general will come around who will accuse the Jews, that they did not want to die. . . . And when this will happen I am sure the Jews will do just like the Negroes are doing, creating disturbances and protest the insult.[85]

If the Yiddish press felt that Jews and blacks often met the same kind of prejudice in the United States of the twentieth century, they felt even more strongly that, in the sweep of history, Jews and blacks had endured similar suffering and similar persecution. The very language used by the press pointed to this. Race riots were usually "pogroms" and lynchings were "autos-da-fé," the ceremony and execution of the fifteenth-century Spanish Inquisition. After the East St. Louis riot, that city occasionally was called Kishinev, a Russian town where, in 1903, over fifty Jews were killed in a pogrom. "Everywhere the same world," noted the *Forward*. Then, after quoting a Talmudic line, the paper noted:

Kishinev and St. Louis—the same soil, the same people. It is a distance of four-and-a-half thousand miles between these two cities and yet they are so close and so similar to each other . . . . Actually twin sisters, which could easily be mistaken for each other. Four-and-a-half thousand miles apart, but the same events in both . . . . The same brutality, the same wildness, the same human beasts. There, in Kishinev, they ripped open peoples' bellies and stuffed them with feathers; here in St. Louis, houses were set on fire and women and children were allowed to burn alive. Which is better? It is a matter of taste: some like things stuffed, others like them roasted. . . . The Anglo-Saxon likes an open fire, broiled steak; this is his national food.

Reports that the Tulsa, Oklahoma, riot of 1921 began when a white girl accused a Negro of rape sounded to the *Forward* like a "blood libel"—the centuries-old accusation that Jews used the blood of Christian children for sacramental purposes, which frequently precipitated pogroms in Russia and elsewhere in Europe. Lynchers and race-rioters were routinely called "the White Hundred," named for the organized anti-Semitic shock troops in the czarist armies. The recognition of the historic parallels caused the Yiddish newspapers to give coverage to the riot in Carteret, New Jersey, far out of proportion to its severity. The image of residents of a town being roused from their sleep and forced to leave their homes, struck a deep chord of recognition in Jews.

The black migration from the South was compared to the exodus from Egypt as well as to the Jewish mass migration from eastern European oppression. In both the North and the South blacks had to live in ghettos, a term which held more than symbolic meanings to Jews. The Yiddish newspapers described Garveyism in the language of Zionism. The anthem sung at Garvey's conventions was called "The Negro Hatikvah" (the "Hatikvah" being the Zionist anthem), and the newspaper claimed that Garvey wanted to take his people out of the Galuth, the Hebrew word for diaspora. [86]

Not only were individual incidents compared and the black situation linguistically described in Jewish terms, but social analysts for the Yiddish press directly addressed themselves to the historic similarity. In 1917, for example, the *Forward* noted:

> The situation of the Negroes in America is very comparable to the situation of the Jews . . . in Russia. The Negro diaspora, the special laws, the decrees, the pogroms and also the Negro complaints, the Negro hopes are very similar to those which we Jews . . . lived through.

Two years later, another *Forward* columnist asked:

> Who has suffered and still suffers to this day from the most brutal form of punishment other than us Jews? Whenever there is an upheaval, all of Israel is oppressed, not just for the deeds of a few Jews, but even for imaginary crimes. And here, in our free state, in our great and progressive democracy, this is the lot of the black race.

Because of these historic parallels, the Yiddish newspapers knew that a special relationship existed, that a special bond mystically drew

Jews and blacks to each other. The consensus in the newspapers was that because Jews had suffered, they understood more deeply the black plight. In 1917, as black Americans cried out against the East St. Louis riot, the *Tageblatt* joined in:

> A Jewish heart is more moved by reading the banners which were carried in the East St. Louis Silent Protest, thinking about the injustices being done to the whole race. Who but a Jew can taste oppression? Who but a Jew knows so well what it means to be dealt out segregation laws and pogroms? Jews who have lived through all of these things in the Old World can well empathize with those who walked in the procession, can feel the oppression which the silent march protested.

Whenever the Yiddish newspapers discussed some Jew who had taken a particularly active role in the movement for black rights, they stressed the firm link between that action and the Jewish history of oppression. [87]

If the Yiddish press believed that Jews should have a special sympathy for blacks and if they felt that in fact most Jews sensed the similarity of history, how then did the newspapers view the other side of the relationship—the black attitude toward Jews? The Yiddish newspapers realized that black anti-Semitism existed, yet they were generally reluctant to discuss it. They tried to minimize anti-Jewish feeling about blacks and went to great lengths to rationalize incidents which might have been interpreted as such.

There were several events reported in which blacks had helped Jews or in which some black organization had spoken out for Jewish rights, and the Yiddish press glowed with pleasure. In one case a black minister in Newport News, Virginia, had prevented the lynching of a Jew. But more important, the Yiddish writers happily announced that a group of blacks had publicly declared themselves against anti-Semitism. When *Crisis* eloquently applauded Louis Brandeis' nomination to the Supreme Court and when organized black meetings condemned Nazi persecution of Jews, the Yiddish press noted: "Negroes feel a certain closeness to Jews, because they know that Jews are a foreign element in Europe and have been persecuted for years by the same dark forces which are persecuting Negroes today." [88]

Just as such items appeared in relatively isolated cases, articles on black hostility towards Jews cropped up rarely. In the 1930s, the Yiddish press began to discuss in guarded and muted terms the topic of black anti-Semitism. Until then there had been only the slightest mention of it. During the 1919 riot in Chicago the *Forward* reported some destruction of Jewish property in the "Black Belt," claiming that it had been done by blacks. In 1922 the Yiddish papers reported that some black leaders were enthusiastic about the possibility of Henry Ford being nominated for president, an act which the journalists believed could only be motivated by anti-Semitism. During this particular incident, the *Forward* told its readers that Jews "hope that the Negroes will not repay the Jews with evil for the friendship that the Jews have shown them." Until 1933, these constituted the only references to Negro anti-Semitism.

The first in a series of incidents which provoked a more full-blown discussion on the subject of black anti-Semitism in the columns of the Yiddish press was the publication of an article in a New York black daily which justified the Nazi persecution of Jews. According to the *Morgen Journal-Tageblatt*, the Negro writer of the article felt that Jews were to blame for their own troubles and that Jewish behavior in Harlem was ground enough for Naziism. The Yiddish press was aghast at this and one editorial suggested that perhaps Jews had gone too far in identifying themselves with blacks:

> The Jew who wakes up every day with the Scottsboro boys on his mind and who tears his clothing in mourning when he hears the Negro spirituals must now be a little more careful with his new "friend" . . . The Negro writer has poured oil on the Jews and sounds like a real Nazi. It is actually shocking that a Negro in America who can feel the taste of oppression and discrimination on his own dark skin, shall be so steeped in hatred of Jews. And in a land where Jews openly and warmly depicted their sympathy to their black neighbors, in a land where Jews were perhaps the only ones to act brotherly towards the oppressed. [89]

Even this incident was quickly dismissed, in spite of a Jewish awareness of the developing menace in Germany.

From September 1934 through March 1935, when the issue of Negro anti-Semitism came to a head in New York, the press persisted in discussing it in cloaked and subtle terms. The crisis was precipitated by a Harlem campaign against white merchants. The goal of the campaign was to force white merchants in the black community, by means of a boycott, to hire black employees, and pickets were thrown up around selected shops. The campaign was led by Sufi Abdul Hamid (Eugene Brown), and its rhetoric was laced with anti-Semitism, since many of the Harlem merchants were Jewish. The Yiddish press reacted quite negatively to Sufi and went to great lengths to show that blacks in Harlem were being stirred up by racketeers and communists and that the bulk of the Negro leadership opposed the picketing of Jewish-owned stores and the boycott against the merchants. Referred to consistently as the "Black Hitler," Sufi's anti-Semitism was seen as part of a worldwide outbreak rather than as a natural outgrowth of black-Jewish economic relations. The Yiddish writers clearly did not consider it a movement indigenous to American blacks or did not want to.

The Yiddish press made only a feeble effort to justify some of the practices of the merchants. All of the newspapers admitted that if Jews did discriminate against blacks, they should be stopped and condemned by the Jewish community. Yet they felt that the employment practices of the Jewish storekeepers did not deserve the pickets and boycott:

> There are very few Jewish businesses where workers and clerks are employed . . . most of the stores are run by the owner himself, helped out by a wife or child. Some may have one helper and some have a helper just on Saturday when there is more business. The few large stores have Jewish and also black salespeople. The pickets have been placed at those stores which have no clerks, or one who is usually a son or a daughter. The stores are poor and shabby. Most of the Jews in Harlem do not own the stores—the stores own them.

Instead, the Yiddish press attempted to expose Sufi as a racketeer, motivated by his own greed. What few blacks followed him, the writers claimed, were goaded on by the shattering effects of the depression, and the Yiddish newspapers viewed the communist speakers who frequented Harlem street corners as provocateurs. Generally the press went to great lengths to distinguish between Sufi's followers and the masses of blacks. Hence Sufi's anti-Semitism was considered artificial and unpopular. [90]

By mid-March of 1935 the Yiddish newspapers could not help but discuss the existence of intense widespread anti-Jewish feeling in Harlem, though they still wanted desperately to downplay it. For three nights, beginning on March 19, rioting ravaged the business district of Harlem. When the fires died down 200 destroyed stores and millions of dollars in property damage severely tested and strained the position of the Yiddish press. Though the Yiddish newspapers referred to the riots as "pogroms" and were sensitive to the fact that Jews had incurred most of the loss, they still minimized the role anti-Semitism played. The *Morgen Journal-Tageblatt* advised its readers: "One must understand. This was a riot against whites, against the businesses of whites. It was not a riot against Jews, it was not a pogrom against Jews. Most of the merchants who suffered were Jews, because the largest number of Harlem storekeepers were Jews." Again, the newspapers blamed the riot on communist agitators, selfish racketeers, and the desperation of the Depression. Here again was the same fear to label the incident anti-Semitic, even though the chief victims of the incident, the merchants themselves, were sure that it was. [91]

Why were the Yiddish newspapers, usually vigilant in spotting anti-Semitism and in watching out for Jewish interests, reluctant to admit its existence in the black communities? Why would the Yiddish newspapers, no doubt read by many of the Harlem Jewish merchants, tend to minimize the extent to which blacks resented Jews as merchants, as employers, as landlords? It was perhaps difficult for the Yiddish newspapers to admit to the existence of black anti-Semitism because, for over twenty years, they had been stressing the intimate bond which existed between Jews and blacks. Because Jewish-black relations had seemed so perfect for Jewish community leaders who were seeking to discover their place in American society, the journalists and editors could not admit that there was something to mar their program.

In the early months of 1935, when black-Jewish conflict in New

York City was becoming acute and as Jews in America were learning of the horrors of Nazi Germany, the *Forward* wrote a moving obituary for Richard Harrison, the star of *The Green Pastures*. In that short editorial the writer expressed that mystical feeling of closeness which perhaps blinded the Yiddish press to unpleasant realities. The writer noted that the philosophy of *The Green Pastures* had made a great impression on most Jews:

> In this present moment of upheaval and unrest, of world catastrophe and world storm, there was no greater pleasure than to be carried away to that far more naive, sinless world, which the play presented. No matter how difficult human life, it became a bit easier when one heard how "God, the Lawd," said that even God "is in no bed of roses," that even God is to be pitied . . . . In this play . . . the souls of two nations are woven together . . . the soul of the Jews and the soul of the Negroes. [92]

For twenty years the Yiddish newspapers had believed that there was an emotional and psychological bond which drew the two groups together. That bond of history, it was felt, could overcome differences in color, differences in class, and differences in religion. The Yiddish press, one of the central institutions of immigrant Jewish life in America, chose in 1935 to try to cling to that view.

Moreover, for twenty years the editors and writers, as leaders of the Yiddish-speaking Jewish world of America, tried to define for their readers a special role for American Jews. Part of that special role and unique mission included extending sympathy and friendship to America's downtrodden. Not even the events of April 1935 caused the Yiddish journalists to abandon that mission.

NOTES

1. David Wolf Silverman, "The Jewish Press: A Quadrilingual Phenomenon," in Martin E. Marty et. al., *The Religious Press in America* (New York: Holt, Rinehart and Winston, 1963), p. 139; Hutchins Hapgood, *The Spirit of the Ghetto: Studies of the Jewish Quarter of New York* (New York: Funk and Wagnalls, 1902).

2. David Druck, *Tzu Der Geshichte Fun Der Yiddisher Prese: In Rusland Un Poilin* (Warsaw: Zichronos, 1920); Joseph Chaiken, *Yiddishe Bleter in Amerike* (New York: M. S. Shkalarsky, 1946); Jacob Shatsky, *Tzu Der Geshichte Fun Der Yiddishe Prese in Amerika* (New York: Yiddish Kultur Gezelshaft, 1934).

3. Alfred McClurg Lee, *The Daily Newspaper in America* (New York: Macmillan, 1937), p. 737.

4. Ronald Sanders, *The Downtown Jews: Portraits of an Immigrant Generation* (New York: Harper and Row, 1969), pp. 97-125; Robert Park, *The Immigrant Press and Its Control* (New York: Harper and Brothers, 1922), pp. 80-83; Milton Doroshkin, *Yiddish in America: Social and Cultural Foundation* (Rutherford, New Jersey: Fairleigh-Dickinson University Press, 1970).

5. Robert Park, *The Immigrant Press*, p. 89.

6. Mordecai Soltes, *The Yiddish Press: An Americanizing Agency* (New York: Teachers College, Columbia University, 1925), pp. 39-44.

7. Yiddish Writers' Union, *Funf Un Zibitzik Yor Yidishe Prese in America: 1870-1945* (New York: Y. L. Peretz Writers Union, 1945), pp. 79-81; Ronald Sanders, *The Downtown Jews*, p. 319; Mordecai Soltes, *The Yiddish Press*, pp. 24-25, 185.

8. Robert Park, *The Immigrant Press*, p. 355; Yiddish Writers' Union, *Funf Un Zibitzik Yor*, pp. 62-68; Mordecai Soltes, *The Yiddish Press*, p. 24.

9. Of all the Yiddish newspapers the *Jewish Daily Forward* has received the most attention from historians and social scientists. Park discussed it more thoroughly than any of the other newspapers. Ronald Sanders' *The Downtown Jews* was largely a study of the *Forward* and Cahan. The "Bintel Brief," a daily *Forward* column meaning a "packet of letters" which gave advice, has been translated, edited and published. See Isaac Metzger, ed., *A Bintel Brief* (New York: Doubleday and Company, 1971).

10. Abraham Cahan, *Bleter Fun Main Leben*, 5 vols. (New York: Forward Press, 1920-1931) has never been translated into English, but is an invaluable source on not only Yiddish journalism but on all aspects of immigrant Jewish life. Abraham Cahan, *The Rise of David Levinsky* (New York: Harper and Brothers, 1917); Hutchins Hapgood, *The Spirit of the Ghetto*, pp. 186-187; Robert Park, *The Immigrant Press*, pp. 101-104.

11. A survey of the Yiddish press demonstrates that there was no equivalent interest and identification with other ethnic or racial groups in the United States.

12. In this footnote and in all the following ones for this chapter, only a sampling of the relevant articles will be cited. *Morgen Journal*, March 29, 1925, p. 5; March 15, 1925, p. 6; *Forward*, August 28, 1932, p. 5; December 7, 1924, p. 11; December 21, 1924, pp. 15-16; January 18, 1925, p. 15; February 26, 1928, p. 13; March 18, 1928, p. 18; April 8, 1928, p. 13; May 3, 1919, p. 1; February 21, 1926, p. 11.

13. *Forward*, July 13, 1916, p. 8; March 21, 1918, p. 1; January 4, 1925, p. 4; August 17, 1928, p. 4.

14. *Tageblatt*, September 4, 1921, p. 4; July 17, 1925, p. 1; September 18, 1924, p. 4; *Morgen Journal*, March 6, 1921, p. 6; December 15, 1920, p. 2; August 10, 1930, p. 5; *Forward*, August 20, 1923, p. 8; May 9, 1926, p. 11.

15. *Tageblatt*, January 3, 1916, p. 5; January 2, 1922, p. 1; July 4, 1922, p. 2; March 25, 1928, p. 8; *Morgen Journal*, January 2, 1917, p. 2; July 10, 1921, p. 1; July 7, 1924, p. 7; *Forward*, November 19, 1919, p. 12; January 2, 1920, p. 1; June 13, 1926, p. 4.

16. *Forward*, August 1, 1915, p. 1; May 23, 1917, p. 8; November 29, 1918, p. 4; *Morgen Journal*, February 10, 1920, p. 1; December 19, 1920, p. 6; September 16, 1921, p. 6; *Tageblatt*, May 2, 1921, p. 1; *Morgen Journal-Tageblatt*, January 2, 1929, p. 1; August 16, 1933, p. 5; October 28, 1934, p. 1.

17. *Forward*, August 26, 1922, p. 6; May 22, 1918, p. 8; October 13, 1919, p. 6; *Tageblatt*, August 25, 1922, p. 1; *Morgen Journal-Tageblatt*, October 17, 1935, p. 5; April 27, 1933, p. 4.

18. *Forward*, December 27, 1915, p. 1; May 23, 1917, p. 8; August 26, 1922, p. 6; *Morgen Journal*, July 15, 1915, p. 2; May 27, 1924, p. 1; September 30, 1920, p. 1; *Tageblatt*, July 20, 1918, p. 1; August 8, 1921, p. 1; June 30, 1922, p. 1; *Morgen Journal-Tageblatt*, February 6, 1935, p. 10; December 6, 1931, p. 2; July 13, 1933, p. 2.

19. *Morgen Journal-Tageblatt*, June 23, 1934, p. 10; May 14, 1934, p. 1; *Forward*, December 2, 1921, p. 1; June 22, 1935, p. 1; April 5, 1925, p. 1; October 5, 1916, p. 1; *Tageblatt*, April 12, 1923, p. 2; *Morgen Journal*, July 9, 1920, p. 1.

20. *Forward*, August 20, 1916, p. 4; May 9, 1922, p. 4; February 26, 1926, p. 4; *Tageblatt*, January 2, 1917, p. 1; October 1, 1919, p. 6; January 4, 1925, p. 4; *Morgen Journal*, May 7, 1922, p. 2; December 19, 1923, p. 1; *Morgen Journal-Tageblatt*, April 27, 1933, p. 4; May 12, 1930, p. 6; December 21, 1934, p. 4.

21. *Tageblatt*, October 14, 1917, p. 8; October 7, 1919, p. 1; February 28, 1924, p. 1; *Morgen Journal*, May 22, 1922, p. 1; November 13, 1927, p. 1; June 14, 1927, p. 1; *Forward*, October 1, 1916, p. 12; August 4, 1921, p. 1; May 12, 1930, p. 1; *Morgen Journal-Tageblatt*, February 2, 1930, p. 1; September 11, 1930, p. 1; December 11, 1931, p. 1.

22. *Morgen Journal*, August 26, 1923, p. 1; *Forward*, December 9, 1933, p. 1; May 18, 1930, p. 1; December 29, 1933, p. 1; *Tageblatt*, December 25, 1925, p. 1; January 29, 1933, p. 1; November 28, 1933, p. 1; *Morgen Journal-Tageblatt*, November 29, 1933, p. 1; December 1, 1933, p. 1; December 1, 1933, p. 4.

23. *Forward*, November 15, 1917, p. 4; February 19, 1928, p. 1; December 5, 1922, p. 4; *Morgen Journal*, July 24, 1921, p. 4; November 2, 1919, p. 1; December 1, 1922, p. 1; *Tageblatt*, May 7, 1919, p. 4; December 20, 1921, p. 2; December 24, 1925, p. 5; *Morgen Journal-Tageblatt*, November 12, 1934, p. 4; October 29, 1934, p. 1; December 11, 1933, p. 5.

24. *Tageblatt*, December 31, 1924, p. 1; August 30, 1926, p. 1; October 2, 1919, p. 1; *Morgen Journal-Tageblatt*, September 13, 1932, p. 2; August 16, 1929, p. 1; *Morgen Journal*, January 9, 1924, p. 8; July 20, 1921, p. 6; February 3, 1926, p. 1; *Forward*, October 16, 1919, p. 1; October 9, 1925, p. 1; December 13, 1928, p. 1; November 21, 1927, p. 1.

25. *Morgen Journal-Tageblatt*, June 7, 1931, p. 1; June 16, 1931, p. 4; June 24, 1931, p. 1; July 21, 1931, p. 1; *Forward*, June 7, 1931, p. 8; January 23, 1932, p. 1; March 26, 1932, p. 4; March 3, 1933, p. 1; April 11, 1933, p. 4.

26. *Tageblatt*, January 7, 1923, p. 1; January 8, 1923, p. 1; May 19, 1921, p. 1; *Forward*, November 15, 1919, p. 1; July 14, 1919, p. 1; September 12, 1927, p. 1; July 6, 1930, p. 1; *Morgen Journal*, January 15, 1923, p. 4; September 19, 1918, p. 6; *Morgen Journal-Tageblatt*, July 6, 1930, p. 1; August 2, 1929, p. 1.

27. *Morgen Journal*, August 21, 1918, p. 8; March 20, 1927, p. 1; July 30, 1918, p. 1; *Forward*, August 6, 1919, p. 8; July 31, 1920, p. 1; June 4, 1920, p. 9; *Tageblatt*, June 21, 1920, p. 1; December 17, 1920, p. 1; March 13, 1921, p. 1; *Morgen Journal-Tageblatt*,

July 21, 1930, p. 3; July 15, 1929, p. 1.

28. *Morgen Journal*, May 30, 1917, p. 1; July 5, 1917, p. 1; July 3, 1917, p. 1; *Tageblatt*, May 31, 1917, p. 1; July 3, 1917, p. 1; July 11, 1917, p. 4; *Forward*, July 3, 1917, p. 1; July 5, 1917, p. 4; July 15, 1917, p. 5.

29. *Forward*, July 31, 1919, p. 3; July 24, 1919, p. 5; June 21, 1920, p. 1; *Tageblatt*, June 3, 1921, p. 1; June 2, 1921, p. 1; July 24, 1919, p. 1; *Morgen Journal*, June 3, 1921, p. 1; August 5, 1919, p. 4; July 30, 1919, p. 1; October 22, 1919, p. 1.

30. *Forward*, April 29, 1926, p. 4; April 27, 1926, p. 8; *Tageblatt*, April 28, 1926, p. 1; *Tageblatt*, April 30, 1926, p. 4.

31. *Forward*, July 12, 1917, p. 8; September 6, 1919, p. 1; July 31, 1919, p. 4; *Tageblatt*, July 29, 1919, p. 6; June 7, 1921, p. 1; *Morgen Journal*, July 29, 1919, p. 4; June 7, 1921, p. 4.

32. *Forward*, June 2, 1927, p. 6; March 1, 1925, p. 4; September 4, 1925, p. 4; *Morgen Journal*, March 31, 1921, p. 4; April 27, 1921, p. 1; *Tageblatt*, April 8, 1921, p. 1; April 7, 1921, p. 1; February 2, 1927, p. 6.

33. *Forward*, March 30, 1921, p. 4; June 8, 1924, p. 16; June 14, 1925, p. 3; October 11, 1925, p. 19; *Tageblatt*, July 27, 1921, p. 1; *Morgen Journal*, June 16, 1919, p. 4.

34. *Morgen Journal*, February 15, 1918, p. 4; *Tageblatt*, June 15, 1919, p. 2; July 11, 1920, p. 2; *Forward*, June 23, 1919, p. 4.

35. *Forward*, October 4, 1921, p. 7; November 19, 1916, p. 8; June 27, 1917, p. 8; *Tageblatt*, August 18, 1921, p. 1; *Morgen Journal*, July 19, 1921, p. 2.

36. *Forward*, October 27, 1923, p. 16; March 16, 1928, p. 10; April 13, 1932, p. 14; *Morgen Journal-Tageblatt*, August 5, 1931, p. 4; August 4, 1931, p. 1; August 5, 1931, p. 1; October 8, 1931, p. 3; August 25, 1930, p. 6.

37. *Morgen Journal-Tageblatt*, August 23, 1933, p. 4; September 1, 1932, p. 2; *Forward*, September 23, 1932, pp. 1-2; August 31, 1932, p. 1; June 8, 1924, p. 4.

38. *Forward*, September 30, 1918, p. 4; August 14, 1924, p. 4; June 22, 1915, p. 1; *Morgen Journal*, July 9, 1915, p. 5; March 15, 1927, p. 10; March 8, 1927, p. 6; *Tageblatt*, July 9, 1920, p. 1; September 20, 1920, p. 1; March 8, 1927, p. 6; *Morgen Journal-Tageblatt*, June 8, 1932, p. 8; June 9, 1929, p. 4.

39. *Forward*, October 30, 1928, p. 4; January 19, 1933, p. 1; July 22, 1930, p. 3; February 24, 1924, p. 4; *Tageblatt*, May 19, 1921, p. 2; *Morgen Journal*, May 31, 1925, p. 5; July 3, 1921, p. 5; September 25, 1921, p. 5; July 12, 1926, p. 1.

40. *Forward*, January 13, 1916, p. 2; June 8, 1921, p. 5; April 3, 1928, p. 8; *Tageblatt*, November 8, 1921, p. 2; *Morgen Journal*, December 4, 1921, p. 5; October 28, 1921, p. 1.

41. *Forward*, March 21, 1916, p. 16; March 15, 1927, p. 11; July 20, 1925, p. 1; *Morgen Journal*, November 7, 1917, p. 5; March 16, 1927, p. 8; *Tageblatt*, November 6, 1917, p. 4; March 11, 1927, p. 1; *Morgen Journal-Tageblatt*, April 21, 1930, p. 12.

42. *Tageblatt*, January 25, 1923, p. 1; January 12, 1923, p. 1; April 3, 1924, p. 1; September 30, 1927, p. 5; *Forward*, April 4, 1924, p. 4; April 10, 1922, p. 4; October 16, 1927, p. 25; *Morgen Journal*, March 7, 1923, p. 1; *Morgen Journal-Tageblatt*, January 16, 1930, p. 3.

43. *Tageblatt*, April 30, 1926, p. 5; *Morgen Journal-Tageblatt*, October 14, 1929, p. 4; November 1, 1932, p. 4; *Forward*, September 18, 1929, p. 6; October 28, 1932, p. 4.

44. *Morgen Journal-Tageblatt*, December 26, 1929, p. 3; December 19, 1929, p. 8; July 22, 1929, p. 6; *Forward*, May 23, 1930, p. 10; March 5, 1924, p. 4; May 23, 1930, p. 10; March 9, 1924, p. 4; *Tageblatt*, February 20, 1920, p. 14; July 6, 1919, p. 4; August 16, 1923, p. 4; *Morgen Journal*, March 9, 1928, p. 7; July 20, 1926, pp. 6-7.

45. *Forward*, November 22, 1917, p. 4; August 26, 1925, p. 4; August 8, 1925, p. 5; January 29, 1933, p. 4; *Morgen Journal*, August 10, 1920, p. 4; April 20, 1925, pp. 6-7; May 3, 1925, p. 5; June 28, 1925, p. 6.

46. *Morgen Journal*, August 10, 1920, p. 4; July 6, 1923, p. 1; April 19, 1923, p. 6; *Forward*, September 18, 1917, p. 3; April 8, 1923, p. 4; August 24, 1926, p. 5; *Morgen Journal-Tageblatt*, July 15, 1931, p. 4.

47. *Forward*, October 1, 1919, p. 1; August 24, 1917, p. 1; December 12, 1917, p. 1; *Tageblatt*, July 28, 1919, p. 1; July 29, 1919, p. 1; August 24, 1917, p. 1; *Morgen Journal*, July 30, 1919, p. 1; July 22, 1919, p. 1; August 26, 1917, p. 1.

48. *Morgen Journal*, December 21, 1921, p. 5; *Tageblatt*, July 25, 1919, p. 1; *Forward*, September 18, 1917, p. 3; December 21, 1918, p. 1.

49. *Tageblatt*, December 8, 1925, p. 5; December 21, 1926, p. 3; June 3, 1920, p. 2; *Forward*, December 5, 1926, p. 15; December 23, 1935, p. 10; December 31, 1918, p. 1; June 23, 1935, p. 12; March 18, 1920, p. 13.

50. *Forward*, December 5, 1926, p. 15; September 6, 1922, p. 1; October 6, 1933, p. 1; *Tageblatt*, August 23, 1927, p. 2; July 1, 1927, p. 4; November 30, 1922, p. 1; *Morgen Journal*, June 22, 1920, p. 1; November 10, 1924, p. 8; *Morgen Journal-Tageblatt*, December 12, 1934, p. 1.

51. *Forward*, August 2, 1920, p. 1; August 18, 1924, p. 2; November 27, 1932, p. 2; *Morgen Journal*, August 17, 1920, p. 1; August 2, 1920, p. 1; September 2, 1924, p. 2; *Tageblatt*, August 18, 1924, p. 1; February 3, 1925, p. 5; August 26, 1927, p. 6.

52. *Forward*, December 6, 1919, p. 15; July 11, 1930, p. 4; April 15, 1918, p. 8; *Tageblatt*, June 3, 1919, p. 1; March 25, 1927, p. 2; March 13, 1927, p. 6; *Morgen Journal*, August 3, 1917, p. 7.

53. *Morgen Journal*, January 19, 1923, p. 8; October 16, 1924, p. 5; November 6, 1922, p. 1; *Morgen Journal-Tageblatt*, July 11, 1929, p. 8; December 30, 1930, p. 1; *Tageblatt*, February 26, 1924, p. 1; October 7, 1924, p. 1; November 6, 1922, p. 2.

54. *Forward*, November 25, 1934, p. 10; November 8, 1923, p. 1; July 10, 1932, p. 9; *Morgen Journal*, December 24, 1925, p. 1; November 12, 1924, p. 5; April 29, 1928, p. 1; May 13, 1928, p. 10; *Morgen Journal-Tageblatt*, August 1, 1930, p. 5; *Tageblatt*, November 6, 1922, p. 2; November 23, 1922, p. 1.

55. *Forward*, November 15, 1915, p. 1; July 8, 1925, p. 21; October 11; *Morgen Journal*, November 16, 1915, p. 5; *Morgen Journal-Tageblatt*, July 15, 1934, p. 5; May 8, 1927, p. 7.

56. *Forward*, August 26, 1925, p. 8; June 28, 1927, p. 6; January 24, 1935, p. 6; January 11, 1927, p. 3; January 7, 1935, p. 8; August 24, 1934, p. 10; July 10, 1923, p. 10; February 10, 1921, p. 1.

57. *Forward*, September 11, 1926, p. 12; January 16, 1927, p. 17; May 15, 1932, p. 12; *Morgen Journal-Tageblatt*, October 14, 1934, p. 3.

58. *Morgen Journal*, May 1, 1925, p. 1; *Forward*, March 12, 1922, p. 3; January 31, 1922, p. 5; February 18, 1921, p. 8; December 31, 1933, p. 5; May 23, 1930, p. 10; *Tage-*

blatt, November 2, 1920, p. 2; February 20, 1921, p. 14.

59. *Forward*, March 26, 1932, p. 15; September 13, 1931, p. 5; October 5, 1932, p. 12; *Tageblatt*, July 23, 1917, p. 4; November 24, 1926, p. 4; *Morgen Journal-Tageblatt*, October 30, 1933, p. 8.

60. *Forward*, April 27, 1931, p. 5; March 7, 1930, p. 3; March 4, 1930, p. 4; March 16, 1935, p. 6; *Morgen Journal-Tageblatt*, March 15, 1935, p. 5; December 11, 1930, p. 6; May 14, 1923, p. 7.

61. *Tageblatt*, July 23, 1917, p. 4; November 24, 1926, p. 4; *Forward*, July 18, 1931, p. 4; May 5, 1923, p. 7; October 21, 1926, p. 6; July 29, 1923, p. 10.

62. *Forward*, September 16, 1928, p. 21; October 15, 1934, p. 4; December 8, 1933, p. 1; *Morgen Journal*, September 5, 1920, p. 2; July 23, 1922, p. 2; May 24, 1925, p. 5; *Tageblatt*, September 16, 1923, p. 8; June 10, 1917, p. 1; June 13, 1924, p. 7; June 13, 1924, p. 7; *Morgen Journal-Tageblatt*, February 6, 1935, p. 3.

63. *Forward*, September 18, 1922, p. 6; November 15, 1928, p. 1; August 9, 1931, p. 6; *Morgen Journal*, June 18, 1928, p. 9; June 2, 1925, p. 2; August 8, 1917, p. 5; *Tageblatt*, April 8, 1928, p. 8; November 2, 1925, p. 6; October 14, 1926, p. 6.

64. *Morgen Journal*, July 20, 1916, p. 7; February 13, 1916, p. 4; July 16, 1917, p. 2; June 19, 1923, p. 2; June 3, 1924, p. 4; July 2, 1925, p. 8; March 21, 1924, p. 12; March 11, 1926, p. 8; August 3, 1928, p. 11.

65. *Tageblatt*, February 25, 1919, p. 1; September 1, 1922, p. 1; March 9, 1923, p. 1; December 8, 1925, p. 1; June 12, 1925, p. 5; April 1, 1928, p. 1; March 21, 1928, p. 1.

66. *Morgen Journal-Tageblatt*, November 18, 1929, p. 5; May 19, 1929, p. 6; April 22, 1929, p. 8; March 27, 1929, p. 6; June 13, 1932, p. 3.

67. *Forward*, June 3, 1915, p. 8; July 29, 1918, p. 8; April 2, 1922, p. 1; June 18, 1923, p. 1; June 1, 1925, p. 1; May 13, 1925, p. 8; May 28, 1928, p. 1.

68. *Tageblatt*, October 22, 1919, p. 1; *Morgen Journal*, February 3, 1926, p. 1; *Morgen Journal-Tageblatt*, August 16, 1929, p. 1; *Forward*, February 3, 1926, p. 1; February 20, 1935, p. 10.

69. *Tageblatt*, October 9, 1923, p. 8; *Forward*, January 31, 1918, p. 1; January 12, 1922, p. 3; *Morgen Journal*, October 10, 1921, p. 4.

70. *Forward*, December 30, 1915, p. 3; December 16, 1921, p. 1; June 21, 1925, p. 8; *Morgen Journal*, March 27, 1919, p. 2; August 9, 1920, p. 1; July 2, 1923, p. 8; *Tageblatt*, July 19, 1925, p. 6; May 13, 1925, p. 1; August 10, 1923, p. 1; *Morgen Journal-Tageblatt*, January 7, 1931, p. 3; April 7, 1929, p. 1; April 15, 1934, p. 3.

71. *Forward*, June 4, 1930, p. 1; January 14, 1922, p. 8; May 10, 1931, p. 1; *Morgen Journal*, January 31, 1917, p. 5; July 3, 1923, p. 12; July 2, 1923, p. 5; *Tageblatt*, August 6, 1925, p. 1; February 6, 1925, p. 1; August 5, 1924, p. 1; *Morgen Journal-Tageblatt*, August 15, 1933, p. 4; March 4, 1935, p. 2.

72. *Forward*, March 16, 1930, p. 18; July 31, 1930, p. 1; December 3, 1922, p. 10; October 23, 1929, p. 8; February 18, 1932, p. 6; July 19, 1932, p. 1; September 23, 1932, p. 4.

73. *Forward*, December 13, 1926, p. 6; April 24, 1931, p. 8; March 16, 1915, p.1; July 13, 1916, p. 8; July 1, 1916, p. 2; *Morgen Journal*, December 16, 1921, p. 1.

74. *Tageblatt*, May 8, 1917, p. 1; *Morgen Journal*, November 26, 1925, p. 4; June 20, 1925, p. 1; *Forward*, October 28, 1925, p. 1; February 13, 1935, p. 1; January 26, 1929, p. 1; *Morgen Journal-Tageblatt*, March 1, 1934, p. 18; September 26, 1932, p. 1; December 4, 1929, p. 7.

75. *Morgen Journal-Tageblatt*, September 21, 1930, p. 2; January 22, 1935, p. 3; November 21, 1929, p. 7; *Tageblatt*, November 30, 1916, p. 1; June 7, 1921, p. 1; June 14, 1921, p. 1; *Forward*, June 3, 1929, p. 1; June 12, 1921, p. 1; April 22, 1928, p. 1; *Morgen Journal*, May 29, 1924, p. 10.

76. *Forward*, May 18, 1921, p. 1; January 23, 1925, p. 1; *Tageblatt*, May 18, 1921, p. 1; *Morgen Journal-Tageblatt*, June 28, 1929, p. 2; November 25, 1930, p.2; November 20, 1930, p. 3.

77. *Tageblatt*, September 15, 1927, p. 1; January 12, 1922, p. 2; March 17, 1924, p. 1; *Morgen Journal*, June 29, 1922, p. 1; July 18, 1927, p. 8; *Morgen Journal-Tageblatt*, May 24, 1929, p. 1; July 16, 1931, p. 1; *Forward*, August 22, 1928, p. 10; March 15, 1922, p. 8; April 13, 1921, p. 8.

78. *Tageblatt*, November 3, 1921, p. 1; June 28, 1920, p. 4; *Morgen Journal*, March 15, 1923, p. 4; April 11, 1921, p. 4; October 8, 1928, p. 8; *Forward*, November 19, 1924, p. 7; March 31, 1922, p. 3; May 16, 1920, p. 5; *Morgen Journal-Tageblatt*, September 1, 1933, p. 4.

79. *Forward*, March 22, 1925, p. 3; December 13, 1933, p. 3; December 17, 1933, p. 9; *Morgen Journal*, September 7, 1924, p. 2; August 29, 1924, p. 2; August 15, 1924, p. 4; *Morgen Journal-Tageblatt*, June 17, 1931, p. 5; July 11, 1929, p. 3; *Tageblatt*, March 4, 1925, p. 10; December 18, 1925, p. 7. See also Howard M. Brotz, *The Black Jews of Harlem: Negro Nationalism and the Dilemmas of Negro Leadership* (New York: Shocken Books, 1964).

80. *Forward*, February 9, 1929, p. 10; August 1, 1922, p. 1; July 10, 1923, p. 10; *Morgen Journal*, August 1, 1921, p. 1; July 10, 1934, p. 5; *Tageblatt*, June 28, 1926, p. 1; *Morgen Journal-Tageblatt*, August 14, 1929, p. 8.

81. *Forward*, January 19, 1932, p. 1; January 23, 1925, p. 1; June 29, 1919, p. 2; *Tageblatt*, January 4, 1927, p. 5; October 12, 1919, p. 2; April 17, 1928, p. 7; *Morgen Journal*, April 9, 1928, p. 7; *Morgen Journal-Tageblatt*, February 5, 1931, p. 4.

82. *Forward*, March 11, 1923, p. 3; August 26, 1917, p. 9; January 30, 1929, p. 1; *Morgen Journal*, December 22, 1924, p. 2; October 10, 1924, p. 1; December 22, 1924, p. 2; *Morgen Journal-Tageblatt*, July 21, 1930, p. 3; *Tageblatt*, October 10, 1924, p. 1.

83. *Forward*, December 2, 1928, p. 25; June 29, 1919, p. 2; May 17, 1916, p. 4; *Tageblatt*, September 7, 1922, p. 4; April 20, 1928, p. 6.

84. *Forward*, October 2, 1927, p. 21; November 21, 1922, p. 4; April 15, 1923, p. 4; August 19, 1928, p. 11; *Tageblatt*, March 15, 1925, p. 4; April 20, 1928, p. 6; April 4, 1922, p. 3; *Morgen Journal*, December 9, 1924, p. 4; July 16, 1925, p. 3.

85. *Forward*, May 29, 1917, p. 5; October 5, 1916, p. 1; October 13, 1923, p. 8; *Morgen Journal*, May 17, 1921, p. 4; June 8, 1923, p. 7; *Tageblatt*, April 30, 1926, p. 5; April 17, 1923, p. 10; *Morgen Journal-Tageblatt*, July 17, 1931, p. 6.

86. *Morgen Journal*, May 7, 1922, p. 1; July 3, 1919, p. 1; May 30, 1917, p. 1; *Forward*, July 28, 1917, p. 12; July 27, 1917, p. 8; *Tageblatt*, July 3, 1917, p. 1; July 4, 1917, p. 1; July 23, 1919, p. 4.

87. *Morgen Journal-Tageblatt*, April 8, 1929, p. 4; September 1, 1933, p. 4; *Forward*, November 8, 1932, p. 10; January 7, 1932, p. 10; *Tageblatt*, March 9, 1916, p. 3; July 31, 1917, p. 4; *Morgen Journal*, June 21, 1925, p. 6, August 10, 1924, p. 4.

88. *Morgen Journal*, October 29, 1920, p. 1; *Tageblatt*, October 29, 1920, p. 2; *Forward*, April 1, 1933, p. 14; March 29, 1918, p. 1.

89. *Forward*, July 31, 1919, p. 1; July 27, 1922, p. 1; *Tageblatt*, March 8, 1923, p. 8;

Morgen Journal-Tageblatt, May 19, 1933, p. 8.

90. *Forward*, September 26, 1934, p. 1; November 1, 1934, p. 1; October 9, 1934, p. 1; *Morgen Journal-Tageblatt*, September 27, 1934, p. 4; October 12, 1934, p. 1; November 1, 1934, p. 1.

91. *Forward*, March 20, 1935, p. 1; March 21, 1935, p. 1; March 22, 1935, p. 4; *Morgen Journal-Tageblatt*, March 21, 1935, pp. 1-2; March 22, 1935, p. 1.

92. *Forward*, March 16, 1935, p. 6.

chapter 3

"TO FIGHT THEIR BATTLES":
ENGLISH-LANGUAGE JEWISH
MAGAZINES AND IMAGES OF BLACKS

Not all American Jews read the Yiddish press; it served an eastern European immigrant audience. For other Jews, the Uptown Jews, the Jews of western European origins, the American-born Jews, an active and vital press existed also. The Yiddish press and the English-language Jewish press demarcated different stages on the road to Americanization. The Yiddish newspapers served Jews taking their first steps on the path to acculturation in America. Middle-class Jews who functioned quite freely in mainstream America read and wrote for the English magazines and journals.

The Yiddish press absorbed itself in questions of racial difference and racism in the United States. Its writers and editors systematically explored the themes of black life as one way of working out questions of their own ambiguous identity and status in American society. The Yiddish journalists used black issues as reflectors of their marginality and played with them to help blend an old world heritage with the realities of modern America. The English-language Jewish writers expressed this same intense interest in blacks. The magazines in which they wrote differed thoroughly from the Yiddish press in format, style, orientation, and audience. Yet the writers evinced this same tendency to use the issues of black oppression and achievement as a path to explore their ambivalence about America and their doubts about the future. These periodicals, like the Yiddish newspapers, used the images of black life as vehicles for self-examination and evaluation.

THE ENGLISH-LANGUAGE JEWISH MAGAZINES

The Yiddish press was highly centralized, based primarily in New York. On the other hand, in the mid-1920s at least ninety-one English-language Jewish journals circulated throughout the United States. Published all across the country, no single city maintained a monopoly. Magazines originated in New York, Chicago, Los Angeles, Detroit, Boston, Philadelphia, Cincinnati, San Francisco, Portland, and Seattle. Two Jewish magazines were based in the South, in Houston and Atlanta. Of these ninety-one periodicals, only one was a daily. The number of weeklies and monthlies was divided equally.[1]

These magazines reached an audience far different from that of the *Forward, Tageblatt,* or *Morgen Journal.* The readership was undoubtedly less working-class, less centered in the garment trades, less immigrant, less socialist, and less orthodox. At least five of the periodicals were published in Cincinnati, the home of Hebrew Union College, the center of Reform Judaism. These included the *American Israelite,* which began in 1854. Like several other Cincinnati journals, its audience spanned the country. Other English Jewish magazines merely served a local community and had a very limited appeal. None of these publications provided general news. They were very specifically Jewish magazines, whose central purpose was to inform readers about the affairs of the Jewish world, the doings of Jewish organizations, the activities of Jewish personalities. In that sense, they served a *more* narrowly Jewish function than the Yiddish dailies. The Yiddish newspapers had three basic purposes: to inform readers about general news of the day since some readers might not have had any other access to it; to report on the events of the Jewish world; to transmit a particular ideology—socialism, Zionism, or religious orthodoxy. The English journals did not need to bother with the first task. Their readers obviously could get regular news elsewhere since they had command of English.

English Jewish magazines concerned themselves much less with ideology than the Yiddish newspapers. Most of the dozen magazines discussed in this study boasted no specific philosophy, no clearly articulated program. Even the official publications of organizations like B'nai Brith expressed no clear political or social line. These were all nonpolitical magazines, trying to appeal to a broad spectrum of

American Jews. Strong philosophical stands would have limited their appeal. They did, however, have an underlying mission: to keep the Jewish world organized and alert; to make American Jews aware of Jewish events and conscious of Jewish problems.

Thus, the magazines advocated purely Jewish goals. Of those discussed here none appeared politically radical, although *Opinion*, edited by New York's liberal Rabbi Stephen Wise and started in 1931, expressed a certain admiration for radicals and sympathy with radical causes. The *Jewish Frontier*, initiated in 1934, the official organ of the Labor Zionist Organization of America, played down the socialist message, at least in the first years of publication, in favor of promoting political Zionism. This was perhaps the most political and ideological of the journals. Most of the magazines steered away from politics and from commentary on the political scene.

Many of the magazines reached out to younger readers. At least one, the *Menorah Journal*, was written specifically for Jewish college students. The readers of the magazines probably came from the middle class, judging from the types of advertisements, the emphasis on American theater and arts, the extensive discussions of expensive vacations, and the large number of social announcements. The content of the magazines provides a clue to readership, as do the issues ignored. The English Jewish magazines paid almost no attention to the Jewish labor movement or to Yiddish culture. The leaders of the immigrant, working-class Jewish world never appeared here. Nor did the magazines express any interest in Jewish radicalism or orthodox Judaism. The heroes of these magazines were Jewish businessmen like Julius Rosenwald, lawyers like Louis Marshall, and Jewish political figures like Herbert Lehman—the American Jews who had achieved prominence on the *American* scene. [2]

Like the Yiddish newspapers, however, these magazines were the products of Jewish history and the culture of the European Jewish experience. For the writers and readers of the Yiddish press, that history was very close and personal. The writers of the English journals, children and grandchildren of immigrants, found it somewhat more distant. How important was that experience for these Americanized, acculturated Jews and how vital was their Jewish identification? How did that history and culture affect their view of American race relations? In spite of their seemingly high level of Americanization, the magazines clearly revealed that their editors, writers and readers were still engaged in the process of defining for themselves a comfortable role in American society. Here, again, the issues of black life proved to be uniquely attractive media in satisfying that quest.

Black Themes and the Quest for Jewish Identity

The kinds of black issues which captivated the magazine writers—black oppression and persecution, black achievement and black potential, the creativity of a distinct black culture—all related to the Jewish quest for identity and were areas of concern to Jews about themselves. Of course, the English-language Jewish journals never explicitly announced that their interest in these particular black themes stemmed from their own search for place and status in American society. In all likelihood, most of these writers and editors did not fully appreciate the positive value black subjects served in pondering the problems of Jewish life in the United States. In each of these areas of interest Jewish writers discussed issues and events which strikingly paralleled the Jewish experience. Jews and blacks were compared frankly and candidly. The writers passionately condemned anti-black Jews, praised Jews active in aiding black causes, and pointed out the historic analogies of oppression and suffering.

Although the English Jewish press was fascinated by certain aspects of the black experience and seized on images of blacks as a means of clarifying the dilemmas of their own identity, they did not universally treat black subjects with sensitivity and respect. There were the occasional black jokes. From 1924 to 1926 the *B'nai Brith Magazine* ran seven jokes which indulged in Negro stereotyping. Typical were:

A negro called at the hospital and said:

"I called to see how mah fren' Joe Brown was getting along."

The nurse said: "Why he's getting along fine. He's convalescing now."

"Well," said the darky, "I'll just sit down and wait til he's through."

Or:

> The Baptist preacher had just finished an enthusiastic exhortation.
>
> "Now brudders an' sisters, come up to de altar and hab yo sins washed away."
>
> All came up but one man.
>
> "Brudder Washington, don't yo' want yo' sins washed away?"
>
> "I done had ma sins washed away."
>
> "Yo has! Where'd yo get hit done?"
>
> "Ober at de Methodist Church."
>
> "Ah, Brudder Washington, you ain't been washed. Yo 'jes been dry cleaned."

As late as 1935, some of the journals still did not capitalize *negro*. A humorous, light, or human interest sketch frequently used the word *darky* or, to be really funny, it might refer to a "gentleman with a dusky complexion."[3]

This occasional use of black stereotyping, which found its way so often in the general American press, illustrates the cross-pressures experienced by the Jewish writers. They had picked up the prevalent images of blacks from the various stimuli of American society. Yet these sporadic, negative cues about blacks were offset by the great personal stake which the writers, as Jews and as spokespeople for a particular segment of American Jewry, had in discussing black issues in a sympathetic and empathetic manner. Overall, blacks usually emerged in admirable roles. The writers stressed the achievements of the black race and condemned racism wherever they saw it.

RACISM IN AMERICA

The widespread brutality toward blacks, especially in the South, surfaced repeatedly in the English-language Jewish magazines. In fact, more than any other series of events or developments concerning the American race situation, these magazines discussed and informed their readers copiously about lynchings, race riots, the activities of the Klan, and the exclusion of blacks from the vast range of American institutions. The choice of topics appeared particularly striking considering that these were not news magazines. They rarely discussed non-Jewish issues or events, since readers got that kind of news from the mainstream press. Proportionate to the amount of space devoted to *any* general news, the English Jewish press covered racism and black victimization even more extensively than the Yiddish press, which reported on the whole range of current events.

While the *Israelite* and all the other Jewish magazines defined their journalistic purpose as exclusively Jewish, they did provide voluminous coverage of racism in American society. They undoubtedly saw a direct link between the goals of Jewish journalism and, for example, lynchings of blacks in the South. They believed that Jews had a special stake in understanding the American persecution of blacks.

Both the *American Israelite* and the *American Hebrew* watched the lynching statistics closely and both, occasionally, published in its entirety Tuskegee's annual report on lynching. Those reports always merited editorial comment. The lynching figures, according to the *American Hebrew*, gave the "English Tories and the German Junkers reason to sneer at America and at all democratic governments." While the magazines registered pleasure when the number of lynchings declined, they believed that change was too slow in coming. They did not believe that a slight decrease in lynching signified a fundamental shift in southern attitudes. Charles Joseph, a columnist for the *American Jewish World*, reported that most American newspapers had glowed with happiness in January 1924, when they reported that 1923 had seen a substantial lessening of lynching. Yet he considered such euphoria unwarranted:

> One will appreciate how naive such a statement [is] when we learn that one of the principal reasons for such higher standards of moral conduct is due to the fact that there were fewer Negroes in the South to lynch, some six hundred thousand having migrated to the North during the past year. Yes, they are becoming quite a God-fearing people, those Southerners.[4]

The English Jewish press spent less space covering the actual details of the brutality of lynching than the Yiddish press. The more middle-class magazines shied away from the gruesome descriptions of blood, burning, mobs, and screams that spread across the pages of the Yiddish papers. Usually, the English-language press expressed its indignation at lynching in cool, reserved tones. The *American Israelite* in 1922 noted that three blacks had burned to death in Texas, although only one had been implicated in a crime. "There is no need for comment. The utter barbarism and lawlessness of the act speaks for itself." The next year, in a succinct but damning item, the *Israelite* recounted "Another negro was burned alive by a mob . . . this time at Yazoo, Mississippi. It was hoped that this relic of barbarism no longer existed in the United States, but it seems that it does, to the shame of the entire country, be it said."[5]

Many of the lynchings took place in Georgia, which the magazines consistently held up as the symbol of American racism and the ultimate in racial depravity. In fact, for several years in the 1920s that state held the record for the largest number of lynchings. More significant for these magazines, it was there in 1915 that Leo Frank had been murdered. The magazines always harked back to that incident when reporting lynchings in Georgia or when conducting a general discussion on the subject. Very cynically, the *Israelite* noted in 1921: "The state of Georgia lost its lead [in lynching] which it had held indisputably for so many years, having been beaten last year by Texas. Still as it came in a very good second, Georgia need not despair regaining its eminence in 1921." When in 1917 the Governor of Kentucky spoke out against lynching and actually placed himself in front of a lynch mob, *The American Hebrew and Jewish Standard* praised him and noted that his actions "will long serve as an example of true Americanism and will tend to offset the base, un-American propaganda of the Dorseys and the Tom Watsons who not only incited mob violence but also shielded the lynchers of an honest man." That "honest man" was Leo Frank, and Dorsey had been the prosecuting attorney for the state of Georgia. The Jewish magazines focused most sharply on lynchings in Georgia for more than coincidental reasons. The Frank case loomed as the most upsetting incident of recent Jewish history in America. While it was an isolated event, it provoked the leaders and the opinionmakers of the American Jewish world to doubt the security and stability of Jewish life in the United States. [6]

In the aftermath of the Frank murder, the *American Jewish World* expressed the hope that the whole epidemic of lynchings would be brought to a swift end by the intervention of the federal government. Throughout the period from the Leo Frank lynching to the 1930s the English Jewish press called vigorously for a federal anti-lynching law. The magazines praised progressive southern efforts to stop lynchings but assessed them as impotent and weak. The goodwill of the South could not be relied upon, and only the federal government commanded ample resources to handle the situation. The magazines berated Congress' failure to act, although they otherwise praised the American legislative process. Such magazines rarely criticized Congress, or the President, or the courts, yet in 1919 the *Israelite* felt compelled to point out that:

> The burning of "niggers," who, by-the-way, are just as much American citizens as their white fellow countrymen, or hanging, or shooting them, without "due process of law," guaranteed by the national constitution is surely as grave an offense as making or selling whiskey. Our national legislative body could find a way to establish prohibition, why can it not do as much for the protection of the lives of American men and women from murderous mobs?

A few years later the *Israelite* ran a direct appeal to the Senate in favor of the Dyer Anti-Lynching Bill. [7]

The activities of the Ku Klux Klan in the 1920s also received heavy news coverage in the *Jewish Tribune*, the *American Hebrew and Jewish Messenger*, and the *American Israelite*. The terror which the Klan inflicted on southern blacks (the *American Israelite* suggested that the organization change its name to the LLL—the Legalized Lynching League) was documented and decried. While the Klan occasionally bore the brunt of jokes, it generally provoked serious discussion and the writers held it up as the epitome of an anti-democratic, violent, and racist organization. Jews had a personal stake in exposing the Klan. In many areas of the country, it stirred up anti-Semitism as well as anti-black sentiment. Yet, the Jewish English magazines launched their crusade against the Klan in the name of blacks, and only subtly and tentatively made the linkage between the Klan's persecution of blacks and American anti-Semitism. In 1922, for example, the *American Israelite* invoked the Georgia image to denounce the Klan. "That modern Ku Klux Klanism should have originated in Georgia and have its headquarters in Atlanta is not to be wondered at. On the contrary it is quite appropriate; the State and city had achieved an unbelievable premiership for lynching, race riots and other mob outbreaks." A writer for the *American Jewish World* also implied the relationship between anti-Semitism and anti-Negro violence when he noted that the Klan was strongest in those parts of the country where orthodox Christian theology held its tightest grip on the population. The Jewish magazines rarely spelled out clearly their own fears about the Klan, and they rarely discussed the Klan's position on Jews. However, they chronicled Klan harassment and persecution of blacks extensively and passionately. [8]

The urban race riots also merited copious attention. The English Jewish magazines all decried the "brutal outbreak of the mob spirit." Again unlike the Yiddish newspapers, these magazines did not dwell on the bloody details but recounted briefly the flaring of riots in East St. Louis, Washington, Chicago, and Tulsa. Unlike the Yiddish newspapers, the English-language periodicals did not consistently employ the terminology of the eastern European Jewish experience. Although riots here were not called pogroms, nor the white mobs the "Black Hundreds," the riots still were condemned in standard American terminology. Since the Russian pogrom experience was much less a personal reality to the writers and readers of these magazines, no need existed to use its language and paint its imagery. The *American Israelite* only once drew the analogy. "Apparently the civilized world cannot do with pogroms," editorialized the Cincinnati-based periodical. "But," it continued, "lest the world be without such tangible evidence of the existence of the devil, our own country has demonstrated its ability to substitute Russia as it was under the . . . Czar and his bureaucracy, by the pogrom which took place in East St. Louis last week."

An intense spirit of disenchantment with the American democratic process pervaded the articles on race riots. The police forces of the various cities, the state militias, and the federal authorities all drew criticism for their failure to respond and for their racism. "If the Federal government," speculated the *Israelite*, "displayed half the energy in putting a stop to mob murder that it has to establish and enforce prohibition, this shameful blot upon our civilization would soon be eradicated." The consensus was that race riots occurred only when the authorities allowed them. After the Tulsa riot had subsided, the *American Hebrew* blamed the mass murders on the municipal government. "A mob never gets out of hand when it has reason to fear determined opposition by the properly constituted authorities." After criticizing the mayor and the police of the Oklahoma city, the same article returned to the underlying reason for the intense interest in race riots. "No one for a moment believes that Leo Frank in Georgia could have been taken from the state penitentiary . . . by a handful of men, and lynched, had not the prison officials . . . failed to offer the proper resistance. No member of the lynching mob was ever punished in Georgia." Six years after the Frank lynching, that event was invoked over and over again in articles and editorials condemning violence against black Americans. [9]

In the early years of the 1930s the American public was barraged by the details of the Scottsboro case. For liberals and radicals it became a cause célèbre—the symbol of American racism, the proof of the anti-black bias in the American legal system, and the evidence of the insecurity of black existence in the South. The English Jewish magazines participated in the publicity campaign for the Scottsboro boys. The *American Israelite* and the *American Hebrew* ran several lengthy articles decrying the denial of justice in Alabama. The *Jewish Frontier* proclaimed that the Supreme Court's decision to overturn the death sentences of the Scottsboro defendants "makes us want to sing for joy." *Opinion* took the lead in chronicling the case. Writers appealed directly to the audience to contribute money for the defense. The magazine proudly included itself among those who believed that "Scottsboro should be made to understand that its official lynching will not be disregarded by the rest of the world and that its concession to mob rule and race prejudice will be branded as infamy." Such intense support did not come out of a direct Jewish interest in the case. The only particularly Jewish element might have been the Jewish defense lawyer, Samuel Leibowitz. The magazines were pleased with Leibowitz's appearance as counsel for the boys but, beyond that, no direct links existed between the case and specific Jewish issues. Yet the Jewish magazines were greatly aroused by the plight of the nine black teenagers. The case caused these organs of Jewish public opinion, usually cautious and guarded, to question the security of their own status in the United States and Europe. [10]

The race riots, the lynchings of the South, the growth of the Ku Klux Klan, and the Scottsboro trials emerged as major news stories of their day. It was not coincidental, though, that of all the developments of the black world the Jewish magazines should have seized on these, given how little non-Jewish news they reported. These issues spoke indirectly but audibly to many of the questions which puzzled Jewish leaders about their own role and future in the United States. They wanted Jews to become an integral part of the American world, yet they questioned the morality of a society which allowed such persecutions to occur. They desired a secure future for Jews in the United States, but they feared that anti-black violence carried with it the seeds of anti-Jewish activity.

A range of events in the years from 1915 to 1935 highlighted the exclusion of blacks from middle-class, bourgeois institutions of American life. These events profoundly impressed the English-language Jewish magazines. The Jews who read these periodicals were also trying to enter these institutions or had already entered them and wanted to ensure their place. It was thus with more than empathy that the American Jewish periodicals reported on the expulsion of Roscoe Conklin Bruce, son of Mississippi's black reconstruction senator, from Harvard's dormitories in 1923. The *Jewish Tribune*, the *American Israelite*, and the *American Jewish World* came out vociferously in favor of admitting Bruce and inveighed against the actions of President A. Lawrence Lowell. The Bruce incident coincided with a heated controversy over the imposition of quotas on Jews at Harvard. The Jewish press naturally decried any kind of Jewish restriction. Thus, when discrimination against the black student was revealed, the Jewish press used it as further ammunition in its crusade against the school's policies. The *Jewish Tribune* called for Lowell's removal from the presidency, to be replaced by someone "whose true Americanism has not been clouded with Fordism or Ku Kluxism." Jews felt the sting of anti-Semitic social discrimination in many middle-class institutions in the opening decades of the century, but Harvard emerged as the symbol of the aloofness and intransigence of the elites. The Bruce incident added reality to that symbol. 11

In the same year the *American Hebrew* and the *Jewish Tribune-Hebrew Standard* expressed dismay that black sculptor Augusta Savage had been refused a scholarship to Fountainbleau School of Fine Art on the grounds that her presence would have made some whites uncomfortable. "If anything should be free of prejudice, it is art and that even art isn't shows to what a low estate we've come," lamented the *Jewish Tribune*. The Savage case, like the Bruce incident, particularly upset Jews who believed that the key to their own mobility and security would be through reward for merit. Similarly, when Walter Cohen, Controller of the Port of New Orleans appointed by President Harding, was barred from his position by southern congressmen because of race, the Jewish magazines were shaken. They pondered the possibility that making bridges to those in power did not ensure acceptance. Prejudice against blacks was so pervasive and deep-seated that it often negated talent and merit. A fear that Jewish talent and merit too would be ignored because of a centuries-old tradition of anti-Semitism underlay the articles on black exclusion. 12

The obsession of the writers and editors of these English Jewish journals with questions of black exclusion clearly stemmed from their own sense of rejection by bourgeois American society. The magazines never discussed discrimination against blacks in its most constant forms. No discussions of segregated streetcars, segregated public facilities, or political disfranchisement graced the pages of these magazines. Those particular issues did not link up to the problems Jews themselves were facing. The exclusion from Harvard, the Savage affair, and the Cohen controversy all struck responsive chords in the Jewish American magazines because they focused on middle-class blacks attempting to enter the elite institutions of the society.

The only constant pattern of black segregation which these magazines discussed at length was housing restriction. They examined Supreme Court decisions affecting restrictive covenants and municipal ordinances setting up legally sanctioned Negro quarters. While magazines like the *American Israelite* expressed some concern over the ecological and sanitary conditions of black neighborhoods, they were more concerned with "the right of a citizen irrespective of color to buy or use property in any locality where he may choose." This issue, like that of Harvard restriction, very directly linked up to the situation of Jews. Jews, too, were victims of restrictive covenants and of somewhat more subtle forms of housing discrimination. The restriction of blacks in the housing market found a sympathetic and receptive audience in the readers and writers of the English-language Jewish magazines. [13]

These Jewish journals did not devote themselves to carrying the news of the day. They had one goal: to serve the Jewish public. Yet they selectively chose to discuss certain black events. They discussed and decried the physical brutality which blacks experienced, partly because this issue spoke to a centuries-old history of anti-Semitic oppression as well as to possibly the most traumatic event in American Jewish history, the Leo Frank case. The exclusion of blacks from universities and from the housing market also caught the attention of the press, since these concerns paralleled the anxieties which Jews were experiencing at that time—the anxiety of feeling qualified, yet restricted, the anguish of being rejected in spite of merit.

ACHIEVEMENTS OF THE BLACK RACE

When in 1928 the Commission on Interracial Co-operation announced a high school essay contest on "America's Tenth Man," the *American Israelite* applauded and said that it was time that "the Negro's part in American history, which . . . is much more creditable than is generally supposed," be considered. The essays "will be helpful to the children of both races, promoting more tolerance and sympathy on the one side and developing wholesome race pride on the other." These same goals also motivated Jewish magazines to devote considerable space to the achievements of black Americans.

They considered the most important areas to be black achievement in the arts and black eductional and scholarly excellence. Significantly, Jews considered themselves particularly talented in these same fields. The writers gave extensive coverage to black theater, black literature, and black music. *The American Jewish World* in 1924 glowingly described a concert given by Roland Hayes, whom the author labeled "another menace to one hundred percent Americanism." Articles on Paul Robeson, the Hall-Johnson Singers, and James

Weldon Johnson pointed to impressive black artistic and literary talents. In 1935, when three black artists won Guggenheim Fellowships (referred to as "The Ultimate Fellowship"), the *American Hebrew* commented that such distinctions and such awards provided additional evidence against theories of racial inferiority or superiority. [14]

Articles on black educational and scholarly achievement echoed this sentiment. The magazines reviewed with great respect speeches and articles by educator Mordecai Johnson, sociologists E. Franklin Frazier and W.E.B. DuBois, and others. The Jewish magazines praised the great passion of blacks for education, since these periodicals adhered to the belief that the road to mobility for blacks—and Jews—lay in education. An *American Jewish World* obituary for Booker Washington in 1915 best expressed the prevalent assumption that the educational attainment of the elite sheds favorable light on the masses. The article went far beyond chronicling Washington's spectacular rise from slavery to international prominence when it noted:

> Should not the life and achievement of such a man teach us all an important lesson that there are no absolutely inferior and superior races in the human family, that the present superior development of a race is due entirely to circumstances and antecedents and opportunities, that will, given the necessary length of time raise the retarded group to the same level. A human group or race, like a mountain range should be judged by its highest peak. A race that produces a Washington or a DuBois is no differently endowed than any other race. [15]

The Jewish writers not only subscribed to the belief that the outstanding achievements of a handful of blacks would further the progress of the race, but they felt that negative action by a few would set back the masses. The *American Israelite* was, for example, quite upset that the first black congressman from a northern city, Oscar De Priest, proved such a disreputable character. The journal asserted, however, that De Priest was not at all "typical of the best of his people." It went on to express the hope that in the future blacks would choose "the best type of leader from the earnest and efficient men and women within its fold." This was exactly the kind of treatment which Jewish criminals, radicals, or "unsavory figures" received in these basically conservative magazines, which yearned to present the world with the image of Jews as a middle-class, respectable group. [16]

Only one article in all of the magazines ever touched on the subject of black crime. The *B'nai Brith Magazine* once discussed Chicago crime statistics and noted that of every 100 juvenile offenders, twenty-three were of "African" descent. The magazine quickly pointed out, however, that the large proportion of black criminals resulted from the "lack of family unity." The Jewish magazines chose to ignore completely the negative images of blacks which prevailed in American society. Instead, they made a concerted effort to show the black contribution to America. These magazines constantly stressed the great strides made by the black race in the generations since Emancipation. In 1921, for example, the *American Jewish World* sang the praises of the "nine million negroes in the United States and their coming up from slavery in the space of a few decades . . . . Thousands of professional men among them; millions of property acquired through industry and thrift, willing to give their blood for the country." The Jewish magazines believed that American blacks had made tremendous progress since slavery days and, in a strange twist of logic, the *American Jewish World* even dismissed criticism of the D. W. Griffith film *The Birth of a Nation*:

> The criticism that it exhibits the Negro in an unfortunate light and that it is calculated to engender racial animosity is fully met by the consideration that it represents the Negro not as he is now at all, but as he was in the days when he had just had the chains broken from him . . . . It . . . is a compliment to the black man of today.

This advancement, as perceived by the magazines, had been possible because they believed "racial inferiority" a meaningless myth and because blacks had firmly set themselves on the course to meet their goals. According to the *Israelite*, "a new colored generation has grown up which contains many men and women of ability and models of citizenship and there is no reason to doubt that this progress will be continuous." The mobility would continue and would crush prevalent

American racial ideas. The Jewish magazines went to great lengths to demonstrate precisely that point. [17]

The magazines maintained a fairly lively interest in the scientific and semi-scientific debate on the nature of racial differences. Many of the participants in the debate were Jewish anthropologists and articles on or by scholars like Melville Herskovits, Franz Boas, and Alexander Goldenweiser graced the pages of these magazines. Yet the interest was much broader; many of the articles spoke directly to the impact of race theory on American blacks. A detailed article in the *Menorah Journal* by Goldenweiser summarized the debate as it stood in 1922, while the *American Israelite* in 1924 examined the work of Boas and Goldenweiser as contrasted with the racist ideologies of other scientists. The writers believed that false notions of inherent racial differences laid the foundation of prejudice. The *American Jewish World* in 1915 quoted from an article in *Howe's Monthly* which claimed that prejudice existed against blacks because of their ignorance, shiftlessness, and immorality. The Jewish magazine categorically rejected this analysis:

> There is not a grain of truth or sense in this . . . . It is not true that the prejudice against the negro is because he is ignorant, etc. This is a most cruel libel against the race. We emphatically deny that all things considered, the negro is of lower morality. . . . One must be both an ignoramus and a fool not to know that the prejudice against the negro is because for generations he was used as a slave . . . and hence the idea of his natural inferiority has developed from his slave condition.

Nearly a decade later Rabbi Lee J. Levinger, writing for the *Israelite*, again attempted to tackle the question of why Americans were prejudiced against blacks and how that related to notions of black inferiority:

> Most white people think that negroes are an inferior race. What are their reasons for this belief? First, that the negroes now in the United States are not wealthy. . . . But that only proves that Negroes came here as slaves. . . . Next, that the Negroes had no great nations in Africa. But this is not even true: the African peoples have had great nations at various times in the past and

the reason why there are no more may be the hot climate, the sparse population, and not intelligence at all. The final reason is usually a judgement of fact, that whites have more intelligence . . . . But even this is a prejudice rather than a proved fact. The means of judging human minds are still very crude.

Jews keenly listened to the debate on racial differences. Periodicals like *The American Jewish World* devoted considerable attention to the impact of that debate on American blacks. As Jews, they had a particular stake in destroying theories of race difference which posited moral and intellectual distinctions between peoples. They reasoned that if blacks, who had come to the United States under such adverse conditions, could begin to progress and advance into the middle class, then an even more optimistic and rosy future might await the American Jew. [18]

THE SPIRIT OF BLACK CULTURE

The English-language Jewish magazines did believe that differences existed between racial and national groups. Those differences did not, however, include biologically transmitted capacities for moral or intellectual growth. The writers recognized the reality and positive value of cultural diversity. All of the magazines firmly asserted that racial and ethnic groups supported distinct cultures. All had different ways of viewing life, reality, the world. The journalists characterized American society and culture as merely a patchwork of a dozen distinct cultures. Among the individual pieces in that patchwork, the English Jewish magazines focused their attention almost exclusively on two—the Jewish, naturally, and the black. While they occasionally alluded to the existence of a vital Italian, German, and Irish cultural life, the journals never gave them the same in-depth treatment that they gave the blacks.

The editors and writers of these magazines used discussions of black cultural life as a mirror in which they could view the vibrance, vitality, and meaning of their own Jewish culture in the American context. The periodicals set their lenses on black literature, music, and theater. Dozens of articles reviewed concerts by Robeson, Hayes, the

Hall-Johnson singers, critiqued the work of Countee Cullen, Sterling Brown, and James Weldon Johnson, and assessed such plays as *The Green Pastures*, and *Run, Little Chillun'!* Many of these articles also attempted to define the nature of black culture in America and to assess how that culture reflected the status of American blacks.

As organs of Jewish opinion, the magazines primarily concerned themselves with the stability of Jewish culture in the United States. As organs of the highly Americanized Jewish world, they wanted that culture to achieve respectability in American society. The meaning of a separate, distinct ethnic culture within a pluralistic society, however, received its clearest and most candid treatment through the medium of black culture. The assumption which underlay all the discussions of black cultural life was that groups possessed special talents, the products of history and circumstance. Each group should preserve that culture. Furthermore, the Jewish writers believed that groups should share their special talents and creative gifts with the society at large. The striving group—be it Jewish or black—should fully exploit its talents as a way of gaining acceptance and recognition in America. If the group or its representatives gave of its best talents to the society, then it might be assured of recognition. Security and higher status came on the heels of that recognition.

The Jewish magazines believed that black Americans had contributed heavily and richly to American culture and art, especially in the field of music. The consensus was that whatever was noteworthy and distinct in American music was the product of black talent. A reviewer for the *American Hebrew* noted in 1929 that "music, in the truly American idiom today is 'blues,' which of course is negroid in origin. Negro spirituals and 'blues' are practically all our worthwhile folk music." While the writers assumed that much of that music was spontaneous and improvised, reviews of performances given by artists like Marian Anderson, Paul Robeson, and Roland Hayes indicated that even in the world of Western, "sophisticated" music, blacks possessed unique talents.

The journalists were, however, most captivated by performances of black music, since that was obviously the special forte of a Robeson or an Anderson. An *Opinion* article covering a Paul Robeson concert at New York's Town Hall in 1932 sadly concluded: "The formal music which Mr. Robeson has introduced in his program has seriously af-

fected his rendition of the Negro songs. He was deprived these spirituals of the abandon and fervor which are absolutely necessary to their
interpretation." While the magazines usually lauded classical performances, they felt that the preservation of the indigenous black culture was of greater importance. The Hall-Johnson choir's rendition of
black music "shows clearly enough what is meant by a genuine expression of national art," asserted a reviewer for *Opinion*. He went on
to note that:

> The dissonance and the quarter tones, the rhythm and the
> frenzy, were magnificent expressions of a people's nature and
> attitude to life. They were as unmistakable as they were inimi-
> table. Whatever of art and training and refining has gone into
> this music, Mr. Johnson emphasized the national note rather
> than disguise it. The audience . . . indicated that they appre-
> ciated not merely the greatness of the performance, but also the
> grandeur of the revelation. [19]

The performance "revealed" to the *Opinion* critic that black culture
constituted a lively and living force. The black artist was responsible
for transmitting this message to all other Americans, who perhaps
might be somewhat less sympathetic to the race. The role of the black
artist was further clarified when *Opinion* called Marian Anderson one
of a "group of fine Negro artists who are interpreting their people to
America."

The Jewish writers believed that they could see a very distinct black
way of looking at the world, a distinct view of both life and death. The
black artist and novelist occupied an excellent position from which to
transmit to the white world the essence of the black view. The black
artist must, however, not *just* express that which was unique to blacks,
but show other Americans the universality of human feelings. A
review of Jessie Fausett's 1932 *The Chinaberry Tree* in *Opinion* noted
that the novel "has tremendous tragic implications—implications
which are peculiarly Negro and yet have an importance that transcends race." The Jewish magazines, then, were interested in two
facets of black culture: that which expressed the national character,
the peculiar genius of the people, that which was unique, as well as
that which stressed the commonality of all people, the similarities

between groups. The periodicals stressed precisely these two goals as the mission of Jewish American artists and of Jewish leaders as a whole: to preserve the unique culture while, at the same time, striving to make it harmonious with the dominant society. It was a monumental task for both the black and the Jewish artists. [20]

Black culture, the black creative spirit, and the black world view stood out from any other. The Jewish magazines most frequently described them with terms like *abandon, enthusiasm, ecstatic, rhythmic*. The Jewish journals believed that blacks, as a result of their historic experience of suffering and oppression, had developed a more acute sense of emotion and heightened feelings. Articles on black theatrical reviews always stressed the highly pitched sense of movement, action, and rhythm which flashed across the stage. A 1927 review of Ethel Waters' show, "Africana," in the *Jewish Tribune* noted that the dancers were extremely spirted and lively:

> Their bronze legs did all sorts of difficult stuff—but somehow, you expect colored dancers to put about fifty times more pep into a performance than the average white girl cares to attempt.

On a more intellectual plane, the *American Hebrew* reviewed a performance of Jewish composer Reuben Goldmark's "A Negro Rhapsody" and noted: "The rhythm of the Negro is vicious, it is of a kinesthetic urge. One sways and bends with it." [21]

At the other extreme of the spectrum of emotions, the Jewish magazines also saw the tragic element as one of the central attributes of Negro culture. The Negro spirituals, which all of the reviewers in these magazines adored, represented the most sonorous expression of an ever-present consciousness of a history of suffering and a present fraught with constant oppression. The black consciousness of this suffering found its way into the dozens of novels and plays which explored that theme and left its mark on the actual manner of delivery. The feeling of suffering inhered in black music and poetry. An *Opinion* review of Sterling Brown's anthology of black verse, *Southern Roads*, noted that so many of the poems focused on the theme of death. "The condition of the Negro has never been pleasant enough to make him value life highly," observed the reviewer. "Heaven, on the other hand, has come to be a very real place where he wants to go—beautiful and without race prejudice." [22]

The Jewish magazines thus portrayed black culture by two polar characteristics: the frenzy of abandon and ecstasy, and the pervasive pathos of suffering. In musical terms, the nervous rhythm of jazz on one end and the melodious mourning of the spirituals on the other characterized these aspects of the culture. A writer for *Opinion* hypothesized that pathos and humor made up the two dominant motifs of black culture. The two characteristics, he believed, were not unrelated. One bore the other. The humor, the abandon, jazz, provided the natural escape from the constant pathos. Usually, a black work of art chose one or the other motif. While the two were closely related, it required profound sensitivity on the part of the artist to mingle the two characteristics without producing a jarring and disjointed effect. The *American Hebrew* reviewer of *Deep Harlem* criticized the play for lacking precisely that sensitivity. "It is perhaps a little too interesting for a musical comedy and is frequently hampered by the seriousness of its theme . . . there is something in that tragic picture of suffering which does not fit with jazz and the common concept of colored comic relief." [23]

Yet, one black play did successfully blend these two motifs of black culture; *The Green Pastures* deeply moved the writers and reviewers of the English Jewish press. Hailed as a monumental work of dramatic creativity, no other work of art—black or white—received such extensive and positive comment. The *American Hebrew* proclaimed that "long after most of the plays of 1930 will have been forgotten, *Green Pastures* will retain a prominent niche in the annals of theatrical history as one of the finest and most impressive dramatic presentations of our generation." The *Jewish Tribune* considered it significant enough to review it before commenting on a new play by George Bernard Shaw which opened at the same time.

While the Jewish press was particularly interested in *The Green Pastures* because it drew from stories of the Old Testament, it also felt that the drama could be an instrument of interpreting black culture to white Americans. The *American Israelite* believed that it "ought to convince our Nordic American culture that American culture is immensely enriched by Negro 'spirituals,' Negro folk-tales and the Negro racial mood." The *B'nai Brith Magazine* believed that *The Green Pastures* had a great deal more to say about the diversity of American culture and the complexity of the American tradition than just pointing out the black cultural gift to American society. The magazine noted that both the 1930 play and James Weldon Johnson's collection of folk-sermons, *God's Trombones*, showed the "intermingling of three elements: naive Negro folk in an oppressed status, American background, and the Bible."[24]

Most reviewers of *The Green Pastures* focused on yet another aspect of black culture which they saw as a certain simplicity and naivete, produced by rural isolation and grinding poverty. The *American Hebrew*, for example, described the play as "a version of the chronicle of the earth as only the naive mind of the Negro in the deep South can conceive it. . . ." An interview with Paul Robeson conducted by a *Jewish Tribune* reporter in 1927 showed that the black baritone shared that view about southern Negroes and their culture. Articles on black religious music, black poetry, and black novels stressed the "grace of the naivete of the colored race." But black culture went far beyond this simple folk tradition. The magazines noted frequently not only the literary and artistic worth of black culture, but its important scholarly and intellectual contributions.

The Jewish journalists perceived a tension in black literature. That tension existed between the artist's desire to represent accurately the lives of the masses, which of necessity called for a tone of unsophistication and simplicity, and the natural tendency of the writer as an intellectual and thinker. The *American Hebrew* believed that poets like Countee Cullen or Claude McKay could bridge this gap between the masses and the elite, between the elemental and the sophisticated. The magazines generally believed that black culture consisted of many complex elements. Not only did it take a certain amount of anthropological insight to be able to see its various parts, but it was undergoing constant change as a result of the contemporary internal migration. The magazines always noted that black plays, written by black playwrights, and novels and poems penned by Negroes achieved greater sensitivity and depicted reality more profoundly than any written by whites. The diverse elements within black culture, the strains of humor and pathos, the tension between simplicity and worldliness were too complex and subtle for most whites to readily understand. Talented blacks thus had the responsibility to serve as mouthpieces for their people and to articulate to the white world the complexity and richness of the culture.[25]

The magazines had carved out this same role for Jewish artists.

Their task included providing the larger society—the Christian society—with an accurate picture of Jews and Jewish life. If black culture was complex, if it carried with it so much tension and ambiguity that whites generally could not appreciate it, then Americans, Christians, would certainly be at a loss trying to understand Jews. In the many articles, reviews, and critiques of black art, the Jewish writers experimented with the notion of a culture-within-a-culture. They considered the problem of how that culture could be part of something larger yet retain its integrity and its vitality. These concerns occupied a central place in the Jewish quest for identity and the Jewish press was fascinated watching another group work out those same problems.

JEWS AND BLACKS: THE BONDS OF EMPATHY

Through the very choices which these Jewish magazines made, in the kinds of black images which they depicted, they were working out questions of their own status. In a subtle and indirect manner they used the themes of black suffering, black achievement, and black cultural life as a vehicle to explore the meaning of their own experiences in America. Often they did not bother with subtlety and in numerous articles made explicit references to the links between their history, culture, values, and the American race problem. These articles, which were candid about the similarities between themselves and blacks, demonstrated even more clearly how the Jewish interest in blacks was shaped by the ambivalent attitudes they held toward America and by their desire to find a comfortable role in the larger society.

Through the hundreds of statements made by these journalists about blacks ran two underlying, though unstated needs: that of carving out for themselves a secure role in America so that they could "belong" and be thought of as worthy members of the sometimes hostile society, and the need to justify the existence of the group as a separate entity. They wanted to become functioning members of the dominant culture, yet also wanted to retain something unique and different, something which distinguished their culture from all others.

One way the English Jewish press sought to meet these needs was to stress the special roles and relationships which they believed should, and did, exist between Jews and blacks. Jewish leaders sought to make themselves interpreters of the Negro to American society and the intermediaries between the white and the black worlds. Nowhere did the Jewish English press state the importance of the role of interpreter more clearly than in articles on Jewish artists and their images of blacks. This emerged especially in several pieces on George Gershwin. Gershwin's ultimate musical goal had been to integrate jazz into the symphonic form, as he believed this blending of musical idiom would lead to the creation of American music of real note. His interest in jazz naturally led him to black themes which he wove into such compositions as *135th Street*, a short opera first performed in 1921, Concerto in F, and his full-length opera, *Porgy and Bess*. The Jewish magazines depicted Gershwin as the interpreter of the black mood to the rest of the world. That role, according to the press, had *everything* to do with Gershwin's ethnic and religious background. The *American Hebrew* in 1925 quoted the young composer, who was convinced that "to write good music one must have feeling. This quality is possessed . . . by the Jewish people. Perhaps the fact that through the centuries the Jews have been an oppressed race, has helped to intensify this feeling." Echoing the composer's assessment, Dr. Abraham Roback, a student of Yiddish literature and a member of Harvard's psychology department, contributed a lengthy article on "Jews and Jazz" to the *Jewish Tribune and Hebrew Standard*. He concluded that Jewish musicians like Gershwin, Reuben Goldmark, the composer of "A Negro Rhapsody," or Louis Gruenberg, the creator of the opera, *Daniel Jazz*, had taken the elemental black themes, rhythms, and musical tones, polished them up, sophisticated them, and made them presentable to the general public. According to Roback:

> The . . . people to bring into the wild gyrations of the original jazz a note of restraint, of anxiety and foreboding were the Jewish song writers who were versatile enough to catch the spirit of Negro music . . . . If you ask what America would have done without the host of Jewish . . . composers, and what the music of the street would have been like, the answer would be that jazz would still have had its day, but it would have been a more puerile and less varied kind of jazz . . . . The original Negro jazz is shapeless and chaotic. In most of the *Jewish versions you can follow motifs.*

This role of interpreter extended far beyond the field of Jewish music, although here the magazines forged the link most strongly and focused most dramatically on the Jewish need for a meaningful role in American society.[26]

The magazines believed that Jews were able to serve as cultural bridges between the white and black worlds because they understood both. As whites, they moved with greater freedom in elite circles than blacks, but as members of a marginal group with a history of oppression, they better understood the tensions, anxieties, and moods of American Negroes. They firmly held that Jews and blacks drew their inspiration and values from the same sources. The Old Testament origin of the black spirituals and the biblical themes dramatized in *The Green Pastures* only confirmed their faith in the existence of a close bond between the two peoples. Historic parallels of segregation and discrimination strengthened this bond. Without being facetious or naive, the magazines sincerely declared that Jews, more than any other group, could and did empathize with black Americans.

Because of that empathy, the black experience had become extremely personal to Jews. The magazine writers, at least, felt that kinship so acutely that they always found a Jewish comparison, a Jewish angle, a Jewish note in black issues. Jewish reviewers of the black arts, for example, repeatedly picked out Jewish analogies in Negro plays, books, and music. Novelist Meyer Levin reviewed the 1933 play, *Run, Little Chillun'!* for *Opinion*.

> To me, the play seemed a revelation out of traditions so deeply akin to our own Jewish traditions that at times it was difficult to keep from rushing onto the stage and joining in the singing, the ecstasy . . . . *Run, Little Chillun'!* is . . . a Chassidic play![27]

What better proof for the magazine writers and editors of their assertion that no whites understood blacks better than the large numbers of Jews who lent their support, energy, and money to help black causes of all kinds. These Jews, Louis Marshall, Herbert Lehman, Arthur and Joel Spingarn, Julius Rosenwald, and many others functioned as intermediaries between the white world, in which they had gained recognition, and the black world, which needed aid. Over ninety articles in these Jewish magazines devoted themselves specifically to discussions of Jewish aid to black causes—to Jewish philan-

thropic work for blacks and to Jewish participation in organizations
like the NAACP. The clear message sounded that Jewish assistance to
blacks was hardly a random, coincidental phenomenon, but stemmed
directly from Jewish tradition.

Black Americans needed champions in a hostile society; Jewish
Americans, on the other hand, wanted a meaningful role so as to
prove themselves to an inhospitable one. Thus, Negro civil rights and
philanthropy seemed proper spheres in which Jews could prove
themselves, demonstrating their generosity, selflessness, and their importance. The significance of the role of champion of the oppressed
was intoned by the *American Israelite*, which addressed black Americans directly and announced in the name of American Jewry, that the
magazine "wishes its colored brethren well and to the extent of its
ability, is always willing to fight their battles." Similarly, *Opinion*
openly stated, when discussing the Scottsboro case, that it took:

> an especial pride in the fact that the chief counsel . . . was a Jew.
> Both as a member of such a group and as an inheritor of his own
> tradition, it is inevitable that the Jew should take active and
> leading parts in all such struggles as that at present being waged
> around the Scottsboro injustice.

Serving as intermediaries for blacks not only grew out of the Jewish
heritage and tradition as defined by these magazines but also figured
in a general Jewish campaign for a more positive public image. By
proving how tolerant, broadminded, and non-ethnocentric Jews were,
the magazines hoped that they could dispel many ancient and deep-
seated prejudices and stereotypes of Jews. On the other hand, the
magazines perceived that by stressing their positive achievements in
the field of human rights, they could prove their Americanism.
Articles on Julius Rosenwald invariably linked the name of the Jewish
philanthropist with Abraham Lincoln. Editorials condemning lynching, race riots, and the Ku Klux Klan always pointed out that these
acts were not only immoral and inhuman but un-American. Thus,
American Jewish leaders involved in a quest for a meaningful identity
and comfortable role in American society found that one way to fulfill
that search was to serve as the intermediaries between blacks and
whites. The Jewish magazines defined a mission for Jews to interpret

the black world to white Americans and to speak for blacks and champion their cause.

If the magazine writers and editors of the English-language Jewish press, who represented the highly Americanized Jewish communities, attempted to find a meaningful role for Jews in American society through the movements for black advancement, they also used the black issue as a way to assert the cultural and ethical differences between Jews and Christians as they saw them. The magazines, and Jewish leaders as a whole, worried about the disintegrating effects of Americanization on future Jewish generations. If American society should prove to be as liberal and as tolerant as promised, then what would be the future of Judaism as a religion and Jewishness as a cultural identity? One way to combat total assimilation and rejection could be to emphasize the special, positive aspects of the Jewish heritage and culture to the next generation. The role of Jews as the special friend of blacks, the Jewish religious precepts which called for social justice and equality, the Jewish history of suffering and oppression, the writers felt all laid the basis for the retention of a distinctly Jewish culture within American society. The problems of American blacks provided an ideal medium by which Jewish leaders could emphasize and expound upon the relevance and virtues of the culture, within the American context. [28]

NOTES

1. The complete list of American Jewish periodicals can be found in *American Jewish Yearbook: 5688, 1925-1926* (Philadelphia: Jewish Publication Society of America), pp. 225-229.

2. *American Jewish World* (Minneapolis), 1915-1924; *American Hebrew* (New York), 1915-1931; *American Hebrew and Jewish Messenger* (New York), 1915-1934; *American Israelite* (Cincinnati), 1917-1935; *Jewish Frontier* (New York), 1934-1935; *Jewish Tribune* (Passaic, New Jersey), 1922-1931; *B'nai Brith Magazine* (Cincinnati), 1924-1935; *Opinion* (New York), 1931-1935; *Menorah Journal* (New York), 1914-1935; *Current Jewish Record* (New York), 1931-1935; *Jewish Layman* (Cincinnati), 1926-1935.

3. *B'nai Brith Magazine*, 39 (December 1924): 120; 40 (April 1925): 256 (May 1925): 288; (June 1925): 320; (December 1925): 100; *Jewish Tribune and Hebrew Standard*, 96 (April 4, 1930): 34; *American Jewish World*, 11 (September 7, 1923): 29.

4. *American Israelite*, 69 (July 13, 1922): 4; *American Hebrew* 100 (January 8, 1920): 7; *American Israelite*, 68 (January 13, 1921): 4; 72 (January 1, 1925): 4; (July 10, 1925): 4; 71 (July 12, 1923): 4; 68 (May 26, 1921): 4; (April 7, 1921): 4; *American Hebrew*, 102 (July 13, 1922): 4; *American Jewish World*, 3 (October 8, 1915): 137; 12 (January 11, 1924): 4; (July 11, 1924): 4; *Jewish Tribune*, 96 (January 9, 1931): 1; 75 (January 6, 1925): 11.

5. *American Israelite*, 69 (May 11, 1922): 3; 64 (December 13, 1917): 4; 65 (April 4, 1918): 4; 66 (July 17, 1919): 4; 66 (July 31, 1919): 4; 68 (December 15, 1921): 7; 70 (August 16, 1923): 4; 72 (January 1, 1925): 4; *American Hebrew and Jewish Messenger*, 97 (January 19, 1917): 358.

6. *American Israelite*, 68 (December 15, 1921): 7; 65 (April 4, 1918): 4; 68 (January 13, 1921): 4; (April 7, 1921): 4; (May 26, 1921): 4; 66 (July 31, 1919): 4; *American Hebrew*, 100 (January 8, 1920): 7; *American Hebrew and Jewish Standard*, 98 (January 19, 1917): 358.

7. *American Jewish World*, 3 (September 10, 1915): 55-56; 14 (July 7, 1922): 5; *American Israelite*, 72 (January 1, 1925): 14; 70 (August 23, 1923): 4; 68 (September 14, 1921): 4; 66 (July 17, 1919): 4; 66 (August 14, 1919): 6; 69 (May 25, 1922): 4.

8. *American Israelite*, 68 (September 15, 1921): 4; 70 (July 12, 1923): 4; 69 (March 30, 1922): 1; 69 (November 16, 1922): 3; 69 (April 20, 1922): 4; *Jewish Tribune and Hebrew Standard*, 81 (June 1, 1923): 33; 86 (August 7, 1925): 32; *American Hebrew and Jewish Messenger*, 101 (December 8, 1922): 148; 100 (September 23, 1921): 430; *Jewish Tribune*, 85 (January 16, 1925): 11; *American Jewish World*, 12 (September 1, 1922): 5.

9. *American Israelite*, 64 (September 13, 1917): 4; 66 (October 30, 1919): 4; 70 (January 25, 1923): 4; 66 (August 14, 1919): 4; 64 (October 25, 1917): 4; 66 (October 2, 1919): 4; 64 (July 12, 1917): 4; *American Jewish World*, 7 (August 15, 1919): 822; *American Hebrew*, 101 (June 16, 1921): 4.

10. *Opinion*, 2 (January 8, 1932): 4; 2 (July 11, 1932): 17; 2 (May 16, 1932): 3-4; 3 (May 1933): 5-6; 3 (December 1933): 29-30; 4 (April 1934); *Jewish Frontier*, 2 (May 1935): 6; *American Israelite*, 80 (April 13, 1933): 1; 80 (June 22, 1933): 4; *American Hebrew and Jewish Messenger*, 134 (December 1, 1933): 45.

11. *Jewish Tribune and Hebrew Standard*, 80 (January 19, 1923): 6, 9; *Jewish Tribune*, 50 (September 8, 1922): 8; 39 (June 23, 1922): 4; *American Jewish World*, 11 (January 19, 1923): 5.

12. *American Hebrew*, 103 (May 18, 1923): 1; 115 (May 10, 1935): 529; *Jewish Tribune and Hebrew Standard*, 81 (May 18, 1923): 11; 80 (March 16, 1922): 9; *American Israelite*, 71 (October 16, 1924): 4; 72 (June 18, 1925): 7; 78 (December 24, 1931): 1; *Jewish Tribune*, 40 (November 10, 1922): 11; *American Jewish World*, 12 (July 4, 1924): 4.

13. *American Israelite*, 73 (August 19, 1926): 1; 64 (November 22, 1917): 4; 71 (December 4, 1924): 8; *American Jewish World*, 7 (January 17, 1919): 328; *Jewish Tribune and Hebrew Standard*, 94 (May 3, 1929): 9.

14. *American Israelite*, 75 (October 4, 1928): 3; *American Jewish World*, 12 (February 1, 1924): 5; *American Hebrew*, 115 (April 5, 1935): 417; *Jewish Tribune*, 91 (July 22, 1927): 2-3; *Jewish Tribune and Hebrew Standard*, 87 (October 30, 1925): 14; *B'nai Brith Magazine*, 46 (February 1932): 134-135; *Opinion*, 4 (February 1934): 32.

15. *American Jewish World*, 3 (November 26, 1915): 248-249; 11 (January 26, 1923): 2; *American Israelite*, 73 (April 19, 1926): 6; *American Jewish World*, 5 (June 15, 1917): 197.

16. *American Israelite*, 76 (April 19, 1929): 4; 69 (April 20, 1922): 1.

17. *B'nai Brith Magazine*, 40 (August 1925): 355; *American Jewish World*, 9 (December 2, 1921): 1; 3 (October 22, 1915): 170; *American Israelite*, 74 (March 10, 1927): 4.

18. *American Israelite*, 71 (June 1924): 7; 75 (October 4, 1928): 3; 73 (September 16, 1926): 1; *Menorah Journal*, 5 (October 1922): 309-316; *American Jewish World*, 3 (December 17, 1915): 296.

19. *American Israelite*, 71 (January 31, 1924): 7; *American Jewish World*, 12 (February 1, 1924): 5; *American Hebrew*, 108 (February 1, 1929): 465; *Opinion*, 2 (April 22, 1932): 12; 2 (February 1, 1932): 17; (April 11, 1932): 18.

20. *Opinion*, 5 (April 11, 1932): 17.

21. *Jewish Tribune*, 91 (July 22, 1927): 13; *American Hebrew*, 107 (November 4, 1927): 939; 113 (May 12, 1933): 456; 109 (May 31, 1929): 67; *Jewish Tribune and Hebrew Standard*, 75 (June 19, 1925): 12; 66 (August 21, 1925): 17; 79 (August 6, 1926): 24; *Opinion*, 3 (April 1933): 37.

22. *Opinion*, 2 (July 18, 1932): 19; 4 (February 1934): 32; *Jewish Tribune and Hebrew Standard*, 90 (March 18, 1927): 3; 87 (October 30, 1925): 14; *Jewish Tribune*, 91 (July 21, 1927): 2-3; *American Hebrew*, 98 (March 9, 1918): 615; 108 (September 7, 1928): 491.

23. *Opinion*, 2 (July 18, 1932): 19; *American Hebrew*, 109 (January 18, 1929): 395; *American Hebrew and Jewish Standard*, 131 (October 14, 1932): 414.

24. *American Israelite*, 77 (May 2, 1930): 4; 79 (January 28, 1932): 6; 77 (September 5, 1930): 1; *Jewish Tribune*, 96 (May 7, 1930): 15; *American Hebrew*, 110 (March 14, 1930): 655; *B'nai Brith Magazine*, 46 (February 1932): 134-135.

25. *Jewish Tribune*, 91 (July 22, 1927): 2-3; *American Hebrew*, 109 (June 28, 1929): 210; 108 (May 4, 1928): 104; 107 (May 20, 1927): 115; *American Jewish World*, 12 (February 8, 1924): 3; *Opinion*, 4 (February 1934): 32; 2 (January 18, 1932): 17; *Jewish Tribune and Hebrew Standard*, 90 (October 4, 1929): 95; 91 (October 21, 1927): 6.

26. *Jewish Tribune and Hebrew Standard*, 88 (January 1, 1926): 4; 111 (September 30, 1927): 5; *Jewish Tribune*, 91 (October 7, 1929): 16; (September 28, 1929): 38; *American Hebrew*, 109 (November 22, 1929): 49; 105 (November 27, 1925): 49; 113 (April 8, 1932): 534; 109 (December 6, 1929): 186; *American Hebrew and Jewish Messenger*, 125 (January 13, 1922): 267; 121 (August 31, 1928): 467; *American Israelite*, 68 (October 27, 1921): 4; 70 (February 22, 1923): 7; 75 (September 7, 1928): 7; 81 (November 29, 1934): 4; *Jewish Tribune and Hebrew Standard*, 111 (September 30, 1927): 5.

27. *Menorah Journal*, 12 (August-September 1926): 424-428; *Opinion*, 3 (July 1933): 29; 3 (April 1933): 37; *American Israelite*, 79 (January 28, 1932): 6; 77 (May 2, 1930): 4; *B'nai Brith Magazine*, 46 (February 1932): 134-137; *Jewish Tribune*, 91 (July 22, 1927): 2-3; *Jewish Tribune and Hebrew Standard*, 90 (March 18, 1927): 3.

28. *Opinion*, 3 (May 1933): 5-6; *Current Jewish Record*, 2 (February 1932): 49-50; *Menorah Journal*, 8 (October 1922): 309-316; *Jewish Layman*, 6 (February 1932): 12; *American Jewish World*, 3 (October 8, 1915): 137; *Jewish Tribune and Hebrew Standard*, 89 (December 10, 1926): *B'nai Brith Magazine*, 46 (February 1932): 132-133; *Jewish Tribune*, 95 (October 4, 1929): 23; 90 (September 15, 1922): 4; *American Hebrew*, 95 (April 30, 1915): 745; *American Israelite*, 73 (December 17, 1926): 4; 77 (July 25, 1930): 4.

chapter 4

"A COVENANT KEPT": JEWS IN THE BLACK CIVIL RIGHTS MOVEMENT

The modern civil rights movement came alive in the first decade of the twentieth century. Sustained and strengthened by blacks and whites in the North who envisioned a society in which black Americans enjoyed full citizenship, its success and survival stemmed largely from its biracial character. In the early twentieth century the civil rights movement was synonymous with the National Association for the Advancement of Colored People. The NAACP functioned as the only nationally based, politically oriented Negro organization.

The origins of the NAACP are well-known. In 1908 William English Walling, a socialist journalist, and his wife Anna Strunsky journeyed to Springfield, Illinois, to investigate a bloody race riot which had swept through the town. Shocked by what they saw there and by the rising tide of race hatred across the country, Walling published an impassioned article in *The Independent*, asking "what large and powerful body of citizens is ready" to reverse the tide? In the next year he brought together a group of other white northerners who drew up a "Call" to action. That "Call" chided white Americans that "Silence . . . means tacit approval. The indifference of the North is . . . responsible for more than one assault upon democracy."

One signer of the "Call" was W.E.B. DuBois, the voice of race militance and the dean of the black intelligentsia. Several years before DuBois had spearheaded the Niagara movement, a black civil rights society which sought to challenge the hegemony of Booker T. Washington and the forces of accommodationism in race relations. Since DuBois could not find financial backers, the movement met a quick demise. So DuBois in 1909 joined forces with the other signers of the

118

"Call," forming the National Negro Committee. Two years later the organization officially adopted its present name.

Historians have pointed out that the civil rights movement attracted two relatively homogeneous groups, blacks and whites. The whites, however, came from at least two distinct sources, each with different social origins and motivations. On the one hand, a large number of white Protestant New Englanders, children and grandchildren of the abolitionists, flocked to the crusade. Oswald Garrison Villard, grandson of William Lloyd Garrison, and Moorfield Storey, a disciple of Charles Sumner, were steeped in the traditions of the nineteenth-century struggle to end slavery. Mary White Ovington, another founder of the NAACP, spent her childhood dreaming about the heroism of the underground railroad and listened to her parents and grandparents reminisce about their role in the abolitionist struggle. Some of these New Englanders, like William E. Walling and Ovington, considered themselves socialists, but their socialism does not in and of itself explain their commitment to racial justice. The Socialist party, like American liberals generally, had not yet adopted civil rights as a central tenet. For Ovington, Villard, Storey, and others the commitment to black civil rights and to the NAACP drew from their personal family heritage and from the tradition of the group with which they identified—the New England Protestant elite.[1]

JEWS IN THE NAACP

The abolitionist tradition cannot, however, explain the motivation of the other identifiable group of whites who helped organize, direct, and fund the National Association for the Advancement of Colored People. The traditions of New England liberalism cannot explain the motives of Stephen Wise, Hungarian-born rabbi whose name appears among the signers of the 1909 "Call," nor did Lillian Wald come out of the milieu of the anti-slavery movement. This daughter of Jewish immigrants from Germany was born in the South, but she too stepped forward and signed the "Call." Emil Hirsch, a German-born rabbi, also signed the 1909 document. So did another Jew, Henry Moskowitz, who had participated in issuing the "Call." Born in Rumania, Moskowitz was a social worker among New York's Jewish immigrants.

Dozens of Jewish Americans subsequently joined the NAACP. Louis Marshall, a noted constitutional lawyer, actively participated in the NAACP's legal projects. He was born in the United States but his parents had emigrated from Germany. Marshall's son-in-law, Jacob Billikopf, himself born in Vilna, Lithuania, served on several of the NAACP's decision-making committees in the 1920s. Herbert Lehman, New York's Democratic governor in the mid-1930s, was the son of German Jewish immigrants. Like Wald, he had spent his early years in the South. Lehman served on the Association's Executive Board and used his influence for the benefit of the movement. The acknowledged leader and spokesperson for America's German Jews was Jacob Schiff, a wealthy financier. Early in the history of the NAACP he helped sustain its shaky finances. Two immigrant Jewish scholars shared their time and expertise with the NAACP: Felix Frankfurter and Franz Boas. Frankfurter, a distinguished jurist and professor of law at Harvard, frequently consulted with the NAACP's legal staff; Franz Boas, the father of modern anthropology, participated in numerous NAACP programs and applied much of his research on the race question to the Association's publicity campaign. Both were immigrants, Frankfurter from Austria and Boas from Germany.[2]

However, of all the Jews who hearkened to the NAACP's message and lent a hand in the Association's activities, Arthur and Joel Spingarn were the most committed. Arthur Spingarn headed the NAACP's legal committee. Under his direction the Association achieved some of its most dramatic and significant victories. His brother, Joel Elias Spingarn, can be considered the most important white in the NAACP and one of the pivotal figures in the early history of the black civil rights movement. From 1912 until his death in 1939 Joel Spingarn's name was synonymous with white liberalism within the ranks of the struggle for black political rights. Spingarn held major leadership positions within the Association, initiated much of the NAACP's policy, devised its strategy and spoke most eloquently in public for the cause of black equality. It was to Joel Spingarn that W.E.B. DuBois dedicated his autobiography in 1940, one year after Spingarn's death: "To Keep the Memory of Joel Spingarn—A Scholar and a Knight."

Joel Spingarn was born in 1875. His father had joined thousands of other Jews emigrating from Austria; his mother was from England.

The Spingarns lived in New York City where they conducted a prosperous trade in tobacco. Joel Spingarn attended New York's public
schools and at twenty-four received a doctorate in literature from
Columbia University. Considered a promising young scholar by his
mentors, on graduation he accepted a teaching position at Columbia.
His dissertation, *History of Literary Criticism in the Renaissance*,
merited publication, and students flocked to the popular young
teacher.

In the early years of the century, while his scholarship led him to
some unorthodox ideas about literature and art, he also began to participate in New York liberal politics. In 1901 he became president of
the Civic Club of New York and in 1908 he ran unsuccessfully for Congress on the Republican ticket. After purchasing an estate in Amenia,
Dutchess County, New York, in 1910 he proceeded to throw himself
into town activities. His first effort saw the establishment of the Heart
of Hope Club, where poor blacks could come for free meals and rec-
reation. Since he had little practical expertise to run such a service, he
sought the help of W.E.B. DuBois, who had just become editor of the
NAACP publication, *Crisis*. This was the first contact between the two
men who were to be life-long friends.

At that point Spingarn primarily saw himself as an academician.
He did not, however, remain one for very long. He had been one of the
first American literary critics to agree with Italian philosopher Bene-
detto Croce on the need to evaluate a work of art independently of
other criteria. This "new criticism" drew vehement censure from the
Columbia faculty and scholars across the country. Generally dissatis-
fied with the drift of Columbia, Spingarn's academic career ended in
1911 when he publicly attacked the university's administration for fir-
ing a member of the philosophy department. Spingarn was summarily
dismissed.

Spingarn abandoned academia completely and devoted most of his
time to the movement for black rights. He totally committed himself
to the NAACP. He became chairman of the board of directors in 1914
and remained in that position until 1918. After wartime military service, he returned to the NAACP and as Treasurer supervised the Association's finances. Then Spingarn assumed the presidency of the
organization. Finally, in 1932 he once again became chairman of the
board and served concurrently as president and chairman.[3]

While Spingarn was more committed to the NAACP than any of the other Jewish participants, many of them exerted considerable effort for the cause. The extent of the Jewish involvement can be seen, for example, by examining the composition of the various governing committees of the Association. Six members of the "Committee of Forty," the executive body of the National Negro Committee, were Jews. The first general committee of the NAACP was composed of forty-five members, of whom seven were Jews. Of the thirty individuals who sat on the Association's first Executive Committee, there were four Jews. Jews made up nearly half the lawyers who served on the NAACP's legal committee through the 1930s. While Jews did not constitute a majority in the upper echelons of the NAACP, they were far out of proportion to their numbers in the population.[4]

These influential and active Jewish members of the NAACP did not have the same motives as DuBois or the other black officials, Walter White, James Weldon Johnson, William Pickens, or Roy Wilkins, who were fighting against their own oppressors. Nor did the traditions of New England abolitionism influence these Jewish civil rights activists. They had their own reasons for being attracted to the cause, their own motives for involvement.

The Jews of the black civil rights movement had a great deal in common with each other. Almost all were the children of immigrants from western Europe, or were themselves German or Austrian immigrants. A few like Henry Moskowitz and Jacob Billikopf had immigrated from eastern Europe, but interacted freely with German Jews. Billikopf, for example, married Louis Marshall's daughter. These Jews were also relatively affluent and successful. They were professionals— lawyers, rabbis, social workers, academicians—and businessmen making up the most visible elite of American Jewry.

One area of difference between them involved their personal definitions of Jewishness and the degree to which they committed themselves to Jewish affairs. Some identified strongly with Judaism and, in fact, chose careers as Jewish community workers. Obviously, the rabbis who chose to join and participate in the NAACP fit this category. Among them could be found Stephen Wise, perhaps the best known American rabbi. He led New York's Free Synagogue which maintained one branch to serve the "uptown" Jews and one for those "downtown." Wise's reputation went beyond New York. A leader of the world Zionist movement, he was an international Jewish figure. Emil Hirsch served Chicago's ultra-Reform Temple Sinai, which included among its members millionaire-philanthropist Julius Rosenwald. Joseph Silverman officiated at Temple Emanu-El in New York, a counterpart of Chicago's Sinai.

The rabbis in the NAACP were not the only ones who had carved out careers for themselves in the Jewish world. While Louis Marshall was a well-known constitutional lawyer, his primary activities included serving as president of the American Jewish Committee. He led and organized many Jewish projects in the United States and Europe. Marshall was, in fact, the closest thing American Jews had to a *Shtadlan*, the European court Jew, who pleaded the Jews' case to those in power. His son-in-law, Jacob Billikopf, also pursued a career in Jewish affairs. A trained social worker, he had directed Jewish social service agencies in Milwaukee, Kansas City, and Philadelphia.

Several of the Jews who joined the NAACP did not define their professional interests in purely Jewish terms but worked most intensely with other Jews. Henry Moskowitz, another social worker, mostly served New York's Jewish immigrants. He acted as an arbitrator in the garment industry and that, again, brought him in contact mainly with Jews. Lillian Wald's Henry Street Settlement operated in the heart of the lower East Side. While the Settlement also ministered to non-Jews, the vast majority of its clients were recent Jewish immigrants. Wald herself did not participate in any specifically Jewish projects, but Moskowitz worked ardently in the Jewish Joint Distribution Committee and the Jewish Social Service Association.

For some of the prominent Jews who lent their names and their time and money to the Association, Jewish affairs did not stem from their professional activities. Felix Frankfurter, for example, a legal scholar by profession, was also an active Zionist who is credited with drafting the Balfour Declaration, the 1918 statement of the British government favoring the establishment of a Jewish homeland in Palestine. Herbert Lehman was also a Zionist and lent a hand in the Palestine Economic Corporation. More important, he organized and directed the Jewish Joint Distribution Committee's relief effort for Jews in post-World War I Europe, in addition to participating in and contributing to dozens of Jewish charities, social service agencies, and schools. Somewhat less involved in specifically Jewish organizations and projects, Franz Boas gave time to organizations like the American Jewish Committee and lectured frequently to Jewish gatherings.

Other Jews in the black civil rights movement basically remained aloof from Jewishness and did not take any role in Jewish affairs. That was true of Herbert J. Seligmann, the NAACP's director of publicity, of Ernest and Martha Gruening, of Arthur Garfield Hays, a member of the NAACP legal team, and of Joel and Arthur Spingarn. These individuals neither rejected Judaism nor actively participated in Jewish life.[5]

Although their personal definitions and means of expressing Jewishness differed, all of the Jews in the NAACP were committed to Americanization and acculturation. Even the most actively Jewish individuals like Marshall or Billikopf believed that Jews must become integrated into the American mainstream. They all believed also that American society must recognize the existence of differences, though it must not equate difference with inferiority. All of them—the Spingarns, Marshall, Wald, Wise—believed that American society would derive strength and culture vitality from the talents of its various groups.[6] Of the many contributions Jews were to make to American society, participation in the quest for black civil rights loomed very high. This can be seen in Jewish efforts for the NAACP's drive for financial stability as well as in the Association's legal efforts, publicity campaigns and political programs.

JEWS AND THE FUNDING OF THE NAACP

The NAACP survived through years of hostile public opinion and a general apathy toward the fate of the Negro because it developed a bold but rational program of combating legal discrimination. But even the most well thought out program could not continue without money. One key to the survival of the National Association for the Advancement of Colored People was its successful drive for financial support from numerous affluent whites. Jews counted themselves among those backers.

Jews were natural potential contributors for two reasons. First, a sizable number of them had enough money to be able to give freely to causes in which they believed. In the first three decades of the twentieth century, American Jewry included such wealthy individuals as Julius Rosenwald, Jacob Schiff, Herbert Lehman, Samuel Fels, Felix Warburg—to name but a few—who could, and did, give to the cause of black equality.

On the other hand, Jews had a long tradition of philanthropy. This tradition, which had theological roots in the Bible and in the Talmud, made charity not only a virtue, but a duty. In Europe, Jews developed extensive philanthropic institutions as a way of "taking care of their own." Because they could not depend on Gentile society, Jewish communities institutionalized charity and made philanthropy the responsibility of all. This philanthropic tradition modified with changing Jewish social conditions, but the heritage of giving to causes lingered on and in America was channeled into the cause of black civil rights, among others.

Jewish donors maintained a constant flow of money from 1910 on to the coffers of the NAACP. Funds came from those already active in Association affairs as well as from Jews who had close ties to Booker Washington, the major black critic of the Association, like Julius Rosenwald and Jacob Schiff.[7] One reason that the NAACP received tens of thousands of dollars from Jews at a time when civil rights for blacks was far from a popular and respectable cause stemmed from the efforts of Jewish activists to use their own personal contacts to persuade other Jews to donate to the Association.

Arthur Spingarn, for one, often served as an intermediary between the NAACP and wealthy Jews, and was always conscious of the potential for even more Jewish support. For example, when he compiled the names of possible NAACP donors in 1920, nineteen of his thirty-five people were Jews. Louis Marshall also personally raised funds for the NAACP among his predominantly Jewish friends. Zionist leader Judge Julian Mack, a member of the NAACP Chicago branch, served as a crucial link to Julius Rosenwald, frequently sending him Association literature. At one point, Jacob Billikopf suggested to Walter White that "Frank Altschul . . . brother-in-law of Herbert Lehman [is] not interested at all in Jewish causes, but may be interested in your cause. Approach him . . . ."[8]

Black officials of the NAACP also realized that Jews could be easily persuaded to give to the Association. So Walter White and James Weldon Johnson systematically consulted with Louis Marshall, Jacob

Billikopf, Arthur Spingarn, and Herbert Lehman on how best to approach potential Jewish donors. White, for example, always checked
with Arthur Spingarn before appealing to Jews for money. "Here is
the new draft of the letter to go to wealthy Jews," wrote White in 1928.
"Will you read it and telephone me your opinion . . . . Kindly complete
the date in connection with the Leo Frank case." White also informed
Spingarn that he had a meeting set up with Baruch Charney Vladeck,
managing editor of the *Jewish Daily Forward*, to discuss fund-raising.[9]

Both Johnson and White kept close watch on obituaries of wealthy
Jews who had left estates to be distributed to charity. In one case,
White wrote to James Marshall, son of Louis, and Jacob Billikopf
about the will of a Simon Straus which bequeathed $100,000 for chari-
table causes. Marshall agreed to speak on behalf of the NAACP and
Billikopf advised him that when approaching the Straus executors,
Marshall should "play up the names of Father, Julius Rosenwald, and
various other Jewish benefactors. The personal element may play a
part in the equation." In a similar situation in October 1933 White
learned that one Madeline Stern had left $10,000 to the Colored
Orphan Asylum of Riverdale, as well as $100,000 to be disbursed to
other charities. He contacted Herbert Lehman's secretary, asking for
Lehman's help in presenting the NAACP's case. Lehman willingly
wrote to Arthur J. Cohen, the executor, noting that such prominent
Jews as Felix Warburg, Samuel Fels, Lillian Wald, and William
Rosenwald had all endorsed the Association's work. Similarly, White
urged Arthur Spingarn, James Marshall, Wise, Billikopf, and Solomon Lowenstein, Executive Director of the Federation of Jewish Philanthropies in New York, to intervene on behalf of the Association.
Consequently, the Stern estate gave $1,000 to the NAACP. [10]

In order to augment Jewish financial support, the Association developed specific strategies to attract it. For example, when the
NAACP turned to Rosenwald for money, it stressed in a not very subtle manner the importance of the NAACP's work for Jews. James Weldon Johnson noted to Rosenwald in 1923 that the Supreme Court's
decision *Moore v. Dempsey*, which ordered a new trial for a group of
Arkansas blacks because the first trial had been conducted in a prejudicial manner, "laid down a principle which . . . might have saved Leo
Frank from being lynched . . . In fact, when Leo Frank was being tried

Mr. Louis Marshall . . . made an attempt to have the Supreme Court adopt the principle that Frank had not received a fair trial." Oswald Garrison Villard in 1915 had also linked the Association with the plight of Leo Frank to attract Rosenwald. [11]

Often the NAACP used the names of Jewish supporters to win the financial support of others. The NAACP launched a massive fund-raising campaign in memory of Louis Marshall, who died in 1929. In early 1930 Walter White approached Jacob Schiff's son, Mortimer, and Samuel Sachs for contributions invoking the names of Jacob Billikopf, Louis Marshall, Julius Rosenwald, and Lillian Wald. At the same time he attempted to interest an executive of the Allied Jewish Campaign in the work of the NAACP and noted in a letter: "You may perhaps remember that our mutual friend Julius Rosenwald introduced me to you at the Memorial Services to the late Louis Marshall at Temple Emanuel." [12]

The proclivity of Jews to give to charity, the use of Jewish members as contacts with other wealthy Jews, and the recognition on the part of the Association's non-Jewish officials that Jews gave more consistently than non-Jews were best illustrated in 1930 when William Rosenwald offered to donate $1,000 annually for three years to the NAACP, providing that four others agreed to do the same. Depression conditions had severely hurt the Association and officials desperately sought sources of revenue to keep the organization afloat. Walter White informed Jacob Billikopf of the financial straits of the organization and Billikopf put Rosenwald in touch with White. Herbert Lehman, Mary Fels, Felix Warburg, and Harold Guinzburg, publisher of Viking Press, all responded within several months. The only non-Jew to do likewise was Edsel Ford. Several other Jewish donors, stimulated by the Rosenwald offer, agreed to give smaller amounts. Altogether, as a result of the Rosenwald plan, the NAACP secured $16,350 for three of the worst years of the Depression.

Jewish periodicals glowed with pride over these contributions and the *Jewish Tribune and Hebrew Standard*, an English-language Jewish magazine, in an editorial entitled, "As It Should Be," best summarized Jewish opinion by noting "no race or creed or any other denomination has contributed proportionately one-half of the support rendered by our people to the advancement of the colored race in its struggle for economic independence." This self-laudatory article concluded with the phrase, *mitzvah gorereth mitzvah!* ("one good deed brings with it another").[13]

Blacks in the NAACP were also conscious of the Jewish response to the Rosenwald offer and they, too, noted the preponderance of Jewish donors. When trying to meet Rosenwald's offer, Walter White contacted Harry Davis, director of the Ohio Civil Service Commission, and informed him that he "had secured one of the four pledges . . . . I do want to get at least one Gentile and one Negro to participate." At one point he attempted to approach Pierre duPont and in a letter to an NAACP colleague asserted: "The clue to Pierre duPont . . . [is] that his wife is a Jewess." The colleague responded that "Pierre's mother was a Jewess and some seem to think that because of that fact he is sympathetic." Still trying to find other donors, White asked, "Are there any influential Catholics in New York who are interested in the NAACP? If so, I would sound them out . . . Failing that, I would advise appealing to some of our potent Jewish friends."[14] Everyone in the NAACP recognized that there was something in the program of the Association and in the kinds of problems it was tackling that struck a responsive chord in Jews.

JEWS AND THE NAACP LEGAL EFFORT

In the courtrooms of America—local, state, and federal—the NAACP achieved its greatest victories. Litigation was the Association's most potent weapon. An array of able and committed lawyers skillfully utilized the Fourteenth Amendment to the Constitution, with its due process and equal protection clauses as well as the Fifteenth Amendment. Many of those lawyers and legal advisers were Jews. In fact, Jews made their greatest impact on the Association in this area. Jews had entered the legal professions in large numbers in the late nineteenth and early twentieth centuries in both western Europe and America. A profession which combined intellectuality and the prospect of monetary reward, the law could open up the channels of power in society. More important, the Jewish religion was based on a legalistic tradition which maintained that the law was ever-changing and always subject to debate. Consequently, many Jews pursued legal careers and some of the most important of these lent their time and their skills to the cause of black political rights. Arthur B. Spingarn, Morris Ernst, Felix Frankfurter, Arthur Garfield Hays, Louis Marshall and James Marshall served on the NAACP's Legal Committee and were involved in some of the Association's most dramatic cases. While the most critical civil rights litigation took place after World War II, a series of cases in the 1920s and 1930s paved the ground for *Sweatt v. Painter* and *Brown v. The Board of Education*.

An NAACP legal case in 1910 actually first attracted the Spingarn brothers to the Association. They had read a newspaper account of the case of Steve Greene, a black farmer from Arkansas who had killed his white landlord in self-defense and had escaped to Chicago. Learning about Greene's plight, Joel Spingarn sent his first donation to the Association, which was conducting the defense, and Arthur Spingarn volunteered his legal services. Arthur Spingarn accepted several early cases for the New York branch of the NAACP and in 1913 assumed full responsibility for the Association's legal work. [15]

The Spingarns took part in one of the earliest NAACP legal battles, an attempt to defeat a Louisville, Kentucky, segregation ordinance. Arthur Spingarn headed the legal committee and he and Joel went to Louisville to build up local support for the case while it was winding its way through the courts. Arthur Spingarn directed the case, *Buchanan v. Warley*, until it reached the Supreme Court, which struck down the residential segregation law in 1917. Spingarn had also been responsible for the NAACP's 1915 victory over the "grandfather clause" in *Guinn v. United States*. [16]

While Arthur Spingarn was behind almost all the Association's legal projects, other Jewish lawyers also participated. Louis Brandeis, for example, whom American Jews considered their greatest legal mind, was never officially affiliated with the NAACP, but in the months before he moved to the Supreme Court he consulted with the Association on its campaign against Jim Crow railroad accommodations. He helped map out the NAACP's strategy in the case and would have pleaded it before the Interstate Commerce Commission had he not gone to the Supreme Court. [17]

Louis Marshall was perhaps the most influential Jewish communal leader of the early twentieth century and he, too, served as a member of the NAACP's legal force. A respected constitutional lawyer, he had unsuccessfully appealed Leo Frank's case before the Supreme Court. The NAACP was most eager to get Marshall to participate in its efforts. As early as 1920 the Association began a major effort to enlist his services, but he did not finally agree to serve until 1923. The incident which finally propelled him into the NAACP was the Arkansas peonage case, formally known as *Moore v. Dempsey*. This case resulted from the organizing efforts of a group of Arkansas black farmers in Phillips County who had tried to secure better prices for their cotton from the white landowners. After an organizing meeting a riot broke out in Elaine, Arkansas, and twelve blacks were sentenced to death on charges of murder. This case interested Louis Marshall so much because the NAACP lawyers, headed by Moorfield Storey, were attempting to use the same principle that he had invoked in trying to secure a new trial for Leo Frank. That principle hinged on the atmosphere in the courtroom, which, Storey argued, made it impossible for the black defendants to get a fair trial. According to Storey, a mob spirit had dominated the courtroom, jeopardizing any chance for impartial justice. Although Marshall did not participate in the case, in 1925, when the Supreme Court ruled in favor of the black farmers, he harked back to his involvement with Frank, musing, "The stone the builders rejected has become the cornerstone of the temple." [18]

Marshall did join the NAACP legal effort in two major cases in the years from 1924 to his death in 1928: *Corrigan v. Buckley* and *Nixon v. Herndon*. The Corrigan case involved an NAACP test of the prevalently used restrictive covenant. In 1921 thirty District of Columbia home owners entered in a restrictive covenant, covering twenty-five lots of land, stipulating that "no part of these properties shall ever be used or occupied by, or sold, leased or given to, any person of the negro race or blood." One of the signers, Irene Corrigan, in 1922 sold her home to a black, Helen Curtis, causing another signer, John Buckley, to sue her.

NAACP lawyers took on the case in 1924 hoping that the precedent of the 1917 Buchanan decision would kill restrictive covenants. Arthur Spingarn and James Weldon Johnson sent Marshall a steady stream of letters detailing the progress of the case through the lower courts and in October 1924 Marshall took charge of Corrigan's defense. Throughout the proceedings Johnson urged Marshall to go beyond the technicalities and try to arouse support for the Association. Marshall, a legal purist, refused. "If I am to argue the case it would to my mind be manifestly improper to discuss the subject at a meeting held for . . . propaganda. What I will say as a lawyer will be more effective if I confine myself to my professional function." Hoping to broaden the scope of Marshall's involvement, Johnson tried to point out to Marshall that the case carried Jewish implications. "In connection with the residential segregation case . . . I wish to call to your attention the enclosed clipping showing that residential segregation by exclusion paragraphs in deeds has already been invoked against Jews . . . It occurs to me that you might be willing to make a statement on the case calling its importance to the attention of Jewish people." While Marshall did not participate in any mass meetings or public rallies, he did keep influential Jews like Julius Rosenwald posted on the Corrigan affair because of its significance for Jews.

Working with Moorfield Storey, Marshall argued that Corrigan had been deprived of her "due process" in disposing of property. Behind Marshall's constitutional arguments rang a fear of the "moment that there is a differentiation in our courts between white and black, Catholic and Protestant, Jew and non-Jew, hatreds and passions will inevitably be aroused and that which has been most noble and exalted and humane in American life will have been shattered." [19]

In 1927 Marshall handled the case of *Nixon v. Herndon*, a decision hailed as a monumental victory by the civil rights movement at the time. This case destroyed the constitutional basis of the white primary in Texas. Dr. Nixon was an El Paso resident who had been denied the right to vote in the Democratic Party primary because he was black. He successfully sued on the basis of the equal protection clause of the Fourteenth Amendment and the Fifteenth Amendment. While Marshall and the NAACP were very pleased with the court's favorable decision, the Texas legislature moved quickly and passed a new primary law circumventing the Nixon decision. Nixon sued once again and Marshall eagerly took on the new case of *Nixon v. Condon*. Marshall died while the case was moving through the courts, but his son James accepted his place on both the Nixon case and the NAACP Legal Committee. [20]

Marshall clearly was very seriously committed to his NAACP work. Just prior to his September 1929 trip to a Jewish meeting in Zurich, where he died, Marshall refused to give in to family pressure and take an extended vacation. He demurred not because of his own legal practice, which he confessed interested him very little, but because "I am working on a very important brief for the National Association for the Advancement of Colored People involving the constitutionality of one of the most important matters that has been brought to the Supreme Court in years." Marshall respected the work of the Association, although he often disagreed with its stand. For example, he seriously questioned the constitutionality of the Dyer Anti-Lynching Law which the NAACP pushed so vigorously in the 1920s. While Marshall maintained that he wanted to fight discrimination against blacks purely because Jim Crow laws and disenfranchisement were unconstitutional and because they affected black Americans adversely (he claimed, for example, that he "would fight the Klan as hard had it spared Jews and was simply 'against Negroes'"), most of his contemporaries—Jews and blacks—saw a direct link between his Jewish identity and his black civil rights work. During his years with the NAACP, English-language Jewish periodicals pointed with great pride to his civil rights work. In an obituary, Alfred Segal, the president of the B'nai Brith, wrote: "To be a Jew was no narrow identity to him; it had to do with all the duties at the common altar. To be a Jew was to be a servant of mankind: to champion the Negro against discrimination." In a lengthy memorial tribute to Marshall, Cyrus Adler, a Jewish historian, speculated: "It may be because he was a Jew and was aware of the oppression to which minorities are subject that he took up the cause of the Negro." [21]

After Marshall's death in 1929 another Jew, Felix Frankfurter, agreed to serve on the NAACP's Legal Committee. While he never handled cases directly for the Association, he often consulted with Walter White on legal matters. White wrote to Frankfurter, for example, about the qualifications of candidates for judgeships, and it was Frankfurter who first recognized the legal talents of William Hastie, a black lawyer who later served on the Circuit Court of Appeals. Hastie had been Frankfurter's student and he advised Walter White that the NAACP "keep . . . [an] eye on a young man named Hastie . . . he is one of the finest students who has ever studied at Harvard." Frankfurter's involvement in the NAACP was quiet and behind the scenes. Rarely did he make public statements about specific cases which the Association was handling. He did, however, lend both advice and prestige to the NAACP's quest for legal and political equality. [22]

This quest, perhaps more than any of the NAACP's efforts, bore fruit in numerous Supreme Court cases which chipped away at the Jim Crow legal structure. Arthur Spingarn, Louis Marshall, James Marshall, Felix Frankfurter, and Louis Brandeis all were moved to lend their time and their talents to the cause of black political and legal equality. They had legal expertise to donate to the movement. More important, they were attracted to goals of the NAACP and obviously sensed some degree of mutual interest in joining in the struggle.

JEWS AND POLITICAL ACTION

The NAACP buttressed its legal work with extensive political activity. From its first years it tried to influence politicians, and here, too, it took advantage of the political contacts of its Jewish members. Many of these Jews willingly brought the NAACP's cause into politics. In 1912, for example, Joel Spingarn, Henry Moskowitz, and Jane Addams tried unsuccessfully to introduce a civil rights plank into the Progressive Party platform. Spingarn was so stung by the party's racial stance he remained aloof from partisan politics for almost twenty-five years. He supported no candidate, Republican or Democrat, until 1936 when he actively went out to stump for Franklin Roosevelt. [23]

Although Spingarn averred politics for over two decades, he did use his political contacts for the benefit of the Association and the cause of black civil rights. This was illustrated most aptly by his attempts to establish a training camp for black officers during World War I. Spingarn openly professed a fervent American nationalism. When war broke out in Europe in 1914 he immediately sided against the Germans and threw himself into the preparedness campaign, hoping to secure a commission when the United States took up arms. Just as eagerly, he hoped blacks would be able to prove their Americanism and their prowess by enthusiastic participation in the war effort and wanted to see blacks become officers. In a *Washington Bee* editorial he asked black readers: "Is it not time that we should have colored heroes who are lieutenants, captains, colonels, and generals?" When General Leonard Wood proposed to Spingarn in January 1917 that a month-long training camp for black officers be established, Spingarn embarked on a personal crusade. He traveled across the country, going to black gatherings, especially on black college campuses, hoping to secure enough volunteers. He successfully persuaded his Dutchess County neighbor, Franklin D. Roosevelt, then Assistant Secretary of the Navy, to endorse the plan. Due in part to Spingarn's efforts, on May 25, 1917, General Wood announced the establishment of the camp for black officers at Fort Des Moines, Iowa. [24]

This had been Joel Spingarn's own effort. Most members of the board of the Association opposed it, since many espoused pacifism and all, except DuBois, considered it segregation. Yet Spingarn willingly ignored the short-range implications of sanctioning segregation because of what he believed to be more far-reaching benefits for American blacks. He believed that the pride which blacks would derive from seeing their own young men in officers' uniforms was worth the price of separate treatment, and that service by Negro officers would help convince many white Americans that blacks deserved all the rights and privileges of citizenship.

Spingarn and other NAACP members worked on numerous other political projects, many involving petitioning those in power. He and several other Jewish activists joined in a protest against D. W. Griffith's film, *The Birth of a Nation*. The 1915 movie, based on Thomas Dixon's novel *The Clansman*, depicted the ravages of Reconstruction on southern whites and the supposed degeneracy of the newly freed slaves. While the Association was committed to combating *all* negative stereotypes of blacks, they found this film particularly odious. In St. Louis, for example, real estate interests pressing for a residential segregation law passed out copies of their literature after showings of the film, and there was at least one reported murder of a black by a white who had just seen the movie. Joel Spingarn, Lillian Wald, and Jacob Schiff worked actively on an NAACP committee which implored the National Board of Censorship in Moving Pictures to withhold sanction of the film. At first the censors supported them, but shortly thereafter the Board reversed itself and approved the movie. [25] Stephen Wise spoke out vehemently against the Board's reversal and Lillian Wald organized an assembly of five hundred to march on the offices of New York Mayor John Puroy Mitchell, who subsequently promised to eliminate the most objectionable scenes from all New York showings. In Boston, Ernest Gruening led an equally successful public appeal to Mayor James Curley. [26]

Jewish leaders commonly wrote to national political figures on behalf of blacks. Louis Marshall protested the exclusion of African immigrants to Senator Reed Smoot of Utah in 1916 and, at the request of James Weldon Johnson, he suggested to President Coolidge that Professor James A. Cobb of Howard University Law School be appointed to a judgeship. Stephen Wise urged President Wilson to end the segregation of blacks in the Federal service. Wise, who had ardently campaigned for Wilson in 1912, noted that Wilson "spoke as a true Southerner when he added, 'White people do not wish to work in too close proximity to the Negro.'" Jacob Schiff also tried to prod Wilson on the same issue:

> May I ask to be permitted to add my voice to that already raised in defense of the inalienable rights of the colored people, who are human beings as we are . . . whom we have no right to humiliate because of the fact, for which they are not responsible, that they have a different color than our own. It is entirely proper that the officers of the National Association for the Advancement of Colored People are asking their fellow citizens to address you, Mr. President, as head of this entire nation, of which the colored people form an integral part, in support of the protest . . . . [27]

Jews in the NAACP and other leaders of the Jewish world also actively supported legislation designed to ease racial tension. They backed bills like the Dyer Anti-Lynching Law, which Congress debated in the early 1920s and which the NAACP lobbied for so vigorously. English-language Jewish periodicals as well as the Yiddish press urged their readers to pressure their representatives to support the bill. The *American Israelite* had directly appealed "to the Senate of the United States," decrying the "killing and burning alive of human beings by mobs." [28] Many Jews also testified for the Dyer Act and for the 1934 Wagner-Costigan Anti-Lynching Bill. Among them were Arthur Spingarn and Arthur Garfield Hays, Rabbi Edward Israel of Har Sinai Congregation, Baltimore, a representative of the Maryland Anti-Lynching Federation, Bernard Flexner, a Zionist leader and social worker, Max Lowenthal, a New York attorney, and Rabbi Julius Mark of Vine Street Temple, Nashville. Jewish writers participated eagerly in the Writers' League Against Lynching which supported the legislation, as did seven national Jewish organizations, and dozens of rabbis from both the South and the North. [29]

A number of Jews in the NAACP tried to exploit their contacts in American politics for the benefit of the civil rights movement. They publicly pressured elected officials to advance certain demands and they supported legislation to secure equal political and legal rights for black Americans. There was little direct political prestige for the elite of American Jewry as a result of its championship of black causes in the political arena. The motivation for its activities must have been more than pure self-service. The goals of the Association and the programs it was advancing rang harmoniously with the needs of American Jewish leaders.

JEWS AND THE NAACP PUBLICITY CAMPAIGN

One way the NAACP marshaled support was through a sophisticated publicity campaign. The Association needed to attract favorable public attention in order to educate the public on problems of racism, and its financial stability depended on arousing the interest and outrage of sympathetic individuals. Because of these needs the NAACP put a great deal of effort into its publicity drives. Conferences, meetings, publications, and lectures all drew public attention to the legal and political plight of black Americans as well as to the successes of the Association. This area of the NAACP called for individuals with writing and journalistic skills and with contacts with newspaper publishers. A number of Jews fit these qualifications and eagerly lent a hand in the NAACP's publicity activities.

One of the chief tools was the Annual Conference. The first meeting of the National Negro Committee in 1909 was a complete disaster. Poor publicity compounded by a snowstorm brought attendance down to seven. Consequently, plans for the 1910 conference began almost a year in advance. Henry Moskowitz and Stephen Wise directed arrangements and economist E.R.A. Seligman of Columbia University, who had addressed the meager crowd in 1909, served on the planning committee. The organizers chose black disfranchisement in the South as the theme of the conference and Jacob Schiff and Franz Boas agreed to speak. This heavy Jewish involvement may explain why the conference passed the "Russian Resolution," which protested the expulsion of Jews from the city of Kiev, Russia. In the first full years of its life, numerous public gatherings heralded the new association, like the one celebrating the one-hundreth birthday of abolitionist Charles Sumner, organized by Wise, Lillian Wald, and Paul Warburg, and at which Jacob Schiff spoke.[30] During the next two decades many Jews would address the annual meetings which highlighted the NAACP's calendar.[31]

Jewish leaders, in fact participated in all kinds of civil rights conferences. In 1919, for example, Stephen Wise was the featured speaker at a mass meeting of the National Conference on Lynching at New York's Ethical Culture Society, and the Jewish Welfare Board and the Council of Jewish Women helped sponsor a 1921 anti-lynching meeting.[32] Horace Kallen, a Jewish philosopher and the leading American advocate of cultural pluralism, appeared at a Pan-African conference in 1919. His speech "Africa and World Democracy" later circulated as an NAACP pamphlet. In 1927 anthropologist Melville Herskovits addressed the Fourth Pan-African Congress and W.E.B. DuBois, Jacques Loeb of the Rockefeller Institute, anthropologists Franz Boas and Robert Lowie, and Henrietta Szold, a Zionist leader, appeared together on a panel of the Socialist Press Club to ponder the nature of race prejudice.[33]

However important those publicity activities were to the Association and the cause of civil rights, they were minor when compared to those of Joel Spingarn. His appearances always drew large crowds and an interested press. In 1913 he embarked on a national speaking tour dubbed "The New Abolitionism" during which he tried to stir up interest in the Association where it did not exist and strengthen faltering branches by invoking the memory and inspiration of the abolitionists. He dared both blacks and whites to come and listen to his fiery rhetoric. In 1914 he and DuBois spoke in Memphis and their local newspaper advertisement called upon "All Those Who Love the Truth and Dare to Hear It." In the same year Spingarn castigated Booker Washington and his accommodationist policies. In Chicago, St. Louis, Memphis, and other cities he stridently called on blacks to reject the Tuskegee approach to race relations. In Baltimore he even urged blacks to begin to defend themselves physically against hostile whites and antagonistic police. Oswald Garrison Villard, who also sat on the platform, arose in annoyance to moderate Spingarn's boldness and stressed the NAACP's insistence on peaceful protest.[34]

Spingarn also used the podium at meetings of elite white groups to deliver the NAACP message. His extensive contacts afforded him many such opportunities. He attended the 1919 convention of the American Legion and tried to block the exclusion of Negro veteran posts from the South. At Chicago's prestigious City Club in 1914 he condemned the introduction of segregated facilities in the federal government. He also attempted to publicize the achievements of the Association to people with wealth and power. He described to the audience a movement "which hopes to emancipate ten million people once more from a condition so closely allied to servitude that it is fair to speak of the emancipation that we would give them as a 'second abolition.'" Spingarn thus stimulated a discussion on the race question among those who might not otherwise have been exposed to the "radical" ideas of the NAACP. For some reason unknown to Spingarn, he was also invited to a 1932 White House conference on hoarding money. Although Spingarn found the situation ironic, he used the national publicity effectively. Inviting him, a representative of the black cause, to a discussion of hoarding, he told the press, was "not unlike inviting a man dying of starvation to listen to a lecture on the dangers of extravagance."

Spingarn was so committed to the NAACP that almost every public act of his was focused on how it would benefit the Association. In March 1913 Joel Spingarn announced the endowment of the Spingarn Medal for the "highest and noblest achievement of an American Negro." He wanted to instill group pride among blacks and shed favorable publicity upon the race. Since the medal would be under the auspices of the NAACP, it would also enhance the Association's image. The prize, estimated at $100, was first awarded in February 1915 to Professor Ernest Just, a Howard University biologist. The Association staged an impressive public ceremony where the scientist received the award from the governor of New York. Spingarn considered the prize so significant a contribution to the cause of black civil rights that in his will he earmarked $20,000 for the continuation of the award, even if the NAACP were to pass out of existence. [35]

The NAACP's quest for public exposure also enlisted the support of Jews who were not Association members. Many Jews, for example, registered with the NAACP Speakers' Bureau. In 1912 four rabbis agreed to introduce Martha Gruening, an NAACP worker, to their congregations and agreed to praise the Association's work. Rabbi Alexander Lyons, an occasional member of the Brooklyn branch of the NAACP, volunteered in 1913 to speak on the subject, "If I Were a Negro." In 1920 and 1934 he reaffirmed his willingness to speak for the "uplift and advancement of your people." In 1919 eight other rabbis offered their services in New York, Philadelphia, New Orleans, St. Paul, Albany, Chicago and Boston. They wanted to orate on such issues as "Why I Am Interested in the Colored Race," "Justice to the Negro," "Negro Contributions to Civilization," "The American Negro," "Racial Facts and Fallacies," and "The Jew, Who Knows What Race Prejudice Is, Can Plead for His Stricken Brother."[36]

Frequently Jewish groups requested NAACP officials to lecture to them on black topics. The Associated Young Man's Hebrew Association of New England wanted an NAACP speaker in 1922. Association representatives appeared also at the Jewish Community Center of Omaha, at Hebrew Union College in Cincinnati, at the Jewish Forum of Missouri, and at dozens of Reform synagogues. Clearly, DuBois was the most popular and most often requested speaker. DuBois spent a day among Jewish groups in Oakland, California, for example, and Rabbi Rudolph Coffee lamented, "It is a pity that so able a man, with so genuine a message, spends but one day in our community. May he return to us . . . Our prayer is that the NAACP realizing the tremendous good such a speaker accomplishes will send other lecturers to us in the course of the years."[37]

Successful publicity also required extensive contacts with the press and here, too, Jews were useful. Herbert J. Seligmann was appointed the Association's director of publicity in 1919 and he handled liaisons between the Association and the press. This included general as well as black newspapers for whom he prepared the NAACP's regular press bulletins. Seligmann's first contact with the Association had been in 1917 when he covered a speech given by James Weldon Johnson at the Inter-Collegiate Socialist Society for the New York *Evening Star*. His work as publicity director involved writing numerous articles for popular and liberal magazines, laying out the Association's position and stressing its achievements.

Seligmann kept watch on the national press and monitored articles about both race relations in general and the NAACP in particular. He reacted quickly to an editorial in *Forum* magazine which asserted that

Judge John Parker's nomination to the Supreme Court had been defeated by the American Federation of Labor. Seligmann countered
this claim, pointing out that the North Carolina segregationist had
been defeated by "the Negro voters of this country, led by the National
Association for the Advancement of Colored People, who carried the
issue to the Senate. It was the Negroes whose power brought about
Parker's rejection and helped to make the present . . . Supreme
Court . . . liberal."

The NAACP frequently sent Seligmann to investigate areas of
racial conflict. He traveled through Mississippi and Tennessee in
1919, to Chicago after that city's riot, and to Haiti in 1920. He routinely traveled hundreds of miles a year for the Association. Seligmann reported back his extensive findings to the board of directors and
eventually used much of that material for his book, *The Negro Faces
America*. [38]

In 1912 Martha Gruening joined the NAACP as an assistant secretary. The Association sent her to investigate the East St. Louis and
Houston race riots and, as with Seligmann, published her findings in
popular magazine articles. Gruening had earlier spearheaded an
NAACP publicity campaign to indict the lynchers of Zach Walker, a
Pennsylvania black. According to Mary White Ovington, Gruening
visited dozens of white homes pleading for money and for a chance to
present the NAACP's case. "There were oceans of ice in the homes
and the offices of New York that Martha visited and the impatient
listeners refused to melt. Occasionally instead of ice she met sympathy
and brought us a check . . . ." Gruening also coauthored an NAACP
pamphlet with DuBois on the 1919 riots and wrote "Reconstruction
and the Ku Klux Klan in South Carolina" for the Association. A committed advocate of the NAACP, in 1911 she had publicly chided suf-
fragist Anna Howard Shaw on the prejudicial treatment of black
women in the suffrage movement. [39]

Martha Gruening's brother Ernest, a journalist, also helped gather
material for the NAACP. He did research on black troops during
World War I and in the 1920s, as managing editor of the *Nation*, was
instrumental in the NAACP's victorious efforts to force United States
troops from Haiti. [40] Earlier, as the newly appointed editor of the
Boston Traveler, Gruening had taken a bold stand for the fair treatment of blacks in the press. He instructed his staff to never slander
blacks and issued guidelines:

In editing stories which involve Negroes please handle as follows: Ask yourself how the story would read if the word Jew, Irishman or Swede was substituted for . . . Negro.

Refer to the color of the individual only when it is of particular and special interest and when the story is manifestly incomplete and inaccurate if the color of the person . . . is concealed . . . In other words I would like the colored people treated with approximately the same fairness we accord other racial groups.[41]

The NAACP was well aware of the importance of the press in shaping racial attitudes. Blacks almost always emerged as criminals while the achievements of blacks rarely merited discussion. Seligmann, as director of publicity, vigilantly surveyed newspapers. He wrote to editors when he felt they had treated blacks unfairly and also praised those who had been particularly fair. Positive articles drew the Association's attention. *Crisis*, for example, was so pleased to see a *New York Times* letter to the editor attacking race prejudice written by Nathan Straus, a prominent Jewish leader and philanthropist, that it reprinted it in full:

Easy to create, it is hard to destroy, sinister of wit, it is weak of wisdom . . . it rules those who give it life. It is a conjured Frankenstein, dominating millions of men. It sits beside the gate of life and takes toll of all that pass . . . It is the monster of the mind. It pollutes thought, serves despair and ravishes right . . . . It is prejudice.[42]

The *New York Times* was perhaps the most influential newspaper in America at that time. It was published and managed by a Jew, Adolph Ochs. While there was no indication that the *Times* was especially sensitive to blacks or any more willing to give the NAACP positive coverage than other newspapers, Jews in the NAACP, on occasion, used their contacts on the paper for the benefit of the Association. At James Weldon Johnson's request, Louis Marshall agreed to show "someone on the *New York Times*" a copy of an NAACP pamphlet on the Klan. Jacob Billikopf heartily agreed with Herbert J. Seligmann that the *Times* should have covered the 1931 DuBois Literary Prize. Billikopf felt he must point it out to avoid similar negligence in the future but confessed to Seligmann: "How I should handle the matter is something I cannot decide at this moment. I think it would be impolitic for me to write to anyone in authority . . . . But I am likely to see most any time Mr. Arthur Sulzberger, son-in-law of Mr. Adolph Ochs, and as diplomatically as I know how I shall refer the incident." [43]

Publicity of all kinds—lecturers, meetings, articles, pamphlets, news releases—were crucial to the NAACP. The very existence of the Association depended on a positive public image and on aroused public discussion of the race question. Many Jews used their skills and their contacts to aid the Association. Seligmann, Louis Marshall, Joel Spingarn, Jacob Billikopf, and Stephen Wise, among others, eagerly sounded out publicly the Association's message.

JEWISH ANTHROPOLOGISTS AND THE CONCEPT OF RACE

In the movement for black political equality, still another group of Jews brought their abilities to bear for the cause: the small but influential group of anthropologists who in the early 1900s were beginning to examine critically the concept of race. In the early years of the century anthropology, a new field, attracted a remarkable number of Jews. Some of them, including Franz Boas, Melville Herskovits, and Alexander A. Goldenweiser, conducted extensive research which eventually discredited the scientific basis of anti-black prejudice. All three of these anthropologists also joined in the civil rights movement and the NAACP consciously used their research findings to advance its goals.

A few years before his death in 1942, Franz Boas, in a foreword to Herbert Seligmann's *Race Against Man*, decried the gap between scientific knowledge and public opinion on the "dogma of racial superiority." Yet when Boas had first entered the field in the late nineteenth century, such a gap had not existed. Scientific research perfectly complemented and reflected prevalent attitudes about black inferiority. Throughout the nineteenth century, scientists and social thinkers, liberals and conservatives generally agreed that superior and inferior races existed. The darker races always fell in the inferior category. The only disagreement which arose focused on what to do about the alleged inferiority. According to one history of the development of the concept of race:

The state of the sciences of biology and anthropology was such in the nineteenth and early twentieth centuries that few men of reputation in the field were willing to hazard the opinion that race theory is useless in explaining the character of peoples. They protested against some of the conclusions of the racists with regard to particular peoples, but they did not reject racism itself.

Scientific and intellectual racism had direct social implications. These scientific principles found their way into the law, which in the South called for the total legal segregation of the races. The writings of scientists of repute who heartily ascribed inherent inequality to dark-skinned people bolstered popular opinion that blacks constituted a biologically inferior group. [44]

Yet in the first three decades of the twentieth century a group of scientists in the newly born field of anthropology actively and vigorously challenged the prevailing concepts of race. Their challenge of biological racism was as significant to the civil rights effort as was the scientific support of racism which laid the cornerstone to the preservation of segregation and inequality. Three of the most eminent of these challengers were Jews. That fact played a central role in turning their interest to the race question and in their hope of shattering prevalent opinion.

Franz Boas was one of the first scientists of "reputation" who examined critically commonly held ideas about racial difference. One history of anthropology has even asserted that "Boas did more to combat race prejudice than any other person in history." [45] Born in Minden, Westphalia, in 1858, Boas grew up in a family of liberals and freethinkers who rejected most of the religious content of Judaism, although his father "retained an emotional affection for the ceremonial . . . without allowing it to influence his intellectual freedom." In spite of the fact that he did not grow up in an intensely Jewish environment, he felt profoundly conscious of his religious background and his minority status in German society. All biographies of Boas include an anecdote (which Boas once told a friend but which has never been further substantiated) that as a student, sitting in a café, he overheard an anti-Semitic remark. This infuriated him and he threw the speaker out, challenging him to a duel. [46]

Boas came to the United States in the 1880s, having abandoned a career as a physical geographer in order to study human cultures and behavior. His anthropological research of the next fifty years ranged over several continents as he studied peoples and cultures in diverse environments. His work hinged on several unifying principles which he laid out in 1927 in an introduction to a monograph, *Primitive Art*: "The one being the fundamental sameness of mental processes in all races and in all cultural forms; the other, the consideration of every cultural phenomenon as the result of historical happenings." These two principles can be considered the cornerstones of Boas' work and especially of his voluminous contribution to the question "What is race?"

To Boas the concept of "race" was extremely ambiguous. It signified merely a "major grouping of mankind, marked off by genetically rooted physical characteristics that reach far back into antiquity." The term could be useful as only *one* tool of analysis, and he was more interested in the changeability of races as a result of contacts with other groups than in racial classifications. In 1925 in an article in the *Nation* entitled "What Is Race?," he dismissed the idea that race consciousness and race hatred were instinctive in human nature, and noted that each "race" had so many variants that any "generalized characterization of race must be misleading." No such things as pure races existed in the Western world, and Europeans or whites who boasted of their own racial purity were mistaken. There was no "Semitic race," just as an "Aryan race" existed in myth only. While Boas accepted the fact that groups differed from one another anatomically, he rejected any consequent attributions of superiority or inferiority.

Characteristics which most people attributed to racial difference Boas saw as products of history and environment. He concluded the 1925 *Nation* article by generalizing: "The behavior of an individual is determined not by his racial affiliation, but by the character of his ancestry and his cultural environment. We may judge of the mental characteristics of families and individuals, but not of races." This environmental emphasis was best demonstrated by his interest in differences between blacks in Africa and America. In Africa, blacks had attained a high degree of civilization. They excelled in crafts and in industry and as active traders. They traveled extensively. Based on observation of their highly organized societies. Boas asserted, "No other race on a similar level of culture has developed as strict methods of legal procedure as the Negro has." Yet in America, where blacks were not treated as individuals but as members of a hated group, they seemed to have lost those characteristics. Boas emphasized that environmental influences caused this change. He pointed to the differences between northern and southern blacks, indicating that northern blacks scored consistently higher on such scales as intelligence tests because of "more favorable social conditions." Racial stratification, which made American blacks seem inferior, was irrational. Supported by faulty thinking and based on ignorance of the scientific nature of race and of black achievements in Africa, it perpetuated itself by legislation which in turn denied adequate educational opportunity to blacks.

In 1931 in his presidential address to the American Association for the Advancement of Science, Boas exhorted his fellow scientists asking: "Will it be better for us to continue as we have . . . or shall we try to recognize the conditions that lead to the fundamental antagonisms which trouble us?" Boas felt that he could not be particularly optimistic about the future of race relations in America, because the myths of racism would long hold sway. At times, in a particularly pessimistic note, he even ventured that the only total solution lay in interracial marriage. This might be the only real answer to anti-Semitism also. In 1921 he speculated: "It would seem that man being what he is, the negro problem will not disappear in America until the negro blood has been so much diluted that it will no longer be recognized just as anti-Semitism will not disappear until the last vestige of the Jew as Jew has disappeared." [47]

Boas wrote for social as well as for scientific reasons. He was deeply concerned with the real human suffering created by racist thinking and eagerly shared his findings with the NAACP. Throughout his career he tried to use his scientific data to influence public policy. He testified, for example, before the Dillingham Commission, against immigration restriction. He lectured frequently at black universities and published in black journals. He was equally concerned with Jewish problems, speaking to Jewish gatherings and consulting with Jewish groups. While Boas believed that the scientist must go where the data leads, he was equally convinced that the scientist had a responsibility to society. To carry out this responsibility Franz Boas actively worked with the NAACP. He spoke at the 1909 Conference of the National Negro Committee and occasionally appeared at other Association ceremonies. In 1923, for example, he delivered a speech at the unveiling of a bust of DuBois at the 135th Street Branch of the New York Public Library. In 1910 Boas wrote an NAACP propaganda pamphlet, "The Real Race Problem From the Point of View of Anthropology." He kept in close touch with the Association and served as a consultant even when he was doing fieldwork. In addition to his direct NAACP work he always had his eye on how anthropology could be used for the advancement of civil rights. [48]

One Boas student, Melville Herskovits, also affiliated himself with the movement for black civil rights. He spoke frequently at black gatherings and addressed the 1927 Pan-African Congress. While he participated less actively than Boas in the NAACP during the first decades of the twentieth century, he taught courses on blacks in America at Columbia in the mid-1920s and at Northwestern beginning in 1926. Interestingly, he also offered courses on race relations at the Chicago Hebrew Institute, a Jewish social settlement. One such course on "Racial Differences" sought to compare black and Jewish problems. He lectured frequently at the Institute on African Culture, on black contributions to American society and on the history of discrimination against blacks. [49] From the beginning of his career in 1923 through the 1930s, Melville Herskovits published at least ten major articles in black journals. He contributed dozens of pieces on the race question to popular magazines. In the five years from 1924 to 1929 alone, he published twenty-nine articles on blacks in the United States, the Western Hemisphere, and Africa.

Although he was not as significant or groundbreaking a scientist as his mentor, his voluminous research on the concept of race, on Africa, and on black-white relations all pointed to a sensitivity to black social problems. One recent study of Herskovits documented the change in his stance on Negro culture from one which assumed that blacks had totally assimilated the dominant white values to one which stressed the retention and survival of Africanisms. The authors believed that the reason his position evolved slowly was because "Herskovits sensed that if a case could be made for the survival of Africanisms among United States Negroes, racists might be able to justify policies of exclusion and segregation by arguing that black Americans had not yet reached the point at which they could qualify as '100 percent American.'"

Herskovits noted in his 1927 monograph, *The American Negro*, that the potential importance of the book lay in its insistence on "how little we are able to define a word [race] that has played such an important role in our political and social life." Herskovits felt that race relations in America were governed by fallacious thinking which "translated into action . . . too often make for tragedy." Like Boas, he questioned the validity of the term *race*, and after exhaustive surveys concluded that it was a meaningless word. To him the "Negro race" was not a biological but a sociological concept, and he asserted that "sociological distinctions are . . . irrational and nonsensical. They exist because they *have* existed." Since racial distinctions were social and not scientific, then the scientist must discard them and convince society to do likewise. [50]

Alexander Goldenweiser, yet another Boas student, also appeared frequently at NAACP events. He addressed Association meetings and penned a glowing introduction to Herbert J. Seligmann's *The Negro Faces America*. He came from a more thoroughly Jewish background than either Boas or Herskovits. Born in Russia, the anthropologist's father was a noted Jewish scholar and an active member of the Kiev Jewish community. [51] While Goldenweiser's writings were largely theoretical, in the 1920s he wrote numerous articles for popular magazines as well as for Jewish and black journals on the meaning of race and on the status of blacks in America. Based not on primary research but synthesizing the findings of others, these lucidly written essays were presented to the educated layperson. One such piece appeared in 1922 in *Menorah Journal*, summarizing recent anthropological discoveries which discredited "the errors of the evolutionary ideology." Goldenweiser stated that

Two generations of painstaking researches by anthropological field workers and of critical muck-raking by humanitarian philosophers were necessary to break down the ramparts of the dogma of racial differences. But once the fog had lifted, the picture that appeared before the eyes of the curious was a different one indeed. It now became clear that the physical differences between the various groups of man were not of such character as to allow for an evolutionary grading.

He echoed Boas and Herskovits in his intellectual and social concerns. Like Boas, he noted that while racial physical differences existed, they had no bearing on mental or moral development. Only race prejudice and discrimination blocked the full intellectual growth of American blacks, and those negative social characteristics attributed to blacks, like laziness, inefficiency, dishonesty, "are the result, not the cause of prejudice." [52]

The civil rights movement and the NAACP recognized the importance of the anthropological work of Boas, Herskovits, and Goldenweiser. Editors opened the pages of *Crisis* and *Opportunity* to them and reviewed their books with great praise. An *Opportunity* review of Herskovits' *Anthropometry of the American Negro* lauded his "fervid and glowing imagination." Editorials in these journals also paraphrased and quoted liberally from the work of these scientists. *Opportunity* devoted an entire editorial to Boas' address before the American Association for the Advancement of Science.

The NAACP also used this anthropological evidence in its crusade for fair representation of blacks in the press. James Weldon Johnson, in an irate letter to a newspaper editor, cited both Goldenweiser and Boas to refute an article which assumed black inferiority. Johnson marshalled to his defense the work of these sympathetic anthropologists and wrote: "Now that statement . . . is explicitly denied by such noted anthropologists as Professor Franz Boas . . . by Dr. Robert H. Lowie and by Dr. Alexander L. Goldenweiser . . . . For a clear statement of the position taken by leaders of modern scientific research, I can refer you to Professor Boas' article in the October *American Mercury* . . . ." Herbert Seligmann relied heavily on the works of Boas, Herskovits, and Goldenweiser for his two books, *The Negro Faces America* (with an introduction by Goldenweiser) and *Race Against Man* (with an introduction by Boas). He dipped deeply into their ideas for a two-part *Opportunity* essay on "Race Prejudice", directly citing Goldenweiser's *Early Civilization: An Introduction to Anthropology*.

These scientists took a radical and bold stance at a time when many respected social thinkers assumed black inferiority. DuBois attributed his earliest interest in Africa to Boas, whom he had heard lecture at Atlanta University on the history of the Sudan. Du Bois claimed that he was so amazed by Boas' presentation that "I began to study Africa for myself." A 1926 *Opportunity* article on African art admitted disbelief at Boas' early research on Africa. "When in 1916 Dr. Franz Boas' consummate attack upon a flourishing system of racial misconceptions (*Mind of Primitive Man*) referred to the cultural achievement of African tribes in their art, industry and folk philosophy, it was information so strange that it could not be appreciated."[53]

Both Franz Boas and Alexander Goldenweiser were conscious of a direct link between Jewish identity and an interest in destroying the foundations of racism. In 1934 Boas addressed a group at Temple Emanu-El, New York, summarizing the latest psychological and anthropological research on race. He then went on to assert that most of the significant research being done in the field "is the product of the effort of Jewish students and scholars." Goldenweiser, in an article in the *Menorah Journal*, claimed that since Jews were separated from the rest of society they not only remained untouched by prevailing prejudice but they were much better able to understand the irrationality of racism than those not alienated from the culture.[54]

A good deal of boasting and self-congratulation undoubtedly found its way in this position. Yet clearly, as Jews, these anthropologists had a special stake in discrediting racist thinking. By the 1920s, racist thinking began to threaten the very existence of German Jewry and anti-Semitic rhetoric, based on a belief in the biological difference of Jews, was being heard in the United States. The same principles which Boas and his students, Herskovits and Goldenweiser, used to discredit anti-black thinking could be employed as effective weapons to combat anti-Jewish sentiment.

JEWISHNESS AND BLACK CIVIL RIGHTS

In the face of the evidence it seems difficult to dismiss the "Jewish" factor in the civil rights movement as purely accidental or random. The sheer number of Jews who flocked to the NAACP and who aided the cause demonstrated that it held a special attraction for Jews. Many of the participants in the early civil rights struggle saw the movement's special lure to Jews. A number of the non-Jews, black and white, who belonged actively to the NAACP were struck by the intensity of the Jewish involvement. Oswald Garrison Villard, for example, paid a lengthy tribute to Jewish participation in the cause in his autobiography:

> Their idealism, their liberalism, their partriotism . . . heartened me in the hardest hours. I have been wholly unable to discover the slightest difference between their support and that of Gentiles, except that they responded more quickly and more generously. I have never appealed to them for aid for the Negro . . . and been rebuffed. And never once have the Jews . . . sought to capitalize upon this.

Black civil rights leaders also were well aware of the Jewish enthusiasm for the crusade. In the early 1930s Walter White searched for at least *one* Gentile to match the Rosenwald offer. He knew that Jews would contribute to the NAACP and he purposely geared many NAACP campaigns to them. In 1934 Roy Wilkins organized a fundraising drive which he "addressed [to] wealthy Hebrew residents of New York . . . They are being appealed to, of course, for Jewish charities and for German refugees, but we might design an appeal pointing out the similarity of the situation of the Negro in this country and the Jew in Germany."

Blacks in the civil rights movement knew that many NAACP leaders were Jews, and that Jews in general sympathized with the Association's cause. William Pickens, for example, did not hesitate to describe Joel Spingarn as a "Jewish gentleman," and DuBois believed that Louis Brandeis' appointment to the Supreme Court would herald a change in court policy on race because "as a Jew [he] knows what it is to be 'despised and rejected of men.'" In 1932 *Crisis* published a biography of physicist Albert Einstein. According to the sketch, Einstein cared about the plight of black people since "he hates prejudice because as a Jew he knows what it means."

Years later, reminiscing about the early civil rights movement, Roy Wilkins was struck by the intensity of the Jewish involvement. He noted:

We've had Rabbi Wise. Rabbi Stephen Wise is one of our supporters and Louis Marshall. We've always had some stalwarts at
work. But, I'll tell you. Jewish people understand this business
of discrimination. They understand very well. They have great
sympathy for those who are fighting it. Jewish people have
another characteristic: they have a tradition of giving to things
in which they believe or wish to support. They don't hang back.
This isn't confined to the NAACP or Urban League or organs of
the AJC or the United Jewish Appeal. They teach their children
to give something. It's part of their religion and a part that
seems pretty well absorbed by them. It is a social response and
responsibility . . . . I have found them to be uniformly generous . . . it has really been a revelation, the way they believe in
giving.

Perhaps DuBois offered the most dramatic opinion by a black leader
on Jews in the civil rights struggle. In an interview with the *Jewish
Daily Forward* DuBois, who had worked so closely with Jews in the
NAACP, told the Yiddish newspaper that "The Negro Race Looks To
Jews For Sympathy and Understanding."[55]

Non-Jews in the movement, blacks and whites, saw that a strong
link bound Jewishness and interest in black civil rights together. They
noted the active participation of the Spingarn brothers, Herbert Lehman, Felix Frankfurter, Louis Marshall, Jacob Billikopf, Stephen
Wise, Lillian Wald, Jacob Schiff and others. Many felt that the Jewish
interest stemmed from a feeling of empathy which existed between
two oppressed minorities. Jews themselves generally stressed empathy
when trying to explain their involvement in the NAACP and civil
rights. A 1926 speech by Louis Marshall to the Association's annual
meeting clearly illustrated this theme. Marshall began by praising the
Association. "It does not crawl. It does not weep. It does not show
weakness. It does not throw itself upon the mercy of the aggressor."
Marshall then went on to draw the historic analogy of suffering.

We [Jews] have had some experience . . . I belong to an ancient
race which has had even longer experience of oppression than
you have. We came out of bondage nearly thirty centuries ago

and we have had trouble ever since. In all parts of the world we have had to fight for our lives, for our existence, for our conscience, for our rights to express ourselves, to believe in God according to our own views. We have been subject to massacres, wholesale massacres, not mere individual lynchings. We have been prevented in some countries from getting an education, from getting any opportunities of earning a livelihood. We were not permitted to own land, or go into the fields of Russia or Poland . . . . We were not permitted to engage in any profession. We had kings and queens . . . against us. But we did not give up. We fought our battles. We went from country to country. The very year that America was discovered, 1492, six hundred thousand of us—all that were in Spain—were driven out . . . . In Russia, in Poland . . . we were subjected to indignities in comparison with which to sit in a "Jim Crow" car is to occupy a palace. Yet we have not given up and we are not going to give up.

Like Marshall, other Jews noted the parallel between the Jewish and black situations. Herskovits taught courses which compared black and Jewish history. Like Marshall, other Jews believed that a history of suffering had predisposed American Jews towards understanding the problems of blacks. Franz Boas believed that direct historic reasons could explain why Jews were in the vanguard of the anthropological attack on racism. The historic bond of suffering which brought Jews into the civil rights movement in all capacities frequently figured as the topic in Jewish religious sermons. A Rabbi Kaplan of Boston noted in a New Year's sermon that he could see a direct link between a past of oppression and "the passion for justice which animates so many leaders among our people . . . . 'I am a Jew' means that our people are sympathetic to the suffering of mankind. Because we have suffered we treat kindly and sympathetically and humanly all the oppressed of every nation."[56]

Both Jews and blacks noted this empathetic attraction to the NAACP. Some Jews also justified their participation in civil rights by reference to traditional Jewish theology, like the Old Testament insistence on social justice. The prophets had thundered against injustice and called upon Jews to set an example to the rest of the world. Amos cried out: "Though you offer me burnt sacrifices . . . I will not accept them; Take away from me the noise of your songs; And let me not hear the melody of your psalteries. But let justice well up as waters and righteousness as a mighty stream." A centuries-old tradition of charity provided yet another motivating factor. Herbert Lehman believed that the Jewish insistence on philanthropy was one of the most significant religious principles that he had learned as a child. That principle, he sensed, remained with him for the rest of his life. It is impossible to measure precisely if theology really made the difference. It is, however, certain that many Jews *believed* it did. [57]

While most Jews attributed their interest in blacks to an empathy which drew together the oppressed, other forces were at work simultaneously. Whether they acknowledged it or not, Jewish participation in the civil rights movement also served them as Jews. In the first place, Jews could often use the crusade for black equality as a forum in which to present their own causes. Louis Marshall, for example, once noted that one reason for his participation in the NAACP legal effort was ". . . in the hope that it may incidentally benefit Jews."

That hope was aptly illustrated in a protracted correspondence between Marshall, DuBois, and James Weldon Johnson in 1924 over the *Crisis'* use of the swastika as a decorative symbol. Like Marshall, a small but growing number of American Jewish leaders had become acutely aware of the dangerous growth of the Nazi Party in Germany by the mid-1920s. Marshall tried to discredit Naziism long before its horrors were known to most. He pleaded with DuBois and Johnson to stop using that symbol, which "no right-thinking Jew can . . . behold . . . without alarm." DuBois hesitated to give in to Marshall's wishes. To him the swastika was merely a beautiful "geometric form." But Marshall, attempting to use his position in the NAACP for the benefit of the Jews, admonished the editor:

Whatever the historical connotation of the symbol may have been, it is now swallowed up in the bitter reality of the present persecution of the Jews. The policies of the Hakenkreuzler, so far as they relate to Jews, are identical with those of the Ku Klux Klan . . . The letters K.K.K. might well be used as a printer's ornament, but these letters, as now employed, would be looked upon as symbolizing support of the accursed doctrines of the organization which has appropriated them . . . . The fact . . .

remains . . . whatever they may have originally betokened, a secondary meaning is now attached to them . . . . That would at least be my interpretation as one of the members of the Board of Directors of the National Association for the Advancement of Colored People.

Marshall and many of the other Jews believed that they could best serve the Jewish cause from their position within the black civil rights movement.[58]

Participation in the struggle for black rights may have been useful to Jews in several other ways. Jews were constantly in search of allies. They occupied, according to their own perceptions, a precarious position in the United States and Europe. Their constant anxiety, while not always conscious, made them believe that they must solidify and ensure their lot in America by building bridges to liberals with power, like those established white Protestants who made up much of the NAACP leadership. The Jews undoubtedly realized that blacks possessed no power, but it was not among them that they were casting about for friends. They were attempting to forge an alliance with the Moorfield Storeys, the Oswald Garrison Villards, the Jane Addams, the Mary White Ovingtons. While they met many of these same people in other progressive reform activities, the black civil rights movement was one more place where they could try to solidify their relations with powerful liberal whites. Jews also used the crusade for black equality as a forum to dispel certain prevalent stereotypes about Jews. For centuries Jews had been plagued by the image of the greedy, clannish miser, always out for himself. In the movement for black legal rights, Jews could prove themselves generous, selfless, tolerant, and humanitarian. These possibilities begin to explain the large Jewish contribution to the movement to grant equal political and legal rights to blacks. In the final analysis, however, the majority of Jews in the NAACP sincerely believed that their commitment to the crusade sprang from a special sympathy and a unique ability to understand the suffering of America's blacks.

NOTES

1. There is no general history of the civil rights movement in the twentieth century. Francis L. Broderick and August Meier, eds., *Negro Protest Thought in the Twentieth*

Century (Indianapolis: Bobbs-Merrill Company, 1965) is a valuable collection of documents. General works which do not detail closely this history of the movement but are of value are John P. Roche, *The Quest for the Dream: The Development of Civil Rights and Human Relations in Modern America* (New York: Macmillan, 1963) and Joseph Robinson, "Organizations Promoting Civil Rights and Liberties," *The Annals of the American Academy of Political and Social Sciences*, ed., Robert Carr (Philadelphia: American Academy of Political and Social Sciences, 1951), pp. 18-26. The best history of the NAACP is Charles F. Kellogg, *N.A.A.C.P.: A History of the National Association for the Advancement of Colored People, 1909-1920* (Baltimore: Johns Hopkins University Press, 1967). The period after 1920 is covered in less adequate studies like Warren D. St. James, *The National Association for the Advancement of Colored People: A Case Study in Pressure Groups* (New York: Exposition Press, 1958); Langston Hughes, *Fight for Freedom: The Story of the N.A.A.C.P.* (New York: W. W. Norton and Company, 1962); and Robert L. Jack, *History of the National Association for the Advancement of Colored People* (Boston: Meador Publishing Company, 1943). Mary White Ovington, a founder of the Association, wrote a very readable account of its early history in *The Walls Came Tumbling Down* (New York: Harcourt, Brace and World, 1947). There are also biographies and autobiographies of W.E.B. DuBois, James Weldon Johnson, Walter White, Oswald Garrison Villard, Moorfield Storey and others. A copy of the "Call" can be found in Kellogg, *N.A.A.C.P.*, pp. 297-299.

2. Emil Hirsch, *My Religion* (New York: Macmillan Company, 1925); David E. Hirsch, *Rabbi Emil G. Hirsch: The Reform Advocate* (Chicago: Whitehall Company, 1968); Robert L. Duffus, *Lillian Wald: Neighbor and Crusader* (New York: Macmillan Company, 1938); Beryl Williams, *Lillian Wald: Angel on Henry Street* (New York: Julian Messner, 1948); Lillian Wald, *The House on Henry Street* (New York: Macmillan Company, 1915); Lillian Wald, *Windows on Henry Street* (Boston: Little, Brown and Company, 1934); Stephen S. Wise, *Challenging Years* (New York: G. P. Putnam's Sons, 1946); "Henry Moskowitz," *Who's Who in American Jewry, 1928* (New York: Jewish Biographical Bureau, 1928), p. 503; Cyrus Adler, *Jacob H. Schiff: His Life and Letters* (Garden City, N.Y.: Doubleday and Company, 1928); Charles Reznikoff, ed., *Louis Marshall, Champion of Liberty: Selected Papers and Addresses*, 2 vols. (Philadelphia: Jewish Publication Society of America, 1957); Morton Rosenstock, *Louis Marshall: Defender of Jewish Rights* (Detroit: Wayne State University Press, 1965); Helen Shirley Thomas, *Felix Frankfurter, Scholar on the Bench* (Baltimore: Johns Hopkins University Press, 1960); Alan Nevins, *Herbert H. Lehman and His Era* (New York: Charles Scribners' Sons, 1963).

3. W.E.B. Du Bois, *Dusk of Dawn: An Essay Toward an Autobiography of a Race Concept* (New York: Harcourt, Brace and World, 1940). B. Joyce Ross, *J. E. Spingarn and the Rise of the N.A.A.C.P.* (New York: Atheneum, 1972) is the only biography of Joel Spingarn. Biographical sketches of him are Oswald Garrison Villard, "Issues and Men," *Nation*, 149 (August 12, 1939): 174; and Lewis Mumford, "Scholar and Gentleman," *Saturday Review of Literature*, 20 (August 5, 1939): 8-9.

4. *Proceedings of the National Negro Conference 1909: New York, May 31 and June 1*, p. 225; *Crisis*, 1 (November 1910): 12; Charles F. Kellogg, *N.A.A.C.P.*, Appendix E, p. 306; NAACP, *Annual Report: 1935* (New York: National Association for the Advancement of Colored People, 1935), p. 12.

5. See Note 2.

6. Stephen S. Wise, *Challenging Years*; Lillian Wald, *The House on Henry Street*; Charles Reznikoff, *Louis Marshall*; B. Joyce Ross, *J. E. Spingarn.*

7. W.E.B. Du Bois, *The Autobiography of W.E.B. DuBois* (New York: International Publishers, 1968), pp. 224-225; Oswald G. Villard to William E. Walling, n.d., [1910], NAACP Admin. Files, C-1; Jacob Schiff to Oswald G. Villard, May 1, 1914, Jacob Schiff Collection, 438, 158; "Contributions to the NAACP," n.d., NAACP Admin. Files, C-1; Julius Rosenwald to William E. Walling, November 16, 1910, NAACP Admin. Files, C-158; "N.A.A.C.P. Annual Budget," March 9, 1928, Copy in Julius Rosenwald Papers, 26; James W. Johnson to Edwin Embree, February 9, 1928, NAACP Admin. Files, C-158; Oswald Villard to Julius Rosenwald, July 21, 1915, NAACP Admin. Files, C-158.

8. Mary Nerney to A. B. Spingarn, February 27, 1914, A. B. Spingarn Collection, 1; A. B. Spingarn to Mary Ovington, October 14, 1920, A. B. Spingarn Collection, 2; Mary Ovington to A. B. Spingarn, October 13, 1920, A. B. Spingarn Collection, 2; Louis Marshall to James Weldon Johnson, August 28, 1924, Louis Marshall Papers, 1596; Walter White to Louis Marshall, April 23, 1925, Louis Marshall Papers, 1597; Julian Mack to Julius Rosenwald, July 19, 1929, NAACP Admin. Files, C-158; Jacob Billikopf to Walter White, January 20, 1936, NAACP Admin. Files, C-159; Felix Frankfurter to Walter White, February 9, 1932, NAACP Admin. Files, C-159.

9. Walter White to A. B. Spingarn, October 26, 1928, A. B. Spingarn Collection, 4; Walter White to A. B. Spingarn, A. B. Spingarn Collection, 6.

10. Julian Mack to Julius Rosenwald, July 19, 1929, NAACP Admin. Files, C-158; Walter White to Louis Marshall, April 23, 1925, Louis Marshall Papers, 1597; Louis Marshall to James W. Johnson, August 28, 1924, Louis Marshall Papers, 1596; Jacob Billikopf to Walter White, January 20, 1936, NAACP Admin. Files, C-159; Walter White to James Marshall, Copy to Jacob Billikopf, September 23, 1930, NAACP Admin. Files, C-296; Jacob Billikopf to James Marshall, September 26, 1930, NAACP Admin. Files, C-296; Walter White to Caroline Flexner, October 3, 1933, NAACP Admin. Files, C-296; Newspaper Clipping, *New York Times*, October 3, 1933; Walter White to Arthur Cohen, October 5, 1933, both in NAACP Admin. Files, C-296; Walter White to Herbert Lehman, December 12, 1934, Herbert Lehman Collection, Corres-Special File; Walter White to A. B. Spingarn, March 25, 1932; William Sidenberg to Walter White, March 28, 1932, both in A. B. Spingarn Collection, 5.

11. James Weldon Johnson to Edwin Embree, February 9, 1928; Oswald Garrison Villard to Julius Rosenwald, July 21, 1915, NAACP, Admin. Files, C-158.

12. James Marshall to Walter White, February 4, 1930, NAACP Admin. Files, C-69; Pamphlet, "To Commemorate and Carry on the Work of Moorfield Storey and Louis Marshall, N.A.A.C.P., 1930," Copy in A. B. Spingarn Collection, 5; Walter White to Mortimer Schiff, January 30, 1930; Walter White to Paul Baerwald, March 11, 1930, both in NAACP Admin. Files, C-15; Walter White to Paul Baerwald, March 18, 1930, A. B. Spingarn Collection, 4.

13. Jacob Billikopf to Walter White, November 25, 1929, NAACP, Admin. Files, C-63; Walter White to A. B. Spingarn, February 3, 1930, A. B. Spingarn Collection, 4; NAACP Press Bulletin, March 25, 1930, NAACP Admin. Files, C-158; *New York Times*, March 10, 1930, p. 4; *N.A.A.C.P.: Twenty-First Annual Report*, 1930, p. 55; William Rosenwald to Herbert Lehman, June 13, 1933, Herbert Lehman Papers,

Corres-Gen; William Rosenwald to Walter White, May 20, 1933, NAACP Admin. Files, C-74; *Jewish Tribune and Hebrew Standard,* June 27, 1930, p. 10.

14. Walter White to Harry Davis, February 5, 1930; Walter White to Isador Martin, February 21, 1930; Henry Patterson to Walter White, March 17, 1930; Henry Patterson to Walter White, April 3, 1930, all in NAACP Admin. Files, C-158.

15. The standard discussion of civil rights activities in the courts is Milton R. Konvitz, *A Century of Civil Rights* (New York: Columbia University Press, 1961), and he does not discuss at all the NAACP cases of the 1920s and 1930s. Loren Miller, *The Peti-* Pantheon Books, 1966) is a good and detailed analysis; Jack Greenberg, *Race Relations and American Law* (New York: Columbia University Press, 1959); Bernard H. Nelson, *The Fourteenth Amendment and the Negro Since 1920* (Washington, D.C.: Catholic University of American Press, 1946); Tom C. Clark and Philip Perlman, *Prejudice and Property: An Historic Brief Against Racial Covenants* (Washington, D.C.: Public Affairs Press, 1948) are also useful. See Oswald G. Villard to J. E. Spingarn, October 7, 1910, J. E. Spingarn Papers. This letter was sent by Villard thanking Spingarn for a $100 donation and on it was penciled in "JES's first interest in NAACP" in Amy Spingarn's handwriting; J. E. Spingarn to Oswald Villard, October 19, 1910, J. E. Spingarn Papers.

16. Blacks occasionally wrote to Arthur Spingarn concerning legal questions. Their inquiries were answered quickly. For example see Hallie Parker to A. B. Spingarn, September 30, 1915; *Louisville Courier Journal,* July 6, 1914; *Buchanan v. Warley,* 245 U.S. *60* (1917); *Guinn v. United States,* 238, U.S. *347* (1915).

17. Board Minutes, NAACP, August 4, 1914; September 13, 1915; February 13, 1917.

18. Morton Rosenstock, *Louis Marshall, Defender of Jewish Rights,* p. 143; Charles Reznikoff, *Louis Marshall,* p. 255; Leonard Dinnerstein, *The Leo Frank Case*; Herbert Seligmann to Louis Marshall, October 23, 1920, Louis Marshall Papers, 1620; Arthur Waskow, *From Race Riot to Sit-In: 1919 and the 1960's* (Garden City, N.Y.: Doubleday and Company, 1966), pp. 121-174; Louis Marshall to Walter White, March 19, 1923, NAACP, Admin. Files, C-69; quoted in Walter White, *A Man Called White* (New York: Viking Press, 1948), p. 53; A. B. Spingarn to Mary Ovington, October 24, 1923, A. B. Spingarn Papers, 2.

19. *Corrigan v. Buckley,* 299 Fed., *899; Corrigan v. Buckley,* 271 U.S. *323; Nixon v. Herndon,* 273 U.S. *536;* J. W. Johnson to A. B. Spingarn, September 16, 1924, NAACP Legal Files, D-98; A. B. Spingarn to J. W. Johnson, September 17, 1924, NAACP Legal Files, D-98; NAACP Press Bulletin, October 31, 1924; Louis Marshall to James W. Johnson, November 10, 1924, Louis Marshall Papers, 1596; J. W. Johnson to L. Marshall, September 24, 1924, NAACP Legal Files, C-98; Marshall to Julius Rosenwald, December 4, 1925, Rosenwald Papers, 26, 13; quoted in Morton Rosenstock, *Louis Marshall,* p. 143; NAACP Press Bulletin January 8, 1926.

20. Herbert J. Seligmann, "The Negro's Influence as a Voter," *Current History,* 28 (May 1928): 230-231; *Crisis,* 34 (July 1927): 224; James W. Johnson to James Cobb, January 8, 1927; J. W. Johnson to A. B. Spingarn, January 16, 1927, both in NAACP Legal Files, D-64; *Nixon v. Condon,* 286 U.S. *73.*

21. Quoted in Charles Reznikoff, *Louis Marshall,* p. xxxix; for example, see the *American Israelite,* January 21, 1926, p. 7; *B'nai Brith Magazine,* 44 (October 1929):

10; Cyrus Adler, "Louis Marshall: A Biographical Sketch," *American Jewish Yearbook, 1930-1931*; Cyrus Adler, *Louis Marshall: A Biographical Sketch* (New York: American Jewish Committee, 1931); Morton Rosenstock, *Louis Marshall*, p. 274.

22. Walter White to Felix Frankfurter, November 6, 1929, Walter White to Felix Frankfurter, January 13, 1932, Felix Frankfurter Collection, 11; cited in Robert L. Zangrando, "The Efforts of the National Association for the Advancement of Colored People to Secure Passage of a Federal Anti-Lynching Law, 1920-1940," (Ph.D. dissertation, University of Pennsylvania, 1963); John Hope Franklin, *From Slavery to Freedom* (New York: Alfred A. Knopf, 1947), p. 430; Walter White, *A Man Called White* (New York: Viking Press, 1948), p. 165.

23. W.E.B. DuBois, *Autobiography*, pp. 263-264; Henry Moskowitz to J. E. Spingarn, August 24, 1912, Spingarn Papers; NAACP Press Release, n.d. [1936], NAACP Admin. Files, C-392.

24. W.E.B. DuBois, *Dusk of Dawn*, p. 256; Poughkeepsie *Sunday Courier*, August 15, 1917; December 16, 1917, Clippings in Spingarn Papers; W.E.B. DuBois, *Autobiography*, pp. 266-268; *Washington Bee*, March 24, 1917, p. 1; F. D. Roosevelt to the Adjutant-General of the Army, March 13, 1917, copy in Spingarn Papers.

25. *Crisis*, 12 (June 1916): 87; Board Minutes, NAACP, September 13, 1915; Jacob Schiff to Oswald G. Villard, February 25, 1915, Jacob Schiff Collection, 445; Stephen Wise, *Challenging Years*, p. 117.

26. Mary C. Nerney to board members, March 18, 1915, in Board Minutes, NAACP, March 23, 1915; *Crisis*, 10 (May 1915): 33; Sherwood Ross, *Gruening of Alaska* (New York: Best Books, 1968), pp. 39-40; *Fighting a Vicious Film: Protest Against the "Birth of a Nation"* (Boston: Boston Branch, NAACP, 1915).

27. Louis Marshall to Reed Smoot, December 20, 1916, Marshall-Immigration Collection, 3; James Weldon Johnson to Louis Marshall, December 31, 1925, Louis Marshall Papers, 81; Louis Marshall to J. W. Johnson, January 2, 1926, Louis Marshall Papers, 1598; Stephen Wise, *Challenging Years*, pp. 172-173; Charles Kellogg, *N.A.A.C.P.*, p. 179.

28. *Jewish Tribune*, 40 (December 1, 1922): 15; *American Israelite*, (May 25, 1922), p. 4.

29. "Alphabetical List of Witnesses to Appear at Hearings on the Costigan-Wagner Anti-Lynching Bill . . . ," February 20-21, 1934, in A. B. Spingarn Collection, 27; Max Lowenthal, A. B. Spingarn Collection, 27; Social Justice Commission of the Central Conference of American Rabbis to Herbert Lehman, November 24, 1932, Herbert Lehman Collection, Gov. Micro, 66, M#.

30. Minutes, National Negro Conference, December 13, 1909, in Board Minutes, NAACP: Minutes, National Negro Conference, February 14, 1910 in Board Minutes, NAACP; "Program National Negro Committee, Second Annual Conference," New York, May 12-14, 1910; *New York Age*, May 10, 1910, p. 8; Charles F. Kellogg, NAACP, p. 56.

31. "Program of the Fifth Annual Conference, April 23-25, 1913,"; "Program of the Thirteenth Annual Conference, June 18-23, 1922"; "Program of the Nineteenth Annual Conference, June 27-July 3, 1928"; A. B. Spingarn Collection, 55.

32. Walter White to Herbert Lehman, May 7, 1930, Lehman Collection, Lt. Gov. Micro.; "Program National Conference on Lynching, May 16, 1919," Lillian Wald

Papers; Memorandum to A. B. Spingarn, March, 1921, A. B. Spingarn Collection, 27; Charles E. Kellogg, *N.A.A.C.P.*, pp. 159-160.

33. W.E.B. DuBois, *Dusk of Dawn*, p. 230; "Felix Adler," in Harris E. Starr, ed., *Dictionary of American Biography, Supplement One*, Vol. 21, pp. 113-114; *Crisis*, 17 (February 1919): 173; Meyer Weinberg, *W.E.B. DuBois: A Reader* (New York: Harper and Row, 1970), p. 385; *Crisis*, 10 (May 1915): 9.

34. *Crisis*, 9 (April 1915): 286; W.E.B. DuBois, *Dusk of Dawn*, pp. 238-239; John W. Day to J. E. Spingarn, January 24, 1914, William M. Trotter to Spingarn, January 28, 1914, Spingarn Collection; *Washington Bee*, January 24, 1914, p. 3; *New York Age*, February 26, 1914; Mary White Ovington, *The Walls Came Tumbling Down*, p. xvi.

35. Board Minutes, NAACP, April 14, 1919, December 8, 1919; NAACP, *Tenth Annual Report*, 1919, p. 43; *City Club Bulletin*, 7 (February 5, 1914): 33-40; NAACP, *Twenty-Third Annual Report*, 1932, p. 45; Board Minutes, NAACP, March 11, 1913, October 7, 1913; Ninth Annual Report: 1918, p. 69; Mary Ovington, *The Walls Came Tumbling Down*, pp. 117-118; Arthur Spingarn to Walter White, August 21, 1939, NAACP Admin. Files, Uncatalogued Material.

36. Oswald Villard to Group of Clergymen, n.d. [1912], Copy, NAACP Admin. Files, C-1; Carl Hermann Voss, *Rabbi and Minister: The Friendship of Stephen S. Wise and John Haynes Holmes* (Cleveland: World Publishing Company, 1964), p. 256; Note from Alexander A. Lyons, February 7, 1913, NAACP, Admin. Files, C-1; Alexander Lyons to A. W. Hunter, August 20, 1920, NAACP Branch Files, G-138; Alexander Lyons to Walter White, December 26, 1934, NAACP, Admin. Files, C-173; Stephen Wise to James W. Johnson, March 9, 1919, NAACP, Admin. Files, C-172; "List of Speakers," n.d. [1919], NAACP, Admin. Files, C-172; "Speakers Bureau Form," March 1919, filled out by Isaac Rypins, Eli Mayer; Alexander Lyons to Mary Ovington, August, 1919, NAACP, Admin. Files, C-172; "Speakers Bureau Form," May 17, 1919, filled out by Rudolph I. Coffee, NAACP, Admin. Files, C-172; Max Heller to J. W. Johnson, May 21, 1919, NAACP, Admin. Files, C-172; "General Report of Harlem Office," March 1923-January, 1924, NAACP, Branch Files, G-139; Mitchell Fisher to James W. Johnson, February 22, 1929, NAACP, Admin. Files, C-172; "Quarter Century Fund Speakers Bureau," n.d. [1934], NAACP, Admin. Files, C-173; Walter White to A. B. Spingarn, January 24, 1935, A. B. Spingarn Collection, 7.

37. Samuel Leff to NAACP Speakers Bureau, August 18, 1922, NAACP, Admin. Files, C-172; William Pickens to A. B. Spingarn, January 2, 1921, A. B. Spingarn Collection, 2; NAACP, *Annual Report: 1929*, p. 10; NAACP, *Annual Report:* 1930, p. 11; *Opportunity*, 6 (March 1929): 93; Julian Greifer to NAACP, December 7, 1934, NAACP, Admin. Files, C-173; George Friedman to Speakers Bureau, January 18, 1934; Mrs. Ernest Lillienthal to Johnson, November 3, 1934, both in NAACP, Admin. Files, C-173; Maurice Bloom to Robert Bagnall, February 1, 1929; Maurice Bloom to Robert Bagnall, February 6, 1929; S. C. Schulenski to J. W. Johnson, November 24, 1930; James W. Johnson to W.E.B. DuBois, NAACP, Admin. Files, C-172; *Crisis*, 26 (May 1923): 34.

38. James W. Johnson, *Along This Way* (New York: DeCapo Press, 1933), pp. 326-327; Herbert J. Seligmann, "The Negro Protest Against Ghetto Conditions," *Current History*, 25 (March 1927): 831-833; "Twenty Years of Negro Progress," *Current History*, 29 (January 1929): 614-621; "Letter to the Editor," *Forum* 76 (December 1931):

xxiv; "Protecting Southern Womanhood," *Nation*, 108 (June 14, 1919): 938-939; "What Is Behind the Negro Uprisings?" *Current Opinion*, 67 (September 1919): 154-155; "The Menace of Race Hatred," *Harper's Magazine*, 140 (March 1920): 537-543; "Slavery in Georgia," *The Nation*, 112 (April 20, 1921): 591; *The Negro Faces America* (New York: Harper and Brothers, 1920); *Race Against Man* (New York: G. P. Putnam's Sons, 1939).

39. Board Minutes, NAACP, February 6, 1912; Martha Gruening, "Democratic Massacres in East St. Louis," *Pearson's Magazine*, 38 (September 1917): 106-108; Board Minutes, NAACP, September 17, 1917; Mary Ovington, *The Walls Came Tumbling Down*, pp. 113-114; *Crisis*, 3 (March 1912): 95-96; *Crisis*, 4 (June 1912): 77.

40. Board Minutes, NAACP, November 12, 1917, December 10, 1917.

41. Sherwood Ross, *Gruening of Alaska* (New York: Best Books, 1968), pp. 34-35.

42. *Crisis*, 9 (December 1914): 81.

43. James W. Johnson to Louis Marshall, October 21, 1927, Louis Marshall Papers, 121; Herbert J. Seligmann to Jacob Billikopf, March 17, 1931, NAACP, Admin. Files, C-63.

44. Herbert Seligmann, *Race Against Man*, p. v. For early histories of anthropology and race theory see John S. Haller, *Outcasts from Evolution: Scientific Attitudes of Racial Inferiority, 1859-1900* (Urbana: University of Illinois Press, 1971); Jacques Barzun, *Race: A Study in Modern Superstition* (New York: Harcourt Brace and Company, 1937); Thomas Gossett, *Race: The History of an Idea in America* (Dallas: Southern Methodist University Press, 1963); Idus A. Newby, *Jim Crow's Defense: Anti-Negro Thought in America, 1900-1930* (Baton Rouge: Louisiana State University Press, 1965); Marvin Harris, *The Rise of Anthropological Theory: A History of Theories of Culture* (New York: Thomas Y. Crowell, 1968); Louis L. Snyder, *Race: A History of Modern Ethnic Theories* (New York: Longmans, Green, and Company, 1939); George W. Stocking, *Race, Culture, and Evolution* (New York: Free Press, 1968); Abram Kardiner and Edward Preble, *They Studied Man* (Cleveland: World Publishing Company, 1961); Margaret Mead and Ruth Bunzel, eds. *The Golden Age of American Anthropology* (New York: George Braziller, 1960); Thomas Gossett, *Race*, p. 410; Jacques Barzun, *Race*, p. 51; Thomas Gossett, *Race*, p. 418; George M. Frederickson, *The Black Image in the White Mind: The Debate on Afro-American Character and Destiny, 1817-1914* (New York: Harper and Row, 1971), p. 330.

45. Thomas Gossett, *Race*, p. 418.

46. For biographies of Boas see Abraham Kardiner and Edward Preble, *They Studied Man*, pp. 232-283; George Stocking, *Race, Culture, and Evolution*, pp. 135-160; Melville Herskovits, *Franz Boas: The Science of Man in the Making* (New York: Charles Scribner's Sons, 1953); A. L. Kroeber and others, *Franz Boas; 1858-1942* (Memoir Series, No. 61, American Anthropological Association, 1943).

47. Boas' full bibliography contains over 625 entries. A complete listing can be found in *The American Anthropologist*, 45 (May 1943). Only a small sample of his works were considered here and those chosen were mostly those dealing with race, many of which were published in popular magazines. Franz Boas, *Primitive Art* (Oslo: Instituttet for Sammenlignende Kulturforskning, Series B, 1927); "What Is a Race?" *Nation*, 120 (January 28, 1925): 89-91; "What the Negro Has Done in Africa," *The Ethical Record*, 5 (March 1904): 106-109; "The Negroes' Past," *Commencement Address at*

Atlanta University, May 31, 1906 (Atlanta University, Leaflet 19); "Aryan and Non-Aryan, *American Mercury*, 32 (September 1934): 163-193; "Race Prejudice from the Scientist's Angle," *Forum*, 98 (August 1937): 90-94; "The Problem of the American Negro," *Yale Review*, 10 (January 1921): 384-395; "Race and Progress," *Science*, 74 (July 3, 1931): 1-8; "Are the Jews a Race?" *The World Tomorrow*, 24 (January 1923): 193-198; *Anthropology and Modern Life* (New York: W. W. Norton and Company, 1928); *Anthropology* (New York: Columbia University Lectures on Science, Philosophy and Art, 1907-1908, No. 10); *The Mind of Primitive Man* (New York: Macmillan Company, 1911); *Race and Democratic Society: Collected Addresses and Papers for Lay Audiences* (New York: J. J. Augustin, 1945); "The Negro and the Demands of Modern Life," *Charities*, 15 (October 1905): 85-88; Foreward to Mary White Ovington, *Half a Man: The Status of the Negro in New York* (New York: Longmans, Green and Company, 1911).

48. *New York Age*, May 19, 1910; *Opportunity*, 1 (February 1923): 32; Herbert Seligmann to F. Boas, June 16, 1919, NAACP, Admin. Files, C-401; "Report of Meeting With Judeans, Temple Emanu-El," March 4, 1934, American Jewish Committee Files, Boas Folder; Franz Boas, *Changes in Bodily Forms of Descendants of Immigrants*, in *Reports of the Immigration Commission* (61 Cong. 2 Sess., Senate Document No. 208, Washington, 1911), pp. 2-7; George Stocking, *Race, Culture and Evolution*, p. 300.

49. "Report of the Meeting of the Harlem Branch," October 7, 1923, NAACP, Branch Files, G-139; Meyer Weinberg, ed., *W.E.B. DuBois: A Reader* (New York: Harper and Row, 1970), p. 245; *Opportunity*, 4 (October 1926): 331; *Chicago Hebrew Observer*, 20 (May 1, 1930): 57, 83-84.

50. The Herskovits papers are unfortunately not available to scholars yet, and he has not received much secondary attention. For a complete bibliography of Herskovits see *American Anthropologist*, 46 (February 1964): 83-109; Norman E. Whitten and John F. Szwed, *Afro-American Anthropology: Contemporary Perspectives* (New York: Free Press, 1970), pp. 23-27; Melville Herskovits, "What Is a Race?" *American Mercury*, 2 (June 1924): 207-210; "The Racial Hysteria," *Opportunity*, 2 (June 1924): 166-168; "A Preliminary Consideration of the Culture Areas of Africa," *American Anthropologist*, 26 (January 1924): 50-63; "Some Observation of the Growth of Colored Boys," *American Journal of Physical Anthropology*, 7 (October 1924): 204-208; "Preliminary Observations in a Study of Negro-White Crossings," *Opportunity*, 3 (March 1925): 69-73; "The Negro's Americanism," in Alain Locke, *The New Negro* (New York: A. and C. Boni, 1925); "The American Negro Is Evolving a New Physical Type," *Current History*, 24 (September 1926): 898-903; "Does the Negro Know His Father: A Study in Negro Genealogies," *Opportunity*, 4 (October 1926): 291-298; "Some Physical Characteristics of the American Negro Population," *Social Forces*, 6 (September 1927): 93-98; "The Art of the Congo," *Opportunity*, 5 (May 1927): 135-136; "Anthropology and Ethnology During 1926," *Opportunity*, 5 (January 1927): 12-13; "Acculturation and the American Negro," *Southwest Political and Social Science Quarterly*, 8 (December 1927): 211-224; "Race Relations in the United States, 1928," *American Journal of Sociology*, 34 (July 1928): 1129-1139; "Wisdom from Africa," *Crisis*, 36 (September 1929): 306-307; "Bush-Negro Art," *The Arts*, 18 (October 1930): 25-37; "Race Relations, 1931," *American Journal of Sociology*, 37 (May 1932): 976-982; "A Footnote to

the History of Negro Slaving," *Opportunity*, 11 (June 1933): 178-181; "What Has Africa Given America?" *The New Republic*, 84 (September 4, 1935): 92-94; *The American Negro: A Study in Racial Crossing* (New York: Alfred A. Knopf, 1928); *The Negro and the Intelligence Test* (Hanover, N.H.: Sociological Press, 1928); *The Anthropometry of the American Negro* (New York: Columbia University Press, 1930).

51. NAACP, *Annual Conference, June 23, 1922*, Program in A. B. Spingarn Collection, 2; Herbert Seligmann, *The Negro Faces America*.

52. Wilson D. Wallis, "Alexander A. Goldenweiser," *American Anthropologist*, 43 (April-June 1941): 250-255; Ruth Bunzel and Margaret Mead, *The Golden Age of American Anthropology*; David H. French, "Goldenweiser, Alexander A.," *International Encyclopedia of the Social Sciences*, 6th ed. (New York: Macmillan, 1968), pp. 196-197; Alexander Goldenweiser, "Concerning Racial Differences," *Menorah Journal*, 8 (October 1922): 309-316; "Racial Theory and the Negro," *Opportunity*, 13 (May 1922): 229-231; "Some Problems of Race and Culture in the United States," *Proceedings of the National Conference of Social Work*, 1922, p. 318; "Are the Races Potentially Equal," *Proceedings of American Philosophical Society*, 63 (1924): 215-221.

53. *Opportunity*, 11 (February 1933): 57; James W. Johnson to Editor, *Post-Standard*, October 20, 1924, NAACP Admin. Files, C-165; H. Seligmann, *The Negro Faces America*; H. Seligmann, *Race Against Man*; *Opportunity*, 3 (February-March 1925): 37-40, 84-85; Walter Wilson, ed., *The Selected Writings of W.E.B. DuBois* (New York: New American Library, 1970), p. 338; *Opportunity*, 4 (May 1926): 142; *Opportunity*, 9 (July 1931): 203.

54. "Memorandum of Talk with Professor Franz Boas by Harry Schneiderman," June 22, 1933, American Jewish Committee, Boas Folder; *Menorah Journal*, 8 (October 1922): 309-316.

55. Oswald G. Villard, *Fighting Years: Memoirs of a Liberal Editor* (New York: Harcourt, Brace and Company, 1939), p. 529; Walter White to A. B. Spingarn, October 11, 1932, A. B. Spingarn Collection, 6; Roy Wilkins to Walter White, September 5, 1934, NAACP Admin. Files, B-170; *Crisis*, 11 (March 1918): 43, 41 (February 1932): 45, 10 (August 1915): 177, 10 (October 1915): 276-278; "Program, National Negro Committee, Second Annual Conference," New York, May 12-14, 1910; NAACP, Annual Report, 1933, p. 10; *Opportunity*, 15 (October 1938), reprint in Herbert Lehman Papers; "Roy Wilkins-June 4, 1957," Lehman Oral History Project: Memoirs by Associates, Part One, pp. 19-20; *Jewish Daily Forward*, August 5, 1923, p. 3.

56. James W. Johnson to Louis Marshall, December 1, 1926, Louis Marshall Papers, 83; Quoted in *Crisis*, 33 (February 1927): 196-197. The following are a few sermons which referred to the Jewish interest in black civil rights: Stephen Wise, "Can American Endure the K.K.K.?" Stephen Wise Papers, 49; Stephen Wise, "Gaudium Certaminis," n.d. Stephen Wise Papers, 7 "What Price Freedom, or Is Liberty Declining?" *A Set of Holiday Sermons: 5690-1929* (Cincinnati: Tract Publishing Company, 1929); Abraham Feldman, *Lights and Shadows: Eight Addresses* (Hartford: 1928); Abraham Feldman, *Religion in Action: Twelve Discourses* (Philadelphia: Oscar Konower, 1923); Henry Berkowitz, "Quenching the Fires of Hate," *A Set of Holiday Sermons* (Cincinnati: Tract Publishing Company, 1922); Jacob H. Kaplan, "I Am a Jew: A Sermon for the Eve of the New Year," *A Set of Holiday Sermons: 5691-1934* (Cincinnati: Tract Publishing Company, 1934), p. 5.

57. Herbert H. Lehman Oral History Project, Part I, p. 4.

58. James W. Johnson to Louis Marshall, August 21, 1924; Louis Marshall to W.E.B. DuBois, August 27, 1924; Louis Marshall to W.E.B. DuBois, September 4, 1924, Louis Marshall Papers, 1596.

chapter 5

"TO SERVE AT THE COMMON ALTAR":
JEWS AND BLACK PHILANTHROPY

Prominent American Jews lent their support—financial and moral—to dozens of philanthropic projects designed to alleviate the dismal economic and social hardships experienced by blacks in the early decades of the twentieth century. Just as the motivation for Jewish activism in the black civil rights movement stemmed in part from preoccupations peculiar to American Jews, so Jewish philanthropists consciously and unconsciously worked for blacks out of peculiarly Jewish motives. Jewish philanthropists like Julius Rosenwald, Jacob Schiff, and Felix Warburg contributed to dozens of black elementary and vocational schools, institutions of higher and professional education, hospitals, orphanages, libraries, settlement houses, and social clubs. Furthermore, many Jewish social workers established and staffed settlement houses in the newly developing black ghettos of northern cities, especially in New York and Chicago. Still other Jews joined, funded, and supported the National Urban League, founded in 1911 to wage "a definite, thorough, and continuous campaign to bring about cooperation among the various social agencies working with Negroes."[1]

Jewish philanthropists were not the only whites concerned with black education and health care, nor did they stand alone in their commitment to ameliorating the economic and social environment which trapped most American blacks. Black causes had, in fact, been a major object of northern white philanthropy since the pre-Civil War era, when Christian groups donated liberally to the education of slaves. This was sustained through the war and Reconstruction, and northern missionaries from various Protestant denominations went south to render educational, medical, and spiritual services to the newly emancipated blacks. Even in the early decades of the twentieth century, when most northern whites and the federal government had lost interest in the plight of black people, numerous white philanthropists retained a lively concern for black education and health care in the South. John D. Rockefeller, Andrew Carnegie, and John F. Slater donated millions to black projects of various kinds.[2]

The age of massive industrial expansion of the late nineteenth and early twentieth century, which saw the rise of the "robber barons" and the multi-millionaire industrialists, coincided with the age of charitable and philanthropic institutionalization. Giving charity to the poor moved from local, disorganized efforts into a highly rationalized procedure, culminating in the growth of the great philanthropic funds and foundations. Charitable trusts had existed since the late nineteenth century for specific purposes. However, in the early twentieth century, dozens of huge foundations like the General Education Board (1902), the Russell Sage Foundation (1907), the Carnegie Corporation of New York (1911), and the Rockefeller Foundation (1913) began to give money to a multitude of projects and programs. Black causes, especially black education, benefited from the endeavors of these institutions.[3]

Jewish philanthropic activities for blacks paralleled the general drift of American philanthropy in the early twentieth century which accelerated support for black institutions. However, a uniquely Jewish note distinguished the millions given by Julius Rosenwald, Jacob Schiff, Felix Warburg and others. Jews clung to a long and intense philanthropic tradition which sprang from both theological roots and from the separateness of Jewish communities in pre-Emancipation Europe. In America, the tradition of giving continued with a new dimension. Many wealthy, Americanized Jews sought to elevate the standard of living of the floods of eastern European Jews as a way to improve their own status in America. While they were sincerely disturbed by the grinding poverty of their coreligionists, they also believed that by raising the level of some Jews, all members of the group would benefit. Jewish philanthropy served as a double-edged sword, growing out of a combination of motives. A mixture of philanthropic motives also underlay the massive gifts given by Jews to black projects, especially educational ones.

BLACK EDUCATION AND JEWISH PHILANTHROPY

No type of black institution merited as much interest and support from Jews as did black education. Blacks themselves had committed vast resources and efforts in this area. Because learning had been almost universally denied to slaves and because American values stressed education as an avenue out of poverty, freed black slaves after the Civil War rushed to the newly created schools staffed by the Freedmen's Bureau and by northern missionaries and teachers. By 1865 over 60 percent of Louisiana's black children between five and twelve were enrolled in school. Five years later the state of Georgia spent over a million dollars a year on black schooling. With the end of Reconstruction in the 1870s, real hope for educational opportunities for blacks faded. When per capita expenditures for white students rose in the late nineteenth century, for blacks they remained frozen or even fell. White teachers' salaries went up in several southern states; black teachers received no increases.[4]

What black educational opportunities existed were limited to elementary and vocational training schools with only a handful of Negro colleges offering higher degrees. This emphasis on rudimentary education found its most articulate mouthpiece in the late nineteenth and early twentieth centuries in Booker T. Washington. The Tuskegeean's stress on basic and technical education, based on the belief that to give black children of the South "mere book education . . . would be . . . a waste of time," won him the respect of white southerners, white northerners, and the masses of southern blacks. Yet in spite of his personal popularity and his political influence, southern black education in 1900 was dismal, characterized by poor facilities, underpaid staffs, and almost no opportunities beyond the early grades. This depressed state of black education brought action from many of the new foundations financed by Protestant millionaires. It also propelled Jewish philanthropists to give.[5]

Julius Rosenwald was perhaps the major white philanthropist to join the crusade for black education. Personally, Rosenwald was closer to Booker T. Washington than any of the others who gave to black education. Rosenwald's parents, German-Jewish immigrants, had risen from poverty to modest comfort in Springfield, Illinois, where he was born in 1862. Although Rosenwald received little formal education, by the 1890s he had attained success in an uncle's clothing firm. He wanted to get rich and set for himself some specific goals. He confided once to a friend that "the aim of my life is to have an income of fifteen thousand dollars a year—five thousand to be used for my personal expenses, five thousand to be laid aside and five thousand to go to charity." Julius Rosenwald achieved that goal handily. He became president of Sears, Roebuck and Company, earning profits spiralling into the millions.

He also met his philanthropic goal many times over, giving generously to Jewish charities in Chicago, in other American Jewish communities, in Europe, and in Palestine. He contributed over $5 million alone to help establish Jewish agricultural colonies in Siberia and donated vast amounts to the arts, museums, libraries, research agencies, and hospitals. In fact, Rosenwald's total philanthropic commitment has been estimated at between $60 million and $70 million.

Rosenwald did not just give away money but espoused a definite philanthropic philosophy. He believed that each generation must fund those institutions that *it* considered most vital. He therefore opposed perpetual endowments which he believed led to bureaucracy and often supported institutions beyond their usefulness. He noted that "more good can be accomplished by expending funds as trustees find opportunities for constructive work than by storing up large sums of money for long periods of time."

One cause which Julius Rosenwald believed that he and his generation ought to finance was black education. While there is no evidence as to exactly when Rosenwald first became interested in black problems, he did grow up in Springfield and greatly admired Lincoln. Early in the twentieth century a cousin discussed the racial situation with him, impressing upon him the gravity of the problems. Rosenwald frequently noted that Booker Washington's autobiography, *Up from Slavery* (1901), stirred him more profoundly than any book he had ever read. Rosenwald's relationship with the Alabama educator began a decade later when the two met in Chicago and Rosenwald made his first donation to Tuskegee.[6]

Rosenwald was impressed with Washington but admired even more the people Washington served, the "people who are compelled to make such sacrifices for the sake of an education for themselves and their children." He heartily subscribed to Washington's philosophy of self-help for blacks, since he believed firmly that charity would never ameliorate black poverty. Training, however, could. His analysis of the race situation was quite simple, admitting that he was

> not a politician and the politics of the Negro question does not interest me. Neither do I profess to be a trained sociologist. But it does not need a special training nor peculiar political sagacity to discern the fact that a very real problem exists in this great mass of uneducated Negroes, barely above the peon class and for whose training no adequate provision has been made by the communities in which they live.

Because southern municipalities and states refused to provide adequate education for blacks, Rosenwald made it a principle never to donate to southern white schools. In a letter justifying his refusal to give to the School for Organic Education in Fairhope, Alabama, he noted, "I am of necessity compelled to confine myself to a given policy and while I am interested in Southern Schools, my activity is confined almost entirely to work for the colored people—not because the whites are not equally deserving, but they already get so much larger share of the money that is expended for school purposes in proportion to the population, and in addition have many other advantages which blacks do not have."[7]

Julius Rosenwald certainly emerged as the most important Jewish—and white—patron of southern black education, but he was not alone. Jacob Schiff, Felix and Paul Warburg, Julian Mack, and Jacob Billikopf played important roles in funding black elementary education and also vocational, higher, and professional learning. All were initially drawn to black projects because of Washington, either after reading about him or meeting him. All of these philanthropists remained steadfastly loyal to Booker T. Washington, accepting and internalizing his philosophy of education. As a result, Jews gave more money to Tuskegee than to any other black school and served on Tuskegee's board of directors from 1912.

Jacob Schiff's interest in Washington and Tuskegee was revealed in 1899 when the Jewish millionaire appeared at a fund-raising rally for Tuskegee at Madison Square Garden. By 1909 Schiff felt close

enough to Washington to write and complain, "I am receiving constant appeals from educational institutions for colored people in the
South, so that I feel entirely at a loss to know where to contribute
properly and justly." Schiff then suggested that he "place annually a
given amount at your disposal, of which a part might go to Tuskegee
and the balance be appropriated toward other Southern educational
institutions for colored people such as under your advice may be entitled to support from me." Such an arrangement suited Washington's needs and put even more power in his hands. From 1909 until his
death in 1915 Washington annually sent Schiff lists of vocational and
training schools he deemed worthy of support. Whenever Schiff received appeals from unfamiliar schools, he always sought and followed Washington's advice. He discussed his friends' as well as his
own donations at some length with the Tuskegeean.[8]

Schiff and Felix Warburg gave primarily to those black educational
projects which reflected Booker Washington's philosophy that "the
worth of work with the hands is an uplifting power in real education."
Schiff gave almost exclusively to vocational schools, partly because he
believed that governments should shoulder the responsibility of elementary education. If this approach ignored the reality that southern
states and municipalities would not provide decent basic education
for blacks, it also echoed the philosophy of Tuskegee that blacks
ought to first develop those critical skills which would make them crucial to the southern economy.

Felix Warburg, also a devotee of Washington's, gave freely to
Tuskegee and other training institutions. He declared in 1919, "I continue to believe that Booker Washington's solution is the correct one,
namely: help the colored people to help themselves. He put the
emphasis on their duties instead of their rights and perhaps that
would be a good thing for all of us to do."[9] These Jewish philanthropists were not unique among whites in their loyalty to Booker Washington. Rockefeller and Carnegie worked through Washington almost exclusively when donating money to black causes. William
Henry Baldwin, a northern white philanthropist who was to inspire a
group of blacks and whites to found the Urban League, once characterized his feelings towards the Tuskegeean: "I almost worship this
man." More than expressing mere admiration for the Tuskegee educator, Baldwin wholeheartedly subscribed to Washington's prescrip-

tion that blacks ought to "avoid social questions; leave politics alone; continue to be patient; live moral lives; live simply; learn to work." [10] Jewish philanthropists, like most northern white elites, were inspired by the example of Tuskegee and worked through Booker Washington when giving to southern black education. Jewish motives for philanthropic work differed from those of Protestants like Rockefeller, Carnegie or Baldwin, yet their tone and their direction all upheld the Washington approach.

The amounts given by Jewish philanthropists to black elementary and vocational schools in the South totalled in the hundreds of thousands of dollars, with Julius Rosenwald unquestionably the most generous benefactor. He was more than a casual giver and kept very close watch on the finances of southern black education. Rosenwald frequently introduced Jewish potential donors to Washington, hoping that the force of Washington's personality would inspire them to give. [11] As Washington's link to affluent Jews across the country, Julius Rosenwald annually suggested the names of possible contributors to Tuskegee. In 1912, for example, he informed Booker Washington that Harry Hart, Max Hart, Joseph Schaffner, Charles Schaffner (all of the clothing firm Hart, Schaffner, and Marx), as well as A. G. Becker, Emanuel Mandel and Levy Mayer should be approached. Washington in turn kept Rosenwald informed as to who had responded and in what amount.

Rosenwald also personally asked wealthy and prominent Jews for their financial assistance to Tuskegee. In 1917, for example, he forwarded to Louis Marshall an article about Tuskegee's achievements, hoping to induce him to contribute, and in 1925 he suggested to the Lehman brothers, Irving, Arthur, and Herbert, that they consider contributing $25,000 to the Alabama school. The Lehmans found this much too extravagant and subsequently donated only $10,000. [12] The Chicago philanthropist also arranged annual visits to Tuskegee to meet with Washington, assess conditions at the Institute, and stimulate others to contribute. Rosenwald brought with him an entourage of dozens of prominent individuals, most of whom were Jewish and who were distinguished by either their wealth or their expertise in education or social service. To mark Rosenwald's visits to Tuskegee, Washington staged huge ceremonies, attended by all the students and staff, who showered Rosenwald with accolades. Rosenwald hoped that the members of his party would be moved by the ceremony, by the demonstrations of gratitude of the students, and the efficiency of the school. [13]

Much of the Jewish interest in black elementary-vocational education was stimulated by Booker Washington. Washington, the shrewd master of public relations, recognized the preponderance of Jewish benefactors to his school as well as to other projects he supported. His contacts with Rosenwald, Warburg, and Schiff exposed him to Jewish history and communal organization. He was fascinated by the Jewish experience, which he saw as one of an oppressed people who nonetheless retained self-pride and achieved material success.

He was, for example, intrigued by Aaron Aaronsohn, the Director of the Jewish Agricultural Experimentation Station in Palestine, whom Rosenwald had brought to Tuskegee. Washington was anxious to have Aaronsohn "stop by Tuskegee and talk to our students on farming. I am sure he can be of great service to us. His ideas put into practice would improve farming conditions . . . in the South."

More important, Washington felt that Jews provided a model and blacks needed to emulate them. In *The Future of the American Negro* (1902), he proclaimed:

> We have a very bright and striking example in the history of the Jews in this and other countries. There is, perhaps, no race that has suffered so much . . . But these people have clung together. They have a certain . . . unity, pride, and love of race; and, as the years go on, they will be more . . . influential in this country—a country where they were once despised . . . . It is largely because the Jewish race has had faith in itself. Unless the Negro learns more and more to imitate the Jew in these matters, to have faith in himself, he cannot expect to have any high degree of success. [14]

It seems likely that Washington's views on the meaning of ethnic group identity and success were reinforced by his contacts with Jewish philanthropists. The Jews with whom he dealt most intimately—Rosenwald, Schiff, Warburg—identified strongly with Jewish life, despite their economic success and acceptance in mainstream America. Washington maintained that black separatism was a necessary expedient in the economic development of the race, recognizing that the corollary of separatism could be the fostering of race pride and achievement through self-help. Washington's admiration for the accomplishments of Jews through self-help and strong group loyalty probably strengthened his faith that separatism could be a useful device in Negro advancement.

There is no doubt that Washington held powerful sway over the Jewish philanthropists, as he did over nearly all white patrons of black education. Yet many of these same Jews gave to causes which countered Booker T. Washington's publicly avowed principles. Both Schiff and Rosenwald counted themselves among the heaviest backers of the NAACP, an organization considered the antithesis of the Tuskegee approach to race relations. They also fostered black universities like Howard, Fisk, and Atlanta which offered a traditional intellectual curriculum and maintained programs in law, medicine, and social work. Although Jews contributed to these institutions and helped direct their educational programs, much of this involvement with black higher education remained dormant until Washington's death in 1915, and it was not until the early 1920s that a significant Jewish contribution began. [15]

The involvement of Jewish philanthropists with Howard University in Washington, D.C., demonstrated that pattern. Rosenwald gave money to Howard after 1915, as did Stephen Wise, Joel Spingarn and others. Wise made the pulpit of the Free Synagogue available to Howard's president, Mordecai Johnson, in 1929 for a successful fund-raising drive and Julian Mack served as a consultant for various Howard projects. Jacob Billikopf and Abraham Flexner sat on the board of trustees of Howard. Billikopf was first elected in 1928 and Flexner in 1930. In 1931 Flexner, an authority on education, became president of the board of trustees and in 1933 Billikopf moved up to the executive committee, becoming chairman in 1935. [16]

Rosenwald was in frequent contact with Howard's president, Mordecai Johnson, who kept him informed about Howard's progress. Rosenwald's interest in Howard was further enhanced by the interest of other Jews. For example, in 1925 Julian Mack and Felix Frankfurter warned Rosenwald that Howard's legal library had become dismally out-of-date and contained far less than the acceptable number of volumes prescribed by the Association of American Law Schools.

Rosenwald agreed to give $2,500 if Howard could raise an additional sum from other donors. Mack responded with a gift of $500. Frankfurter then helped select the books to be purchased. All three agreed that the major black university in America should stand on an equal footing with all other universities and that Howard lawyers should be as fully trained as lawyers from any other law school.

Julius Rosenwald also donated $25,000 to Howard University's medical school in 1927. This time Abraham Flexner provided the additional sum. Flexner had been interested in the school's medical training long before he became a trustee. In his general report on the conditions of medical education in the United States, published in 1910, Flexner suggested that Freedmen's Hospital become an integral part of Howard's medical school. He realized that black physicians primarily served other blacks and this, to him, constituted a grave responsibility. Howard medical students would be responsible for the "physical life of 10,000,000 of their people." Therefore, the medical training offered at Howard had to be as good as that offered anywhere in the United States.

This was consistent with Flexner's general opposition to parochial education. In a 1933 speech to the trustees of Howard, Flexner declared that institution's task was to educate citizens, who just happened to be black:

> There is no such thing as a university especially created for any race or denomination. The university is devoted to teaching competent young men and women... It is devoted to expanding the bounds of human knowledge in every field ... Is there any such thing as Baptist science or Negro science, or Jewish science, white science or colored science? [17]

Flexner's efforts to upgrade Howard's medical school and Mack, Frankfurter, and Rosenwald's attempts to equalize Howard's law school with other institutions were part of a policy that seemed nonpaternalistic, certainly in the context of the times, and which did not seek to reinforce a racial status quo. It assumed that black students could become as good doctors or lawyers as white students if only the resources were provided. The Jewish philanthropists saw that as their task.

Jewish contributors demonstrated this same confidence and mission by donating to Fisk University. Rosenwald made his first gift to the Nashville school, W.E.B. DuBois' alma mater, in 1924 when he gave $25,000. Two years later he went to Fisk to participate in university ceremonies, and he and his son Lessing, as well as Harry and Max Hart, Julian Mack and Max Epstein, conducted a campaign for Fisk in Chicago. Felix Warburg, a great admirer of Booker Washington, contributed to Fisk as early as 1912 when the Tuskegeean was still alive and helped raise funds for the school among his associates. Samuel Sachs served on Fisk's board of trustees in the 1930s and also donated thousands of dollars. Even Lillian Wald, who usually found herself preoccupied with trying to raise money for her own settlement, helped map out a fund-raising strategy for Fisk. [18] Atlanta University received a sizable donation from Jacob Schiff as early as 1909. Both Lillian Wald and Jacob Billikopf helped to organize a school of social work there which, they hoped, would create a cadre of black social workers in the south. Like Fisk and Howard, Atlanta University also received substantial amounts of money from Julius Rosenwald. [19] Besides providing substantial financial support to black universities and professional schools, prominent American Jews also encouraged the growth of a black professional class by endowing scholarships for black students. Samuel Sachs endowed a scholarship to be administered through the Urban League for "the development and training of some Negro man or woman especially fitted for social and civic service to the community." Dr. Bernard Herstein established the Rachel Herstein Scholarship for black graduates of New York's public schools and asked the NAACP to administer it.

Jews interested in black higher education wanted to help in the creation of a black middle and professional class. They wanted capable black students to receive an education that was rigorous and traditional, in no way inferior to the standards in white schools. They all believed that black university students should train themselves not just to serve other blacks but to serve the community at large. Reality, however, dictated that if blacks did not become doctors, social workers, lawyers, those vital services would be largely denied to blacks in both the South and the North. The black university thus bore a heavy responsibility for offering the very best training, and its white supporters believed that it could be done. [20]

Although an almost unbridgeable gulf separated this philosophy of black education with Booker Washington's notion that blacks should cast down their buckets where they were, the Julius Rosenwald Fund attempted to combine both approaches. The Fund considered every aspect of southern black education. It supported universities and other institutions of higher learning, funded training and vocational schools, and offered fellowships to black students, scholars, and intellectuals. It built, staffed, and equipped thousands of elementary schools for black children in the South. In fact, according to one history of black education, "No foundation ever cast a more benevolent shadow across the path of the Negro school."

The Rosenwald Fund began as an experiment in 1912 when Rosenwald first began a massive program of building black elementary schools. In three years over 300 schools were built, so Rosenwald decided to formalize the experiment and at the same time broaden the scope of its activities. The Fund, chartered in 1917 "for the well-being of mankind," was at first controlled directly by the Rosenwald family and by Tuskegee, which housed its southern offices. In 1920 the Fund's headquarters moved to Nashville and in 1928 control shifted from Rosenwald to the board of trustees under Edwin Embree, formerly a director of the Rockefeller Fund. Up to 1928, however, the activities of the Fund and of Rosenwald were indistinguishable.

Perhaps the most widely celebrated program undertaken by the Fund was the construction of elementary schools for black children mentioned above, an undertaking stemming directly from the Rosenwald-Washington friendship. By July 1932 the Fund had established 5,357 schools, serving 663,615 students. Of all black school children in the South, 25 to 40 percent were educated in Rosenwald schools, which received funding from four sources. The Rosenwald Fund agreed to give part of the money if the local community would give part, if blacks themselves would give another part, and local whites yet another. From 1920 to 1929, 3,824 schools were erected at a cost estimated at over $20 million. The largest single source of money was the local communities which gave almost $13 million, while individual whites raised the least, about $800,000. Blacks contributed almost $3.5 million, and the Rosenwald Fund contributed over $3 million. Julius Rosenwald insisted on this arrangement so that blacks would not think of the program as charity but would participate intimately in funding their own education. Rosenwald also hoped to awaken the southern white communities to their responsibility to educate black citizens. [21]

The Rosenwald Fund also very actively fostered black university education. It supported Howard, Fisk and Atlanta, and Dillard in New Orleans. It also contributed substantial amounts to fifteen other private black colleges in the South and to seven black state colleges. The Fund conducted massive teacher-training programs to staff the black elementary schools. Like most philanthropists of the day, Rosenwald attempted to apply business principles to philanthropy and tried to make black higher education more efficient. He encouraged the consolidation of the many small black colleges which had been notoriously inefficient into larger, supposedly more manageable institutions. [22]

When giving money to black education Jews like Rosenwald, Schiff, and Warburg acted like most northern white philanthropists. They accepted Booker T. Washington's philosophy of Negro education and gave most frequently and generously to elementary and vocational schools. Yet they were also acting out of a Jewish tradition which stressed both the importance of charity and the centrality of education. All of them identified strongly with their Jewishness and were always conscious of the Jewish implications of all of their actions.

BLACK HEALTH AND JEWISH PHILANTHROPY

Jewish philanthropists also attempted to raise the level of health care for blacks which at the time was grossly inadequate. Poverty and segregation had created poor health facilities throughout the country, in the North just as in the South. In the early decades of the twentieth century, the black mortality rate significantly outpaced the white. In 1930 the average life expectancy for blacks was 48.5 years, for whites it was 60.9. In 1937 only 35 percent of all southern black infants were delivered by a physician compared to 90 percent of southern white babies. Segregated hospitals and negligible state appropriations for those which served blacks led to these dismal health conditions in the South. Civil rights groups frequently charged that publicly supported northern hospitals also practiced segregation and openly discriminated against black patients. As late as 1938 a white American had a fourteen times better chance of receiving proper medical attention than a black. The problems of black health were exacerbated by a paucity of black doctors, dentists, and nurses. Few medical schools would admit blacks, and through the 1930s only two medical schools trained Negro physicians: Meharry Medical School in Nashville and Howard University.[23]

Jewish philanthropists took a keen interest in these depressing health conditions and made real efforts to change them. The Julius Rosenwald Fund particularly concerned itself with black medical care. From 1920 to 1942 the Fund contributed $1,701,928 to various black health projects. The Fund envisioned developing three regional black medical centers in Chicago, New Orleans, and rural Alabama.

The Provident Hospital project in Chicago was one of the Fund's most ambitious undertakings. Founded in 1891, the hospital initially served an interracial clientele, but by World War I, with the massive influx of blacks into Chicago, the South Side hospital became strictly black. Rosenwald, whose donations to Provident began in 1912, attempted to arrange a system whereby the University of Chicago, of which he was a trustee, used Provident for teaching and in turn provided it with nurses, doctors, and interns. Just as Rosenwald believed that black universities must train students with rigor and excellence, so he felt that black medical facilities and personnel must live up to high standards. Flint-Goodrich Hospital, an affiliate of Dillard University in New Orleans, also benefited from Rosenwald's philanthropy and the Fund arranged for white specialists and medical experts to serve as consultants. The rural health project of Macon County fell under the direct administration of Tuskegee, and the Fund instituted programs there on the control of venereal disease and tuberculosis. It also established sorely needed prenatal and pediatric clinics.

The Fund contributed substantially to black hospitals and medical facilities across the country in Baltimore, Philadelphia, New Orleans, Knoxville, St. Louis, Savannah, Richmond, Birmingham, Louisville, Cincinnati and New York City. Each of these hospitals reflected Julius Rosenwald's philosophy of charity and race relations. First, he believed that just as blacks must themselves help in financing the rural schools, so local black communities should aid in hospital building campaigns. New Orleans blacks, for instance, successfully collected

$300,000 for a new hospital and Rosenwald matched the amount. Second, he asserted that black health problems were everybody's problems. In a ground-breaking ceremony for one hospital, Rosenwald blasted discriminatory medical practices and declared that: "Disease is not a thing that can be segregated. The germs of tuberculosis and typhoid fever and measles do not obey Jim Crow laws. If a nation cannot endure half free and half slave, it is equally true that a community cannot keep healthy with one half well and the other half harboring contagious diseases." In a 1928 letter to Dr. J.M.T. Finney, director of Baltimore's Black Provident Hospital, Rosenwald restated his attitude toward the problems of and prospects for black medical care as the responsibility of all:

> If colored doctors and nurses are to have the teaching and stimulus which will enable them to reach high standards, white physicians must encourage them by counsel and service: white citizens must help if adequate funds are to be provided for Negro hospitals and health. And it is well to remember that germs recognize no color line and that disease in one group threatens the health of all. [24]

Julius Rosenwald's philosophy of black philanthropy met its most sustained and serious public criticism in the field of black medical care. Late in 1930 Rosenwald was condemned by a group of black doctors from New York for his "policy of financing and advocating separate [medical] institutions for American citizens of Negro descent." The board of directors of the NAACP echoed this charge. Whereas Rosenwald, the Fund, and its president, Edwin Embree, had consistently justified their policy of building black hospitals on the grounds that black doctors and nurses faced insurmountable difficulty in getting appointments in general hospitals, the Manhattan Medical Society, the association of New York black physicians, maintained that a "'Jim Crow' set up per se produces a sense of servility, suppresses inspiration and creates artificial and dishonest standards." The Rosenwald Fund claimed that in funding and creating black hospitals it was imitating the large number of Jewish hospitals established to circumvent anti-Semitic discrimination in both state and private institutions. The black doctors rejected this analogy, noting that religious and cultural reasons had led in part to the creation of Jewish hospitals. The doctors also noted that Jewish students, too, faced limitations in medical school admissions, but they pointedly asked: "Why has not Mr. Rosenwald established a Jewish medical school for these Jewish candidates . . ."

Rosenwald believed in the possibility of excellence despite segregation, but by the 1930s a large number of articulate black professionals refused to accept the philosophy that was so reminiscent of the early policies of Tuskegee. Rosenwald's orientation had not changed fundamentally since 1912, when Washington still wielded power and the Chicago Jewish philanthropist made his first contribution to Provident Hospital. [25]

Where Rosenwald aided the drive for black medical care by donating money, Lillian Wald directly and actively participated in the movement to improve the health of New York's black population through her work with the Visiting Nurses Association, an offshoot of the Henry Street Settlement. By 1926, 15.5 percent of the people served by the Visiting Nurses were black. A nursing center had been established on 136th Street, the heart of black Harlem, and a black nurse, Josephine Prescott, served as nursing supervisor. Her staff included eighteen black nurses and four black nursing students. By 1929 the Harlem unit of the nursing project was the largest in New York.

Lillian Wald, like Abraham Flexner and Julius Rosenwald, realized the pervasiveness of prejudice and while white nurses occasionally took care of black patients and black nurses went to white homes, Wald recognized "the objections of the colored families and the white families when this is done . . ." and did it only rarely. "We, of course, make no distinctions between races, but the field opens up, and we are making our services available to the colored nurses as we have always been happy to do," Wald wrote in 1925 in an appeal for funds for Lincoln Hospital. She did not equate the all black facility in Harlem with segregation, but felt that the program gave black medical professionals a "fair play to demonstrate their potential power to participate in the advancement of their race . . . and the [white race] marches with them." Wald claimed that she first considered expanding her nursing work to Harlem when a black nurse, a Howard graduate, came to her "wanting an appointment to work with her people."

Her expertise was often sought for nursing and nursing education projects for blacks. When the Robert Shaw House in Boston was looking for a "colored head worker," its director, Alice Tapley, contacted Wald. Wald agreed that a health center in a black neighborhood should be directed by a black, adding that her experiences with black nurses had proven uniformly excellent. George Hall, a black physician who served on the Illinois Commission on Race Relations, wrote to Wald in 1920 and admitted that he had been impressed by the "splendid arrangement of the nursing forces in New York" and expressed warm approval of "your interest in the colored nurses, as indicated by the number in service under your charge." Wald even tried to carry her black health concerns to the politically oriented NAACP. In 1914 she took a major role in an NAACP investigation of discrimination against black nursing students at New York's Bellevue Hospital, and in 1918 proposed that the NAACP consider tackling problems of public health among blacks in the South and launch a campaign to educate black women for public health work there. [26]

JEWISH SOCIAL WORK AND BLACKS

Julius Rosenwald and other Jewish philanthropists genuinely believed that giving money would not in itself eliminate the problems of racism and poverty. They believed, however, that a rational, organized program of social service could be crucial and might be provided by the newly created profession of social work. Many Jewish social workers in Chicago and New York, funded by Jewish philanthropists, provided extensive social services and settlement work to black communities.

The social work and settlement movement began in America in the late nineteenth century. Inspired by the example of Oxford University students, who in 1884 moved into London's East End and founded Toynbee Hall, the social settlement impulse spread to the United States. In 1889 Jane Addams and Ellen Gates Starr established Hull House to serve Chicago's immigrants. In the same year College Settlement in New York began operation, and Lillian Wald moved to Henry Street in 1893. Jews were attracted early to the field. Besides the individual activities of Wald, Henry Moskowitz, Jacob Billikopf,

Minnie Lowe and other Jewish social workers, an elaborate network of Jewish social work agencies developed early in the twentieth century. Between 1895 and 1910 the number of Jewish social settlements rose from four to twenty-four, and hundreds of Jewish agencies dispensed services of all kinds. Just as Jewish philanthropists shifted without great difficulty from purely Jewish to black causes, so Jewish social workers did not hesitate to join the effort to eliminate black poverty and disorganization. Significantly, two of the Jewish signers of the NAACP "Call" were professional social workers—Wald and Moskowitz. Jewish social work institutions publicly committed themselves to the cause of black equality. They vigorously supported anti-lynching legislation, for example, and in 1928 the Association of Jewish Charities and Settlement Workers boycotted the Annual Meeting of the National Conference of Social Work in Memphis because blacks were to be segregated there. In both Chicago and New York, Jewish social workers opened the doors of their settlement houses to blacks, and Jewish philanthropists helped fund social work programs which served blacks. [27]

In Chicago the two key Jews involved in black social work were Julius Rosenwald and Salmon O. Levinson. Rosenwald generously funded the interracial Frederick Douglass Center and the Wendell Phillips Settlement whose clients were exclusively black. The *Chicago Defender* in 1915 revealed a sizeable Rosenwald gift to the Phillips Settlement and glowed, "As for Mr. Rosenwald, long ago we have run out of words that would adequately express how dear to the hearts he is of the people he is trying to aid." Rosenwald generously backed dozens of other social work projects among Chicago's black population, including a variety of agencies serving children, the sick and the aged.

Rosenwald also gave to the Abraham Lincoln Center, an integrated settlement house on the South Side, which by 1932 worked with an equal number of blacks and whites. For most of its history a Unitarian minister, Jenkin Lloyd Jones, directed its operations. On Jones' death in 1917, Salmon O. Levinson, a Jewish associate of Rosenwald, took over direction of the center. Levinson's major role at the Lincoln Center involved fund-raising, since a professional staff handled the actual educational and recreational programs. Levinson solicited contributions most frequently and extensively from Chicago's Jews, emphasizing that his was one of the few agencies in the city which catered to blacks. Although in 1928 he lamented that "I have not had much luck in my public endeavors with my own coreligionists. Perhaps I am a poor solicitor," twenty of the thirty-three individuals who responded to Levinson's appeal in that year were Jewish. Their contributions amounted to over $3,000. Twenty-four of the twenty-nine donors who responded to Levinson in 1929 were Jewish. [28]

In Chicago, Rosenwald's donations to a large number of black projects and Levinson's administration of the Abraham Lincoln Center exemplified Jewish involvement in black social work. Neither took a real role in shaping policy or designing programs for the black people being served. However, in New York Lillian Wald personally directed Henry Street Settlement's program for blacks. Four years after she first opened the doors of the institution, she established Stillman House, a branch in the San Juan Hill District, Manhattan's black neighborhood. It ran a program similar to that of her original lower East Side settlement, employing a cadre of nurses, offering courses of all kinds, supporting a vocational training program, maintaining a library, sponsoring athletic clubs, maintaining playroom and playground facilities, and running a summer camp for black children. In 1909 Wald established the Lincoln Day Nursery in the same neighborhood. That nursery merged with Stillman House a few years later and became Lincoln House.

By 1925 Wald had a staff that was one-fifth black and sponsored a full range of integrated activities. To Walter White she boasted in 1935, "We have no segregated classes," though there was a "chorus made up of colored men and women. This was organized through a colored committee consisting largely of the ministers of colored churches in the neighborhood." The philosophy of the settlement, which did "not [try] to superimpose organizations and activities so much as to encourage them and offer them facilities. Our . . . Jewish Mothers' Club [is a] case in point; . . . in our general festivals and activities, all groups come together and participate," occasionally created all-black or all-Jewish activities. In spite of this orientation, the settlement did make special efforts for blacks. Black speakers appeared frequently at the house and an Urban League Club met there. The Settlement also sponsored black dramatic presentations, and black children at Stillman House had Uncle Remus stories read to them. [29]

Like most social workers at the time, Wald believed strongly in sociological research as a tool for social change. The settlement conducted frequent statistical investigations of the racial situation of the various neighborhoods. A 1922 study of the ethnic and racial makeup of the Columbus Hill section was the first major survey of a black residential area of New York. In 1928 a much more detailed report was issued on "Negro Families Recently Moved into the Neighborhood of the Henry Settlement." Wald designed the survey to ensure the settlement's traditional flexibility of program, feeling that the directors must understand the social fabric of the neighborhood and appreciate the situation of those who used its facilities.

The survey found, among other things, that Jews and blacks frequently occupied the same tenement buildings under fairly amicable conditions. According to the Henry Street Settlement report, each group did have some complaints about the other:

> The complaint of the Negro is that the Jews are so avaricious and so dirty, while the complaint of the Jewish families against the colored is that they are not as exacting with the landlords concerning the condition of the houses as they should be. And that as a result the houses are not kept in the condition they formerly were. In many cases this is very true, and will no doubt be a factor in causing those Jewish families to join the exodus from the neighborhood.

Because of the Settlement's extensive research Wald had the reputation of being an expert on black social conditions in New York, and she frequently addressed meetings concerned with race relations. She advised various black groups like the Circle for Negro War Relief on strategy and personally raised money for numerous black social service causes. As a result of her reputation for fairness and concern, blacks often turned to her with specific discrimination grievances. In 1908, for example, a black resident of Columbus Hill appealed to her about a case of police brutality against a black child. Within four days Wald had contacted the Police Commissioner, urging him to investigate the allegation.

Social workers and black leaders generally praised Wald's interracial work. Eugene Kinckle Jones of the Urban League, for example, asserted that he could think of no other "settlement house anywhere in America that is doing so much for the people surrounding it and that is being as efficiently managed for the colored people as is Lincoln House." He went on to praise the fact that black adults as well as children used its facilities, and concluded, "Miss Wald, may I express to you personally the appreciation that the colored people of New York have for the many things that you have done to further their interest here." [30]

Other Jews less systematically joined in black social service efforts. Isaac Silberstein was on the board of directors of the Harlem Children's Fresh Air Fund, which listed among its supporters Irwin Strassberger, Sidney S. Cohen, and Herbert Lehman. While governor, Lehman maintained a lively interest in the fund and donated regularly and liberally to it and to myriad other black social projects. Professor Morris Loeb of New York University served on the board of directors of the Free Kindergarten for Colored Children as early as 1895. [31]

As in all other areas of black philanthropy, Julius Rosenwald took the lead in funding recreational and social service agencies for black Americans. Most widely hailed of these projects was his scheme for financing black YMCAs. In 1910 Rosenwald met with Jesse Mooreland and other representatives of the national YMCA to find out what the agency provided for black city dwellers. Shocked to learn that there was not one fully equipped facility anywhere in the country which blacks could use, Rosenwald offered to donate $25,000 to any city which could raise three times that amount to build YMCAs for blacks. Rosenwald noted that he had long been disturbed by the lack of adequate recreational facilities for blacks, and since "they have not yet, in their own ranks, a sufficient number of people whose means would enable them to establish and adequately equip such institutions, . . . it is . . . in my judgement, the duty of the white people of this country irrespective of their religious beliefs, to supply this need." Altogether twenty-five YMCAs and two YWCAs were built at a cost of over $5 million. An additional fifty communities tried unsuccessfully to match the Rosenwald offer.

From around the country scores of letters poured into Julius Rosenwald's office from blacks and whites, from Jews and non-Jews, hailing the YMCA offer. Most people found it noteworthy that a Jew would fund a black, Christian project. Black leaders and organized groups joined in the crescendo of praise for Rosenwald. Only one discordant note was sounded. A black newspaper in Cleveland ran a long article about the "Jim Crow YMCAs," which it claimed were a "Magnificent Monument to Race Prejudice, Intolerance, Inhumanity, and White American Christian Hypocrisy . . . ." The writer thought Rosenwald's motives to be purely mercenary, and blasting the philanthropist, he asked if Rosenwald would give money "to a Yiddish YMCA?" Rosenwald never answered this editorial, but his massive donations to dozens of specifically Jewish institutions like the Chicago Hebrew Institute were well known.[32]

This criticism did not stimulate a great controversy among blacks, nor did Rosenwald seriously reconsider the goals of his philanthropy as a result of it. But it did foreshadow the criticism levelled at the Jewish philanthropist in the 1930s by the black medical association. This also spoke to the fact that Julius Rosenwald and the other white philanthropists—Jews and Christians alike—accepted segregation, albeit reluctantly, if that was the only way blacks could receive certain crucial services.

JEWS AND THE URBAN LEAGUE

Jewish social service work with blacks as well as Jewish efforts in black education and health care point to a clear pattern of Jewish commitment. This same commitment can be seen in Jewish involvement in the Urban League, which was founded in New York in 1911 as a response to the appalling economic conditions endured by newly arrived black migrants from the rural South. The League was an amalgamation of three earlier, weaker organizations. The National League for the Protection of Colored Women, begun in 1905, attempted to "prevent friendless, penniless and inefficient Negro women from being sent north by irresponsible agencies . . . ." In 1906 an interracial group created the Committee for Improving the Industrial Conditions of Negroes in New York (CIICNNY), which concerned itself with the dismal employment situation among New York blacks. When, in 1910, it was proposed that the CIICNNY go into the field of social work, yet another urban black agency was created, the Committee on Urban Conditions Among Negroes. This agency

trained black women for social work jobs and conducted various research projects on black living conditions in New York.

All three organizations maintained close ties to Booker T. Washington as did the National Urban League, the product of their fusion,
which strove for expanding economic opportunities for blacks. It
sought first to investigate the actual industrial and social conditions
blacks faced. The League saw itself also as a training institution for
black communal and social workers. Its vague and general goals
allowed it to move into all areas of American life which affected "the
industrial, economic, social and spiritual conditions among
Negroes."[33] The Urban League differed from the NAACP in that it
focused on questions of economic opportunity for blacks instead of
legal rights. It rarely used the tools of litigation on behalf of blacks but
conducted surveys, gathered statistics and actually dispensed social
services. Generally, it assumed a less radical posture than the
NAACP. While its focus differed from the civil rights organization,
Urban League leaders and members bore a striking resemblance to
those of the NAACP. Both consisted primarily of educated blacks,
mainly based in the North, as well as professional elite whites. The
whites were either descended from abolitionist families or were German Jews, usually the children of immigrants.

The first chairman of the National Urban League was Columbia
University economist Edwin R. A. Seligman. In 1911 Ruth Baldwin, a
wealthy New York reformer, persuaded Seligman to accept the position. Seligman had been a founder and Board Chairman of the Committee on Urban Conditions Among Negroes. Descended from one of
the wealthiest and most prestigious Jewish families in America, which
was also one of the most Americanized, Seligman maintained little or
no active identification with Jewish life. A vigorous participant in
many New York reform movements since the beginning of the century, he seldom attended Urban League Board meetings and was only
marginally involved. Lillian Wald had been a member of one of the
parent organizations of the League, the CIICNNY.[34]

Other Jews occupied strategic positions within the Urban League
but significantly fewer appeared here than in the NAACP. Besides
Wald and Seligman, the first executive board of the League included
Abraham Lefkowitz, a pioneer organizer of New York City's teachers,
and Felix Adler, founder of Ethical Culture, an extreme offshoot of

Reform Judaism. Lefkowitz was particularly active and rarely missed a board meeting. By 1914 they had been joined by George Seligman, brother of the economist, and Ella Sachs Plotz. In the 1920s Julius Rosenwald became a member of the executive board, as did Dorothy Straus.[35]

Across the country Jews actively participated in the League's various branches. The League's Chicago branch, for example, established in 1917, marshalled much Jewish support, and like most organized efforts for blacks in Chicago, it received the support—moral and financial—of Julius Rosenwald and many of his associates. The Chicago branch depended heavily on the millionaire-philanthropist for its basic survival. Rosenwald rarely exerted his influence over actual League programs, but he did try to use his monetary support as a lever to alter administrative arrangements. Like most business-oriented philanthropists of the day, he tried to apply business principles to non-business institutions. In the Chicago branch of the Urban League, Rosenwald and his son-in-law Alfred K. Stern attempted to fuse the League with the NAACP. They believed that this would be more efficient. They also hoped it would cut the power of the League's executive secretary, Eugene Kinckle Jones, whom Rosenwald and Stern both disliked. When the rest of the board of the Chicago branch rejected the plan in 1929, Rosenwald withdrew his support from the group. Before actually leaving the League, Stern warned Rosenwald that he would surely meet severe criticism for his actions. He cautioned Rosenwald, "You should be prepared, if you withdraw . . . to have pressure brought to bear on you . . . by . . . the Jewish members of the Board . . . particularly Mr. Harry D. Oppenheimer and Mrs. Emil Levy . . . ." Serious financial repercussions accompanied Rosenwald and Stern's actions, but other Jews continued to support the group. In 1932, for example, six Jews served as officials of the Chicago branch: Levy and Oppenheimer, the Treasurer Edgar Greenbaum, Mrs. Max Adler, Mrs. Arthur Oppenheimer, and Rabbi Louis I. Mann.[36]

Jews participated in Urban League leadership activities around the country and in the New York national office. They also offered their services to the League and aided its many projects in various ways. In 1915, for example, Isaac Seligman, Joseph Auerbach, and Sam Lewisohn, wealthy New York Jewish businessmen, worked with the League on a program of investing in Harlem housing in an attempt to stabilize

black residence there. In 1920 the League sponsored a health campaign in Harlem and James Hubert, Executive Secretary of the New
York chapter, successfully persuaded Lillian Wald to help. Just as
Jewish members of the NAACP used their influence and contacts for
the benefit of the Association, so did Jews in the Urban League.
E.R.A. Seligman, for example, persuaded Columbia University officials to waive certain admission requirements for black social work
students being sponsored by the League. Harry Oppenheimer used
his influence to persuade Cook County Judge Harry Horner to support the Chicago branch in 1930.[37]

Jews appeared often at Urban League events and sponsored many
of its programs. In 1931 Jacob Billikopf, Julius Rosenwald, and Sam
Lewisohn sponsored an Urban League conference on black unemployment, and Herbert Lehman lent his support to a League charity
ball in Harlem in 1932. Much of this sponsorship was obviously purely
ceremonial, but Jews also made massive financial contributions to the
League which served more than symbolic value. Many of the Jews who
gave regularly to the NAACP and to black education also donated
money to the League, with Julius Rosenwald leading the list of benefactors. Paul and Felix Warburg, George, Edwin, and Isaac Seligman, Jacob Schiff, Felix Adler, and Benjamin Altman of the New
York department store all gave substantial amounts.[38]

Again, as in the funding of the NAACP and black education, Jews
never stood alone as sole benefactors, but their donations were large
and constant. Most Jewish philanthropists made few ideological distinctions between the various causes. The same people who gave to the
Urban League also donated to the NAACP and to scores of black educational, medical, and recreational projects.

JEWISHNESS AND BLACK PHILANTHROPY

Why did so many Jews devote both money and effort to black philanthropic causes? The sheer number of Jews involved in black philanthropy suggests that this pattern of involvement did not emerge
accidentally. The Jewish presence made itself felt in black philanthropy far out of proportion to the number of Jews in the population
who could donate money or share their expertise with these enter-

prises. That Jews concentrated most heavily in educational activities, the area that most closely mirrored their own tradition, is instructive. The commitment of Jewish philanthropists to black education undoubtedly stemmed in part from the great power and prestige of Booker T. Washington and in part from the widespread American belief that education paved the ultimate path to social mobility. But successful American Jews had long attributed their own achievements to educational attainments and consistently prescribed education for those Jews making their way out of poverty into the mainstream of American life. It was only natural that Jewish philanthropists, once they had determined to help black people, would put most of their resources into education, just as they did for their coreligionists from the ghettos of eastern Europe.

But why did they show this interest in blacks in the first place? Few of the philanthropists themselves answered this question explicitly. Few stopped to ponder the meaning of their contributions, yet when one examines Julius Rosenwald's ideas about the position of Jews in America and the response of prominent Jews to Rosenwald's black philanthropy, one can get some appreciation of the peculiarly Jewish motives in these activities.

Intensely conscious of his Jewishness, Julius Rosenwald gave freely to Jewish causes of all kinds. He made his own religious affiliation very clear and was very sensitive about questions of the status of Jews in the United States. The extent of American anti-Semitism troubled him. During the years of the Leo Frank case he cautiously watched the events unfolding in Georgia and anxiously discussed their implications with other Jewish leaders.

Rosenwald recognized that the negative actions of some Jews reflected badly on all. To an aspiring Jewish politician he nervously wrote in 1913: "I am not in the least anxious to see many Jews in politics or even on the bench . . . ." Likewise, he believed that the good deeds and achievements of a handful elevated the status of the whole group. He sensed that society always interpreted the behavior of individual Jews as indicative of certain Jewish traits, either positive or negative. To a student at the University of Chicago worried about anti-Semitism on campus, he admonished, "All persons of the religion to which they belong are likely to be judged by their conduct and, therefore, it is important that young Jewish men and Jewish women at the college conduct themselves well. They should demean themselves favorably and participate in college activities." While the roots of Rosenwald's interest in blacks extended far deeper than just a desire for favorable recognition of Jewish benevolence, that factor figured unmistakably in his thoughts and actions. [39]

Other successful Jews echoed this theme. They commonly wrote to Rosenwald and praised his work with blacks *because* it contributed to the good name and hence to the welfare of American Jews. A Chicago Jewish attorney, Julius Stern, wrote to Rosenwald about the reaction of a group of Christians to the 1911 YMCA offer. "Some remarks . . . made in my hearing yesterday among non-Jews, showed such keen appreciation by them of your actions as an individual and as a representative member of our Jewish community." Stern noted that Rosenwald's actions "brought credit upon yourself . . . and upon the Jewish people." At the same time, another Jew, Alfred Decker, declared: "What impresses me . . . is your . . . assisting a race that is discriminated against like our own." [40]

The same attitude was evinced universally by the English-language Jewish press from the earliest years of Rosenwald's philanthropic interest in blacks until his death in 1931. From 1915 to 1931, over fifty-six articles dealing specifically with Rosenwald's black philanthropy appeared in eight magazines. Some of the articles were purely descriptive, recounting the millions he spent, calling him the "American Jewish Prince of Philanthropists." These articles unabashedly declared that "Julius Rosenwald was the greatest friend the negro has had since Abraham Lincoln." Most magazines considered his interest in blacks in America quite unusual but very laudatory. "In a world that despised the Negro he was his generous protector," boasted the *B'nai Brith News.*

Jewish journalists did not hesitate to assert the element of self-interest, that Rosenwald's efforts for blacks helped Jews at the same time. The *American Hebrew* stridently asserted twice that, "by helping the colored people in this country, Mr. Rosenwald doubtless also serves Judaism, in that he tends therefore to disabuse the anti-Semitic Gentile mind as to the alleged clannishness of the Jew." When Rosenwald helped salvage a black insurance firm from imminent doom in 1924, the *American Israelite* used the event as a platform to attack American anti-Semitism: "Here's an item for Ford's Folly. A group of

Nordics in the South—white, 100 percent, American money lenders—
were about to stop Herman E. Perry, Negro financier of Atlanta . . .
when a JEW by the name of Julius Rosenwald stepped in."

Most periodicals urged their readers to follow Rosenwald's example and give to black causes, claiming that his actions were not coincidental but part of a larger pattern of Jewish action. In these frequently
chauvinistic articles, a definite link was drawn between Rosenwald's
concern for blacks and his Jewish origins. One magazine noted in
1928:

> In Mr. Rosenwald serving the stranger we see the performance
> of the highest mission of the Jew. The mission of the Jew is to
> contribute to mankind of his idealism and enrich the world with
> his age-old experience as a civilized human being—to serve at
> the common altar.

In a memorial service for the Chicago philanthropist, the rabbi of
Rosenwald's congregation, Rabbi Louis Mann, also drew the connection:

> By helping the Negro, Rosenwald was motivated both intellectu-
> ally and emotionally . . . . Rosenwald's devotion to the cause of
> uplifting the Negro was, in the light of . . . emotional motivation,
> one of the most intensely Jewish things that Rosenwald ever
> did . . . his passionate interest in helping the black man was a
> practical application of Hillel's golden rule and but an ethical
> paraphrasing of "remember the stranger for ye, too, were
> strangers." A white man who accepted the burden of the black
> man! A Jew who built Young Men's Christian Associations! An
> American who loved men of all nations. [41]

Jews were proud of Rosenwald and his involvement in the world of
black philanthropy, just as they pointed with pride to efforts of Schiff,
Wald, Warburg, and the other Jews who aided black social and economic causes. It was not an abstract pride, but a feeling that the specific actions of the few would enhance the status of the many. They believed, however, beyond a doubt that Jewish concern for blacks was
unique, that no other ethnic group could equal it, and that it grew
directly from the fertile soil of Jewish history and culture.

NOTES

1. National League on Urban Conditions Among Negroes, *Annual Report for 1910-1911*, p. 2; Nancy J. Weiss, *The National Urban League: 1910-1940* (New York: Oxford University Press, 1974).

2. Ullin W. Leavell, *Philanthropy in Negro Education* (Nashville: George Peabody College for Teachers, 1930); Robert M. Lester, *Forty Years of Carnegie Giving* (New York: Charles Scribner's Sons, 1941); Allan Nevins, *Study in Power: John D. Rockefeller, Industrialist and Philanthropist* (New York: Charles Scribner's Sons, 1953).

3. Robert H. Bremner, *American Philanthropy* (Chicago: University of Chicago Press, 1960), pp. 105-142.

4. Henry Allen Bullock, *A History of Negro Education in the South: From 1619 to the Present* (New York: Praeger Publishers, 1970); Horace Mann Bond, *Negro Education in Alabama: A Study in Cotton and Steel* (Washington, D.C.: Associated Publishers, 1939); Horace Mann Bond, *The Education of the Negro in the American Social Order* (Englewood Cliffs, N.J.: Prentice-Hall, 1934); Hugh Brown, *A History of the Education of Negroes in North Carolina* (Raleigh: Irving Swain Press, 1961); Dwight Holmes, *The Evolution of the Negro College* (New York: Teachers' College, Columbia University, 1934) are useful surveys of black education. On the educational work of the Freedman's Bureau see William S. McFeely, *Yankee Stepfather: General O. O. Howard and 'the Freedmen* (New Haven: Yale University Press, 1968) and George R. Bentley, *A History of the Freedman's Bureau* (Philadelphia: University of Pennsylvania Press, 1955). See also W.E.B. DuBois, "The Negro Common School," in *Crisis*, 35 (September 1926): 493-501.

5. Sanuel R. Spencer, *Booker T. Washington and the Negro's Place in American Life* (Boston: Little, Brown and Company, 1955); Emma L. Thornbrough, *Booker T. Washington* (Englewood Cliffs, N.J.: Prentice-Hall, 1964); Louis R. Harlan, *Booker T. Washington: The Making of a Black Leader, 1856-1901* (New York: Oxford University Press, 1972); Booker T. Washington, *Working with the Hands* (New York: Doubleday, Page and Company, 1904); Booker T. Washington, *Up from Slavery* (New York: Doubleday, Page and Company, 1901).

6. There is no real biography of Rosenwald. The closest is an authorized biography by M. R. Werner, *Julius Rosenwald: The Life of a Practical Humanitarian* (New York: Harper and Row, 1939). Edwin Embree and Julia Waxman, *Investment in People: The Story of the Julius Rosenwald Fund* (New York: Harper and Brothers, 1949) contains useful biographical materials, but deals more with the workings of the Julius Rosenwald Fund. One reason for the lack of any real interpretive biography is that the massive collection of Rosenwald papers is catalogued by charity and reveals very little of the person. His charitable work is summarized well in Robert P. Frazen, "The Public Life of Julius Rosenwald" (M.A. Thesis, Hebrew Union College, 1964); for statements by Rosenwald see *Atlantic Monthly*, May 1929, pp. 599-606; see also clipping, *Chicago Record*, February 9, 1912, Rosenwald Papers, Notebook I.

7. Julius Rosenwald to Booker Washington, August 20, 1914, Booker Washington Papers, 772; *Christian Century*, July 15, 1927, pp. 847-848; Julius Rosenwald to W. J. Hoggson, n.d., Rosenwald Papers, Notebook III, 1; Julius Rosenwald, "You Can't

Keep a Man in the Ditch Without Staying in with Him," *Colliers Magazine*, 76 (July 4, 1925), p. 23.

8. Cyrus Adler, *Jacob H. Schiff: His Life and Letters*, Vol 2 (Garden City, N.Y.: Doubleday and Company, 1928), pp. 314-318; Tuskegee Institute, *Bulletin: Principal's Annual Report, 1930, 1934, 1935*; Jacob Schiff to Booker Washington, July 3, 1912, Jacob Schiff Papers, 677; Jacob Schiff to Booker Washington, June 16, 1909; Booker Washington to Jacob Schiff, June 18, 1909; July 9, 1909; December 29, 1909; December 21, 1909, n.d., 1909, all in Booker Washington Papers, 47; Samuel Spencer, *Booker T. Washington*, p. 165.

9. Jacob Schiff to Oswald Garrison Villard, December 9, 1909, Jacob Schiff Papers, 677; Booker T. Washington, *Working with the Hands*, p. 30; Felix Warburg to Frank Trumbull, February 14, 1919, Felix Warburg Papers, 188.

10. Mary White Ovington, *The Walls Came Tumbling Down* (New York: Harcourt, Brace and World, 1947), p. 76; William H. Baldwin, Jr., "The Present Problem of Negro Education," *Journal of Social Science*, 37 (1899): p. 56.

11. Emmett Scott to Julius Rosenwald, November 1, 1915, Booker T. Washington Papers, 78; "Hampton-Tuskegee Endowment Fund," March 16, 1925, Julius Rosenwald Papers, 17, 8; "Hampton-Tuskegee Endowment Fund," October 17, 1928, Julius Rosenwald Papers, 17, 4; Charlotte Thorn to Julius Rosenwald, March 28, 1921, Julius Rosenwald Papers, 15, 1; *American Israelite*, 54 (June 23, 1927): 3.

12. Julius Rosenwald to Louis Marshall, April 9, 1917; Louis Marshall to Julius Rosenwald, April 27, 1917, Louis Marshall Papers, 50-R; Arthur Lehman to Julius Rosenwald, April 14, 1925, Julius Rosenwald Papers, 17, 6; Henry Sachs to Julius Rosenwald, April 14, 1925, Julius Rosenwald Papers, 17, 8; Julius Rosenwald to Booker Washington, March 15, 1912, Booker Washington Papers, 62; Julius Rosenwald to Booker Washington, October 28, 1914, Booker T. Washington Papers, 72; James Loeb to Booker Washington, August 8, 1904, Booker Washington Papers, 711; Booker Washington to Julius Rosenwald, April 2, 1913, Booker Washington Papers, 66; Booker Washington to Julius Rosenwald, December 8, 1914, Booker Washington Papers, 72; Julius Rosenwald to Booker T. Washington, April 11, 1912, Booker Washington Papers, 62.

13. Booker Washington to Jacob Schiff, February 3, 1911; Jacob Schiff to Booker Washington, February 3, 1911, Booker Washington Papers, 55; "Trip to Tuskegee," n.d. [1912], Booker Washington Papers, 62; "Members of the Tuskegee Chicago Party, February 18-23, 1913," Julius Rosenwald Papers, 53, 12; "Special Party Taken to Tuskegee by Julius Rosenwald, 1915," Booker T. Washington Papers, 711; Booker Washington to William Graves, January 17, 1915, Julius Rosenwald Papers, 39, 24; *American Jewish World*, 6 (August 2, 1918): 798.

14. Booker Washington to Julius Rosenwald, January 11, 1913, Booker Washington Papers, 66; Booker T. Washington, *The Future of the American Negro* (Boston: Small, Maynard and Company, 1899), p. 182.

15. Howard University, *Financial Report, 1921-1922; 1922-1923* (Washington, D.C.: Howard University Press, 1922, 1923); Mordecai Johnson to Julius Rosenwald, March 13, 1929, Julius Rosenwald Papers, 19, 7; Julian Mack to Julius Rosenwald, February 20, 1922, Julius Rosenwald Papers, 19, 2; Howard University, *Catalogue*

(Washington, D.C.: Howard University Press, 1915), p. 15.

16. Walter Dyson, *Howard University: The Capstone of Negro Education, A History: 1867-1940* (Washington, D.C.: The Graduate School of Howard University, 1941); Rayford Logan, *Howard University: The First Hundred Years* (New York: New York University Press, 1969); Dwight O. W. Holmes, "Fifty Years of Howard University," *Journal of Negro History*, 3 (April 1918): 123-138; (October 1918): 368-380; Howard University, *Catalogue, 1915*, p. 15; *Catalogue, 1928*, p. 12; *Catalogue, 1930*, pp. 13-14; *Catalogue, 1933*, p. 12; *Catalogue*, 1931, p. 11; Mordecai Johnson to Julius Rosenwald, December 26, 1928, Julius Rosenwald Papers, 19, 2; Jacob Billikopf to Claude Barnett, April 7, 1931, NAACP, Admin. Files, C-63; William Graves to Julian Mack, February 15, 1926, Julius Rosenwald Papers, 19, 6; Julian Mack to Lessing Rosenwald, February 8, 1926, Julius Rosenwald Papers, 19, 7; "Resolutions," February 11, 1926, Julius Rosenwald Papers, 19, 6.

17. Walter Dyson, *Howard University*, pp. 258, 392-393; Abraham Flexner to Julius Rosenwald, November 7, 1927, Abraham Flexner Papers, 13; *Crisis*, 38 (April 1933): 126.

18. Julius Rosenwald to F. A. McKenzie, August 25, 1917, Julius Rosenwald Papers, 14, 32; "Fisk University Million Dollar Endowment Fund, June 5, 1924," list of donors in Rosenwald Papers, 14, 30; William Baldwin to Julius Rosenwald, July 3, 1924, Julius Rosenwald Papers, 24, 30; Ben Hooper to Felix Warburg, May 11, 1912, Felix Warburg Papers, 163; L. Hollingsworth Wood to Felix Warburg, June 21, 1918, Felix Warburg Papers, 184a; *Jewish Tribune and Hebrew Standard*, 89 (December 17, 1926): 9; L. Hollingsworth Wood to Lillian Wald, June 26, 1918, Wald Papers, 27.

19. Jacob Schiff to Booker Washington, July 9, 1909, Booker T. Washington Papers, 47; Forrester B. Washington to Lillian Wald, April 21, 1928, Wald Papers, 27; Forrester Washington to Julius Rosenwald, January 5, 1928; March 13, 1928, Julius Rosenwald Papers 3, 2; Julius Rosenwald to Myron Adams, May 29, 1922, Julius Rosenwald Papers, 3, 3.

20. *Opportunity*, 1 (March 1923): 32; Bernard Herstein to Roy Wilkins, July 18, 1935, July 29, 1936, NAACP, Admin. Files, C-293; *American Hebrew*, 110 (December 5, 1930): 92; *American Israelite*, 57 (February 7, 1930): 6; Alfred K. Stern to W. C. Kelly, March 18, 1930, National Urban League Papers, 4, 7.

21. Edwin Embree and Julia Waxman, *Investment in People*; Henry Bullock, *A History of Negro Education*, p. 127; Horace Mann Bond, *The Education of the Negro*, pp. 142-143; Ullin W. Leavell, *Philanthropy in Negro Education*, pp. 137-146; 76-82; 109-118; *Journal of Negro History*, 17 (April 1932): 237-239; Horace Mann Bond, *Negro Education in Alabama*, pp. 278-286; Charles H. Wilson, *Education for Negroes in Mississippi Since 1910* (Boston: Meador Publishing Company, 1947), pp. 64-70; *School and Society*, 21 (June 6, 1925): 676-677; 30 (December 28, 1929): 878; 27 (November 17, 1928): 616; *Literary Digest* 94 (August 13, 1927): 27-28; *Journal of Negro History*, 7 (April 1922): 230-231.

22. Edwin Embree and Julia Waxman, *Investment in People*, pp. 68-106; Robert L. Owens, "Financial Assistance for Negro College Students in America: A Social Historical Interpretation of the Philosophy of Negro Higher Education," (Ph.D. dissertation, State University of Iowa, 1954).

23. Montague Cobb, *Medical Care and the Plight of the Negro* (New York: NAACP,

1947); Herbert M. Morais, *The History of the Negro in Medicine* (New York: Publishers Company, 1967); Dietrich C. Reitzes, *Negroes and Medicine* (Cambridge: Harvard University Press, 1958); Michael M. Davis, "Problems of Health Services for Negroes," *Journal of Negro Education*, 6 (July 1937): 438-449; Gunnar Myrdal, *An American Dilemma*, Vol. 1 (New York: Harper and Row, 1944), p. 162; William Graves to Julius Rosenwald, December 13, 1912, Rosenwald Papers, 31, 8; H. M. Green, "Hospitals and Public Health Facilities for Negroes," *Proceedings of the National Conference of Social Work: 1928*, pp. 178-180; Charles S. Johnson, *The Negro College Graduate* (Chapel Hill: University of North Carolina Press, 1938), p. 137.

24. Henry Sachs to Julius Rosenwald, April 14, 1925, Julius Rosenwald Papers, 17, 8; Allan H. Spear, *Black Chicago: The Making of a Negro Ghetto, 1890-1920* (Chicago: University of Chicago Press, 1967), pp. 97-100; Edwin Embree and Julia Waxman, *Investment in People*, pp. 110-111, 269-271; Julius Rosenwald to T.M.T. Finney, September 26, 1928, Julius Rosenwald Papers, 31, 6; "A Medical Center for Negroes," *Opportunity*, 7 (February 1930): 58.

25. Speech to the American Hospital Association, September 30, 1930, copy in Julius Rosenwald Papers, 1, 25; "Equal Opportunity—No More—No Less: An Open Letter to Mr. Edwin Embree, President of the Julius Rosenwald Fund, Chicago, Illinois from the Manhattan Medical Society," January 28, 1931, Copy in Herbert Lehman Papers, Lt. Gov-Micro; W.E.B. DuBois, "Resolution for the N.A.A.C.P. Board of Directors," n.d., Herbert Lehman Papers, Lt. Gov-Micro; NAACP, *Annual Report*, 1931, p. 5; *American Israelite*, 57 (December 18, 1930): 5; *American Israelite*, 58 (February 5, 1931): 1; (August 20, 1931): 5.

26. Henry Street Settlement, Report (New York: Harry Powers, 1926), pp. 35-39; Lillian Wald to Mrs. Schuyler-Warren, December 3, 1929, Wald Papers, 27; Lillian Wald to National Organization for Public Health Nursing, April 30, 1930, Lillian Wald Collection; Lillian Wald to Mrs. Van Santwood Merle-Smith, March 6, 1925, Lillian Wald Collection; George Hall to Lillian Wald, June 3, 1920, Lillian Wald Papers, 27; Lillian Wald to Adah B. Thomas, April 11, 1929, Lillian Wald Collection; Lillian Wald to New York Colored Mission, January 24, 1910, Lillian Wald Papers, 27; Herbert Lehman to Belle Davis, February 28, 1933, Herbert Lehman Papers-Donations, 1933; Belle Davis to Lillian Wald, January 3, 1928; Lillian Wald to Belle Davis, January 4, 1928, Lillian Wald Papers, 27; Lillian Wald to Mrs. David Levy, April 16, 1930, Lillian Wald Collection; Alice Tapley to Lillian Wald, February 25, 1927, Lillian Wald to Mary Brinsmeade, August 14, 1914, August 18, 1914; Lillian Wald to John Shillady, February 25, 1918, Lillian Wald Papers, 27.

27. Allen F. Davis, *Spearheads for Reform: The Social Settlements and the Progressive Movement, 1890-1914* (New York: Oxford University Press, 1967); Roy Lubove, *The Professional Altruist: The Emergence of Social Work As a Career, 1880-1930* (Cambridge, Mass.: Harvard University Press, 1965); Clarke Chambers, *Seedtime of Reform: American Social Service and Social Action, 1918-1933* (Minneapolis: University of Minnesota Press, 1963); Jane Addams, *Twenty Years at Hull House* (New York: Macmillan, 1910); Lillian Wald, *The House on Henry Street*; Lillian Wald, *Windows on Henry Street*; Boris D. Bogen, "Settlement Work Among Jews," *Charities*, 10 (January 3, 1903): 1-2; Herman D. Stein, "Jewish Social Work in the United States, 1654-1954" (Ph.D. dissertation, Columbia University, 1958); *The History of American*

Jewish Social Welfare (Philadelphia: Jewish Publication Society of America, 1966); there is very little on social workers and blacks; see Steven J. Diner, "Chicago Social Workers and Blacks in the Progressive Era," *Social Service Review*, 44 (December 1970): 393-410; unidentified newspaper clipping, May 12, 1928, Urban League Papers, 13, 85.

28. William Graves to Celia Parker Woolley, February 27, 1915; Newspaper Clipping, February 21, 1914, Julius Rosenwald Papers, 30, 16; "Report" Abraham Lincoln Center, n.d.; J. M. Artman to William Graves, October 19, 1922; C. W. Reese to William Graves, n.d., Julius Rosenwald Papers, 24, 2; Salmon O. Levinson to Morris Rosenwald, December 13, 1920; Salmon O. Levinson to William Nussbaum, Sam Meyer, David Blum, December 4, 1928; L. Levinson to Sol Kline, February 27, 1928; "Subscribers Through Mr. Levinson, 1927," "Subscribers Through Mr. Levinson, 1928," "Subscribers Through Mr. Levinson, 1929," Salmon O. Levinson Papers, 56.

29. Frances Blascoer, *Colored School Children in New York* (New York: Public Education Association of the City of New York, 1915), pp. 174-175; Lillian Wald to Clara Berenberger, May 23, 1926; "Memorandum for Miss Wald," January 30, 1925; R. J. Elzy to Karl Hesley, March 10, 1931, Lillian Wald Papers, 27; Lillian Wald to M. Canerly, April 21, 1937, Lillian Wald Collection; Lillian Wald to Walter White, May 20, 1935, NAACP Admin. Files, C-362.

30. "Sociological Survey of the Negro Population of Columbus Hill of New York City," October 14, 1922; "Survey of Negro Families Recently Moved into the Neighborhood of Henry Street Settlement, New York City, p. 9, Lillian Wald Papers, 27; Elizabeth Tyler to Lillian Wald, July 10, 1908; Lillian Wald to Elizabeth Tyler, July 10, 1908; James Hubert to Lillian Wald, December 10, 1926, December 15, 1926; "Report of Conference on 'Scope of Vocational Work in New York City and Its Application to the Colored Child, December 22, 1919,'" Lillian Wald Papers, 27; Eugene K. Jones to Lillian Wald, May 21, 1918, Lillian Wald Papers, 45; Lillian Wald to Mr. Gilman, October 23, 1919, Wald Collection.

31. "Thirteenth Annual Report of the Negro Fresh Air Committee," Summer, 1918; Clipping, *New York Evening Post*, November 27, 1912; Lillian Wald to Sojourner Truth House, May 22, 1915; July 5, 1912; June 24, 1913; October 12, 1913; March 26, 1914; May 25, 1915; Lillian Wald to Mary W. Ovington, January 6, 1920, Lillian Wald Papers, 27; George Harris to William Crawford, August 17, 1931, Herbert Lehman Papers, Lt. Gov-Micro.

32. George Arthur, *Life on the Negro Frontier* (New York: Association Press, 1934), pp. 35-42; Jesse E. Moorland, "The Young Men's Christian Association Among Negroes," *Journal of Negro History*, 9 (April 1924): 127-138; Jesse O. Thomas, *My Story in Black and White* (New York: Exposition Press, 1967), p. 49; Julius Rosenwald to YMCA of Chicago, n.d., 1910; Henry Gittler to Julius Rosenwald, January 2, 1911; Belle Donalds to Julius Rosenwald, January 2, 1911; Julius Stern to Julius Rosenwald, January 5, 1911; Alfred Decker to Julius Rosenwald, January 2, 1911, Julius Rosenwald Papers, 10, 21; Clipping, *Cleveland Gazette*, June 28, 1913, Julius Rosenwald Papers, Notebook III, I; Jesse Moorland to Julius Rosenwald, May 22, 1911, Julius Rosenwald Papers, 10, 21; Jesse Moorland to Jacob Billikopf, May 19, 1932, Julius Rosenwald Papers, 3, 19.

33. The major monograph on the Urban League is Nancy J. Weiss, *The National*

Urban League: 1910-1940. See also L. Hollingsworth Wood, "The Urban League Movement," *Journal of Negro History,* 9 (April 1924): 117-126; Guichard Parris and Lester Brooks, *Blacks in the City: A History of The National Urban League* (Boston: Little, Brown and Company, 1971); National Urban League, *Bulletin,* 3 (November 1913): 7.

34. Ruth Baldwin to E.R.A. Seligman, October 23, 1910, E.R.A. Seligman Papers; Ruth Baldwin to E.R.A. Seligman, October 23, 1912; National Urban League, *First Annual Report,* p. 10.

35. National Urban League, *Annual Report, 1910-1911*; Executive Board List, n.d., Urban League Papers, 5, 8; Urban League, "Board Minutes, 1914"; "National Urban League, 1927," Julius Rosenwald Papers, 27, 18; "Board of Directors-Brooklyn Urban League: Newspaper Clipping, *Columbus* (Ohio) *Dispatch,* October 11, 1934 in Urban League Papers, 13, 86; "Affiliated Organizations," Urban League Papers, 5, 5.

36. Arvarh E. Strickland, *History of the Chicago Urban League* (Urbana: University of Illinois Press, 1966); Chicago Urban League, *Two Decades of Service* (Chicago: Chicago Urban League, 1936); T. A. Hill to Julius Rosenwald, January 19, 1917; Julian Mack to William Graves, January 27, 1917; William Graves to T. Arnold Hill, April 10, 1917; H. Oppenheimer to William Graves, February 7, 1917; Harry Oppenheimer to William Graves, February 25, 1920, Julius Rosenwald Papers, 3, 17; Alban Foster to Salmon O. Levinson, October 8, 1927, Salmon O. Levinson Papers, 21; *Chicago Defender,* January 28, 1928; Arvarh Strickland, *History of the Chicago Urban League,* pp. 98-101; Nancy J. Weiss, *The National Urban League,* p. 160; Alfred K. Stern to Julius Rosenwald, October 15, 1929, Julius Rosenwald Papers, 9, 17.

37. National Urban League, *Annual Report,* 1910-11; James Hubert to Lillian Wald, April 20, 1920, Lillian Wald Papers, 27; National Urban League, *Annual Report,* 1910-1911, p. 20; Henry Horner to Julius Rosenwald, April 22, 1930, Julius Rosenwald Papers, 9, 18; T. Arnold Hill, "Report: Fort Wayne, Indiana," February 1, 1929; T. Arnold Hill to Meyer Jacobstein, March 10, 1931, March 11, 1931, March 12, 1931, National Urban League Papers, 4, 1.

38. Proposed Unemployment Conference, n.d., 1931, National Urban League Papers, 4, 3; Herbert Lehman to James Hubert, November 1, 1932, Herbert Lehman Papers, Lt. Gov-Micro; National Urban League, Annual Conference, January 13-14, 1920, p. 14; "List of Persons Giving Since Mr. Rosenwald's Last Check," April 16, 1918, Julius Rosenwald Papers, 9, 13; Felix Warburg to L. Hollingsworth Wood, February 13, 1920, Felix Warburg Collection, 190a; "Mrs. George Seligman," *Opportunity,* 9 (March 1931): 71; T. Arnold Hill to Herbert Lehman, January 24, 1934, Herbert Lehman Papers; *American Hebrew* 107 (August 10, 1928): 401.

39. Telegram, Julius Rosenwald to Booker Washington, March 1, 1912, Booker Washington Papers, 62; Cyrus Adler, "Julius Rosenwald," *Jewish Social Service Quarterly* (March 1932): 125-126; Leo Frank to Julius Rosenwald, July 11, 1915; Louis Marshall to Julius Rosenwald, Julius Rosenwald Papers, 15, 15; Louis Marshall to Julius Rosenwald, n.d., Julius Rosenwald Papers, 31, 1; Julius Rosenwald to Elijah Zaline, January 9, 1913, Julius Rosenwald Papers, 23, 5; Harold Kramer, November 7, 1928, Julius Rosenwald Papers, 31, 1.

40. Julius Stern to Julius Rosenwald, January 5, 1911; Alfred Decker to Julius Rosenwald, January 2, 1911, Julius Rosenwald Papers, 10, 21; Edward Flexner to Julius

Rosenwald, January 17, 1921, Julius Rosenwald Papers, 247.

41. *B'nai Brith Magazine*, 130 (February 1932): 130; *Jewish Tribune* 95 (October 4, 1929): 23; *American Hebrew*, 105 (July 3, 1925), 262; 106 (August 12, 1927): 457; *American Israelite*, 51 (December 25, 1924): 5; 47 (December 30, 1920): 4; 51 (August 28, 1924): 4; *B'nai Brith Magazine*, 142 (August 1928): 360; 146 (February 1932): 132-133.

chapter 6

"OUR EXPLOITED NEGRO BROTHERS":
JEWISH LABOR AND THE
ORGANIZATION OF BLACK WORKERS

Yet another group of Jews joined in the struggle to ameliorate black social and economic life and this group, too, acted out of the peculiar needs of Jews. In the garment factories of New York, Chicago, Philadelphia, and Baltimore, Jewish and black workers labored side by side. They belonged to the same unions and aided each other in the quest for economic security. Leaders of Jewish labor strove actively to bring the benefits of unionization to the masses of workers both within the garment industry and without. A world of difference separated them from Jews like the Spingarns, or Lillian Wald, or Jacob Schiff, or Julius Rosenwald. Almost all of the union organizers were immigrants from Russia, Poland, or Lithuania. Almost all were socialists who interpreted human activities as a continuous class struggle. However, like those Jews who joined the NAACP or the Urban League or gave money to Tuskegee, Jewish labor leaders occupied themselves with securing the status of the Jews in the United States. They, too, were alarmed at rising anti-Semitism in both Europe and America in the decades between the two world wars. Like Rosenwald, Lehman, and Wise, eastern European-born, Yiddish-speaking labor leaders found the issue of black discrimination and the plight of Negro Americans a useful forum in which to work out certain pressures of Jewish acculturation to America.

For working-class Jews an element of economic self-interest also entered into the drive to unionize black workers. Since a significant number of blacks labored in the garment industry, the leaders of the International Ladies' Garment Workers' Union (ILGWU) and the Amalgamated Clothing Workers Union felt that they could not afford to ignore blacks. Yet the way they organized black needle-workers

and their efforts to encourage the unionization of blacks in other industries indicated that their vision was shaped not by *purely* economic
concerns.

The policies followed by the leadership of the ILGWU and the
Amalgamated toward blacks departed quite dramatically from the
traditional practices of American organized labor. Hostility towards
black workers had long characterized the stance of the American Federation of Labor and of its president, Samuel Gompers. A number of
the trade unions affiliated with it openly excluded blacks from membership. This pattern had been set long before the A. F. of L. was
formed in 1886; throughout the nineteenth century most organized
workers' organizations refused to admit blacks.[1]

Racism in American unions was exacerbated by the common practice of management hiring black strikebreakers. In any number of industries, black workers were brought in to replace protesting laborers.
This served to accentuate already pervasive anti-black feeling, which
forced blacks always to work for lower wages than other workers.
Blacks won the hatred of their fellow steelworkers, railroad men and
meat-packers for not honoring strikes and picket lines and because
many black leaders unequivocally sided with anti-union forces. One
black newspaper, *The Colored American*, claimed that, "there is
seldom a time when a strike is justifiable. The attempt to break up
another man's business . . . is revolutionary and anarchistic." Booker
T. Washington pointed out proudly that his race was "not given to
strikes and lockouts."[2]

The leadership of the garment workers' unions attempted to break
this vicious cycle for blacks working in the needle trades. In 1935 the
Negro Labor Conference of New York issued a special resolution com-
mending the "officers and members of the International Ladies Garment Workers Union upon its edifying example of labor solidarity—
regardless of race, creed, or color."[3] One possible explanation for this
policy of racial liberalism in the ILGWU and, to a lesser extent, in the
Amalgamated (the major union in the men's clothing industry) may
lie in the socialism of the leadership and most of the membership.
Like David Dubinsky, Sidney Hillman, Benjamin Schlesinger, Morris
Sigman, Baruch Charney Vladeck, and Abraham Baroff, many had
been converted to socialism in eastern Europe, where they had thrown
themselves into the Bund, the Jewish socialist labor federation

founded in Vilna in 1897. When they arrived in America, many of them fleeing czarist repression of labor radicals, they found themselves attracted to the left wing of the American labor movement and carried on here the traditions of the Bund.[4] Jewish labor organization in America took its first feeble steps in the mid-1880s with the short-lived Yiddisher Arbeter Farayn in New York. In 1888 a more significant and certainly more durable Jewish labor group was founded. The United Hebrew Trades (Faraynikte Yiddishe Geverkshaftn) consisted of Jewish laborers representing a variety of trades and crafts including typesetters, actors, singers, tailors, garment cutters, and furriers. The UHT eagerly plunged into the socialist activities of New York.[5]

The most significant Jewish socialist labor organization was the International Ladies' Garment Workers' Union, founded in 1900. From its earliest years through the mid-1930s, the socialism of the leaders and of much of the rank and file shaped many union programs. It succeeded in organizing everyone in the industry, regardless of skill, and avoided the pitfall of concentrating only on elite workers. It actively supported socialist political campaigns and candidates until the New Deal, and as a result defined for itself a social mission much broader than the A. F. of L.'s "bread-and-butter" unionism.[6] The Amalgamated Clothing Workers, founded in 1914 and directed by Sidney Hillman, did not belong to the A. F. of L. The Federation recognized, instead, the older, more conservative United Garment Workers.[7]

The leaders of both the ILGWU and the Amalgamated, as well as organizers of the United Hebrew Trades and other Jewish labor groups, were socialists and that ideology shaped much of their policy. The active support they gave to socialist political candidates, especially Eugene V. Debs (the ILGWU's Yiddish radio station was named for Debs—WEVD), their vigorous participation in radical efforts of all kinds, and their commitment to industrial unionism accentuated their sharp differences with the A. F. of L. over the purposes of trade unionism. The ILGWU's racial policies through the mid-1930s also differed from the A. F. of L.'s and seemed like the natural consequence of its socialist vision. Yet the answer is not so simple or one-sided. A number of socialist-dominated unions, like the United Brewery Workers, did not make special efforts to unionize blacks. Even powerful socialist unions in socialist-governed Milwaukee, for example, not only failed to design special programs to bring in black members but constructed a consistent pattern of discrimination no different from those of non-socialist unions. The Socialist Party itself hedged on the race question. It made few serious attempts to attract blacks and almost no blacks held even minor positions of leadership within the SPA or the SLP. Eugene V. Debs' American Railway Union explicitly barred blacks, and although Debs went on to vigorously champion the cause of black equality, the Social Party remained tinged with the heritage of ARU's exclusion.[8]

A commitment to socialism, then, does not in and of itself explain the particular racial policies adopted by the ILGWU and by other Jewish labor groups. It obviously was one important factor in determining the course they chose. The centuries-old history of Jewish oppression and the contemporary anxieties of Jewish leaders about the status of American Jews perhaps figured as even more crucial factors.

The history of black unionization and of the Jewish labor movement in the first three decades of the twentieth century yields numerous examples of the special efforts exerted by Jewish labor groups *for* blacks and the public recognition *by* blacks of that Jewish effort. In 1921, for example, the Arbeter Ring (Workmen's Circle), a Jewish-Yiddishist socialist mutual aid society for workers, refused to become chartered in several southern states because the incorporation papers stated that membership must be limited to whites. It was not that they wanted, or even expected, blacks to join the Arbeter Ring, but they did not want to sanction racism in even the most minor way. In 1925 such predominantly Jewish unions as the ILGWU, the United Cloth Hat and Cap Makers, and the Furriers' Union all sent May Day greetings to A. Philip Randolph's black socialist magazine, *The Messenger*. Various Locals of the Amalgamated extended their warm wishes to "Our Exploited Negro Brothers," "To Our Black Fellow Workers," and "To the Oppressed Black Toilers." These scattered acts and the more thoroughgoing policies of the garment trade unions received the attention of black leaders. Jewish labor activists were no doubt thrilled when in 1935 the New York Negro Labor Conference heartily congratulated the "officers and members of the International Ladies' Garment Workers' Union upon its edifying example of labor solidarity...." It went on to express the "hope that other labor units will emulate its example for the general good of all labor."[9]

The Jewish interest in black workers manifested itself in two ways. First, Jewish leaders actively supported black efforts to unionize themselves. Second, Jewish labor unions, especially the ILGWU, developed extensive programs to attract black workers into their ranks. In both areas Jewishness emerged as an important motivating factor and in both areas Jews went out of their way to publicize their endeavors for black workers.

JEWISH AID TO BLACK UNIONS

In the first decades of the twentieth century black workers largely stood outside organized labor. They had little or no chance to reap the benefits of the growing strength and respectability of trade unionism. Among those Americans who were concerned about the mounting isolation of the black worker could be counted numerous Jews from both within and without the labor movement. Acting on this concern and motivated by both economic and psychological impulses, Jews attempted to help black workers help themselves. This can be demonstrated clearly by examining Jewish assistance to A. Philip Randolph's Brotherhood of Sleeping Car Porters and also in the heavy Jewish involvement with the Harlem Labor Conference in the mid-1930s.

In 1925, A. Philip Randolph, a black socialist prominent in Harlem and in radical circles, began organizing the Pullman porters. Randolph, a highly controversial figure, had migrated from Florida to Harlem in the early years of the twentieth century, and in 1912 he joined the Socialist Party in Harlem. As a New York socialist, he came in frequent and, it seems, amicable contact with Jews of the same political stripe. In 1917 he and Chandler Owens, an associate, engineered Morris Hillquit's mayoral campaign in Harlem. They claimed that the Jewish socialist was the only candidate that "any self-respecting Negro could vote for" and they actively canvassed the black community on Hillquit's behalf. Randolph and Owens in 1920 assumed leadership of the National Association for the Promotion of Labor Unionism among Negroes. On the advisory board of this short-lived body they found themselves working with Hillquit, as well as with Joseph Schlossberg of the Amalgamated Clothing Workers Union,

Rose Schneiderman of the ILGWU, and I. A. Shiplacoff of the International Pocketbook Workers' Union.

Randolph, who was a very charismatic and flamboyant leader,
often assumed a non-conventional posture. By the time the United
States had entered World War I, he had become the editor of *The
Messenger*, touted as "The Only Radical Negro Magazine in America," and as "The Only Magazine of Scientific Radicalism in the
World Published by Negroes." *The Messenger* provided a forum for
the young militant blacks of Harlem and attracted the attention of
many black writers, artists, and intellectuals. It launched a scathing
critique of American racism and vehemently condemned United
States participation in the war. Before the United States Post Office
denied Randolph's magazine second-class mailing privileges, Randolph had the chance to write as a socialist and as a militant black
that his opposition would not "be drowned by prayers of patriotism.
The[ir] gospel of obey and trust has been replaced by one of rebel and
demand."[10]

Wartime suppression of most socialist publications, a general national decline in radicalism in the 1920s, and the growth of Marcus
Garvey's Back-to-Africa movement all led to the virtual demise of *The
Messenger*. At the very point when Randolph's career as a journalist
was fading, a delegation from the ineffective Porters Athletic Association approached him to assume the herculean task of organizing the
Pullman porters. After a few months of research and deliberation
Randolph agreed, partially because he saw porters as the perfect
agents to spread unionism and socialism among blacks.

In August 1925 Randolph officially assumed the presidency of the
newly created Brotherhood of Sleeping Car Porters, amid distrust and
suspicion from the Pullman Company and with the open condemnation of the elite of the black community. Earlier attempts to organize
the porters had never met success. Any stirrings of unionization were
blocked by the repression of the Pullman Company and a lack of
interest or support from the labor movement. The nature of the porters' work provided one more obstacle to organization. Since they
rode the trains and worked in small, dispersed units, the porters had
few opportunities for communication among themselves. This made
organizing much more difficult than in factory situations.[11]

Once in control of the Brotherhood, Randolph appealed to Con-

gress, which was then debating legislation concerning railroad workers. Randolph wanted Congress and the public to learn about the
paltry wages, the tedious hours of humiliation and hard work endured
by the porters, as well as the Pullman Company's intransigent refusal
to recognize any labor group other than a puppet company union. The
congressman whom Randolph approached to speak in behalf of the
porters in the House of Representatives was Emanuel Celler, a Jew
who represented a predominantly Jewish district in Brooklyn. Celler
agreed and submitted a resolution instructing the Labor Committee
to "investigate the wages, hours, and conditions of employment of the
Pullman porters." When the Rules Committee killed the Celler resolution Randolph attempted to take the porters' cause to the Board of
Mediation, created by the 1926 Railway Labor Act. Several Jewish
lawyers served as the Brotherhood's counsel: Samuel Untermyer,
Louis Waldman, Morris Ernst, and Morris Hillquit. Untermyer and
Waldman advised Randolph that, under existing law, the Brotherhood had no legal case against the yellow-dog contracts which the
company circulated among the workers. They suggested, instead, that
the union educate the porters never to sign such statements.

Through the first decade of the union's life Jewish leaders found
their way into its affairs. For example, when the Brotherhood was having jurisdictional quarrels with another union, the Hotel Alliance,
leaders of the United Hebrew Trades stepped in to mediate. In 1930 a
dispute between two black labor organizers of the Brotherhood,
Frank Crosswaith and Roy Lancaster, threatened the stability of the
union and I. A. Shiplacoff, a Jewish labor leader from the International Pocketbook Makers' Union, served on the panel formed to adjudi-
cate. [12] Jewish leaders from outside organized labor also gave money
to the cause of the sleeping car porters' union. Herbert Lehman
counted himself among the many Jewish donors at a time when the
porters' cause was far from respectable. Rabbi Stephen Wise also
supported the union and Randolph often consulted with him on strategy and public relations. Wise publicly commended Randolph's work
and extended his greetings to Randolph and the Brotherhood,
stating:

I like the Brotherhood of Sleeping Car Porters because it sym-
bolizes the earnest will of thousands of men to render their ser-

vice to the public under conditions which guarantee to the membership work and wages that shall make possible the best service on their part. Our business is to make America great and to keep it free. God help all of us to move vigorously and constructively towards that end!

Wise also put Randolph in contact with other influential and affluent Jews who might be sympathetic to the porters' cause. Thus, Jewish aid to Randolph was not insignificant; it was well-known and it came early. The *Jewish Daily Bulletin* even noted with glee that Henry Ford's anti-Semitic *Dearborn Independent* claimed that Jews were the real power behind A. Philip Randolph. [13] Jewish organs of public opinion wanted to be linked in the public's mind with Randolph and his heroic efforts.

The warm response extended by Jewish leaders to Randolph in the 1920s and 1930s was echoed by other Jews within the labor movement. Abraham Lefkowitz, an Urban League officer and a founder of the New York Teachers' Union, thought of the porters in Randolph's ranks as "heroic men who are fighting for a living wage in order that they may not have to be the recipients of charity." Lefkowitz went on to wish that

> my colored brothers will realize that they have the privilege of fighting for things worth while. The Pullman Company will always place the rights of property above the rights of humanity and self interest above social interest . . . [but] your men will have to contend with the added difficulty of race prejudice of his mistaken and miseducated white brothers, even in the industrial field . . . but . . . Let your men bear in mind that the eyes of America are upon them. Fight on, your fellow workers are with you.

Few American workers evinced this solidarity with the porters; few American workers would be willing to claim that they were with Randolph; yet the leaders of Jewish labor did not hesitate to publicize that they were. The Workmen's Circle yearly gave money to the Brotherhood and had earlier supported *The Messenger*. The leaders of the Arbeter Ring invited Randolph to several of their conventions in the

1920s where he graphically drew the parallels between the black and the Jewish experience. (Randolph was one of few non-Yiddish-speaking personalities to address this group.) From 1922, ILGWU conventions praised Randolph's activities, and each year the union voted to add money to his coffers. The 1922 convention declared Randolph and Chandler Owens "class-conscious and intelligent Negroes." *The Messenger* was heralded as the "only Negro publication in America which supports the organized workers both on the industrial and political fields." Individual ILGWU locals also contributed money to the organization of the Pullman porters, and the union's official publication, *Justice*, praised *The Messenger* and told the garment workers: "If you want the Negro workers in your shop to *join the Union*, to become members of the great army of organized labor, ask them to read *The Messenger*." Committees from Randolph's magazine attended meetings of the ILGWU General Executive Board. [14] *Fortschritt*, published by the Amalgamated Clothing Workers, carried appeals by Randolph and Owens for money and in 1920 the Yiddish labor publication went on to editorialize:

> The Negro workers are a great and growing force in industry. They will cooperate . . . with their fellow workers of other races only to the extent that they are educated . . . *The Messenger* is doing this work and is entitled to our support."

Jewish labor leaders actively joined in yet another effort to organize black workers, the Harlem Labor Committee, and once again were extremely pleased by the amount of publicity that their participation generated. The Harlem Labor Committee, founded in 1935, was a federation of all black trade unionists in New York City and served as a nucleus for further unionization drives among blacks. The chairman of the committee was Frank Crosswaith, an associate of Randolph and a prominent figure in black labor circles. He also served as the general organizer for the International Ladies' Garment Workers' Union. The Harlem Committee functioned for several months as a purely black group. In that period it secured admission for a handful of blacks into a dozen New York unions. The group, however, decided that it could be more effective if it extended its scope and reached out to sympathetic white trade unionists. Consequently, in July 1935 an enlarged Harlem Labor Committee met. Among its vice-presidents were Morris Feinstone, the Executive Secretary of the United Hebrew Trades and Julius Hochman, an ILGWU vice-president and a leader of the dressmakers' union. Among the sponsoring and participating organizations were the Joint Board of the Amalgamated Clothing Workers, Local #10 of the ILGWU and Locals #25, 66, 91, 35, 102, 22, 60, 89, 19953, 142, and 38. The Capmakers' Union Local #1, the Cleaners', Dyers', and Pressers' Union, the Joint Council Knit Goods Workers' Union, the Joint Board Cloak, Suit, and Shirtmakers' Union and the Joint Board Dress and Waistmakers Union of the ILGWU also sent representatives, as did the Pocketbook Workers International Union. Seven branches of the Workmen's Circle were represented at the organizing meeting and they maintained a lively interest in the progress of the group. Its headquarters, the Harlem Labor Center, happened to be at the offices of the West Harlem branch of the Dressmakers' Union, Local #22 of the ILGWU.

Jewish labor leaders featured prominently in the formation of the Harlem group, and Crosswaith and the other black unionists claimed that they had been inspired by the example of Jewish labor. In Crosswaith's call to local unions to join the Harlem Labor Committee, he stated that "the invaluable service which the United Hebrew Trades and the Women's Trade Union League are rendering to labor among their respective groups may be duplicated among Negro workers." The purpose of the Harlem Labor Committee was "to create the agency which will apply the principles of the United Hebrew Trades . . . to the problems of the Negro workers." While Jewish laborists were searching for more than just public recognition, they greeted such statements with satisfaction. They had also been gratified when Randolph and Owens had written to the Socialist *Call* in 1920:

Upon a careful and critical survey of unions in New York and in other sections of the country, the editors of *The Messenger* have found that the Jewish workers are some of the most class-conscious, and, too, the most sympathetic with the colored workers' strivings on the industrial field. We have yet to find a single group of Jewish workers manifesting unconcern or hostility to bringing their colored brothers into their unions. In fact, there is always a readiness, a willingness, an eagerness to extend the hand of fellowship, of brotherhood and good will to their fellow workers. [15]

Jewish leaders, both within and without the labor movement, had little to gain directly in aiding A. Philip Randolph and the organization of the Pullman porters. Jewish assistance to the Harlem Labor Conference might have had some minor significance for certain locals of the ILGWU, but it attracted far more attention from Jewish labor leaders than warranted by the number of blacks in the garment trades. Jews lent their time, energy, and money to the various black unionization efforts out of more than purely economic self-interest. Like all other Jewish efforts for black causes, this aid stemmed from a variety of motives and fulfilled many psychological needs of Jews as a marginal group in American society. As with all other Jewish efforts for black causes, Jews sought to publicize their achievements and link their name openly with the struggle for black advancement.

"SUPPORTING WORDS BY PROPER ACTION": JEWS, BLACKS AND THE GARMENT UNIONS

While black workers never approached being a majority in the garment trade, their numbers were certainly significant. Needlework had been a traditional occupation for blacks since antebellum slavery. After emancipation sizable numbers of black men and women earned a living by sewing. The early censuses of the twentieth century revealed large numbers of Negro tailors and seamstresses in northern cities, as well as in the South. However, in the early decades of the century these black workers were not found in industry; in the 1910 Census of Negro Population, 38,148 black women were listed as dressmakers, none of whom worked in factories.

Most of the black women who did find employment in garment factories in 1922 clustered in semi-skilled positions, but some blacks worked in every part of the garment-making process. Blacks labored on every type of garment, made with every kind of fabric, and at least one-fifth occupied the more skilled positions, such as sewing machine operators. Yet even after blacks in the garment trades had been substantially unionized, the largest number still remained in the least skilled and least desirable jobs. Few blacks cut out garments because to become a cutter, a worker had to have a friend or relative in the craft who would teach him. Outsiders—including women—rarely could break into the craft. In the 1920s and 1930s a number of blacks worked as finishers, examiners, drapers and cleaners, with a significant number, especially of the men, as pressers. Pressing was considered the least desirable task, although it was by no means limited to blacks.

Blacks labored in all kinds of clothing shops but predominated in women's apparel, especially in establishments producing dresses. This branch of the industry grew most rapidly, so it needed more unskilled and semi-skilled hands. On the other hand, few blacks worked in the women's cloak and suit industry which had been a declining trade since World War I and never needed additional labor. [16] By 1930 the number of blacks in the women's clothing industry had increased. According to the Census, 35,400 blacks found jobs in the needle trades, an equal number of men and women. The ILGWU estimated that by 1930 New York City shops accounted for some 20,000 black garment workers. [17]

As the number of blacks in the trade increased, especially in New York, after 1920, the number of blacks in the International Ladies' Garment Workers' Union gradually rose. From 1900 to 1910 there were no black members on the union rolls. The first detailed study of black membership in the ILGWU, carried out by the Urban League in 1925 as part of a larger study of trade unions and blacks, computed that of nine ILGWU locals, three stated that they kept no figures on their racial composition, while six others reported a total of 1,348 black members, comprising about 1.7 percent of their total membership. In 1929 the ILGWU discovered that of 4,000 black women working in some 3,500 dress shops in New York, only 200 were union members. By 1935, 6,704 blacks belonged to Manhattan locals and blacks made up about 4.4 percent of the clothing unions. In 1937 the figure had risen to 5 percent. [18]

The ILGWU never relegated blacks to segregated locals, although some branches of locals had only black members. This resulted from the particular manner in which the union broke itself down. The ILGWU sanctioned four kinds of locals. There were craft locals, such as the pressers or the cutters or the finishers. There were language locals, Yiddish, Italian, or Polish, which occasionally cut across craft lines. If enough members of a particular language group concentrated in a particular craft, they could then form a Yiddish cloakmakers' or an Italian dressmakers' local. Other locals, like the Knitted Garment Workers or the Whitegood Workers, united all workers in a particular trade and included cutters, pressers, hemmers, and operators of all languages. The ILGWU also had industrial locals in small towns where it had too few members to warrant a more detailed breakdown. A local in a large city had any number of branches, divided along language or residential lines. Thus, in New York, the Harlem Dressmakers, of Local #22, was all black because there were enough dressmakers in Harlem to constitute a branch and all happened to be black.

The problem of ethnic and racial diversity troubled the ILGWU long before blacks entered the trade in large numbers. Special organizers were hired in 1910 to work among Italians and Poles and continued through the 1920s. The leadership recognized that immigrant workers responded best to members of their own ethnic group, and the ILGWU sanctioned the division of the union into language-ethnic groups as a way to appeal most to members. While this ethnic breakdown occasionally loomed as an obstacle to worker solidarity, it was chosen as the most effective vehicle to reach the largest numbers of workers. English was used in the mass meetings or where no one language predominated. In the 1920s Rose Schneiderman, an ILGWU organizer, insisted that Local #62, the Undergarment Workers, change from Yiddish to English in its meetings so that the black women could understand and participate. Blacks were thus encouraged to join a union which readily accepted differences between groups and viewed ethnic distinctions as a bridgeable gulf between workers. [19]

The first record of blacks in the ILGWU in 1909 coincided with the year of the great dressmakers' strike, and the fervor of the protesting workers reportedly impressed one black woman so much that she declared: "It's a good thing, this strike is, it makes you feel like a real grown-up person . . . But I wish I'd feel about it like them Jew girls do. Why their eyes flash fire as soon as they commence to talk about the strike—and a lot of talk they can put up—at times they make a body feel like two cents." Mary White Ovington remarked in *Half A Man*, her 1911 study of blacks in New York, that during this strike the Jewish dressmakers were "ready to accept the colored worker. Jewish girls are especially tolerant. They believe that good character and decent manners should count, not color." The dressmakers' union began to include blacks in 1909 and by 1925 it had sixty black members.

Other ILGWU locals recorded their first black members in 1910. The shirtwaist strike of that year attracted some blacks to the union, and Ovington was convinced that black participation in the strike was:

profoundly important in its breaking down of feeling between nationalities, its union of all working women in a common cause, that the colored girl, while very slightly concerned in the strike itself, may profit by the more generous feeling it engendered.

In that same year blacks entered the Childrens' Dress, Bathrobe and House Dress Makers' Union #91 as well as some scattered locals of the Furriers' Union. [20]

Blacks often entered the union by a circuitous path. Brought as strikebreakers into the women's clothing factories in a particular city, they often remained after the dispute was settled. The ILGWU then went about trying to unionize the former strikebreakers as a way to ensure a cohesive work force. In Chicago in 1917 black strikebreakers were used, but as soon as the strike subsided, they joined the union. Thus, by 1920 a number of the all-black dress shops in Chicago had been organized by the ILGWU. Similarly, in Philadelphia blacks were first employed as strikebreakers in the industry in 1921. They later gained a foothold in the trade and then were unionized by the ILGWU.

In the late 1920s a fierce split developed between the union leadership and its left wing, both of which were predominantly Jewish. Both groups struggled to win the support of the black workers in the trade. In 1928 the left wing broke off and organized the rival Needle Trade Workers' Industrial Union. This short-lived group maintained an aggressive, but not very successful program for signing up black members. Its actions, however, stimulated the regular unionists to increase their efforts among black workers. The massive organizational drive of the ILGWU in 1933, spurred also by the National Recovery Act, greatly augmented the number of blacks in the union. Local #22, the dressmakers, had 4,000 black members out of 28,000, and Local #40, the Dress Pressers Union, also contained a substantial number. [21]

This trend was not random and grew as much out of the ILGWU's aggressive efforts as it did out of a natural tendency for all new workers to flock to the union ranks. A 1931 study of labor unions and blacks noted this ILGWU effort which "has tried hard to gain the confidence of the Negro worker. It has not only employed Negro organizers, but has made it a practice to push the Negro forward wherever possible and to encourage him to take an active part in organization affairs." As early as 1920 the ILGWU, conscious of the increasing number of black garment workers, realized the need to adopt an aggressive policy to bring them under the union's umbrella. It noted in its convention that year:

A new class of workers, colored women, have begun to enter the various industries controlled by our organization. We note with satisfaction that our General Executive Board has taken cognizance of this fact and has started a campaign among these colored workers. Your committee recommends that the incoming General Executive Board continue this campaign and bring them under the banner of our International.

In the decade of the 1920s the ILGWU began to exert special efforts to attract blacks to its ranks. Besides passing resounding resolutions, which often proved difficult to implement, almost every year in all the various cities where the ILGWU functioned, its leaders attempted to actualize the mandate to unionize black workers. Even earlier, in 1917, when the union was trying to make headway in Baltimore, a special black organizer came on the union payroll to assist "in organizing the colored workers." Sam Smith was a black minister who worked in a dress shop and the black workers in Baltimore reportedly "show[ed] a very keen interest in the movement." Thousands of dollars were spent on black organizing in Baltimore and for three years the ILGWU kept a black organizer in their employ. [22]

The women's garment trade had an even larger base in Chicago than in Baltimore, and here, too, the ILGWU took special steps to organize black workers. According to one history of black participation in trade unions in Chicago, "The International . . . instead of fighting these newcomers [blacks] and trying to eliminate them from the trade . . . accepted them as a permanent part of the industry and made every effort to organize them. Those who came into the union were given full equality." The Industrial Secretary of the Urban League noted in 1923 that, as a result of the ILGWU's special efforts, most of the interracial garment shops in Chicago were fully unionized and one Chicago ILGWU organizer asserted that "every effort should be undertaken to educate the colored race . . . we have an open door for every worker regardless of nationality or color . . . . "

In Chicago the ILGWU met opposition from the shop owners, who naturally wanted to continue to employ non-unionized black labor. Management not only resorted to the trick of bringing in black strike-breakers but, in several instances, fired blacks for joining the union. In one case the owners locked out all unionized Negro workers and tried to convince the union to replace them with whites. The ILGWU refused and struck the shop. Opposition to ILGWU organizers was not limited to employers; the elite of Chicago's black community also tried to stand in the way. When black leaders in 1921 actually did the recruiting of the strikebreakers, the union began to realize that their hostility could negate all organizational work with blacks who, at that time, made up over 20 percent of the garment trade in Chicago. The ILGWU, in turn, launched a massive campaign to woo the black press, churches and professional groups. This strategy had some success and the union appointed the head of the Armstrong Association, a local black uplift group, as a full-time organizer. The ILGWU's problems with Chicago's black elite did not, however, end quickly, and in the early 1930s, the Chicago Urban League once again recruited strikebreakers in an ILGWU strike against the Nelli Ann Dress Shop. [23]

In 1934, continuing in their struggle, the ILGWU again made vigorous efforts to attract blacks in Chicago, focusing on the workers in Sopkins Apron factories. A black organizer, Frank Crosswaith, was dispatched by the ILGWU to Chicago to lead the drive to unionize the Sopkins workers. He and the rest of the ILGWU leadership based the union appeal on both class and race issues. It detailed the exploitation of the black workers in the shops in handbills and circulars and chided them: "Why are you still the victims of these injustices? Is it because you are colored? Or is it because you are not organized?" The official union communique went on to lay the blame on both racism and non-unionization:

> Your boss tries to make you believe that he is doing you a favor by permitting you to slave for him, because you are colored. If you have any race pride or self respect you would resent this insult of the boss. But you can only resent it effectively through United Action. We had to resent it in our shops. WE ORGANIZED. And that is why we have recaptured our pride, saved our self-respect, increased our wages, reduced our hours of work, stopped chiseling and improved our conditions. YOU CAN DO LIKEWISE, BUT ONLY THROUGH ORGANIZATION.

The Sopkins strike and the Union's intense rhetoric rekindled anti-union sentiment in bourgeois black circles in Chicago. The black clergy and the *Chicago Defender* launched a massive campaign on the South Side to prove that black workers were "loyal" to their jobs. The Sopkins incident stirred up a furor in both black and ILGWU circles. Yet it serves to exemplify the many special organizing efforts in Chicago undertaken by the leaders of the women's clothing workers' union in its attempts to bring black laborers under the protection and control of the union. [24]

The center of the garment trade and the headquarters of the ILGWU was New York City, and it was here that the union developed its most vigorous and dynamic programs for bringing in black workers. A 1931 study, *The Black Worker*, by Sterling Spero and Abraham Harris, found this fact noteworthy. "It is extraordinary," the authors mused, "to find an organization going out of its way to organize a group which is an unimportant strategically as the Negro is in New York."

In 1922 the New York ILGWU staged its first special meeting for black workers in the dress and waist shops. Julius Hochman, the vice-president of the ILGWU and a leader of the dressmakers, Grace

Campbell, a black garment worker, and A. Philip Randolph all addressed the meeting. This was not Randolph's first appearance at an
ILGWU event. He and Chandler Owens were frequently present and
according to the union's magazine, *Justice*, "assisted the organization
at mass meetings or during strikes." In 1923 three special mass meetings were held for the same purpose, to win over black workers. Randolph addressed all three assemblies and his fiery reputation attracted large crowds. The union leaders were pleased with their first efforts
among blacks and one officer of the Dress and Waist workers noted
proudly:

> The tide of unionism is slowly though thoroughly reaching . . .
> the women workers of the Negro race employed in our industry
> who have in former years been regarded by the employers as a
> bulwark of defense against the Union and who for a long time
> were immune to the message of organized labor. In the last year
> a number of Negro workers have joined the Union and have
> thereby improved their condition in the shops.

The January 1923 meeting for black dressmakers not only featured
Randolph, but also enlisted the services of a Harlem minister,
Reverend Charles Miller, who appeared at several ILGWU meetings
over the course of the next few years.

New York ILGWU locals proved somewhat more successful in
establishing amicable relations with the city's black elite than with
similar groups in Chicago. A 1929 unionization drive received the
warm support of the New York Urban League. It allowed a special
ILGWU committee on black workers which had been established that
year to be housed at its headquarters. The ILGWU frequently used
Harlem churches and social halls for union meetings and organizational drives. When Charles Zimmerman became president of Local
#22 in 1933 he immediately established contact with the Urban
League, the NAACP, and the Harlem branch of the YMCA to solicit
their support for his organizing efforts among black dressmakers. [25]

One weapon the union used to increase the number of black members was to hire permanent black organizers. While black recruiters
had been employed in Chicago and Baltimore on a temporary basis
from the beginning of the decade, the 1925 ILGWU convention re-

solved that "it might be well to consider the employment of special Negro organizers to bring the message of unionism closer to these workers." One such fulltime staff person, hired as a result of a 1929 study which indicated that the union had been less than successful in attracting blacks, was Floria Pinckney, a graduate of Brookwood Labor College and an active member of the Women's Trade Union League. She addressed scores of meetings of black garment workers, answering questions about the union, and serving as a liaison between the ILGWU and black organizations. As late as 1936 she still worked for the union. In October, 1934 the ILGWU hired yet another full-time black organizer, Frank Crosswaith. Crosswaith had been closely associated with A. Philip Randolph, participated actively in black socialist affairs, and edited the Negro Labor News Service. Crosswaith had long known and worked with Jewish socialists and labor leaders. He first met Morris Hillquit in 1914 and ardently admired him. Crosswaith carried the union's message to black workers in New York, Chicago, and wherever the union sent him. He constantly tried to show black workers in the clothing industry that

> the thousands of Negro garment workers now enjoying membership in the happy family of the ILGWU are . . . blazing a new trail. They are now an integral part of this great army of organized labor struggling to win for all workers, regardless of race, creed, sex or color a fairer share of the products of their labor . . .

In a speech to the Dress Pressers, Local #69, Crosswaith suggested that "there are innumerable instances on record where these organizations [the ILGWU and the Amalgamated] have literally bent backwards . . . to show a preference to Negro members. In many of the shops and factories where members of these unions are employed, Negro chairmen and chairladies can be found presiding over the destiny of their white fellow workers." [26]

The union leadership itself appealed directly to black workers, freely using the race issue to win their support. All the special meetings and drives of the 1930s emphasized the theme that blacks constituted the most exploited and abused element within the labor force and direct appeals were made to blacks on the basis of both of worker solidarity and race progress. In 1934 David Dubinsky, addressing a pressers' rally in Harlem, exhorted the assembled:

You, colored workers, were exploited and mistreated in the shops worse than any other group . . . the distinction between black and white still runs deep through every walk of life except our labor movement . . . They used to say that Negroes are an unorganizable element. You are a living argument against this assertion. It is quite clear . . . that you have the same desire to live comfortably and to fight for decent living conditions as people of all other races.

The ILGWU geared many cultural and educational activities to blacks and this reinforced the union message. In 1919 the ILGWU sponsored a lecture by Kelly Miller of Howard University, whom *Justice* described as the "ablest colored man in the United States." Appearances by Chandler Owens and A. Philip Randolph at ILGWU meetings were common. In 1931 James Weldon Johnson lectured at Unity House, the union's Pennsylvania mountain resort, and Lester Granger, the Industrial Secretary of the Urban League, sent blacks to the ILGWU to take courses on blacks and the labor movement. The union's educational department offered several courses in Negro history in the United States and on blacks and the development of American labor. In October 1935 the ILGWU, with the Negro Labor Conference, sponsored a symposium on "The Negro in the Labor Movement," chaired by Frank Crosswaith and featuring Julius Hochman of Local #22, as well as Randolph and several other New York black trade unionists. These special educational programs all attempted to point out the close relationship between unionism and race advancement and, more important, the link between Jewish unionism and black economic security. [27]

Official ILGWU literature aimed at blacks was clearly propagandistic. It made a point, for example, of stressing the active involvement of blacks in union affairs. Blacks were photographed prominently participating in ILGWU classes and clubs. Blacks could be seen on the pages of *Justice*, in pictures depicting vacations at Unity House, and in union-sponsored plays, concerts, classes and athletic events. The publications of the union *never* mentioned the existence of black strikebreakers and always went out of their way to note the dynamic presence of blacks at ILGWU strikes and events. In 1914 a union reporter noted that "streams of women of all nationalities, hues, and races . . . negro women, Italian, German . . . were pouring into the improvised polling place" to vote in union elections. In 1916 Abraham Baroff of the Waist and Dressmakers' Union described a parade in which "negro girls and women were marching side by side" with the white workers. ILGWU rhetoric glowed with accounts of "tens of thousands . . . marching through the streets . . . of New York. Among them men and women, young and old . . . white and colored . . . . " ILGWU publications stressed the interracial make-up of the union. In 1935 a series of profiles of ILGWU members in *Justice* played up the ethnic diversity of the union and prominently featured such black members as "Hazel—An Operator," "Esther—A Finisher," "Mabel—A Finisher," and "Bessie—An Operator." Esther, the finisher featured on October 15, was described as a "strange kind of 'foreigner.' Esther is a Southerner. Born in the United States, she is reviled by her fellow citizens. Esther is a dressmaker and a worker, like the rest of us. That is her passport to her new country, to the land of the working class."

The ILGWU was highly conscious and sensitive about its public image on the race question. It carefully aligned itself with all moves to unionize black labor. It supported and cultivated extensive dealings with A. Philip Randolph and was one of the few A. F. of L. unions to take the initiative in the formation of the Negro Labor Conference of 1935. Yearly it condemned racial discrimination in the American Federation of Labor, and its delegates to the A. F. of L. annual meetings frequently pleaded the case of the unorganized black workers. ILGWU conventions passed resolutions decrying racism in general. They spoke out against lynching and voted to contribute money to help the Scottsboro boys.[28] The ILGWU also contributed money to numerous other black causes and endeavors. The Joint Board of the Waist and Dressmakers' Union in 1923 voted to support a New York group, the African Blood Brotherhood, which was about to publish a magazine "for the purposes of spreading among the Negro workers the ideas of trade Unionism." ILGWU propaganda on the race issue and the vaunting of its own egalitarian policies most dramatically surfaced in 1934 when the union met in Chicago to hold its yearly convention. At the last minute it was discovered that the Medinah Temple, where the meetings were to be held, maintained discriminatory practices against blacks. With fanfare and bravado the newly elected president of the ILGWU, David Dubinsky, led the union in a mass exodus from the hall to the Morrison Hotel. The ILGWU publicly labeled the Medinah Temple a "Jim Crow hotel," and Dubinsky proclaimed, "we are a labor union and we do not share in racial prejudices. We are committed to the principle of equality and justice and resistance to oppression. It was natural for us to resist this discrimination. . . . It was just a case of supporting words by proper action." *Justice* asserted that the Medinah incident was "the first instance on record of a big labor organization . . . actively and demonstratively taking sides on behalf of racial equality in the labor movement." An official history of the union, published in 1935, echoed this and quoted a black delegate as she left Medinah hall:

> The union has meant a great deal to us. It has improved our condition of toil but more than that, our union has turned the noble phrase of solidarity and fraternity of all labor into a reality. From the union we have received that protection, recognition, and human treatment which a capitalist society has denied us. [29]

Much of the ILGWU propaganda was clearly heavy-handed and self-laudatory. Yet the union was willing to put action behind rhetoric and really organize black workers in the trade. It was ready to design special programs to attract blacks into its locals, and blacks were frequently elected to positions of some power and responsibility within its ranks. The union's upper leadership in these years remained entirely Jewish, but blacks moved into offices of some importance in the locals. As early as 1918 two black women served on the executive board of Philadelphia's Local #15. In 1925 a black woman was reelected to #22's executive board, although it was unclear exactly when she had first been elected. In the same year Local #132, the Cloak Button Workers, elected a black president, Frank Hall. Particularly striking was the fact that the local was not predominantly black, nor did blacks compose a significant minority. The number of black officers increased in the years of the NRA drive, 1934 and 1935. Local #25, the Blouse and Waist Makers, had three blacks on the executive board, six shop chairladies, and a black member of this local was elected a delegate to the ILGWU's 1934 Annual Meeting.

Local #91, which encompassed many of the miscellaneous ladies' garment trades, had both a black chairman and an executive board member. In the Ladies' Neckwear Workers Local #142 three blacks served on the board and several were chairladies. There was one black chairlady in 1935 in Local #66, representing the Bonnaz, Singer and Hand Embroiderers, Tuckers, Stitchers, and Pleaters' Union, a local comprising the most highly skilled workers, and Local #62, the Whitegood Workers, elected five black shop chairladies.

The Dressmakers' Local #22 contained more black members in positions of authority than any ILGWU unit. The local was approximately 9.5 percent black in membership and in 1932 it elected a black woman to the executive board and four more in 1934. In 1935 they were joined by two additional black women. One of these, Edith Ransom, served not only on the executive board but was the business agent for the local. Numerous black chairladies were also elected in Local #22. [30]

The International Ladies' Garment Workers' Union, the largest Jewish-dominated trade union in America, committed itself to bringing black needle workers into its ranks. It designed special programs for blacks. It waged a vigorous propaganda campaign to convince black workers that its professions of racial equality were sincere. Blacks were able to achieve a modest amount of power within its ranks. The other predominantly Jewish garment union, the Amalgamated Clothing Workers, developed less comprehensive and less extensive programs for black workers. Fewer blacks labored in the men's clothing industry because men's clothing required fewer unskilled and semi-skilled workers. Employers had greater difficulty using blacks as strikebreakers or as cheap labor because it was a less diffuse industry than the women's and broke down into fewer small shops. Instead, men's clothing centered in a limited number of large plants where the union exerted greater control over employers. It tended to be an overcrowded field which did not expand rapidly, and there were fewer surges in production when massive numbers of new workers were required.

The Amalgamated's formal position on race was non-discriminatory. Its leaders like Joseph Schlossberg and Sidney Hillman participated in general efforts to organize black workers in spite of the fact that these efforts would have had little or no impact on their own industry. The handful of blacks in the industry was unionized, was never excluded from Union benefits and never shunted into segregated locals. The largest number of blacks in the Amalgamated were pressers, the least skilled and the least desirable position. Yet according to union statistics, in unionized shops pressers received higher wages than operators to compensate for the unpleasantness of the work.

Some figures on blacks in the Amalgamated emerged from a 1936 study on blacks and trade unions. Local #11, for example, recorded no black members nor had any ever applied for membership. Yet the secretary of the local believed that "Negroes should be organized as workers rather than as Negro workers." Local #158 of the Amalgamated, the Wholesale Clothing Clerks, on the other hand, had twenty-five black members out of 1,500. Blacks had belonged to that local since its founding in 1933. One black sat on its executive board and the local officials noted that blacks had participated amicably with white workers in a number of strikes. Organized in 1918, Local #243, the Shirt Makers and Pressers' local, claimed that it began organizing black workers before it had organized anyone else. In spite of such efforts, only twenty-five black women were involved. A similarly scanty representation can be seen among the Neckwear Makers in Local #250, where eighty-five black members belonged out of a general membership of 2,800. This local had employed Frank Crosswaith on several occasions to stimulate black membership, and blacks had moved up to some positions of minor leadership. Since 1918 blacks had joined strikes organized by Local #250.[31] Like the ILGWU the Amalgamated felt the need to employ full-time black organizers and did so in Chicago in 1919. Black members were reported in locals in Baltimore, Cincinnati, Richmond, and Camden, New Jersey. Finally, the 1920 Amalgamated convention passed a resolution declaring that "such jobs as running elevators, cleaning buildings and assisting in the packing and shipping rooms are essential to the industry." These tasks were performed primarily by blacks and the ACWA set about to organize the workers.

The leadership of the Amalgamated thus positively identified itself with the cause of black unionization. It also participated in the Harlem Labor Conference, supported A. Philip Randolph, and carried on some limited organizational work with its own black workers. Since there were so few blacks in the trade, it had little else to do. The same was true of some of the smaller needle trade unions with heavy Jewish membership and leadership such as the Cloth, Hat, Cap and Millinery Workers' Union, which organized the few blacks it could and generally supported the cause of blacks in the labor movement. This was also the case with the International Fur and Leather Goods Workers. The Secretary-Manager of the Millinery Blockers, Local #42 of the United Hatters, Cap and Milliner Workers' Union, Max Goldman, noted that of the 300 members of his local, 100 were blacks. This local maintained a non-discriminatory policy and claimed, "As we find them in the shops, we take them in . . . These are all expert millinery blockers." While few of the blacks held elective positions in Local #42, they did participate eagerly in strikes, serving as voluntary strike organizers. The local had met with some resistance from black workers initially but it brought in Frank Crosswaith to encourage the blacks to join the union.[32]

The Amalgamated's limited work with its black workers elicited praise from many blacks who surveyed the labor situation. But it was the ILGWU with its extensive black programs which black labor leaders heralded. In labor circles in general the ILGWU had the reputation of being one of the most egalitarian labor unions, and the Negro Labor Conference congratulated the ILGWU for its bold and vigorous efforts. Charles Franklin, who studied the black labor scene of New York in the 1930s, also lauded the union. After describing ILGWU policy in detail, he proclaimed that in that union blacks and whites "together they are participating in the privileges and responsibilities of union membership and are fighting to gain and maintain desirable standards of employment. An example well worth the emulation of other labor unions in Manhattan and in the United States!" Frank Crosswaith, who had worked for the ILGWU, the Amalgamated and some of the other smaller needle unions, shared this positive assessment of its policies. Addressing the 1934 ILGWU convention, Crosswaith told the predominantly Jewish audience: "You have written in the record of American labor a page so grand, a page so cadent and so fragrant, that not the wrinkles of time nor the music of years will ever be able to dull the luster of that record . . . ."; and the dean of black organized labor, A. Philip Randolph, added his voice of tribute to the "brotherhood displayed by the Jewish workers."[33]

THE JEWISH FACTOR AND THE UNION LEADERSHIP

Why did the leaders of the Jewish unions work so actively for the organization of black workers? Like the Jewish philanthropists and civil rights activists, Jewish labor leaders did not always speak explicitly to this issue, nor did they systematically work out the various strands of motivation. Nonetheless, the official union publications of the ILGWU and the Amalgamated, *Justice* and *Fortschritt*, mirrored the thinking of the top union leadership and provide a key to determining motivation.

The Jewish union leaders had at least three crucial identities and roles in the years before 1935. They were union leaders, concerned with the immediate improvement of wages and conditions of their constituents; they were socialists, committed to the replacement of capitalism with state ownership of the means of production; and they were Jews, acutely conscious of the history of their group and sensitive to its needs in America. All of these identities woven together help explain their interest in blacks. An analysis of the Jewish labor press reveals, however, that *the* pivotal identity motivating Jewish labor leaders to assist black workers was their Jewishness. Furthermore, the history of non-Jewish socialism and unionization supports this conclusion.

In some ways the racial stance of the Jewish unions, and especially of the ILGWU, constituted sound unionism and economic pragmatism. A significant number of black workers had made their way into the ladies' garment trade and therefore, economic self-interest dictated that the union organize them. However, many Jews from the Amalgamated, from the Arbeter Ring and from other Jewish labor groups which had few or no black workers in their ranks, also committed themselves to the organization of black laborers. They had no immediate economic stake in supporting A. Philip Randolph's work with the Pullman porters. Furthermore, many unions in a position analogous to that of the ILGWU responded to unorganized blacks with hostility and antagonism. Most American unions did not go out of their way to organize former strikebreakers, with the possible exception of the United Mine Workers. [34]

Many contemporary commentators thought that the ILGWU's socialist ideology led to its commitment to black workers, but sup-

port for blacks did not *inevitably* follow from organized American socialism. The Socialist Party itself hedged on the race issue in order to
win southern support. Socialist-dominated labor unions like the
brewers made no efforts to organize blacks, and by the mid-1930s the
ILGWU and the Amalgamated, under David Dubinsky and Sidney
Hillman, had begun to move away from socialism toward embracing
the New Deal liberalism of the Democratic Party. Their commitment
to black workers, however, did not diminish, but rather intensified.
Clearly, socialism and organizing black workers were not directly
linked.

The publications of the socialist Jewish unions commented constantly on the conditions of blacks in the United States, but paid very
little or no attention to the social, economic, and political conditions
of other minorities in the society. The interest expressed in black life
and culture far outpaced interest in any other group, except in Jews
themselves. Numerous articles detailed the conditions of blacks in
America, North and South, while they put forward no commensurate
coverage of women, Italians, Irish, Poles, or Oriental Americans.

Were the commitment to the socialism pivotal in motivating Jewish labor leaders' interest in blacks, then one would expect Jewish
labor publications to pose a relatively consistent class analysis of
black oppression. Many of the discussions of black life were, in fact,
occasionally posed in these terms, but no thorough analysis of race
ever emerged. In discussions of the epidemic of race riots from 1916 to
1919, the Jewish labor press equivocated on the causes of the riots.
Stunned by outbreaks of race conflicts like the East St. Louis, Washington, Chicago, and Tulsa riots, the Jewish labor press viewed them
not as isolated incidents but as part of a growing "War Between
White and Black Americans." S. Yanofsky, a frequent writer for *Justice*, perceived a direct connection between World War I, which most
ILGWU leaders opposed, and the outbursts of racial violence. In his
view, war service had caused "negroes . . . to feel that they were created
for something better than lynch victims for white folks and instead of
enduring with the necessary martyr-meekness . . . they began to
answer with pistol shots." Yanofsky was convinced that in both
Washington and Chicago blacks should be congratulated for ration-
ally defending themselves against whites. The Jewish labor magazines
wanted to know who the whites were who had attacked the black dis-

tricts of these various industrial cities. One writer for *Fortschritt* implied that workers were responsible for the horrors of East St. Louis, and he particularly indicted the American Federation of Labor. Samuel Gompers had publicly stated that the importation of black strikebreakers had precipitated the riots and the *Fortschritt* article noted that Gompers, the "labor, sweet as sugar old man . . . is too old to fight in the streets. He does not have the strength to take a direct part in the pogroms . . . He pours oil on the fire. He just prods the others." Morris Zisskind, an Amalgamated organizer in Chicago, felt, however, that in the case of the Chicago riot organized labor should not take the blame and that the fault lay with the unorganized workers of the cities. In *Fortschritt* he said he hoped that "the Jewish workers shall not remain with the impression that the white organized laborers in Chicago were involved in the riots." Not only was "the hatred against the Negroes strongest among the ignorant, uncivilized white, unorganized workers," but the employers, the owners of the stockyards, must be blamed because they purposely kept blacks from joining the unions. The real estate "patriots" shared a burden of the guilt, as did the black churches and politicians who maintained an anti-union stance. *Justice* reflected on the whole series of race riots and blamed the capitalists who were "paving the way for a race war in America, compared with which all the recent riots are but harmless pastimes."[35] A thoroughly orthodox socialist analysis would have blamed the riot squarely on capitalism. These writers, however, saw the issue more in terms of a long-standing racial-ethnic prejudice than in terms of class warfare and antagonism.

Jewish labor publications also reacted to the great migration to the North out of a less than strictly socialist framework. From a purely economic point of view, the migration increased the labor pool and depressed wages and was not likely to advance socialism. Instead, poor and uneducated blacks, taking cues from many anti-union and anti-socialist black leaders, were likely to hinder the class struggle. Furthermore, their presence would exacerbate racial conflict which in turn interfered with the process of creating class solidarity. Yet both *Fortschritt* and *Justice* heralded the migration as a positive step for blacks. *Justice* compared the migration to a heroic strike of black farm laborers, and neither periodical seemed upset at the prospect of thousands of blacks streaming into the northern industrial cities.

Again, they reacted in a less than rational and calculatedly socialist way: their concern for the oppressed masses of rural blacks allowed them to overcome any fears about blacks retarding the development of class consciousness.

These publications never showed concern over the potential threat blacks might pose to the socialist movement or to the stability of working conditions in the North. In fact they went out of their way to prove what excellent unionists blacks could be. Max Danish of *Justice* asserted:

> There is no reason on earth . . . why the labor movement of America should not open its gates wide to the Negro workers and show them a cordial fraternal attitude. Of the response to such willingness to admit Negro workers on terms of equality into the labor union, there can be little doubt. Then instead of a liability, the masses of colored workers . . . will become an asset to the labor movement. The story of the rise of labor unionism in many of the trades with a preponderence of foreign workers who at one time were deemed unorganizable and are now among the best divisions of organized labor in the country, is an excellent example to have in mind.

The organizing efforts of black laborers were painted in heroic terms. Naturally, A. Philip Randolph's work with the porters merited special attention and a 1928 speech by Urban League economist Ira De A. Reid on New York's Yiddish radio station, WEVD, concerning "The Decline of the Negro Strikebreaker," was greeted by *Justice* as a call to the A. F. of L. to change its policy and to stop thinking of blacks merely as opponents of organized labor.

The ILGWU, an affiliate of the A. F. of L., generally criticized the Federation's policies on race, but it felt compelled to herald frequent dramatic changes. In 1918 *Justice* asserted that "the American Federation of Labor which has discriminated against the Negro and forced them to establish independent unions, has seen its mistake and is seeking to correct it." It reported in 1919 that the Virginia Federation of Labor had placed a black on its executive committee and that, in the pre-riot weeks in Chicago, the Chicago Federation of Labor had begun to wage a concerted campaign to bring blacks into the stockyards unions. Even Gompers, who usually came out as a villain par excellence in the columns of *Justice*, received praise in connection with a 1921 conference to set up a "board of adjustment for the colored freight handlers and station employees." [36]

On yet another issue the Jewish labor magazines adopted a stand which did not indicate a systematic class interpretation of the racial situation in the United States. The issue of lynching and, more generally, the analysis of the nature of southern society was a major preoccupation. Max Danish, for example, described southerners as "very strong for . . . race riots, broiling of negroes, lynching parties of the Ku Klux Klan variety or otherwise and such other outdoor sports." The reporters of *Justice* and *Fortschritt* detailed lynching after lynching, using these incidents as a vehicle to totally condemn the South. Yet they never discussed the economic basis of southern life, the conflict between the planter and poor white class or the economic tensions which led to outbursts of racial violence. Lynchings, to them, grew out of race hatred, not class antipathy. Perhaps more striking was the analysis of the Leo Frank lynching. The newspapers saw the Frank case as just one link in an endless chain of lynchings. The lynching of Frank fit the all too clear pattern. *Fortschritt* noted:

> The day after Frank was lynched . . . three Negroes were lynched in the state of Alabama. A few weeks ago a Negro was burnt alive in Texas. Lynchings in the Southern states are a frequent occurrence and the public is amused by them. It is told, that to the burning of a Negro, the best citizens of the town come, dressed in holiday clothing. For them it is an interesting sport.

Both publications were appalled by the Frank murder. In passionate terms, the writers cried out against the injustice and brutality. Leo Frank was a capitalist, but the newspapers *never* noted this. They reacted to Frank not as socialists but as Jews. [37]

The contents of the official Jewish union publications suggest that Jewish identity among these union leaders often overshadowed either union or socialist identity, and that their intense interest in blacks was rarely couched in either unionist or socialist terms. The magazines and the Jewish labor leaders themselves in speeches and other writings often pointed out the ethnic motivation for their concern. Both *Justice* and *Fortschritt* gave a peculiarly Jewish twist to their discussions of the riots, the "pogroms." Just as Christians in Europe had believed that "there can never be an unjustified pogrom against a Jew," *Fortschritt* noted that "many Americans believed that the 'pogrom' in East St. Louis, Illinois, was a just one, because it was against Negroes. It was just, because they should not have had black skin." The same article which indicted Samuel Gompers expressed shame that Gompers, a Jew, had acted just like an "anti-semitic Russian hooligan." [38] Writers for these magazines and other Jewish labor leaders believed that as Jews they felt a certain bond of empathy with exploited blacks. They believed that their Jewish identity enabled them to work vigorously for the unionization of blacks, that a history of oppression had predisposed them to dealing sensitively and sympathetically with America's oppressed workers. Reminiscing about the labor movement in the early 1930s, Charles Zimmerman, who led Local #22's drive to attract black members, noted that the Jewish labor leaders and rank and file members had all "been subjected to persecution in the old country. They came here to look for a free society. They had escaped pogroms." That history of oppression had made them more aware of the plight of blacks. Zimmerman noted that an egalitarian "spirit was infused in the masses of Jewish workers." [39] This perception of Jewish empathy for blacks, noted by Zimmerman and invoked again and again in the pages of *Justice* and *Fortschritt*, was noted also by black labor activists. Randolph attributed Jewish vigor in working with Negro laborers to two facts. First, Jews possessed a "deeper and more fundamental understanding of the class struggle." Secondly, Jewish workers shared with blacks a "history that is complete with unspeakable outrages . . . they have drunk the bitter dregs of the cup of persecution."

This emphasis on empathy bore a striking similarity to the thinking of Jews like Stephen Wise, Louis Marshall, or Julius Rosenwald, who also believed that they had been drawn to the cause of black civil rights and black philanthropy because a past of suffering had attuned them to the needs of others.

The Jewish labor unionists came from a very different milieu than the middle-class, Americanized Jews who joined the NAACP or donated money to Tuskegee. They were, to a person, born in eastern Europe and had worked their way out of the garment factories to positions of leadership in the Jewish labor movement. Like their more affluent coreligionists, they hoped to solve the problems of Jewish identity in American society. Like the Marshalls, Wises, Schiffs, and Walds, they were attempting to carve out for themselves, as leaders of the Jewish world, a comfortable role in American society. Like the more affluent Jews, they wanted American society to recognize the special contributions they were offering—as Jews. Like their "western European" fellow Jews they were seeking to demonstrate that Jews had a special mission in America. In their case it was to organize the unorganizable, to lend a hand to the friendless of the labor force.

Obviously, both socialism and unionism were important determinants of the Jewish labor leaders' stance on race. Their roles as union leaders and socialists shaped the particular form of their interest and involvement. However, neither of these factors explains why they became interested in blacks in the first place. Many other socialists and labor leaders remained indifferent and hostile, while many anti-socialist and anti-unionist Jews actively worked for blacks through other media—the civil rights movement and through philanthropic and social service endeavors. Clearly, there was something about being Jewish in America in these years that caused these labor leaders to support black causes as they did.

NOTES

1. Leon F. Litwack, *North of Slavery: The Negro in the Free States, 1790-1860* (Chicago: University of Chicago Press, 1961), pp. 153-167; Oscar Handlin, *Boston's Immigrants, 1790-1880* (Cambridge: Harvard University Press, 1941), p. 132; Robert Ernst, "The Economic Status of New York City Negroes, 1850-1863," *Negro History Bulletin*, 12 (March 1949): 139-141; Sumner E. Madison, "The Labor Movement and the Negro During Reconstruction," *Journal of Negro History*, 33 (October 1948): 429; Gerald Grob, *Workers and Utopia: A Study of Ideological Conflict in the American Labor Movement, 1865-1900* (Evanston, Ill.: Northwestern University Press, 1961); Sidney H. Kessler, "The Organization of Negroes in the Knights of Labor," *Journal of Negro History*, 37 (July 1952): 248-275; Marc Karson and Ronald Radosh, "The American Federation of Labor and the Negro Worker, 1894-1949," in Julius Jacobson, ed., *The Negro and the American Labor Movement* (Garden City, N.Y.: Doubleday and Company, 1968), pp. 155-158.

2. Chicago Commission on Race Relations, *The Negro in Chicago* (Chicago: University of Chicago Press, 1922); Elliot M. Rudwick, *Race Riot at East St. Louis, July 2,*

1917 (Carbondale: Southern Illinois University Press, 1964); William M. Tuttle, *Race Riot: Chicago in the Red Summer of 1919* (New York: Atheneum, 1970); Arthur Waskow, *From Race Riot to Sit-In; 1919 and the 1960's: A Study in the Connections Between Conflict and Violence* (Garden City, N.Y.: Doubleday and Company, 1966), pp. 38-104; August Meier and Elliot Rudwick, "Attitudes of Negro Leaders Towards the American Labor Movement from the Civil War to World War One," in Julius Jacobson, *The Negro and the American Labor Movement, pp.* 27-48.

3. Charles L. Franklin, *The Negro Labor Unionist of New York: Problems and Conditions Among Negroes in the Labor Unions in Manhattan with Special Reference to the N.R.A. Situation* (New York: Columbia University Press, 1936), p. 152.

4. Hertz Burgin, *Geshichte Fun Der Yiddisher Arbeter Bavegung in America* (New York: United Hebrew Trades, 1915); A. Menes, "Di Yidishe Arbeter Bavegung in Rusland Fun Onhaib 70er Bizn Soif 90er Yorn," *Historishe Shriftn* (Vilna: 1932); N. A. Buchbinder, *Geshichte Fun Yiddisher Arbeter Bavegung in Russland* (Vilna: 1931); Elias Tcherikower, *The Early Jewish Labor Movement in the United States* (New York: YIVO, 1961); Bernard Weinstein, *Di Yiddishe Unions in America* (New York: United Hebrew Trades, 1929); Melech Epstein, *Jewish Labor in USA: 1914-1952* (New York: Trade Union Sponsoring Committee, 1953), pp. 364-401.

5. Abraham M. Rogoff, *Formative Years of the Jewish Labor Movement in the United States: 1890-1900* (Ann Arbor: Edwards Brothers, 1945); H. Lang and M. Feinstone, eds., *Geverkshaftn: Zamelbuch Tsu Fuftsik Yor Fun Di Farainikte Yiddishe Geverkshaftn* (New York: United Hebrew Trades, 1938); Brernard Weinstein, *Fertzig Yor in Der Yiddisher Arbeter Bavegung* (New York: Vecker Press, 1924); J. Kaminsky, *Fertzig Yor Arbeter Ring: A Geshichte in Bilder* (New York: National Executive Committee of the Workmen's Circle, 1925); Melvyn Dubofsky, "Organized Labor and the Immigrant in New York City, 1900-1918," *Labor History*, 2 (Spring 1961): 182-201.

6. Lewis L. Lorwin, *The Women's Garment Workers: A History of the International Ladies' Garment Workers' Union* (New Yrk: B. W. Huebsch, 1924); B. Hoffman, *Fuftzig Yor Clokmacher Union: 1886-1936* (New York: Cloak Operators' Local 117, 1936); J. M. Budish and George Soule, *The New Unionism in the Clothing Industry* (New York: Harcourt, Brace, 1920); Joel I. Seidman, *The Needle Trades* (New York: Farrar, Rinehart and Company, 1942); Benjamin Stolberg, *Tailor's Progress: The Story of a Famous Union and the Men who Made It* (Garden City, N.Y.: Doubleday, Doran, 1942); Aaron Antonovsky, *The Early Jewish Labor Movement in the United States* (New York: YIVO, 1961); Hyman Berman, "Era of Protocol: A Chapter in the History of the International Ladies' Garment Workers' Union, 1910-1916" (Ph.D. dissertation, Columbia University, 1955); Abraham Bisno, *Union Pioneer: An Autobiographical Account of Bisno's Early Life and the Beginnings of Unionism in the Women's Garment Industry* (Madison: University of Wisconsin Press, 1967); Rose Schneiderman, *All For One* (New York: P. S. Eriksson, 1967); Will Herberg, "Jewish Labor Movement in the United States: Early Years to World War I," *Industrial and Labor Relations Review*, 5 (July 1952): 501-523.

7. Will Herberg, "Jewish Labor Movement in the United States: World War I to the Present," *Industrial and Labor Relations Review*, 6 (October 1952): 44-66; Melech Epstein, *Jewish Labor in USA* (Amalgamated Clothing Workers of America, Research

Department) *The Clothing Workers of Chicago, 1910-1922* (Chicago: Amalgamated Clothing Workers, 1922); Mathew Josephson, *Sidney Hillman: Statesman of American Labor* (New York: Doubleday and Company, 1952); Joseph Schlossberg, *The Workers and Their World: Aspects of the Workers' Struggle at Home and Abroad* (New York: American Labor Party Committee, 1935); Elden La Mar, *The Clothing Workers in Philadelphia: History of Their Struggles for Union and Security* (Philadelphia: Philadelphia Joint Board, Amalgamated Clothing Workers of America, 1940); Barbara W. Newell, *Chicago and the Labor Movement: Metropolitan Unionism in the 1930's* (Urbana: University of Illinois Press, 1961), pp. 54-78; Irving Bernstein, *Turbulent Years: A History of the American Worker, 1933-1941* (Boston: Houghton Mifflin, 1970), pp. 66-89.

8. Ray Ginger, *The Bending Cross: A Biography of Eugene V. Debs* (New Brunswick, N.J.: Rutgers University Press, 1949), pp. 106-107, 231-232; David A. Shannon, *The Socialist Party of America: A History* (New York: Macmillan, 1955), pp. 50-53; James Weinstein, *The Decline of Socialism in America, 1912-1925* (New York: Monthly Review Press, 1967), pp. 63-73; Thomas W. Gavett, *Development of the Labor Movement in Milwaukee* (Madison: University of Wisconsin Press, 1965).

9. *Kultur Und Leben* (May-June 1969): 7; *The Messenger*, 7 (May 1925): 1-7; Charles L. Franklin, *The Negro Labor Unionist*, p. 152.

10. Jervis Anderson, *A. Philip Randolph: A Biographical Portrait* (New York: Harcourt Brace Jovanovich, 1972), p. 98.

11. Brailsford R. Brazeal, *The Brotherhood of Sleeping Car Porters: Its Origins and Development* (New York: Harper and Brothers, 1946); Jervis Anderson, *A. Philip Randolph*, pp. 151-186.

12. Jervis Anderson, *A. Philip Randolph*, pp. 80, 92-95; U.S. House of Representatives, Resolution 238, 69th Cong. 1st Sess, April 26, 1926; B. Brazeal, The *Brotherhood*, p. 33; American Federation of Labor, *Convention Proceedings, 1929*, Resolution 32, p. 137; B. Brazeal, *The Brotherhood*, p. 58.

13. Herbert Lehman to A. Philip Randolph, September 19, 1935, Herbert Lehman Papers; A. Philip Randolph to Stephen Wise, June 15, 1927; June 28, 1926; September 3, 1926; May 18, 1927; December 10, 1928; September 28, 1928; Stephen Wise to A. Philip Randolph, May 19, 1927; June 1, 1927; June 20, 1927; December 6, 1928; September 13, 1930; April 21, 1927, Stephen Wise Papers, 71; *Jewish Daily Bulletin*, July 29, 1925.

14. *The Messenger*, 8 (October 1926): 315; Abraham Sachs, *Di Geschichte Fun Der Arbeiter Ring: 1892-1925* (New York: National Executive Committee of the Workmen's Circle, 1925), pp. 694, 712, 730, 754; Y. Kaminsky, *Fertzig Yor Arbeter Ring: 1892-1925*, p. 71; *Der Fraynd*, 22 (September 1931): 28; International Ladies' Garment Workers' Union, *Report and Proceedings of the Seventeenth Convention*, p. 250; *Report and Proceedings of the Sixteenth Convention*, p. 82; *Report and Proceedings of the Twentieth Convention*, pp. 53-54, 139-140; *Justice*, 5 (June 29, 1923): 139-140; 5 (August 6, 1923): 3; 4 (October 6, 1922): 8; *The Messenger*, 7 (May 1925).

15. Charles Franklin, *The Negro Labor Unionist*, pp. 142-149, 157-158; "Call to Local Unions," n.d., 1935, National Urban League Papers, 4,3; Stephen Wise, *Challenging Years*, p. 118. Jews had been involved in similar earlier projects. In 1919 Morris

Hillquit, Jacob Panken, Joseph Schlossberg, and Abraham Shiplacoff had been active in the National Association for the Promotion of Labor Unionism Among Negroes. See *The National Civic Federation Review*, 4 (March 25, 1919): 13, 20. In 1925 the Trade Union Committee for Organizing Negro Workers received considerable aid from Abraham Baroff, an ILGWU official. See *Justice*, 7 (August 7, 1925): 4; 7 (June 12, 1925): 3; Circular from Abraham Baroff, May 7, 1925, National Urban League Papers, 4, 4.

16. George E. Haynes, *The Negro at Work in New York City* (New York: Columbia University Press, 1912), p. 72; Allan Spear, *Black Chicago*, p. 111; U.S. Department of Labor, Women's Bureau, *Negro Women in Industry* (Washington, D.C.: Government Printing Office, 1922), pp. 32-34.

17. Lazare Teper, *The Women's Garment Industry* (New York: Educational Department, ILGWU, 1937), p. 7.

18. Ira DeA. Reid, *Negro Membership in American Labor Unions* (New York: Alexander Press, 1930), p. 101; *Justice*, 3 (January 14, 1921): 3; Lewis Lorwin, *The Women's Garment Workers*, p. 149; "Labor Union Survey," International Tuckers, Hemstitchers, Pleaters; Dressmakers' Union of Greater New York; Shirtmakers Union No. 23; Ladies' Tailors Custom Dressmakers, Union No. 91; Dressmakers' Union; Millinery Workers' Union; Ladies' Tailors and Custom Dressmakers' No. 38; Amalgamated Clothing Workers of America; Joint Board of Furriers No. 1, 5, 10, 15, Urban League Papers, 6, 98; Charles Franklin, *The Negro Labor Unionist*, p. 115; Jack Hardy, *The Clothing Workers: A Study of the Conditions and Struggles in the Needle Trades* (New York: International Publishers, 1935); Lazare Teper, *The Women's Garment Industry* (New York: Educational Department, ILGWU, 1937), p. 7.

19. ILGWU, *Structure and Functioning* (New York: Educational Department, ILGWU, 1934), pp. 9-10, 13; ILGWU, *Report and Proceedings of the Tenth Convention*, p. 100, 121; Harry Lang, *"62": Biography of a Union* (New York: Undergarment and Negligee Workers' Union, Local 62, ILGWU, 1940), p. 166.

20. Quoted in Moses Rischin, *The Promised City*, p. 249; "Labor Union Survey," Dressmakers' Union of Greater New York, Urban League Papers, 6, 88; Mary White Ovington, *Half a Man: The Status of the Negro in New York* (New York: Longmans, Green and Company, 1911), p. 163; "Labor Union Survey," Childrens' Dress, Bath Robe and House Dress Makers' Union; Joint Board Furriers Union, Urban League Papers, 6, 88.

21. Chicago Commission on Race Relations, *The Negro in Chicago*, pp. 414-415; Sterling Spero and Abraham Harris, *The Black Worker* (New York: Columbia University Press, 1931), pp. 343-344, 339; Irving Bernstein, *The Turbulent Years*, p. 87.

22. ILGWU, *Report and Proceedings of the Fifteenth Convention*, pp. 134, 90, 50-51; ILGWU, *Report and Proceedings of the Sixteenth Convention*, p. 78; *Report and Proceedings of the Seventeenth Convention*, pp. 106-107; *Report and Proceedings of the Nineteenth Convention*, p. 266; *Justice*, 5 (July 6, 1923): 7; *The Ladies' Garment Worker*, 8 (June 1917): 14-16; Sterling Spero and Abraham Harris, *The Black Worker*, p. 340; ILGWU, *Report and Proceedings of the Fifteenth Convention*, p. 36.

23. Chicago Commission on Race Relations, *The Negro in Chicago*, pp. 414-415; *Opportunity*, 1 (February 1923): 15-16; 2 (August 1924): 242; *Justice*, 7 (March 23, 1925): 8; Wilfred Carsel, *A History of the Chicago Ladies' Garment Union* (Chicago:

Normandie House, 1940), p. 10; Sterling Spero and Abraham Harris, *The Black Worker*, pp. 339-340; Barbara Newell, *Chicago and the Labor Movement*, p. 239.

24. "A Message to the Workers in Sopkins' Shops," n.d., Urban League Papers, 4, 4; *Justice*, 13 (February 1934): 16; *Crisis*, 42 (April 1935): 103-114; 42 (June 1935): 167-187; 42 (May 1935): 153-154; *Opportunity*, 13 (May 1935): 142-144.

25. Sterling Spero and Abraham Harris, *The Black Worker*, p. 342; *Justice*, 4 (March 10, 1922): 8; 4 (October 6, 1922): 8; 5 (January 5, 1923): 11; 5 (January 12, 1923): 1; 5 (August 3, 1923): 11; 5 (May 25, 1923): 11; 5 (January 12, 1923): 1; ILGWU, *Report and Proceedings of the Seventeenth Convention*, p. 82; Charles Franklin, *The Negro Labor Unionist*, p. 115; Charles Zimmerman, private interview held at Local 22, ILGWU, New York, New York, December 1973.

26. ILGWU, *Report and Proceedings of the Eighteenth Convention*, pp. 137-138; *Justice*, 11 (September 27, 1929): 3; *Justice*, 12 (February 28, 1930): 2; *Opportunity*, 7 (December 1929): 389; *Justice*, 11 (September 27, 1929): 1-2; Lester B. Granger to Sidney Hillman, June 4, 1936, Urban League Papers, 4, 3; *Justice*, 11 (December 20, 1929): 5; Frank Crosswaith to Algernon Lee, July 30, 1929, Morris Hillquit Papers, 1; "Negro Labor News Service: Press Release," February 7, 1931, Socialist Party Papers, 12; *Justice*, 16 (October 1934): 11-12; 16 (November 1934): 7; 17 (January 1935): 5.

27. *Justice*, 13 (September 1931): 13; 12 (December 5, 1930): 2; 12 (November 21, 1930): 7; 16 (December 1934): 28; 16 (May-June 1934): 11; 13 (October 1931): 9; 16 (March 1934): 4; 16 (January 1934): 9; 17 (January 15, 1935): 12; 17 (August 1935): 6; 1 (March 15, 1919): 7; 2 (July 23, 1920): 2; *Opportunity*, 7 (April 1934): 107-110; T. Arnold Hill To David Dubinsky, July 23, 1935, Urban League Papers, 41.

28. Mark Starr to Lester Granger, November 13, 1935, Urban League Papers, 4, 4; Circular from Mark Starr, September 14, 1935, Urban League Papers, 4, 3; ILGWU, Educational Department, *The Story of the I.L.G.W.U.* (New York: ILGWU, 1935): 16; *Report and Proceedings of the Seventeenth Convention*, pp. 107-108; Ryllis Lynip, *Growing Up: Twenty-One Years of Education with the I.L.G.W.U.* (New York: Educational Department, ILGWU, 1938); Herman Feldman, *Racial Factors in American Industry* (New York: Harper and Brothers, 1931), pp. 222-223.

29. *Justice*, 17 (July 15, 1935): 8; 17 (August 1, 1935): 16; 16 (July 1934): 6; 5 (June 22, 1923): 11; 2 (August 6, 1920): 3; 5 (June 29, 1923): 11; 5 (June 15, 1923): 11; 17 (September 15, 1935): 7; 17 (March 15, 1935): 5; 17 (July 15, 1935): 5; 17 (October 15, 1935): 6; 16 (July 1934): 16; ILGWU, *Report and Proceedings of the Twenty-Sixth Convention*, p. 166; *Report and Proceedings of the Twenty-Fourth Convention*, pp. 53-54, 139-140; *Report and Proceedings of the Nineteenth Convention*, p. 250; *Report and Proceedings of the Twenty-Sixth Convention*, pp. 97, 124, 145-146; *Report and Proceedings of the Twenty-Ninth Convention*, pp. 103, 145; Max Danish, *The World of David Dubinsky* (Cleveland: World Publishing Company, 1957); ILGWU, Educational Department, *The Story of the I.L.G.W.U.* (New York: ILGWU, 1935), p. 29.

30. Clipping from *Report and Proceedings of the Thirty-Eighth Annual Convention of the A. F. of L.*, June 6, 1918, Urban League Papers, 1, 1; *Justice*, 7 (August 28, 1925); 7 (February 13, 1925): 2; 17 (February 1, 1935): 5; 16 (May-June 1934): 24; 17 (January 1, 1935): 3; Trade Union Committee Report, n.d., 1925, Urban League Papers, 4, 8; Charles Franklin, *The Negro Labor Unionist*, pp. 201-203, 310-318; Benjamin Stolberg, *Tailor's Progress*, p. 43; *Our Union at Work: A Study of the Activities of Dress-*

makers' *Union Local 22, I.L.G.W.U., from April, 1935, to April, 1937, Based on the Report of the Executive Board* (New York: Dressmakers' Union Local 22, 1937); *The Present Economic Position of the Negro Woman Worker* (Mimeographed Report, U.S. Department of Labor, 1935), p. 6; *Opportunity*, 12 (April 1934): 52-58; St. Clair Drake and Horace Cayton, *Black Metropolis: A Study of Negro Life in a Northern City* (New York: Harcourt, Brace, 1945), p. 327.

31. Matthew Josephson, *Sidney Hillman*; Herbert R. Northrup, *Organized Labor and the Negro* (New York: Harper and Brothers, 1944), p. 123; F. Ray Marshall, *The Negro and Organized Labor* (New York: John Wiley and Sons, 1965), p. 1; "Labor Union Survey," Urban League Papers, 6, 8; Herman Feldman, *Racial Factors*, p. 223; Charles Franklin, *The Negro Trade Unionist*, pp. 305-307.

32. Sterling Spero and Abraham Harris, *The Black Worker*, pp. 346, 347; Herbert Northrup, *Organized Labor*, pp. 129-133; Charles Franklin, *The Negro Labor Unionist*, pp. 333-334, 363, 387-388; *Opportunity*, 6 (August 1929): 257.

33. Lester B. Granger, *New Trade Union Movements and the Negro Worker* (Mimeographed Report Issued by the Negro Workers' Councils, September 23, 1937), p. 2; Barbara Newell, *Chicago and the Labor Movement*, p. 239; Quoted in Charles Franklin, *The Negro Labor Unionist*, p. 152, 267-269, 235-236; *Justice*, 17 (August 1935): 1; 16 (July 1934): 13; ILGWU, *Report and Proceedings of the Twenty-Sixth Convention*, pp. 248-250; *Opportunity*, 12 (November 1934): 340-342.

34. Herbert Gutman, "The Negro and the United Mine Workers of America," in Julius Jacobson, ed., *The Negro and the American Labor Movement*, pp. 49-127.

35. *Justice*, 3 (July 26, 1919): 2; 2 (August 2, 1919): 7; (October 11, 1919): 3; *Fortschritt*, 3 (July 27, 1917): 4; (July 6, 1919): 5; 5 (July 6, 1919): 4; 5 (August 8, 1919): 4.

36. *Justice*, 5 (June 22, 1923): 9; 7 (February 27, 1925): 8; 3 (April 8, 1921): 2; 9 (October 28, 1927): 7; 5 (July 13, 1923): 11; 5 (May 11, 1923): 2; 1 (July 26, 1919): 7; *Fortschritt*, 5 (July 12, 1918): 12; (August 22, 1919): 5; *Ladies' Garment Worker*, 10 (March 1918): 2.

37. *Fortschritt*, 1 (August 27, 1915): 4; 6 (July 23, 1920): 6; 8 (January 19, 1923): 7; *Justice*, 1 (August 23, 1919): 2; 1 (November 21, 1919): 2; 3 (December 23, 1921): 2; 4 (April 7, 1922): 3; 5 (April 20, 1923): 9.

38. *Justice*, 5 (May 11, 1923): 9; 5 (April 10, 1923): 9; 6 (February 22, 1924): 8; 5 (November 9, 1923): 4; 13 (September 1931): 8; 10 (February 17, 1928): 5; *Fortschritt*, 3 (July 27, 1917): 4; (July 6, 1919): 5; 2 (September 8, 1916): 7.

39. Interview with Charles Zimmerman, Local 22, ILGWU, New York, New York, December 1973.

conclusion

BLACKS AND THE
JEWISH QUEST FOR IDENTITY

Throughout the first decades of the twentieth century the leaders of American Jewry went to great lengths to link their names and their fate in American society with blacks. They not only expended time, influence and their economic resources for various black endeavors—civil rights, philanthropy, social service, labor organizing—but they made sure that their actions were well publicized. On the surface this was less than rational behavior in a country where blacks were reviled by all classes, scorned in all sections. In a nation that maintained a separate legal and political system on the basis of race, why did Jews align with the major victims of that system?

This behavior grew out of the historic roots of Jewish culture and the contemporary status of Jews in their "almost promised land." The involvement with blacks and the keen interest displayed in their plight fulfilled the needs of a group seeking to complete the process of adapting an old culture to a new environment.

Forging a Jewish-black alliance provided several handy tools in completing the task. Jews and blacks shared many concerns. Restrictive housing covenants were used with the same heavy hand to keep Gentile neighborhoods *Judenrein* as they were to keep other areas "lily white." Quotas in colleges and universities slammed the doors on Jewish students with the same rudeness and animosity that excluded blacks.

As many of the Jewish leaders saw it, taking up the cause of blacks provided American Jews with a mission in their new country, a special role which they believed they were uniquely suited to carry out. Their history of suffering, their centuries of exclusion from the mainstreams of national culture—be it German, Polish, Russian, or French—had predisposed them to understand the real needs of a similarly situated group. It was important that someone serve as the middleman between the oppressor and the oppressed, and Jewish leaders eagerly moved into that position. In doing this they believed they were not only helping blacks, but at the same time serving the larger society, contributing to the good and welfare of all. This service might possibly bring in its wake certain benefits for American Jews. It would win them thanks and recognition for doing a crucial job which no one else would—or could—do. That, in turn, could be of immense help in stabilizing the social and political lot of Jews.

Jewish motivation for involvement with blacks, however, was much more complex and significantly more subtle than this, and can be best understood in light of a variety of unconscious needs which came together, propelling Jews into the struggle for black rights.

The issues of black exclusion and oppression provided a stalking horse for American Jewish leaders who were constantly on guard, worrying about the power of anti-Semitic forces in both the United States and Europe. While out of fear they consistently tried to downplay the extent of anti-Jewish action and sentiment in America, they held up the indisputably worse position of blacks as an apt illustration of the negative forces which had also crushed the dreams of an immigrant generation. Analyzing the rhetoric which Jews used when inveighing against racism also helps in probing the more subtle roots of their involvement. Being "good" to blacks, dealing sensitively and sympathetically with them was perceived as a natural outgrowth of the Jewish tradition, and as ethnic group leaders they had a real stake in the preservation of that tradition. They believed that their efforts and concerns for American blacks set Jews apart from other Americans, apart from most Christians. This became, in effect, the American version of the "Chosen People" notion, the American adaptation of the message from Mount Sinai. While Jewish leaders clearly wanted to retain the separateness and integrity of their group, they also felt compelled to prove to America that Jews were not unassimilable, that Jews were not going to remain an alien unalterable group, and here again the imagery of black oppression proved a handy issue. When decrying racism, Jews could orate about how American they had become, how fundamentally they had internalized the principles of the Constitution, the Declaration of Independence, how well-versed they were with the "true" meaning of American history. In fact, they came to assume the posture that they—Jews, who were one, or at most two, generations out of the ghettos of Europe—had internalized those principles and had learned that history better than the "real" Americans.

The Jewish preoccupation with security and overwhelming need for recognition were felt most acutely in the early decades of the twentieth century when the Jewish population of America was stabilizing and at the same time groping for a comfortable niche in American life. The use of black issues as a vehicle to bring American Jewry through the confusing and tortuous path toward accommodation also emerged most strongly in this period. In analyzing the drift of the American Jewish scene and the current of race relations, 1935 emerges as a symbolic date when these two phenomena ceased to operate together. That is not to say that Jewish interest and involvement with blacks ground to a sharp halt in the middle of the 1930s. On the contrary, as we measure the pulse of the civil rights movement and black philanthropic and social projects in the 1940s, 1950s, and 1960s, Jewish support stands undiminished. The leaders of American Jewry continued to lend their time, their money, and their moral support to the heightening struggle for political and legal equality. No one in the 1960s was surprised to see rabbis and Jewish communal leaders joining sit-ins and striding along on marches. No one thought it unusual that the American Jewish world threw itself unequivocally behind the final push for comprehensive civil rights legislation. No one doubted that Jews too "had a dream."

Nor should it be assumed that the Harlem race riot of 1935 ripped asunder an otherwise healthy alliance. While the anti-Semitic cries which resounded in the streets seemed so jarring when set against the chronicles of the decades of Jewish activism in black affairs, it should be kept in mind that discussions of black anti-Semitism remained muted and hushed in both Jewish and black circles until the late 1960s. Occasional hints of black resentment of Jewish merchants surfaced, but disappeared just as quickly. It was in 1935 that the seeds for the disintegration of the black-Jewish alliance were sown. Those seeds were produced as much by the success of that alliance as by the rush of historic events beyond the control of either Jews or blacks.

Since the beginning of the twentieth century Jews had been prodding mainstream liberal institutions to wake up and take note of the extent of black oppression and the legitimacy of black demands. Even before World War I Jews, who had joined the black civil rights movement and the crusade to improve black social and economic conditions, tried to use their strategic middle position to plead the case of blacks to those with "real" power and influence in political parties, in labor unions, in government. By the mid-1930s these efforts were bearing their first tender fruit. The national political coalition within the Democratic party forged during the New Deal began to court the traditionally Republican black voter. By the end of the Second World War blacks had become a major element in any Democratic presidential victory and held a sizable voting bloc in many northern cities. Only twenty years separate 1915 from 1935, but a light year divides Woodrow Wilson's unabashed racism from the first overtures of Franklin Roosevelt and the New Deal coalition. Similarly, 1935 heralded an important shift in the attitude of organized labor toward black workers. In that year the A. F. of L.'s Committee on Industrial Organizations began to move towards the massive unionization drives in the big industries—auto, steel, mining, among others. It was this CIO that set out to organize black laborers. For the first time in the history of American labor in the twentieth century, a major union body held up organizing blacks as a primary goal. Furthermore, in the five years before the outbreak of World War II the Supreme Court added its opinion on the place of blacks in American life and decisions like *Missouri v. Canada* (1936) began to erode the constitutional doctrine of "separate but equal" that was finally struck down in the 1954 Brown decision.

In 1915 the number of institutions and prominent Americans willing to respond to a call for equalizing the races could be counted on the fingers of the hands. By the 1930s the number had increased manifold. In 1915 Jews had been atypical among whites in their public commitment to black civil rights. Twenty years later they had a good deal of company. Consequently, blacks did not have to rely upon Jews nearly as much as they had before. Jews could no longer reasonably claim to be the only group in America that responded sympathetically to black demands. Blacks no longer needed to rely so heavily on Jews as mouthpieces, not only because they now had other white allies but because they were beginning to feel confident about speaking for themselves. They could now expect many people with power and influence to listen to what they had to say. From the mid-1930s this escalating assertiveness of the black leadership also changed the nature of the Jewish-black alliance. By the mid-1930s, for example, power in the NAACP came more into black hands. In late 1934 the Association elected Louis Wright its first black board chairman. In 1935, after a ten-year battle, the Pullman company recognized A. Philip Randolph's Brotherhood of Sleeping Car Porters. The steady accretion of black recognition brought with it a decline in the need for Jewish support.

The Jewish-black alliance had emerged from the almost total weakness of one party. That weakness began to fade as the educational level of blacks rose and as traditional bars to blacks were beginning to fall. The achievement of these goals served to make the alliance obsolete. Jews, in concert with others of a like mind, had wanted to make American political and social institutions sensitive to blacks. Jews, especially those involved with black education, strove to see the creation of a black leadership class. With those two missions partly accomplished, or at least launched, the need for the middlemen, for the white pleaders, Jews or non-Jews, began to diminish.

Just as the legal and political conditions of black Americans went through intense changes in the years preceding World War II, Jewish life also altered in response to new realities. If blacks welcomed Jewish involvement in civil rights and philanthropy because of their need for outside allies and friends with influence, Jews undertook these activities largely because they were insecure in America. That insecurity was diminishing, however. If the "Roosevelt revolution" drew blacks into the Democratic Party and acknowledged the legitimacy of their demands, it also enhanced the influence of Jewish liberal politicians and union leaders. Did Jews really have to worry about their role in American life when a president could openly demand that his advisers clear their decisions "with Sidney?" (Sidney Hillman of the Amalgamated Clothing Workers Union indisputably served as Roosevelt's liaison and lifeline to organized labor.) Two decades earlier, Wilson's nomination of Louis Brandeis to the Supreme Court constituted a bold and daring step. Anti-Semites from the upper echelons of business and politics did everything in their power to try to block the

Brandeis appointment. By 1932 two Jews sat on the high court; by 1939 there were three. On the eve of World War II Jews were also putting their stamp on so much of the culture of the nation—literature, art, cinema, theater, music, academia—that to be Jewish was becoming less and less of a handicap or a barrier to recognition. And those Jews like George Gershwin, Mike Gold, Edna Ferber, Raphael Soyer, Paul Muni, Ben Shahn, to cite but a few, did not feel compelled to hide or camouflage their Jewish background. In fact, many of them believed that much of their artistic and intellectual inspiration had been nurtured and drawn from that tradition.

This is hardly to say that anti-Jewish feeling in America had abated and that Jews, by 1935, were completely at ease in the United States. On the contrary, the pace of anti-Semitism was quickening. Between 1934 and 1939, 105 anti-Semitic organizations were formed compared with a merger fourteen which had surfaced in the years from 1915 to 1933. Despite such a mushrooming of anti-Jewish activity, by the 1930s anti-Semitism was clearly unrespectable and limited to fringe groups. Instead of being penned by heroes like Henry Ford or spewed forth by politically powerful individuals like Tom Watson, anti-Semitic propaganda was being churned out by the Father Coughlins and others clearly outside the mainstream of American thought. Anti-Semitism, while lacking respectability, was still quite evident. Despite the flourishing of anti-Jewish groups, most of which were born of the desperation of the depression, American Jews began to wield a modicum of power and were finding their way into many highly visible and influential circles in American life. One contemporary Jewish writer summarized that "in 1935, we may still say that on the whole the future of Jewry in America, though it has its dangers and weaknesses, still seems sound and hopeful."

Yet the 1930s witnessed the most devastating chapter in the history of world Jewry. In the 1930s the center of world Jewry shifted completely to the United States. It shifted not because of migration. It shifted not because of new cultural or intellectual forces drifting eastward from New York. America achieved this distinction by default. In the 1930s and early 1940s the Jews of Europe and the communities in which they lived were destroyed—both literally and figuratively. The devastation of the Holocaust, beginning with the passage of the Nuremberg Laws of September 1935 which stripped the Jews of Germany of all rights, looms as the single most profound event in the two thousand-year history of the Jewish people. All other events pale in light of Auschwitz and Bergen-Belsen. No other issue even approaches the shattering impact of World War II and its searing memory on the consciousness of Jews. From then on all actions, all thoughts, all activities would have a single point of reference. From then on all American Jewish leaders would search their own souls to find out if they had done as much as they could to prevent it; if they could do enough in the future to stem a second Holocaust. The impotence of Jewish leaders in Europe and in America to do anything to save those six million people who had been the heart of Jewry caused a very profound reaction. Not only can we see that Jews began to turn inward, to direct their emotions and their energies to their own concerns, but they became more open and blatant about their goal—the survival of the group. If that clearly articulated and single-mindedly espoused goal was best served by serving others—blacks, for example—so be it. If that goal was served best by serving themselves—so be it, without shame, without embarrassment.

From the ashes of Holocaust yet another profound event in the history of Jewry grew—the creation of a politically independent Jewish state in 1948. The role of American Jews in that creation is a story which has been told elsewhere, but from that point on the Jewish quest for security and survival became wrapped up in Israel. Whatever other effects Israel has had on the Jewish communities of America, it has provided them with a unifying issue which transcends all divisions, which bridges all rifts. Given a greater degree of Jewish unity coupled with the lingering memory of the devastation of the Holocaust, American Jewish leaders have been constantly reassessing priorities. All actions must inevitably and clearly succor the struggle for the survival of this group in the United States as an identifiably potent group, flexing its muscle in the economic, political, and cultural life of the nation, and in Israel as a secure independent state. Thus, while Jewish leaders continued their support of black civil rights and of black social service projects long into the 1960s, they did so with a different heart than before World War II. In the pre-Holocaust years they sided with blacks partly out of a reticence to tackle anti-Semitism. After the war a strident and aggressive search to expose and ferret out anti-Semitism, no matter how minor, wherever and whenever it raised its head, replaced the timidity. Before American Jews learned about Dachau, and the Warsaw Ghetto, and the crematoria and gas chambers, they went to great lengths to prove that they were not self-serving; that their motives for involvement in black affairs stemmed only from the historic bonds of empathy and commiseration. After the destruction of European Jewry and the birth of Israel, Jewish leaders openly and unabashedly talked about self-interest: how would participation in black causes "help" Jews? Was donating time, money, and emotion to CORE or SNCC or the NAACP "good" for Jews? When in the later years of the 1960s it became less than obvious that such behavior was worthwhile from a Jewish standpoint, American Jews, with a certain degree of sadness and with memories of the past, backed off and began to look elsewhere to satisfy their quest for security and survival.

bibliography

PRIMARY SOURCES

Manuscripts

American Jewish Committee Files. American Jewish Committee. New York, New York.
American Jewish Congress Papers. YIVO Institute, New York, New York.
Felix Frankfurter Papers. Manuscript Division, Library of Congress, Washington, D.C.
Morris Hillquit Papers. Wisconsin State Historical Society, Madison, Wisconsin.
Jewish Communists in the United States Files. YIVO Institute, New York, New York.
Horace Kallen Papers. YIVO Institute, New York, New York.
Labor Zionist Organization Papers, YIVO Institute, New York, New York.
Herbert Lehman Papers. Columbia University, New York, New York.
Salmon O. Levinson Papers. Department of Special Collections, University of Chicago Libraries, Chicago, Illinois.
Meyer London Papers. Tamiment Institute, New York, New York.
Louis Marshall Immigration Collection. American Jewish Historical Society, Brandeis University, Waltham, Massachusetts.
Louis Marshall Papers. American Jewish Archives, Hebrew Union College, Cincinnati, Ohio.
National Association for the Advancement of Colored People Papers. Manuscript Division, Library of Congress, Washington, D.C.
National Urban League Papers. Manuscript Division, Library of Congress, Washington, D.C.
Julius Rosenwald Papers. Department of Special Collections, University of Chicago Libraries, Chicago, Illinois.
Jacob Schiff Papers. American Jewish Archives, Hebrew Union College, Cincinnati, Ohio.
Edwin R. A. Seligman Papers. Columbia University, Manuscript Division, New York, New York.
Socialist Party of America Papers. Wisconsin State Historical Society, Madison, Wisconsin.

Arthur B. Spingarn Papers. Manuscript Division, Library of Congress, Washington, D.C.

Joel E. Spingarn Collection. Howard University Library, Manuscript Division, Washington, D.C.

Joel E. Spingarn Papers. New York Public Library, Manuscript Division, New York, New York.

Baruch Charney Vladeck Papers. Tamiment Institute, New York, New York.

Lillian Wald Collection. New York Public Library, Manuscript Division, New York, New York.

Lillian Wald Papers. Columbia University, Manuscript Division, New York, New York.

Felix Warburg Papers. American Jewish Archives, Hebrew Union College, Cincinnati, Ohio.

Booker T. Washington Papers. Manuscript Division, Library of Congress, Washington, D.C.

Stephen Wise Papers. American Jewish Historical Society, Brandeis University, Waltham, Massachusetts.

Zionist Organization of America Papers. YIVO Institute, New York, New York.

Other Unpublished Primary Sources

Granger, Lester B. "New Trade Union Movements and the Negro Worker." Mimeographed. Negro Workers' Councils, September 23, 1937. Located, U. S. Department of Labor Library, Washington, D.C.

Joint Committee on National Recovery. "The Present Economic Position of the Negro Woman Worker." Mimeographed. 1935. Located, U. S. Department of Labor Library, Washington, D.C.

Newspapers and Periodicals

American Hebrew. 1915-1931.
American Hebrew and Jewish Messenger. 1915-1924.
American Israelite. 1917-1935.
American Jewish World. 1915-1924.
B'nai Brith Magazine. 1924-1935.
Boston Daily Atlas. 1853.
Chicago Defender. January 28, 1928.
Crisis. 1910-1935.
Current Jewish Record. 1931-1935.
Fortschritt. 1915-1935.
Der Fraynd. 1915-1935.
Jewish Daily Bulletin. July 29, 1925.
Jewish Daily Forward, 1915-1935.
Jewish Frontier. 1934-1935.
Jewish Layman. 1926-1935.
Jewish Tribune. 1922-1931.
Jewish Tribune and Hebrew Standard. 1932-1935.

Journal of Jewish Communal Service. 1924-1935.
Justice. 1918-1935.
Kinder Journal. 1921-1935.
Ladies' Garment Worker. 1914-1918.
Literary Digest. August 13, 1927.
Menorah Journal. 1914-1935.
The Messenger. 1919-1928.
Morgen Journal. 1915-1928.
Morgen Journal-Yiddishe Tageblatt. 1928-1935.
National Civic Federation Review. 1919.
New York Age. May 10, 1910.
New York News. December 30, 1922.
New York Times. March 10, 1930, September 15, 1931, November 13, 1932, April 8,
    1933, October 3, 1933.
Observer. Scattered.
Opinion. 1931-1935.
Opportunity. 1922-1935.
Poughkeepsie Sunday Courier. August 15, 1917.
School and Society. June 6, 1925, November 17, 1928, December 20, 1929.
St. Louis Argus. September 27, 1929.
Der Vecker. 1921-1935.
Washington Bee. January 24, 1914, March 24, 1917.
Yiddishe Tageblatt. 1915-1928.
Zukunft. 1914-1935.

Autobiographies, Letters and Memoirs

Adler, Cyrus. *Jacob H. Schiff: His Life and Letters.* Garden City, N.Y.: Doubleday and
    Company, 1928.
Baruch, Bernard. *My Own Story.* New York: Henry Holt and Company, 1957.
Cahan, Abraham. *Bletter Fun Mein Leben.* 5 vols. New York: Forward Press, 1920-
    1931.
Du Bois, W.E.B. *The Autobiography of W.E.B. DuBois: A Soliloquy on Viewing My
    Life from the Last Decade of Its First Century.* New York: International Pub-
    lishers, 1968.
Hays, Arthur Garfield. *City Lawyers: The Autobiography of a Law Practice.* New York:
    Simon and Schuster, 1942.
Hirsch, Emil. *My Religion.* New York: Macmillan Company, 1925.
Johnson, James Weldon. *Along This Way.* New York: De Capo Press, 1933.
Moton, Robert Russa. *Finding a Way Out: An Autobiography.* Garden City: Double-
    day, Page, and Company, 1920.
Ovington, Mary White. *The Walls Came Tumbling Down.* New York: Harcourt, Brace
    and World, 1947.
Phillips, Harlan. *Felix Frankfurter Reminisces.* New York: Reynal and Company,
    1960.

Pickens, William. *Bursting Bonds*. Boston: Jordan and More Press, 1923.

Polier, Justine Wise, and James W. Wise. *The Personal Letters of Stephen Wise*. Boston: Beacon Press, 1956.

Reznikoff, Charles (ed.). *Louis Marshall, Champion of Liberty: Selected Papers and Addresses*. 2 vols. Philadelphia: Jewish Publication Society of America, 1957.

Schneiderman, Rose. *All for One*. New York: P. S. Eriksson, 1967.

Villard, Oswald Garrison. *Fighting Years: Memoirs of a Liberal Editor*. New York: Harcourt, Brace, and Company, 1939.

Wald, Lillian. *The House on Henry Street*. New York: Holt and Company, 1915.

Wald, Lillian. *Windows on Henry Street*. Boston: Little, Brown, 1934.

Washington, Booker T. *My Larger Education: Being Chapters from My Experience*. Garden City: Doubleday, Page and Company, 1911.

Washington, Booker T. *Up from Slavery*. New York: Doubleday, Page and Company, 1901.

White, Walter. *A Man Called White*. New York: Viking Press, 1948.

Wise, Stephen S. *Challenging Years*. New York: G. P. Putnam's Sons, 1946.

Other Writings by Participants

Boas, Franz. "Race Problems in America." *Science*, 5 (May 28, 1909): 839-49.

———. *Anthropology* (New York: Columbia University Press, 1908.)

———. *Anthropology and Modern Life*. New York: W. W. Norton and Company, 1928.

———. "Are the Jews a Race?" *The World Tomorrow*, 10 (January 1923): 5-6.

———. "Aryans and Non-Aryans." *American Mercury*, 32 (June 1934): 219-223.

———. *Changes in the Bodily Forms of Descendants of Immigrants: Reports of the Immigration Commission*. 61 Cong., 2 Sess. Senate Document, No. 208. Washington, D.C., 1911.

———. *The Mind of Primitive Man*. New York: Macmillan Company, 1911.

———. "The Negro and the Demands of Modern Life." *Charities*, 15 (October 1905): 85-88.

———. "The Negroes' Past." *Commencement Address at Atlanta University, May 31, 1906*. Atlanta: Atlanta University Leaflet, 19.

———. "Race Prejudice from the Scientist's Angle." *Forum*, 98 (August 1937): 90-94.

———. *Primitive Art*. Oslo: Instituttet for Sammenlignende Kulturforskning, Series B, 1927.

———. "The Problem of the American Negro." *Yale Review*, 10 (January 1921): 384-395.

———. "The Question of Racial Purity." *American Mercury*, 3 (October 1924): 163-169.

———. *Race and Democratic Society: Collected Addresses and Papers for Lay Audiences*. New York: J. J. Augustine, 1945.

———. "Race and Progress." *Science*, 74 (July 3, 1931): 1-8.

———. "What Is a Race?" *Nation*, 120 (January 28, 1925): 89-91.

———. "What the Negro Has Done in Africa." *The Ethical Record*, 5 (March 1904): 106-109.

Cahan, Abraham. *The Rise of David Levinsky*. New York: Harper and Brothers, 1917.

Du Bois, W.E.B. *The Amenia Conference: An Historic Negro Gathering*. Amenia, New York: Privately Printed, Troutbeck Press, 1925.

———. *Dusk of Dawn: An Essay Toward an Autobiography of a Race Concept*. New York: Harcourt, Brace, 1940.

———. *The Souls of Black Folk: Essays and Sketches*. Chicago: A. C. McClurg and Company, 1903.

Goldenweiser, Alexander A. "Are the Races Potentially Equal?" *Proceedings of the American Philosophical Society*, 63 (1924): 215-221.

———. "Concerning Racial Difference." *Menorah Journal*, 8 (October 1922): 309-316.

———. "Racial Theory and the Negro." *Opportunity*, 13 (May 1922): 229-231.

———. "Some Problems of Race and Culture in the United States." *Proceedings of the National Conference of Social Work* (1922): 473-476.

Gruening, Martha. "Democratic Massacres in East St. Louis." *Pearson's Magazine*, 38 (September 1917): 106-108.

Herskovits, Melville J. "Acculturation and the American Negro." *Southwest Political and Social Science Quarterly*, 8 (December 1927): 211-224.

———. *The American Negro: A Study in Racial Crossing*. New York: Alfred A. Knopf, 1928.

———. "The American Negro Is Evolving a New Physical Type." *Current History*, 24 (September 1926): 898-903.

———. "Anthropology and Ethnology During 1926." *Opportunity*, 5 (January 1927): 12-13.

———. *The Anthropometry of the American Negro*. New York: Columbia University Press, 1930.

———. "The Art of the Congo." *Opportunity*, 5 (May 1927): 135-136.

———. "Bush-Negro Art." *The Arts*, 18 (October 1930): 25-37.

———. "The Color Line." *American Mercury*, 6 (October 1925): 204-208.

———. "Does the Negro Know His Father: A Study in Negro Genealogies." *Opportunity*, 4 (October 1926): 306-310.

———. "A Footnote to the History of Negro Slaving." *Opportunity*, 11 (June 1933): 178-181.

———. *The Negro and the Intelligence Tests*. Hanover, N.H.: Sociological Press, 1928.

———. "Negro Art: African and American." *Social Forces*, 5 (December 1926): 291-298.

———. "A Preliminary Consideration of the Culture Areas of Africa." *American Anthropologist*, 26 (January 1924): 50-63.

———. "Preliminary Observations in a Study of Negro-White Crossings." *Opportunity*, 3 (March 1925): 69-73.

———. "Race Relations." *American Journal of Sociology*, 34 (July 1928): 1129-1139.

———. "Race Relations." *American Journal of Sociology*, 37 (May 1932): 976-982.

———. "The Racial Hysteria." *Opportunity*, 2 (June 1924): 166-168.

———. "Some Observations on the Growth of Colored Boys." *American Journal of Physical Anthropology*, 7 (October 1924): 439-446.

———. "Some Physical Characteristics of the American Negro Population." *Social Forces*, 6 (September 1927): 93-98.

———. "What Has Africa Given America?" *New Republic*, 84 (September 4, 1935): 92-94.

———. "What Is a Race?" *American Mercury*, 2 (June 1924): 207-210.

———. "Wisdom from Africa." *Crisis*, 36 (September 1929): 306-308.

Johnson, James Weldon. *Negro Americans, What Now?* New York: Viking Press, 1938.

Ovington, Mary White. *Half a Man: The Status of the Negro in New York*. New York: Longmans, Green and Company, 1911.

Rosenwald, Julius. "Principles of Public Giving." *Atlantic Monthly*, 143 (May 1929): 599-606.

———. "You Can't Keep a Man in the Ditch Without Staying in with Him." *Colliers Magazine*, 76 (July 4, 1925): 23.

Seligmann, Herbert J. "The Menace of Race Hatred." *Harper's Magazine*, 140 (March 1920): 537-543.

———. *The Negro Faces America*. New York: Harper and Brothers, 1920.

———. "The Negro's Influence As a Voter." *Current History*, 28 (May 1928): 230-231.

———. "The Negro Protest Against Ghetto Conditions." *Current History*, 25 (March 1927): 831-833.

———. "Protecting Southern Womanhood." *Nation*, 108 (June 14, 1919): 938-939.

———. *Race Against Man*. New York: G. P. Putnam's Sons, 1939.

———. "Slavery in Georgia, A.D. 1921." *Nation*, 112 (April 20, 1921): 591.

———. "Twenty Years of Negro Progress." *Current History*, 29 (January 1929): 614-621.

———. "What Is Behind the Negro Uprisings?" *Current Opinion*, 67 (September 1919): 154-155.

Stern, Alfred K. "Decent Housing for Negroes." *American City*, 40 (March 1929): 102-103.

Washington, Booker T. *The Future of the American Negro*. Boston: Small, Maynard and Company, 1899.

———. *Tuskegee and Its People: Their Ideals and Achievements*. New York: D. Appleton & Co., 1905.

———. *Working with the Hands*. New York: Doubleday, Page and Company, 1904.

Weinberg, Meyer. *W.E.B. DuBois: A Reader*. New York: Harper and Row, 1970.

White, Walter F. *Rope and Faggot: A Biography of Judge Lynch*. New York: Alfred A. Knopf, 1929.

Wilson, Walter (ed.). *The Selected Writings of W.E.B. Du Bois*. New York: New American Library, 1970.

Reports and Publications of Organizations

Amalgamated Clothing Workers of America. *Report of the General Executive Board and Proceedings of the . . . Biennial Convention*. 1914-1935.

Amalgamated Clothing Workers of America, Research Department. *The Clothing Workers of Chicago, 1910-1922*. Chicago: Amalgamated Clothing Workers, 1922.

American Federation of Labor. *Convention Proceedings.* 1929.
American Jewish Committee. *American Jewish Yearbook.* 1914-1935.
Boston Branch, National Association for the Advancement of Colored People. *Fighting a Vicious Film: The Protest Against the "Birth of a Nation."* Boston: NAACP, 1915.
Directory of Jewish National and Local Organizations in the United States. Philadelphia: Jewish Publication Society of America, 1919.
Henry Street Settlement. *Report.* 1926.
Howard University. *Catalogue.* 1915-1935.
————. *Financial Reports.* 1915-1935.
International Ladies' Garment Workers' Union. *Report of the General Executive Board to the Annual Convention.* 1914-1935.
————. Educational Department. *The Story of the I.L.G.W.U.* New York: ILGWU, 1935.
————. *Structure and Functioning.* New York: Abco Press, 1934.
Lynip, Ryllis. *Growing Up: Twenty-One Years of Education with the I.L.G.W.U.* New York: Educational Department, ILGWU, 1938.
National Association for the Advancement of Colored People. *Annual Report.* 1910-1935.
National Urban League. *Annual Report.* 1910-1935.
————. *Bulletin.* 1910-1935.
————. Department of Research and Community Projects. *Negro Membership in American Labor Unions.* New York: National Urban League, 1930.
Our Union At Work: A Study of the Activities of Dressmakers' Union Local 22, I.L.G.W.U. from April, 1935 to April, 1937, Based on the Report of the Executive Board. New York: Dressmakers' Union Local 22, 1937.
Proceedings of the National Conference of Social Work. 1928.
Proceedings of the National Negro Conference, 1909: New York, May 31 and June 1.
Teper, Lazare. *The Women's Garment Industry.* New York: Educational Department, ILGWU, 1937.
Tuskegee Institute. *Bulletin: Principal's Annual Reports.* 1912-1935.

Sermons

Berkowitz, Henry. *A Set of Holiday Sermons: 5683-1922.* Cincinnati: Tract Publishing Company, 1922.
Feldman, Abraham J. *Lights and Shadows: Eight Addresses.* Hartford, Connecticut: Privately Published, 1928.
————. *Religion in Action: Twelve Discourses.* Philadelphia: Oscar Klonower, 1923.
Kaplan, Israel. *A Set of Holiday Sermons: 5690-1929.* Cincinnati: Tract Publishing Company, 1929.
Kaplan, Jacob. *A Set of Holiday Sermons: 5695-1934.* Cincinnati: Tract Publishing Company, 1934.
Levi, Harry. *A Rabbi Speaks.* Boston: Chapple Publishing Company, 1930.
————. *The Great Adventure and Other Addresses.* Boston: Privately Published, 1929.

Court Cases

Buchanan v. Warley, 245 U.S. 60 (1917).
Corrigan v. Buckley, 299 Fed., 899; 271, U.S. 323.
Guinn v. United States, 238 U.S. 347 (1915).
Nixon v. Condon, 286 U.S. 73 (1929).
Nixon v. Herndon, 273 U.S. 536 (1927).

Government Documents

U.S. Department of Labor, Division of Negro Economics. *The Negro at Work During the World War and During Reconstruction.* Bulletin No. 20. Washington: Government Printing Office, 1922.
————. Women's Bureau. *Negro Women in Industry.* Washington: Government Printing Office, 1922.
U.S. Office of Education. *Survey of Negro Colleges and Universities.* Washington: Government Printing Office, 1929.

Interviews

Interview with Mr. Charles Zimmerman, Retired President, Local 22, International Ladies' Garment Workers' Union, December 26, 1973.

Other Primary Sources

Addams, Jane. *Twenty Years at Hull House.* New York: Macmillan Company, 1910.
Arthur, George. *Life on the Negro Frontier.* New York: Association Press, 1934.
Blascoer, Frances. *Colored School Children in New York.* New York: Public Education Association of the City of New York, 1915.
Bogen, Boris. "Settlement Work Among Jews." *Charities,* 10 (January 3, 1903): 1-2.
Chicago Commission on Race Relations. *The Negro in Chicago: A Study of Race Relations and a Race Riot.* Chicago: University of Chicago Press, 1922.
Davis, Benjamin J. *Communist Councilman from Harlem* (Autobiographical notes written in a federal penitentiary). New York: International Publishers, 1969.
Feldman, Herman. *Racial Factors in American Industry.* New York: Harper and Brothers, 1931.
Franklin, Charles L. *The Negro Labor Unionist of New York: Problems and Conditions Among Negroes in the Labor Unions in Manhattan with Special Reference to the N.R.A. and Post-N.R.A. Situation.* New York: Columbia University Press, 1936.
Hapgood, Hutchins. *The Spirit of the Ghetto: Studies of the Jewish Quarter of New York.* New York: Funk and Wagnalls, 1902.
Hardy, Jack. *The Clothing Workers: A Study of the Conditions and Struggles in the Needle Trades.* New York: International Publishers, 1935.
Haynes, George E. *The Negro at Work in New York City, A Study in Economic Progress.* New York: Columbia University Press, 1912.
Herndon, Angelo. *Let Me Live.* New York: Arno Press, 1969.
Herzl, Theodore. *Altneuland.* New York: Bloch Publishing Company, 1941.

Jewish Communal Register of Greater New York, 1917. New York: Bureau of Jewish Social Research, 1918.

Jewish Communal Survey of Greater New York, 1928. New York: Bureau of Jewish Social Research, 1928.

Joseph, Samuel. *Jewish Immigration to the United States: From 1881-1910.* New York: Columbia University Press, 1914.

"Julius Rosenwald." *Journal of Negro History,* 17 (April 1932): 237-239.

Karpf, Maurice J. *Jewish Community Organization in the United States: An Outline of Types of Organizations, Activities, and Problems.* New York: Bloch Publishing Company, 1938.

Levinger, Lee J. *The Jewish Student in America: A Study Made by the Research Bureau of the B'nai Brith Hillel Foundation.* Cincinnati: B'nai Brith, 1937.

Lewisohn, Ludwig. *Up Stream: An American Chronicle.* New York: Boni and Liveright, 1922.

Lilienthal, David. "A Trial of Two Races." *Outlook,* 141 (December 23, 1925): 629-630.

————. "Has the Negro the Right of Self-Defense?" *Nation,* 121 (December 23, 1925): 724-725.

Linfield, Harry. *Statistics of Jews and Jewish Organizations: Historical Review of Ten Censuses, 1850-1937.* New York: American Jewish Committee, 1939.

Locke, Alain. *The New Negro.* New York: A. and C. Boni, 1925.

Metzger, Isaac. *A Bintel Brief.* New York: Doubleday and Company, 1971.

Moorland, Jesse E. "The Young Men's Christian Association Among Negroes." *Journal of Negro History,* 9 (April 1924): 127-138.

"The Most Beautiful Picture in America." *Christian Century,* 44 (July 15, 1927): 847-848.

Park, Robert, and Herbert Miller. *Old World Traits Transplanted.* New York: Harper and Brothers, 1921.

Park, Robert. *The Immigrant Press and Its Control.* New York: Harper and Brothers, 1922.

Reid, Ira De A. *Negro Membership in American Labor Unions.* New York: Alexander Press, 1930.

Soltes, Mordecai. *The Yiddish Press: An Americanizing Agency.* New York: Teachers' College, Columbia University, 1925.

Spero, Sterling, and Abraham Harris. *The Black Worker, A Study of the Negro and the Labor Movement.* New York: Columbia University Press, 1931.

Thomas, Jesse O. *My Story in Black and White.* New York: Exposition Press, 1967.

Who's Who in American Jewry, 1928. New York: Jewish Biographical Bureau, 1928.

Wood, L. Hollingsworth. "The Urban League Movement." *Journal of Negro History,* 9 (April 1924): 117-126.

SECONDARY SOURCES

Jewish-Black Relations

Baldwin, James. *Notes of a Native Son.* Boston: Beacon Press, 1955.

Bender, Eugene. "Reflections on Negro-Jewish Relationships: The Historical Dimension." *Phylon*, 30 (Spring 1969): 56-65.

Berson, Lenora E. *The Negroes and the Jews.* New York: Random House, 1971.

Brotz, Howard M. *The Black Jews of Harlem: Negro Nationalism and the Dilemmas of Negro Leadership.* New York: Free Press, 1964.

Cohen, Henry. *Justice, Justice: A Jewish View of the Black Revolution.* New York: Union of American Hebrew Congregations, 1968.

Cronbach, Abraham. *The Bible and Our Social Outlook.* Cincinnati: Union of American Hebrew Congregations, 1941.

Cruse, Harold. *The Crisis of the Negro Intellectual: From Its Origin to the Present.* New York: William Morrow and Company, 1967.

Geltman, Max. *The Confrontation: Black Power, Anti-Semitism and the Myth of Integration.* Englewood Cliffs, N.J.: Prentice-Hall, 1970.

Halpern, Ben. *Jews and Blacks: The Classic Minorities.* New York: Herder and Herder, 1971.

Hentoff, Nat. *Black Anti-Semitism and Jewish Racism.* New York: R. W. Baron, 1969.

Katz, Shlomo. *Negro and Jew, An Encounter in America: A Symposium.* New York: Macmillan, 1967.

Kohler, Max J. *The Jews and the Anti-Slavery Movement.* New York: American Jewish Historical Society, 1896.

Korn, Bertram. *American Jewry and the Civil War.* Cleveland: World Publishing Company, 1961.

————. *Jews and Negro Slavery in the Old South, 1789-1865.* Elkins Park, Penn.: Reform Congregation Keneseth Israel, 1961.

Negro-Jewish Relations in the United States: Papers and Proceedings of a Conference Convened by the Conference on Jewish Social Studies. New York: Citadel Press, 1966.

Pickard, Kate E. R. *The Kidnapped and the Ransomed.* Syracuse: William T. Hamilton, 1856.

Ruchames, Louis. "The Abolitionists and the Jews." *Publications of the American Jewish Historical Society,* 42 (December 1952): 131-155.

Solomon, Gus. *The Jewish Role in the American Civil Rights Movement.* London: World Jewish Congress, 1967.

Teller, Judd. "Jews and Blacks: Together." *National Jewish Monthly.* 84 (January 1970): 21-22.

Vorspan, Albert, and Eugene J. Lipman. *Justice and Judaism.* New York: Union of American Hebrew Congregations, 1956.

Weisbord, Robert, and Arthur Stein. *Bittersweet Encounter: The Afro-American and the American Jew.* Westport, Conn.: Negro Universities Press, 1970.

Weiss-Rosmarin, Trude. "Black-Jew Hatred in Historical Perspective." *Jewish Spectator,* 34 (January 1969): 2-5.

Studies of Jewish History

Anti-Defamation League. *Not the Work of a Day: The Story of the Anti-Defamation League of B'nai Brith.* New York: Anti-Defamation League, 1965.

Antonovsky, Aaron. *The Early Jewish Labor Movement in the United States.* New York: YIVO Institute for Jewish Records, 1961.

Baron, Salo W. *The Russian Jew: Under Tsars and Soviets.* New York: Macmillan, 1964.

Bell, Daniel. "The Grass Roots of American Jew Hatred." *Jewish Frontier,* 11 (June 1944): 15-20.

Berman, Hyman. "Era of the Protocol: A Chapter in the History of the International Ladies' Garment Workers' Union, 1910-1916." Ph.D Dissertation, Columbia University, 1955.

Bernheimer, Charles Seligman. *Half a Century in Community Service.* New York: Association Press, 1948.

Birmingham, Stephen. *"Our Crowd": The Great Jewish Families of New York.* New York: Harper and Row, 1967.

Bisno, Abraham. *Union Pioneer: An Autobiographical Account of Bisno's Early Life and the Beginnings of Unionism in the Women's Garment Industry.* Madison: University of Wisconsin Press, 1967.

Bogen, Boris. *Jewish Philanthropy: An Exploration of Principles and Methods of Jewish Social Service in the United States.* New York: The Macmillan Company, 1917.

Borchsenius, Paul. *The Three Rings: The History of the Spanish Jews.* London: George Allen and Unwin, 1963.

Brandes, Joseph. *Immigrants to Freedom: Jewish Communities in Rural New Jersey Since 1882.* Philadelphia: University of Pennsylvania Press, 1971.

Bregstone, Philip P. *Chicago and Its Jews: A Cultural History.* Chicago: Privately Published, 1933.

Broun, Heywood C. *Christians Only: A Study in Prejudice.* New York: Vanguard Press, 1931.

Buchbinder, N. A. *Geshichte Fun Yiddisher Arbeter Bavegung in Russland.* Vilna, 1931.

Budish, J. M., and George Soule. *The New Unionism in the Clothing Industry.* New York: Harcourt, Brace and Howe, 1920.

Burgin, Hertz. *Die Geschichte Fun der Yiddisher Arbeiter, Bewegung.* New York: United Hebrew Trades, 1915.

Chaiken, Joseph. *Yiddishe bleter in Amerike.* New York: M. Shkalarsky, 1946.

Cohen, Naomi. *Not Free to Desist: The American Jewish Committee, 1906-1966.* Philadelphia: Jewish Publication Society of America, 1972.

Dawidowicz, Lucy. ed. *The Golden Tradition: Jewish Life and Thought in Eastern Europe.* New York: Holt, Rinehart and Winston, 1967.

Dinnerstein, Leonard. *The Leo Frank Case.* New York: Columbia University Press, 1968.

Doroshkin, Milton. *Yiddish in America: Social and Cultural Foundations.* Rutherford, N.J.: Fairleigh Dickinson University Press, 1970.

Druck, David. *Tzu Der Geshichte Fun Der Yiddisher Prese: In Rusland Un Poilen.* Warsaw: Zichronos, 1920.

Dubnow, S. N. *History of the Jews in Russia and Poland.* Translated by I. Friedlander. 3 vols. Philadelphia: Jewish Publication Society of America, 1916-1920.

Epstein, Benjamin R., and Arnold Forster. *"Some of My Best Friends . . . "* New York:

Farrar, Straus and Cudahy, 1962.

Epstein, Melech. *Jewish Labor in U.S.A.: 1914-1952.* New York: Trade Union Sponsoring Committee, 1953.

Federation of Jewish Philanthropies of New York. *The Jewish Population of the New York Area, 1900-1975.* New York: Federation of Jewish Philanthropies, 1959.

Fine, David M. "Attitudes Towards Acculturation in the English Fiction of the Jewish Immigrant, 1900-1917." *American Jewish Historical Quarterly,* 43 (September 1973).

Frankel, Lee K. *Jewish Charities.* Philadelphia: American Academy of Political and Social Science, 1903.

Friedman, Theodore, and Robert Gordis (eds.). *Jewish Life in America.* New York: Horizon Press, 1955.

Frisch, Ephraim. *An Historical Survey of Jewish Philanthropy from the Earliest Times to the Nineteenth Century.* New York: Macmillan, 1924.

Fuchs, Lawrence H. *The Political Behavior of American Jews.* New York: Free Press, 1956.

Glazer, Nathan. *American Judaism.* Chicago: University of Chicago Press, 1957.

Goldberg, Nathan. *Occupational Patterns of American Jewry.* New York: Jewish Theological Seminary and Peoples' University Press, 1947.

Goodman, Paul. *Moses Montefiore.* Philadelphia: Jewish Publication Society of America, 1925.

Goren, Arthur. *New York Jews and the Quest for Community: The Kehillah Experiment, 1908-1922.* New York: Columbia University Press, 1970.

Grayzel, Solomon. *A History of the Contemporary Jews from 1900 to the Present.* Philadelphia: Jewish Publication Society of America, 1960.

Halperin, Samuel. *The Political World of American Zionism.* Detroit: Wayne State University Press, 1961.

Halpern, Ben. *The Idea of the Jewish State.* Cambridge: Harvard University Press, 1969.

Handlin, Oscar. *Adventure in Freedom: Three Hundred Years of Jewish Life in America.* New York: McGraw-Hill Book Company, 1954.

————. *A Continuing Task: The American Jewish Joint Distribution Committee, 1914-1964.* New York: Random House, 1964.

Herberg, Will. "Jewish Labor Movement in the United States." *Industrial & Labor Relations Review,* 5 (July 1952): 501-523; 6 (October 1952): 44-66.

Hertzberg, Arthur. *The Zionist Idea: A Historical Analysis and Reader.* New York: Doubleday and Company, 1959.

Higham, John. "Social Discrimination Against Jews in America, 1830-1930." *Publications of the American Jewish Historical Society,* 47 (1957): 1-33.

Hirschler, Eric E., ed. *Jews from Germany in the United States.* New York: Farrar, Straus, and Cudahy, 1955.

The History of American Jewish Social Welfare. Philadelphia: Jewish Publication Society of America, 1966.

Hoffman, B. *Fuftsig yor Klokmakher Yunyon: 1886-1936.* New York: ILGWU, Cloak Operators' Local 117, 1936.

Howe, Irving. *World of Our Fathers.* New York: Harcourt Brace, 1976.

Hyman, Joseph. *Twenty-Five Years of American Aid to Jews Overseas: A Record of the Joint Distribution Committee.* New York: Joint Distribution Committee, 1939.

Janowsky, Oscar I. (ed.). *The American Jew: A Composite Portrait.* New York: Harper and Brothers, 1942.

Joseph, Samuel. *History of the Baron de Hirsch Fund: The Americanization of the Jewish Immigrant.* Philadelphia: Jewish Publication Society of America, 1935.

Kallen, Horace M. *Jewish Education and the Future of the American Jewish Community.* New York: American Association for Jewish Education, 1944.

Kaminsky, J. *Fertzig Yor Arbeter Ring: A Geshichte in Bilder.* New York: National Executive Committee of the Workmen's Circle, 1925.

Kaplan, Mordecai M. *The Future of the American Jew.* New York: Macmillan, 1948.

————. *Judaism as a Civilization: Toward a Reconstruction of American-Jewish Life.* New York: Reconstructionist Press, 1957.

Kirsch, Guido. *In Search of Freedom: A History of American Jews from Czechoslovakia.* London: E. Goldston, 1949.

Kramer, Judith, and Seymour Leventman. *Children of the Gilded Ghetto: Conflict Resolution of Three Generations of American Jews.* Hamden, Conn.: Archon Books, 1961.

Krauskopf, Joseph. *The Jews and Moors in Spain.* Kansas City: M. Berkowitz and Company, 1887.

Kultur Und Leben, 15 (May-June 1969): 7.

La Mar, Elden. *The Clothing Workers in Philadelphia: History of Their Struggles for Union and Security.* Philadelphia: Philadelphia Joint Board, Amalgamated Clothing Workers of America, 1940.

Lang, Harry. *"62": Biography of a Union.* New York: Undergarment and Negligee Workers' Union, Local 62, ILGWU, 1940.

Lang, H., and M. Feinstone (eds.). *Geverkshaften: Zamelbuch Tsu Fuftsik Yor Fun Di Farainikte Yiddishe Geverkshaftn.* New York: United Hebrew Trades, 1938.

Levinger, Lee J. *Anti-Semitism in the United States: Its History and Causes.* New York: Bloch Publishing Company, 1925.

————. *Anti-Semitism Yesterday and Tomorrow.* New York: Macmillan, 1936.

Lewisohn, Ludwig. *The American Jew: Character and Destiny.* New York: Farrar, Straus, 1950.

Liebman, Charles S. *The Ambivalent American Jew: Politics, Religion, and Family in American Jewish Life.* Philadelphia: Jewish Publication Society of America, 1973.

Lorwin, Lewis L. *The Women's Garment Workers: A History of the International Ladies' Garment Workers' Union.* New York: B. W. Huebsch, 1924.

Lowenthal, Marvin. *The Jews of Germany: A Story of Sixteen Centuries.* New York: Longmans, Green and Company, 1936.

Lurie, Harry L. *A Heritage Affirmed: The Jewish Federation Movement in America.* Philadelphia: Jewish Publication Society of America, 1961.

Mandel, Irving. "The Attitude of the American Jewish Community to East European Immigration." *American Jewish Archives,* 3 (June 1950): 73-85.

Marcus, Jacob Rader. *Jews in American Life.* New York: American Jewish Committee, 1946.

McWilliams, Carey. *A Mask for Privilege: Anti-Semitism in America.* Boston: Little,

Brown, 1948.

Menes, A. "Di Yiddishe Arbeter Bavegung in Rusland Fun Onhaib 70er Bizn Soif 90er Yorn." *Historishe Shriftn.* Vilna: 1932.

Meyer, Isidore S. (ed.). *Early History of Zionism in America.* New York: American Jewish Historical Society, 1958.

Panitz, Esther. "The Polarity of American Jewish Attitudes Towards Immigration, 1870-1891," in Abraham J. Karp (ed.), *The Jewish Experience in America,* Vol. 4. Waltham, Mass.: American Jewish Historical Society, 1969.

————. "In Defense of the Jewish Immigrant: 1891-1924." *American Jewish Historical Quarterly,* 53 (December 1963): 99-130.

Perlman, Selig. "Jewish American Unionism: Its Birth Pangs and Contributions to the General American Labor Movement," in Abraham J. Karp (ed.), *The Jewish Experience in America,* Vol. 4. Waltham, Mass.: American Jewish Historical Society, 1969.

Ringer, Benjamin. *The Edge of Friendliness: A Study of Jewish-Gentile Relations.* New York: Basic Books, 1967.

Rischin, Moses. "The Jewish Labor Movement in America: A Social Interpretation." *Labor History,* 4 (Fall 1963): 227-247.

————. *The Promised City: New York's Jews, 1870-1914.* Cambridge: Harvard University Press, 1962.

Robin, Frederick W. and Selma G. Hirsh. *The Pursuit of Equality: A Half Century with the American Jewish Committee.* New York: Crown Publishers, 1957.

Robinson, Sophia, ed. *Jewish Population Studies.* New York: Conference on Jewish Relations, 1943.

Rogoff, Abraham. *Formative Years of the Jewish Labor Movement in the United States: 1890-1900.* Ann Arbor: Edwards Brothers, 1945.

Ronch, Isaac. *Amerike in der Yiddisher Literatur.* New York: I. E. Ronch Book Committee, 1945.

Rose, Peter I. (ed.). *The Ghetto and Beyond: Essays on Jewish Life in America.* New York: Random House, 1969.

Rosenberg, Stuart E. *America Is Different: The Search for Jewish Identity.* New York: T. Nelson, 1964.

Roth, Cecil. *The Spanish Inquisition.* London: R. Hale, 1937.

Rothman, Jack. *Minority Group Identification and Intergroup Relations: An Examination of Kurt Lewin's Theory of Jewish Group Identity.* Chicago: Research Institute for Group Work in Jewish Agencies, 1965.

Sachs, Abraham. *Di Geschichte fun Arbeiter Ring: 1892-1925.* New York: National Executive Committee of the Workmen's Circle, 1925.

Sanders, Ronald. *The Downtown Jews: Portraits of an Immigrant Generation.* New York: Harper and Row, 1969.

Schachner, Nathan. *The Price of Liberty: A History of the American Jewish Committee,* New York: American Jewish Committee, 1948.

Schlossberg, Joseph. *The Workers and Their World: Aspects of the Workers' Struggle at Home and Abroad.* New York: American Labor Party Committee, 1935.

Seidman, Joel. *The Needle Trades.* New York: Farrar and Rinehart, 1942.

Shapiro, Judah J. *The Friendly Society: A History of the Workmen's Circle.* New York:

Media Judaica, 1970.

Shapiro, Yonathan, *Leadership of the American Zionist Organization, 1897-1930.* Urbana: University of Illinois Press, 1971.

Shatzky, Jacob. *Tzu Der Geshichte Fun Der Yiddishe Prese in America.* New York: Yiddisher Kultur Gezelshaft, 1934.

Sherman, Charles Bezalel. *Yidn Un Andere Etnishe Grupes in Die Farenigte Shtaten.* New York: Unzer Veg, 1948.

Silverman, David W. "The Jewish Press: A Quadrilingual Phenomenon," in Martin E. Marty et al., *The Religious Press in America.* New York: Holt, Rinehart and Winston, 1963.

Sklare, Marshall. *America's Jews.* New York: Random House, 1971.

Sklare, Marshall, Joseph Greenblum, and Benjamin Ringer. *Not Quite at Home: How an American Jewish Community Lives with Itself and Its Neighbors.* New York: Institute of Human Relations Press, 1969.

Stein, Herman D. "Jewish Social Work in the United States, 1654-1954." Ph.D. Dissertation, Columbia University, 1958.

Stolberg, Benjamin. *Tailor's Progress: The Story of a Famous Union and the Men Who Made It.* Garden City, N.Y.: Doubleday, Doran and Company, 1944.

Strong, Donald S. *Organized Anti-Semitism in America: The Rise of Group Prejudice During the Decade 1930-1940.* Washington, D.C.: American Council on Public Affairs, 1941.

Szajkowski, Zosa. *The Attitude of American Jews to World War I, The Russian Revolutions of 1917, and to Communism, 1914-1945.* New York: Ktav Publishing House, 1972.

Tcherikower, Elias. *The Early Jewish Labor Movement in the United States.* New York: YNO Institute for Jewish Research, 1961.

Teller, Judd. *Strangers and Natives: The Evolution of the American Jew from 1921 to the Present.* New York: Delacorte Press, 1968.

Trachtenberg, Joshua. *Jewish Magic and Superstition: A Study in Folk Religion.* New York: Behrman Jewish Book House, 1939.

Weinstein, Bernard. *Fertzig Yor in Der Yiddisher Arbeter Bavegung.* New York: Vecker Press, 1924.

Weyl, Nathaniel. *The Jew in American Politics.* New Rochelle, N.Y.: Arlington House, 1968.

Wiernik, Peter. *History of the Jews in America.* New York: Jewish Press, 1912.

Wirth, Louis, *The Ghetto.* Chicago: University of Chicago Press, 1928.

Yiddish Writers' Union. *Funf Un Zibitzik Yor Yiddishe Prese in America: 1870-1945.* Y. L. Peretz Writers' Union, 1945.

Yinger, John Milton. *Anti-Semitism: A Case Study in Prejudice and Discrimination.* New York: Freedom Books, 1964.

Zborowski, Mark, and Elizabeth Herzog. *Life Is with People.* New York: International Universities Press, 1952.

Zhitnik, Abraham. *Dos Hartz Fun Folk.* New York: 1928.

Biographies of American Jews

Adler, Cyrus. *Louis Marshall: A Biographical Sketch.* New York: American Jewish Committee, 1931.

Boom, Kathleen. "Julius Rosenwald's Aid to Education in the South." Ph.D. Dissertation, University of Chicago, 1950.

Danish, Max. *The World of David Dubinsky.* Cleveland: World Publishing Company, 1957.

Duffus, Robert L. *Lillian Wald: Neighbor and Crusader.* New York: Macmillan, 1938.

Edwin Robert Anderson Seligman, 1861-1931: Addresses Delivered at the Memorial Meeting. Stamford, Conn.: Overbrook Press, 1942.

Embree, Edwin, and Julia Waxman. *Investment in People: The Story of the Julius Rosenwald Fund.* New York: Harper and Brothers, 1949.

Epstein, Melech. *Profiles of Eleven: Profiles of Eleven Men Who Guided the Destiny of an Immigrant Society.* Detroit: Wayne State University Press, 1965.

Frazen, Robert P. "The Public Life of Julius Rosenwald." Master's Thesis, Hebrew Union College, 1964.

French, David H. "Goldenweiser, Alexander A." *International Encyclopedia of the Social Sciences.* 6th ed. New York: Macmillan Company, 1968, pp. 196-197.

Gillis, Adolph. *Ludwig Lewisohn: The Artist and His Message.* New York: Duffield and Green, 1933.

Herskovits, Melville. *Franz Boas: The Science of Man in the Making.* New York: Charles Scribner's Sons, 1953.

Hirsch. David E. *Rabbi Emil G. Hirsch: The Reform Advocate.* Chicago: Whitehall Company, 1968.

Josephson, Matthew. *Sidney Hillman: Statesman of American Labor.* New York: Doubleday, 1952.

The Julius Rosenwald Centennial. Chicago: University of Chicago Press, 1963.

Kroeber, A. L., and others. *Franz Boas: 1858-1942.* Memoir Series 61, American Anthropological Association, 1943.

Lief, Alfred. *Brandeis: The Personal History of an American Ideal.* New York: Stackpole Sons, 1936.

Mandell, Fred. "Ludwig Lewisohn: An Intellectual Biography." Ph.D. Dissertation, University of Chicago, 1972.

Mason, Alpheus T. *Brandeis: A Free Man's Life.* New York: Viking Press, 1946.

Mumford, Lewis. "Scholar and Gentleman." *Saturday Review of Literature,* 20 (August 5, 1939): 8-9.

Nevins, Allan. *Herbert H. Lehman and His Era.* New York: Charles Scribner's Sons, 1963.

Paley, William. *Not Guilty! The Story of Samuel Leibowitz.* New York: G. P. Putnam's Sons, 1933.

Reynolds, Quentin. *Courtroom: The Story of Samuel S. Leibowitz.* New York: Farrar, Straus and Cudahy, 1950.

Rogoff, Hillel. *An East Side Epic: The Life and Work of Meyer London.* New York: Vanguard Press, 1930.

Rosenstock, Morton. *Louis Marshall: Defender of Jewish Rights.* Detroit: Wayne State University Press, 1965.
Ross, B. Joyce. *J. E. Spingarn and the Rise of the NAACP.* New York: Atheneum, 1972.
Ross, Sherwood. *Gruening of Alaska.* New York: Best Books, 1968.
Thomas, Helen Shirley. *Felix Frankfurter: Scholar on the Bench.* Baltimore: Johns Hopkins University Press, 1960.
Urofsky, Melvin I. *A Mind of One Piece: Brandeis and American Reform.* New York: Scribner's, 1971.
Villard, Oswald Garrison. "Issues and Men." *Nation,* 149 (August 12, 1939): 174.
Voss, Hermann. *Rabbi and Minister: The Friendship of Stephen S. Wise and John Haynes Holmes.* Cleveland: World Publishing Company, 1964.
Wallis, Wilson D. "Alexander A. Goldenweiser." *American Anthropologist,* 43 (April-June 1941): 250-255.
Werner, M. R. *Julius Rosenwald: The Life of a Practical Humanitarian.* New York: Harper and Row, 1939.
Williams, Beryl. *Lillian Wald: Angel on Henry Street.* New York: Julian Messner, 1948.

Studies of Black History

Badger, Henry G. *Statistics of Negro Colleges and Universities: Students, Staff, and Finances, 1900-1950.* Washington, D.C.: Federal Security Agency, Office of Education, 1951.
Baldwin, William H. "The Present Problem of Negro Education," *Journal of Social Science,* 37 (1899): 56.
Bentley, George R. *A History of the Freedman's Bureau.* Philadelphia: University of Pennsylvania Press, 1955.
Berger, Morroe. *Equality by Statute: The Revolution in Civil Rights.* Garden City, New York: Doubleday and Company, 1967.
Bond, Horace Mann. *The Education of the Negro in the American Social Order.* New York: Prentice-Hall, 1934.
———. *Negro Education in Alabama: A Study in Cotton and Steel.* Washington, D.C.: Associated Publishers, 1939.
Brazeal, Brailsford R. *The Brotherhood of Sleeping Car Porters: Its Origin and Development.* New York: Harper and Brothers, 1946.
Broderick, Francis L. and August Meier (eds.). *Negro Protest Thought in the Twentieth Century.* Indianapolis: Bobbs-Merrill Company, 1965.
Brown, Hugh V. *E-Qual-ity Education in North Carolina Among Negroes.* Raleigh: Irving Swain Press, 1964.
———. *A History of the Education of Negroes in North Carolina.* Raleigh: Irving Swain Press, 1961.
Bullock, Henry Allen. *A History of Negro Education in the South: From 1619 to the Present.* New York: Praeger Publishers, 1970.
Carter, Dan T. *Scottsboro: A Tragedy of the American South.* New York: Oxford University Press, 1969.
Clark, Tom C., and Philip Perlman. *Prejudice and Property: An Historic Brief Against*

Racial Covenants. Washington, D.C.: Public Affairs Press, 1948.

Cobb, Montague. *Medical Care and the Plight of the Negro.* New York: National Association for the Advancement of Colored People, 1947.

Davis, Michael M. "Problems of Health Services for Negroes." *Journal of Negro Education,* 6 (July 1937): 438-449.

Diner, Steven J. "Chicago Social Workers and Blacks in the Progressive Era." *Social Service Review,* 44 (December 1970): 393-410.

Dann, Martin E. (ed.). *The Black Press, 1827-1890: The Quest for National Identity.* New York: G. P. Putnam's Sons, 1971.

Drake, St. Clair, and Horace Cayton. *Black Metropolis: A Study of Negro Life in a Northern City.* New York: Harcourt, Brace, 1945.

Dyson, Walter. *Howard University: The Capstone of Negro Education, A History: 1867-1940.* Washington, D.C.: The Graduate School of Howard University, 1941.

Ernst, Robert. "The Economic Status of New York City Negroes 1850-1863." *Negro History Bulletin,* 12 (March 1949): 139-141.

Fisher, Miles Mark. *Negro Slave Songs in the United States.* Ithaca: Cornell University Press, 1953.

Franklin, John Hope. *From Slavery to Freedom: A History of American Negroes.* New York: A. A. Knopf, 1947.

Frederickson, George. *The Black Image in the White Mind: The Debate on Afro-American Character and Destiny, 1817-1914.* New York: Harper and Row, 1971.

Gallagher, Buell. *American Caste and the Negro College.* New York: Columbia University Press, 1938.

Gosnell, Harold F. *Negro Politicians: The Rise of Negro Politics in Chicago.* Chicago: University of Chicago Press, 1935.

Gossett, Thomas. *Race: The History of an Idea in America.* Dallas: Southern Methodist University Press, 1963.

Greenberg, Jack. *Race Relations and American Law.* New York: Columbia University Press, 1959.

Haller, John S. *Outcasts from Evolution: Scientific Attitudes of Racial Inferiority, 1859-1900.* Urbana: University of Illinois Press, 1971.

Hauser, Philip M. "Demographic Factors in the Integration of the Negro." *Daedalus,* (Fall 1965): 847-877.

Holmes, Dwight O. W. "Fifty Years of Howard University." *Journal of Negro History,* 3 (April 1918): 123-138; (October 1918): 368-380.

———. *The Evolution of the Negro College.* New York: Teachers' College, Columbia University, 1934.

Huggins, Nathan. *Harlem Renaissance.* New York: Oxford University Press, 1971.

Hughes, Langston. *Fight for Freedom: The Story of the NAACP.* New York: W. W. Norton and Company, 1962.

Jack, Robert L. *History of the National Association for the Advancement of Colored People.* Boston: Meador Publishing Company, 1943.

Johnson, Charles S. *The Negro College Graduate.* Chapel Hill: University of North Carolina Press, 1938.

Karson, Marc, and Ronald Radosh. "The American Federation of Labor and the

Negro Worker, 1894-1949," in Julius Jacobson, *The Negro and the American Labor Movement.* Garden City, New York: Doubleday, 1968.

Kellogg, Charles F. *NAACP: A History of the National Association for the Advancement of Colored People, 1909-1920.* Baltimore: Johns Hopkins University Press, 1967.

Kennedy, Louise V. *The Negro Reasant Turns Cityward: Effects of Recent Migrations to Northern Centers.* New York: Columbia University Press, 1930.

Kessler, Sidney H. "The Organization of Negroes in the Knights of Labor." *Journal of Negro History,* 37 (July 1952): 248-275.

Konvitz, Milton R. *A Century of Civil Rights.* New York: Columbia University Press, 1961.

Leavell, Ullin W. *Philanthropy in Negro Education.* Nashville: George Peabody College for Teachers, 1930.

Litwack, Leon F. *North of Slavery: The Negro in the Free States, 1790-1860.* Chicago: University of Chicago Press, 1961.

Logan, Rayford. *The Betrayal of the Negro: From Rutherford B. Hayes to Woodrow Wilson.* New York: Collier Books, 1965.

————. *Howard University: The First Hundred Years.* New York: New York University Press, 1969.

Madison, Sumner E. "The Labor Movement and the Negro During Reconstruction." *Journal of Negro History,* 33 (October 1948): 426-468.

Marshall, F. Ray. *The Negro and Organized Labor.* New York: John Wiley and Sons, 1965.

McFeely, William S. *Yankee Stepfather: General O. O. Howard and the Freedmen.* New Haven: Yale University Press, 1968.

Meier, August, and Elliot Rudwick. "Attitudes of Negro Leaders Towards the American Labor Movement from the Civil War to World War One," in Julius Jacobson (ed.). *The Negro and the American Labor Movement.* Garden City, N.Y.: Doubleday, 1968.

————. *From Plantation to Ghetto: An Interpretive History of American Negroes.* New York: Hill and Wang, 1966.

Miller, Loren. *The Petitioners: The Story of the Supreme Court of the United States and the Negro.* New York: Pantheon Books, 1966.

Morais, Herbert M. *The History of the Negro in Medicine.* New York: Publishers Company, 1967.

Myrdal, Gunnar. *An American Dilemma: The Negro Problem and a Modern Democracy.* New York: Harper and Row, 1944.

National Urban League. *The Urban League Story, 1910-1960.* New York: National Urban League, 1961.

Nelson, Bernard H. *The Fourteenth Amendment and the Negro Since 1920.* Washington, D.C.: Catholic University of America Press, 1946.

Newby, I. A. *Jim Crow's Defense: Anti-Negro Thought in America, 1900-1930.* Baton Rouge: Louisiana State University Press, 1965.

Northrup, Herbert R. *Organized Labor and the Negro.* New York: Harper and Brothers, 1944.

Osofsky, Gilbert. *Harlem: The Making of a Ghetto: Negro New York, 1890-1930*. New York: Harper and Row, 1966.

Owens, Robert L. "Financial Assistance for Negro College Students in America: A Social Historical Interpretation of the Philosophy of Negro Higher Education." Ph.D. Dissertation, State University of Iowa, 1954.

Parris, Guichard, and Lester Brooks. *Blacks in the City: A History of the National Urban League*. Boston: Little, Brown, 1971.

Range, Willard. *The Rise and Progress of Negro Colleges in Georgia, 1865-1949*. Athens: University of Georgia Press, 1951.

Record, Wilson. *The Negro and the Communist Party*. Chapel Hill: University of North Carolina Press, 1951.

————. *Race and Radicalism: The NAACP and the Communist Party in Conflict*. Ithaca: Cornell University Press, 1964.

Reitzes, Deitrich C. *Negroes and Medicine*. Cambridge: Harvard University Press, 1958.

Robinson, Joseph. "Organizations Promoting Civil Rights and Liberties." *The Annals of the American Academy of Political and Social Science*. ed. Robert K. Carr. Philadelphia: American Academy of Political and Social Science, 1951.

Ross, Frank A., and Louise V. Kennedy. *A Bibliography of Negro Migration*. New York: Columbia University Press, 1934.

Rudwick, Elliot. *Race Riot at East St. Louis, July 2, 1917*. Carbondale: Southern Illinois University Press, 1964.

Scheiner, Seth M. *Negro Mecca: A History of the Negro in New York City, 1865-1920*. New York: New York University Press, 1965.

Snyder, Louis V. *Race: A History of Modern Ethnic Theories*. New York: Longmans, Green, and Company, 1939.

Spear, Allan H. *Black Chicago: The Making of a Negro Ghetto, 1890-1920*. Chicago: University of Chicago Press, 1967.

St. James, Warren D. *The National Association for the Advancement of Colored People: A Case Study in Pressure Groups*. New York: Exposition Press, 1958.

Strickland, Arvarh E. *History of the Chicago Urban League*. Urbana: University of Illinois Press, 1966.

Tatum, Elbert. *The Changed Political Thought of the Negro: 1915-1940*. New York: Exposition Press, 1951.

Tuttle, William M. *Race Riot: Chicago in the Red Summer of 1919*. New York: Atheneum, 1970.

Waskow, Arthur. *From Race Riot to Sit-In: 1919 and the 1960's, A Study in the Connections Between Conflict and Violence*. Garden City, New York: Doubleday and Company, 1966.

Weiss, Nancy J. *The National Urban League, 1910-1940*. New York: Oxford University Press, 1974.

Wesley, Charles H. *Negro Labor in the United States, 1850-1925: A Study in American Economic History*. New York: Vanguard Press, 1927.

Whitten, Norman E., and John F. Szwed. *Afro-American Anthropology: Contemporary Perspectives*. New York: Free Press, 1970.

Wilson, Charles H. *Education for Negroes in Mississippi Since 1910.* Boston: Meador Publishing Company, 1947.
Woodson, Carter G. *A Century of Negro Migration.* Washington, D.C.: The Association for the Study of Negro Life and History, 1918.
Woodward, C. Vann. *The Strange Career of Jim Crow.* New York: Oxford University Press, 1955.
————. *Tom Watson: Agrarian Rebel.* New York: Macmillan, 1938.
Wynn, Daniel W. *The NAACP Versus Negro Revolutionary Protest: A Comparative Study of the Effectiveness of Each Movement.* New York: Exposition Press, 1955.
Zangrando, Robert L. "The Efforts of the National Association for the Advancement of Colored People to Secure Passage of a Federal Anti-Lynching Law, 1920-1940." Ph.D. Dissertation, University of Pennsylvania, 1963.

Biographies of American Blacks

Anderson, Jervis. *A. Philip Randolph: A Biographical Portrait.* New York: Harcourt, Brace, Jovanovich, 1972.
Bradford, Sarah Elizabeth. *Harriet Tubman, The Moses of Her People.* New York: J. J. Little and Company, 1901.
Broderick, Francis. *W.E.B. Du Bois: Negro Leader in a Time of Crisis.* Stanford: Stanford University Press, 1959.
Cronon, E. David. *Black Moses: The Story of Marcus Garvey and the Universal Negro Improvement Association.* Madison: University of Wisconsin Press, 1955.
Harlan, Louis R. *Booker T. Washington: The Making of a Black Leader, 1856-1901.* New York: Oxford University Press, 1972.
Rudwick, Elliot. *W.E.B. Du Bois: Propagandist of the Negro Protest.* New York: Atheneum, 1968.
————. *W.E.B. Du Bois: A Study in Minority Group Leadership.* Philadelphia: University of Pennsylvania Press, 1960.
Scott, Emmett J. and Lyman Beecher Stowe. *Booker T. Washington: Builder of a Civilization.* New York: Doubleday, Page and Company, 1916.
Spencer, Samuel R. *Booker T. Washington and the Negro's Place in American Life.* Boston: Little, Brown, 1955.
Thornbrough, Emma. *Booker T. Washington.* Englewood Cliffs, New Jersey: Prentice-Hall, 1969.

Other Secondary Studies

Baltzell, E. Digby. *The Protestant Establishment: Aristocracy and Caste in America.* New York: Random House, 1964.
Barbash, Jack. "Ethnic Factors in the Development of the American Labor Movement," in Industrial Relations Research, *Interpreting the Labor Movement.* Madison: Industrial Relations Research Association, 1952.
Barzun, Jacques. *Race: A Study in Modern Superstition.* New York: Harcourt, Brace and Company, 1937.

Berger, Meyer. *The Story of the New York Times, 1851-1951.* New York: Simon and Schuster, 1951.

Bernstein, Irving. *Turbulent Years: A History of the American Worker, 1933-1941.* Boston: Houghton Mifflin, 1970.

Bremner, Robert. *American Philanthropy.* Chicago: University of Chicago Press, 1960.

Carsel, Wilfred. *A History of the Chicago Ladies' Garment Union.* Chicago: Normandy House, 1940.

Chalmers, David. *Hooded Americanism: The First Century of the KKK, 1865-1965.* Garden City, N.Y.: Doubleday, 1965.

Chambers, Clarke A. *Seedtime of Reform: American Social Service and Social Action, 1918-1933.* Minneapolis: University of Minnesota Press, 1963.

Davis, Allen F. *Spearheads for Reform: The Social Settlements and the Progressive Movement, 1890-1914.* New York: Oxford University Press, 1967.

Davis, Elmer H. *History of the New York Times, 1851-1921.* New York: New York Times, 1921.

Dubofsky, Melvyn. "Organized Labor and the Immigrant in New York City, 1900-1918." *Labor History,* 2 (Spring 1961): 182-201.

Gavett, Thomas W. *The Development of the Labor Movement in Milwaukee.* Madison: University of Wisconsin Press, 1965.

Ginger, Ray. *Eugene V. Debs: The Making of an American Radical.* New York: Collier Books, 1962.

Glazer, Nathan. *The Social Basis of American Communism.* New York: Harcourt, Brace, 1961.

Grob, Gerald. *Workers and Utopia: A Study of Ideological Conflict in the American Labor Movement, 1865-1900.* Evanston: Northwestern University Press, 1961.

Handlin, Oscar. *Boston's Immigrants: 1790-1880: A Study in Acculturation.* Cambridge: Harvard University Press, 1941.

Harris, Marvin. *The Rise of Anthropological Theory: A History of Theories of Culture.* New York: Thomas Y. Crowell, 1968.

Higham, John. *Strangers in the Land: Patterns of American Nativism, 1860-1925.* New Brunswick, N.J.: Rutgers University Press, 1955.

Hofstadter, Richard. *The Age of Reform, From Bryan to F.D.R.* New York: Vintage Books, 1955.

Jackson, Kenneth T. *The Ku Klux Klan in the City, 1915-1930.* New York: Oxford University Press, 1967.

Kardiner, Abram, and Edward Preble. *They Studied Man.* Cleveland: World Publishing Company, 1961.

Laslett, John H. M. *Labor and the Left: A Study of Socialist and Radical Influences in the American Labor Movement, 1881-1924.* New York: Basic Books, 1970.

Lee, Alfred McClug. *The Daily Newspaper in America: The Evolution of a Social Instrument.* New York: The Macmillan Company, 1937.

Lester, Robert M. *Forty Years of Carnegie Giving.* New York: Charles Scribner's Sons, 1941.

Lubove, Roy. *The Professional Altruist: The Emergence of Social Work as a Career, 1880-1930.* Cambridge, Mass.: Harvard University Press, 1965.

Mead, Margaret, and Ruth Bunzel (eds.). *The Golden Age of American Anthropology.* New York: George Braziller, 1960.

Nestor, Louis P. *Labor Relations in the Laundry Industry.* New York: Privately Printed, 1950.

Nevins, Allan. *Study in Power: John D. Rockefeller, Industrialist and Philanthropist.* New York: Charles Scribner's Sons, 1953.

Newell, Barbara W. *Chicago and the Labor Movement: Metropolitan Unionism in the 1930's.* Urbana: University of Illinois Press, 1961.

Nugent, Walter. *The Tolerant Populists.* Chicago: University of Chicago Press, 1963.

Park, Robert E. *Race and Culture: Essays in the Sociology of Contemporary Man.* New York: Free Press, 1950.

Rayack, Elton. "The Effect of Unionism on Wages in the Men's Clothing Industry, 1911-1955." Ph.D. Dissertation, University of Chicago, 1957.

Rischin, Moses, "Labor Goes Middle Class." *Antioch Review*, 13 (June 1953): 191-201.

Roche, John P. *The Quest for the Dream: The Development of Civil Rights and Human Relations in Modern America.* New York: Macmillan, 1963.

Saenger, Gerhart. "Minority Personality and Adjustment." *Transactions of the New York Academy of Science*, 14 (March 1952): 204-208.

Saposs, David J. *Left Wing Unionism: A Study of Radical Policies and Tactics.* New York: International Publishers, 1926.

Shannon, David A. *The Socialist Party of America: A History.* New York: The Macmillan Company, 1955.

Stocking, George W. *Race, Culture and Evolution.* New York: Free Press, 1968.

Stonequist, Everett. *The Marginal Man.* New York: Charles Scribner's Sons, 1937.

Sulzberger, C. L. *A Long Row of Candles: Memoirs and Diaries, 1934-1954.* New York: Macmillan, 1969.

Weinstein, James. *The Decline of Socialism in America, 1912-1925.* New York: Monthly Review Press, 1967.

index

267

About the Author

Hasia R. Diner, assistant professor of history at the University of Maryland, specializes in Women's History and Ethnic History. She is currently writing a book entitled *Women and Urban Society.*